D0432382

NAVIGATION FOR OFFSHORE AND OCEAN SAILORS

NAVIGATION FOR OFFSHORE AND OCEAN SAILORS

DAVID DERRICK

DAVID & CHARLES
Newton Abbot London North Pomfret (Vt)

British Library Cataloguing in Publication Data

Derrick, David
Navigation for offshore and ocean sailors.
1. Navigation
2. Yachts and yachting
I. Title
623.89'0247971 VK555

ISBN 0-7153-8086-9

Typeset by ABM Typographics Limited, Hull
and printed in Great Britain
by Ebenezer Baylis & Son Limited, The Trinity Press,
Worcester, and London
for David & Charles (Publishers) Limited
Brunel House Newton Abbot Devon

Published in the United States of America
by David & Charles Inc
North Pomfret Vermont 05053 USA

Contents

Acknowledgements

The author and publishers would like to thank the Controller of Her Majesty's Stationery Office for permission to reproduce extracts from the following: the *Nautical Almanac* in Appendices 1-7; the *Sight Reduction Tables for Air Navigation*, Vol. 1, in Appendix 9 and the *Sight Reduction Tables for Air Navigation*, Vol 3, in Appendices 10 and 11.

They also wish to thank Thomas Reed Publications for kind permission to reproduce part of the 1979 edition of *Reed's Nautical Almanac* in Appendix 8.

The chapter-head illustrations, the sextant (Fig 11) and the charts were all drawn by Jennifer Johnson.

Glossary of Abbreviations used in Diagrams

AP	Assumed Position
CT	Civil Twilight
CZD	Calculated Zenith Distance
DWE	Deck Watch Error
DWT	Deck Watch Time
EP	Estimated Position
GC	Great Circle
GD	Greenwich Date
GHA	Greenwich Hour Angle
GHAMS	Greenwich Hour Angle of the Mean Sun
GMT	Greenwich Mean Time
GOAT	Greater Observed Angle Towards
GP	Geographical Position
Hc	Calculated Altitude
HE	Height of Eye
HP	Horizontal Parallax
IE	Index Error
ITP	Intercept Terminal Position
LHA	Local Hour Angle
LHAMS	Local Hour Angle of the Mean Sun
LL	Lower Limb
LMT	Local Mean Time
MP	Meridian Passage
MPP	Most Probable Position
$\underline{\odot}$	Sun, lower limb
$\overline{\odot}$	Sun, upper limb
PZX	The navigational spherical angle
SA	Sextant altitude
SD	Semi-diameter
SHA	Sidereal Hour Angle
SRT	Sight Reduction Tables
TA	True Altitude
TRS	Tropical Revolving Storm
UL	Upper Limb
X	A heavenly body
Z	The observer's zenith
Zn	Azimuth
ZD	Zenith Distance
ZT	Zone Time

Introduction

It has been said that the science of navigation is planning where to go, whereas the art lies in finding out where you are. Since celestial navigation is rarely used for passage planning, save for the rather general case of 'following the sun', the early chapters of this book will concern themselves with the artistic side; that is, the art of establishing a position on the surface of the earth—usually at sea—with minimum reference outside of the vessel concerned.

Celestial navigation is not the exclusive preserve of the long-distance sailor, and it may be used with just as much success and satisfaction on quite modest passages. For anyone to whom a passage of a hundred miles between landfalls does not present a great navigation problem, to master the art of celestial navigation is but a small and easy step, the results of which can be used to advantage on such relatively short passages, apart from its more natural use while crossing the oceans.

All things worth doing seem to need a little effort in order to derive maximum enjoyment and ease of use, and navigation is no exception. Initial efforts have to be directed towards learning a few basic facts. These are mainly definitions and explanations of the terms used. At first they might appear dry and boring, but they are essential and do not take very long to master, particularly if that distant, idyllic anchorage is kept in mind.

The reader is assumed to have a knowledge of navigation up to the standard of the RYA Yachtmaster (Offshore). That is, he is capable of navigating on passages lasting a couple of days, allowing for tides and leeway, and using normal land-based aids such as lights and radio beacons. Successful assimilation of the contents of this book will take him to the RYA Yachtmaster (Ocean) standard.

Most of the theory is dealt with in Chapter 1 and to some may appear daunting. Do not lose heart. Many people have learnt to navigate with no theoretical knowledge whatsoever. Some people, and I am one of them, find subjects such as navigation easier to approach via the theory, whereas there are those who find it easier to get on with the practice. Perhaps readers from both groups will find time to read, or re-read, that chapter while sailing the Pacific!

The taking of a sight involves the navigator in 'shooting' with a sextant, timing that event with a chronometer, reducing the sight using the *Nautical Almanac* and *Sight Reduction Tables*, and, finally, plotting the resultant position line on the chart. These 'tools' and the plotting are considered in succeeding chapters in as much detail as is possible without embarking on particular sights.

After this general introduction to sights and plotting, each type of sight is considered individually and in detail. The object has been to conclude each of these chapters with two worked examples, one with full explanatory notes, the other with no notes, and finally to present the reader with some exercises to be worked using the tables from the appendices and checking the answers with those which appear at the end of the book.

The next stage is to consider the checking of the compass, great-circle sailing and meteorology, the latter chapter dealing fully with the avoidance of tropical revolving storms–those not always uncommon, but always indescribably dangerous, phenomena which pervade the tropical sailing areas.

The final two chapters are an encouragement to utilise a few winter evenings planning a passage or two and completing a navigational exercise. If the reader reaches thus far successfully, he should be well capable of navigating at sea. All that remains is to pack the 'tools' and go.

1 The Earth and the Celestial Sphere

Celestial navigation is based on the observation of heavenly bodies. The observation is made with a sextant, an instrument for measuring angles, a fuller explanation of which appears in Chapter 4.

The heavenly bodies used are the sun and moon, Venus, Mars, Jupiter and Saturn and any of fifty-seven stars. The angle measured, correctly referred to as the *altitude*, is that between the heavenly body and the sea horizon vertically below it. With a little arithmetical dexterity this altitude can be converted to OĈX in Fig 1, where O is the position of the observer on the surface of the earth, C is the centre of the earth and X is the heavenly body.

To make use of this altitude it is necessary to know the precise position of the heavenly body. Although it is far from the case in reality, due to the vast distances involved, no significant errors are introduced to our navigation by imagining that all the heavenly bodies are on the

X
O
C
EARTH
C CENTRE OF EARTH
O OBSERVER
X HEAVENLY BODY

Fig 1

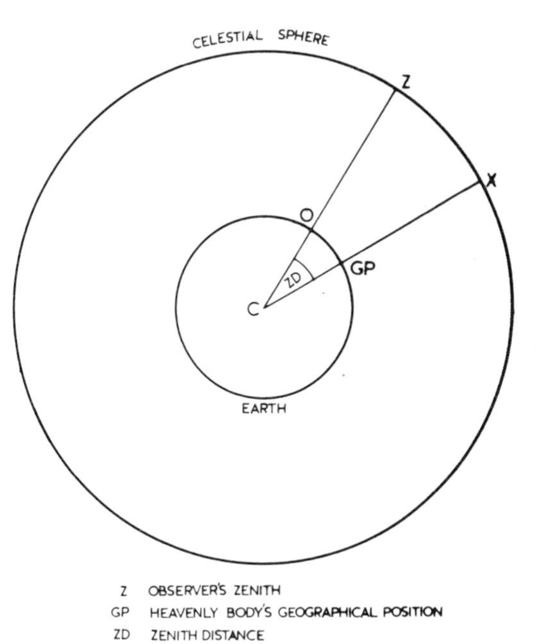

Fig 2

surface of a very large sphere, at the centre of which is the earth. This is the *celestial sphere*, illustrated in Fig 2, where two new terms are introduced.

The point, GP, where CX cuts the surface of the earth is known as the *geographical position* of the heavenly body. Z is the point where the projection of CO meets the celestial sphere. This is the observer's *zenith*. The angle $Z\hat{C}X$ is, of course, the same as $O\hat{C}X$, referred to above. ZX is the 'distance' between the heavenly body and the observer's zenith, so $Z\hat{C}X$ is known as the *zenith distance*.

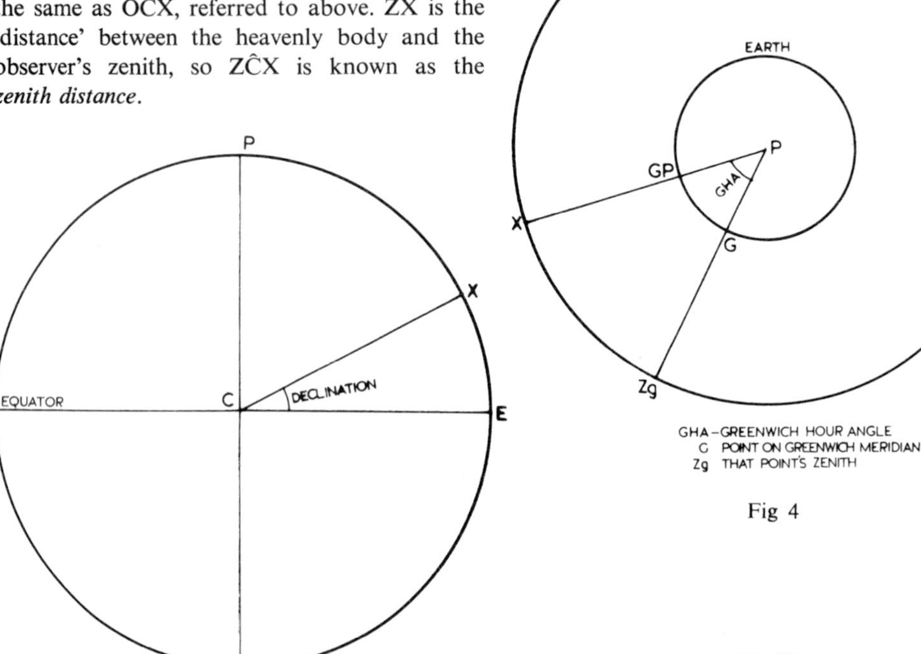

P CELESTIAL POLE

Fig 3

GHA–GREENWICH HOUR ANGLE
G POINT ON GREENWICH MERIDIAN
Zg THAT POINT'S ZENITH

Fig 4

Fig 3 shows a great-circle section through the centre of the celestial sphere (and, of course, that of the earth), its poles, which are extensions of the terrestrial poles, and a heavenly body. The *celestial equator* is in the same plane as its terrestrial equivalent. $X\hat{C}E$ is the *declination* of the heavenly body. This declination bears a certain resemblance to terrestrial latitude and, in the same way is named either north or south, depending on its position in relation to the equator. For example, during summer in the northern hemisphere the sun is north of the equator, so its declination is named north. Conversely, during the winter in the northern hemisphere, the sun being south of the equator is said to have a southerly declination. The declination of all heavenly bodies is forever changing, though the rate at which it changes varies greatly from body to body.

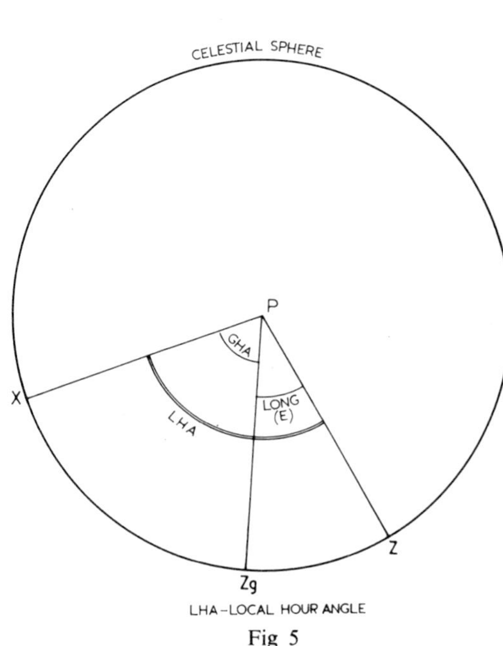

LHA–LOCAL HOUR ANGLE

Fig 5

Fig 4 gives a 'bird's eye view' from above the north pole (P). G is on the terrestrial Greenwich meridian and Zg is its zenith on the celestial sphere. XP̂Zg is the *Greenwich hour angle* (GHA) of the heavenly body (X). This angle, in some ways, is the equivalent of terrestrial longitude, but differs in one important aspect. Whereas longitude is measured 0°–180° both east and west, GHA is always measured in a westerly direction 0°–359°59.′9 and never has a cardinal sign.

The angular displacement between the observer's meridian and that of the heavenly body is the *local hour angle* (LHA). Like GHA, LHA is measured in a westerly direction only, up to 359°59.′9. The 'hour' part of the terms Greenwich hour angle and local hour angle may be a little confusing, but it is there because in circumstances not within the scope of this book, these angles are expressed in units of time.

Fig 5 represents a view from above the celestial pole. The GHA of the heavenly body is XP̂Zg, the longitude of the observer is ZP̂Zg, and the LHA is XP̂Z. In this particular case, then:

$$\text{LHA} = \text{GHA} + \text{LONG (E)}$$

In Fig 6 the observer's longitude is westerly, and in this case, the LHA (XP̂Z) is the difference between the GHA (XP̂Zg) and the longitude (ZP̂Zg):

$$\text{LHA} = \text{GHA} - \text{LONG (W)}$$

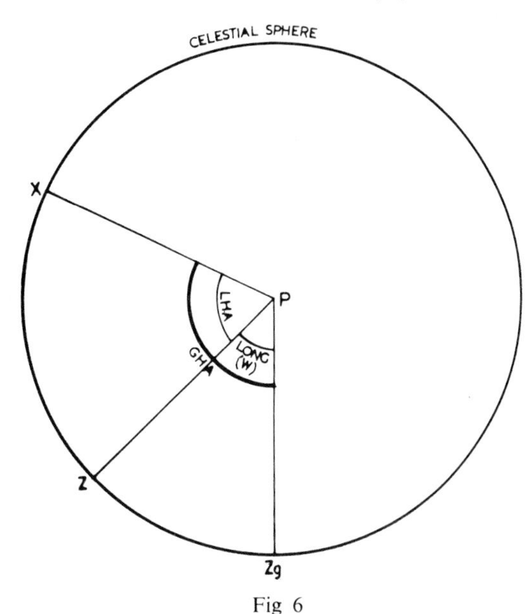

Fig 6

Fig 7

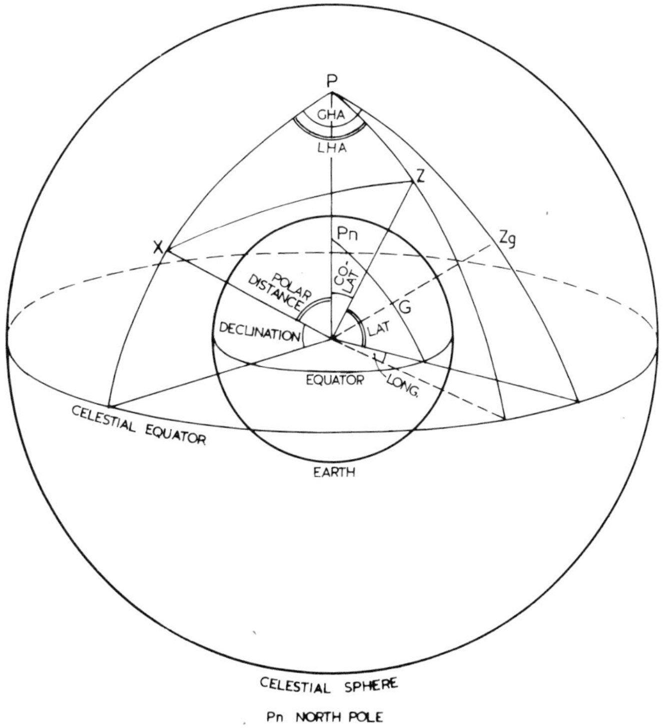

CELESTIAL SPHERE

Pn NORTH POLE

The rule for converting a Greenwich hour angle to a local hour angle is to add easterly longitude or subtract westerly longitude.

In certain circumstances it will be necessary to add or subtract 360° to avoid negative quantities or angles greater than 360°, but these additions and subtractions will have no effect on the eventual trigonometry.

Before moving on, it might be as well to draw what is at first sight a rather complicated diagram of the earth and the celestial sphere, illustrating all the angles and positions already described, and making two small additions (see Fig 7, p13).

Co-latitude is the complement of latitude (90°–latitude). *Polar distance* is the complement of declination (90°–declination). These two new angles are introduced because they have a more direct bearing on the spherical triangle PZX, the solution to which is the ultimate key to the navigational problem.

There are yet two more additions to the celestial sphere which will now be considered separately, rather than complicate Fig 7 beyond recognition.

The apparent path of the sun around the celestial sphere is the *ecliptic*. The plane of its great circle makes an angle of about 23½° with the celestial (and terrestrial) equator, due to the 'tilt' of the earth's axis. The ecliptic thus cuts the celestial equator in two points. The point which most concerns the navigator is that through which the sun passes on about 21st March each year. Known as the *First Point of Aries*, it is often denoted by the Ram's horns ♈, and just as often abbreviated to a simple Aries.

The *sidereal hour angle* (SHA) of a heavenly body is the angular displacement westwards of the meridian through that body, from the meridian through the First Point of Aries. Though each heavenly body has a sidereal hour angle, it is a quantity of particular interest when considering the stars.

The PZX triangle

To consider the PZX triangle in detail, it is best to begin with a simplified version (Fig 9) of Fig 7.

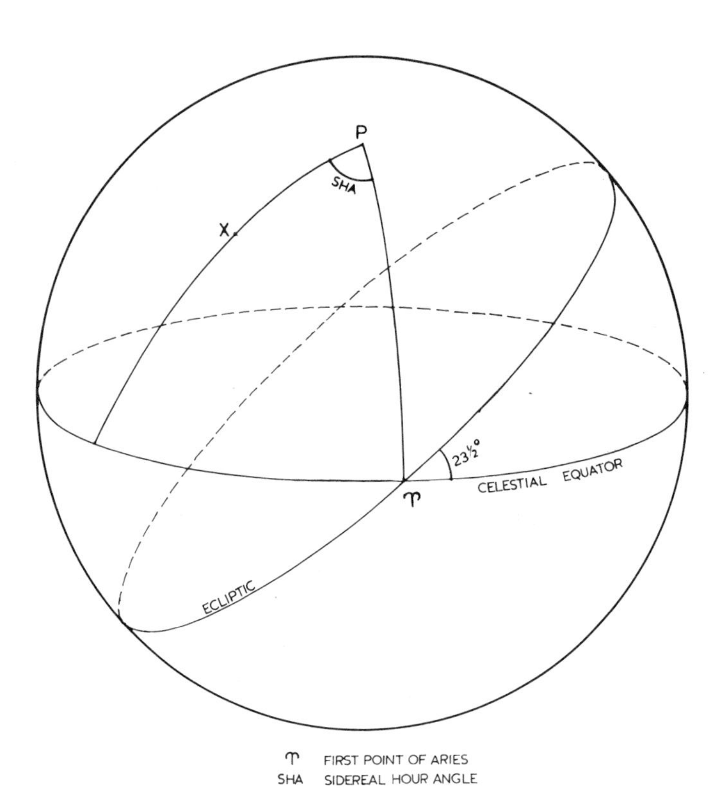

Fig 8

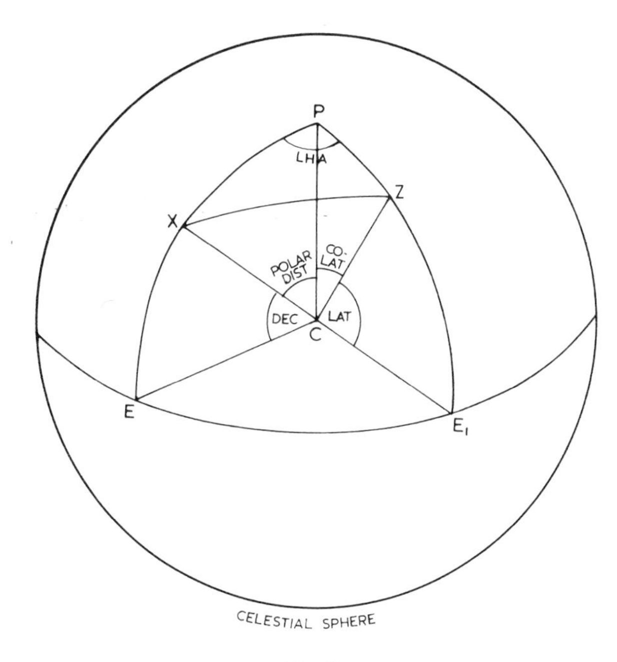

Fig 9

The position of the Pole is fixed. For a given moment in time, the position of the heavenly body (X) is fixed by declination and GHA.

Assuming such a fixed position for the heavenly body, its geographical position could be plotted on a chart by converting the declination and GHA to latitude and longitude. The bearing and distance of the observer from this position would then fix his position.

The true bearing of the heavenly body (X) could be taken by the observer with a compass, and from there it would be but a short step to calculate $P\hat{X}Z$, the bearing of the observer from the geographical position of the heavenly body. Incidentally, the true bearing of the heavenly body from the observer is known as its *azimuth.*

As explained earlier, $Z\hat{C}X$ is the zenith distance, a quantity which once again is but a short arithmetical step or two removed from the altitude as measured with the sextant. This zenith distance, if considered as angular minutes, is equivalent to nautical miles on the surface of the earth.

Thus, having plotted the geographical position of the heavenly body on a chart, the plotting of his bearing and distance would determine the position of the observer. Theoretically, then, the position of the observer may be deduced if the position of the heavenly body, its zenith distance and azimuth are known.

The *Nautical Almanac* tabulates the position of each of the navigational heavenly bodies for each second of the year. Provided the time of the observation is known precisely, the declination and GHA of the body may be extracted from the *Almanac.*

By using a set of tables in the *Nautical Almanac*, the altitude of a heavenly body as measured with a sextant can be readily converted to the zenith distance.

The azimuth of the body can be measured with a compass, but in practice it is calculated by solving the PZX triangle, a relatively easy problem using the *Sight Reduction Tables.* This calculation is used not for the azimuth alone, but also to compare the measured zenith distance with the theoretical zenith distance. This comparison is necessary to overcome a plotting problem, a full explanation being given in Chapter 5.

2 The Nautical Almanac

The *Nautical Almanac* is an annual publication by Her Majesty's Stationery Office, being produced jointly by British and American authorities. Any one almanac covers one calendar year and provides all the data required for navigation at sea. Though relevant to only one particular year, within each issue of the *Almanac* there is information enabling it to be of use during the following year.

Most of the *Almanac* is concerned with the positions of the navigational heavenly bodies, but it also contains sundry other information such as a calendar, a list of standard times kept in various countries, tables containing the corrections to be applied to observed altitudes, rising and setting times of the sun and the moon, and twilight times.

Extracts from various sections of the 1980 *Nautical Almanac* appear in Appendices 1–7. This information was valid only for 1980 and should *not* be used for navigation. The extracts are, of course, to be used to work the examples and exercises in this book.

In order that the *Nautical Almanac* may be of international, world-wide use, all the timings therein are in Greenwich mean time, further consideration to which is given in the next chapter.

Greenwich hour angle

Advantage is taken of the very slow movement of the stars to avoid the tabulation of the Greenwich hour angles of all 57. Instead, the GHA of Aries is tabulated. The sidereal hour angle of each star changes so slowly that it need only be tabulated once for each three-day period, with a consequent saving of space. The GHA of a star for a particular time is obtained by adding its sidereal hour angle to the Greenwich hour angle of Aries (see Chapter 1):

$$\text{GHA star} = \text{SHA star} + \text{GHA Aries}$$

For the remaining bodies–the sun, moon and planets–the sidereal hour angles are constantly changing at different rates, so it is as easy to tabulate the sum of the sidereal hour angles of these bodies and GHA Aries. The GHA of the individual bodies is tabulated.

To keep the *Almanac* to a manageable size, the Greenwich hour angles are tabulated only once for each hour and interpolation tables give increments to be added for each subsequent minute and second.

Unfortunately, the rate of change of GHA is not constant. Not only does it vary from body to body, but also from hour to hour. The interpolation tables assume fixed hourly rates of change for each of the various bodies:

Sun and Planets	15°00.′0
Aries	15°02.′5
Moon	14°19.′0

These 'Increment & Correction' tables (App 6) give the proportion of these figures for each minute and second to be added to the GHA for the tabulated hour. For example, the increment to be added to a tabulated GHA of the sun (or a planet) for 28m 00s is 7°00.′0; that for the moon for 28m 24s is 6°46.′6.

The difference between the assumed hourly rates given above and the actual change for a given hour is tabulated as a 'v' figure adjacent to the hourly GHA. In all cases other than Venus, whose hourly rate of change may be less than that assumed for the planets (15°00.′0), 'v' is positive. A further correction must be applied to the GHA, that proportion of 'v' corresponding to the number of minutes within the hour. This is extracted from the right-hand side of the Increment & Correction table under 'v or d' and 'Corrn'. For example, when v=2.′0, the correction to be applied for 29m is 1.′0; when v=6.′7 the correction to be applied for 30m is 3.′4.

Strictly speaking, the correction should be extracted from the column for the nearest minute, but the values of 'v' are such that it is sufficiently accurate not only to ignore the seconds, but to use the column to which reference is already being made for the increment for the minutes and seconds.

Declination

The First Point of Aries, being an imaginary heavenly body on the celestial equator, has no declination. The declinations of the real heavenly bodies are tabulated at hourly intervals, and, once again, it is necessary to interpolate for the minutes within the hour. (The hourly rate of change of declination is always such that the odd seconds may be ignored.) The rate of change of declination for a particular hour is tabulated as a 'd' figure, and the correction is found by using it in exactly the same way as the 'v' figure. The arithmetical sign of the 'd' correction, which may be either positive or negative, is determined by inspection of the declination for the following hour and deciding whether it is increasing or decreasing.

Daily pages

The hour-by-hour information is contained within the daily pages, some extracts of which appear in App 3. The lay-out of the *Almanac* is such that all the information for a three-day period appears on a double-page spread. The left-hand page deals with the stars and the planets, and the right-hand page with the sun and the moon.

ARIES

The GHA for Aries is tabulated for each hour. 'v' is zero. At the foot of the GHA column is the time of the Meridian Passage of Aries for the middle day of the three. (Meridian passage is when the GHA is zero.)

PLANETS

Adjacent to each of the four names is a figure representing the planet's stellar magnitude–the lower the number, the brighter the body. The GHA is tabulated for each hour, and it is sufficiently accurate to give one average hourly rate of change for the three-day period. 'v' appears at the foot of the GHA column. Note that Venus may have a negative 'v' figure.

Declination is tabulated at hourly intervals, but note that the cardinal sign and the whole number of degrees appear only once at the beginning of each six-hour block. The hourly rate of change is, once again, such that it is sufficient to give an average for the three-day period, and it appears at the foot of the declination column as a 'd' figure. At the bottom right-hand corner of this left-hand page are the SHAs and meridian passage times of each of the four planets for the middle of the three-day period.

STARS

The relative movement of the stars is such that it is sufficient to tabulate just one value for each of SHA and declination for the three-day period.

SUN

Once more the GHA is tabulated for each hour, but 'v' is so small as to be insignificant and is thus not tabulated. At the foot of the GHA column is a figure for SD. It is the angular semi-diameter of the sun expressed in minutes, and is a quantity required for certain calculations to be met later.

Declination requires one average figure for 'd' for the three-day period.

MOON

The moon, unlike all the other navigational heavenly bodies, revolves around–and quite close to–the earth. Consequently its rate of movement is high when compared with the others.

GHA is tabulated for each hour, as is a 'v' figure. Declination is also tabulated hourly along with a 'd' figure. The semi-diameter of the moon is given for each day at the foot of the column. HP is a figure for Horizontal Parallax, to be used when correcting altitudes.

The remainder of the right-hand page is concerned with sunrise, sunset, moonrise, moonset, twilights and meridian passages of the sun and moon–all of which, along with the un-explained entries, will be dealt with in a more appropriate context.

Here is an example of the use of the *Almanac*:

What is the GHA and declination of the sun at 09h 28m 48s GMT on 24th February 1980?

From the *Nautical Almanac*, daily pages 24th–26th February (App 3), adjacent to 09h in the '24th' block, in the column headed 'Sun', are found the values of both GHA and declination for that time. At the foot of the declination column will be found the 'd' figure, the average hourly rate of change of declination for the three-day period. By reference to the declination for 10h, note is made that the declination is decreasing, so 'd' is made negative. So the three quantities extracted from the daily pages are:

GHA 311°39.′2 Declination 9°42.′7 S d = –0.′9

Turning next to the 'Increment & Correction' table (App 6), in the 28m block, adjacent to 48s, the increment for the sun's GHA is found to be 7°12.′0. In the same 28m block, adjacent to 0.′9 in the 'v or d' column will be found a correction of 0.′4. This is the correction to be applied to the declination. More concisely, the extraction would look like this:

GHA 09h	311° 39.′2
28m 48s	+ 7° 12.′0
GHA 09h 28m 48s	318° 51.′2

NB GHA is always increasing, so the increment is always added. If the total GHA had exceeded 360°, 360° would have been subtracted.

Dec 09h	9° 42.′7 S
d= 0.′9, 28m	– 0.′4
Dec 09h 28m 48s	9° 42.′3 S

NB The 'd' correction should, theoretically, be extracted from the 29m block, but no significant error is introduced by using the block to which reference is already being made.

Here is another example:

What is the GHA and declination of the moon at 18h 35m 56s on 23rd September 1980?

GHA 18h	280° 44.′9	App 3—Moon
35m 56s	+ 8° 34.′4	App 6—Moon
v= 7.′5	+ 4.′4	App 6
GHA	289° 23.′7	

(NB 'v' is found on the daily pages, adjacent to GHA. In the case of the moon, 'v' is always positive.)

Dec 18h	6° 19.′1 S	App 3—Moon
d= 12.1	– 7.′2	App 6
Dec	6° 11.′9 S	

NB 'd' is on the daily pages adjacent to the declination. It is negative because the declination for the next hour, 19h, is 6° 07.′0 S; ie it is decreasing.

All that remains before closing this chapter is to offer the reader a few exercises. Take care, be meticulous with detail, refer to the text when necessary. Virtually every sight will require the extraction of GHA and declination from the *Nautical Almanac*, and this is the time to ensure that the process is fully understood.

Exercises

1. On 22nd June 1980 at 15h 32m 16s GMT an observation was made of the sun. What was its GHA and declination at that time?
2. What was the GHA and declination of Venus at 03h 29m 18s on 25th February 1980?
3. What was the GHA and declination of the star Sirius on 22nd June 1980 at 12h 30m 48s?
4. What was the GHA and declination of the moon on 24th February 1980 at 08h 32m 08s?

3 Measurement of Time

The sun, supplying as it does heat and light to earth, has always been the basic timepiece for the human race. As the earth moves along its orbit around the sun, or–more in keeping with the navigator's conception of the celestial sphere–as the sun moves around the earth, so the seasons come and go. One such complete revolution or cycle is known as a year, and is one basic unit of time. Another basic unit is the period of revolution of the earth about its own axis. This, of course, is a day. A day is defined as the interval which elapses between two successive transits of the sun (or any other heavenly body) across the same meridian.

Unfortunately, the apparent speed of the sun around the celestial sphere is not constant, so the sun is not a perfect timepiece. This irregularity means that the interval between two successive transits of the sun across the same meridian is not constant. Thus the *apparent solar day* is not a fixed interval.

To overcome the problem of the varying length of the apparent solar day, a *mean sun* is introduced. This hypothetical mean sun is thought of as completing one full orbit of the celestial sphere in the same time as the true sun, but with the refinement of travelling at a constant speed. Thus the *mean solar day*–that is, the interval between two successive transits of the mean sun across the same meridian–is of fixed duration.

The mean solar day is divided into 24 *mean solar hours*, each of which is divided into 60 *mean solar minutes*, which are in turn divided into 60 *mean solar seconds*. This *mean solar time* is the time in everyday use, but the prefix 'mean solar' is not used.

For many reasons it is more convenient to change days at midnight, whereas logically the days should change at noon when the mean sun crosses the meridian. To effect the change of day at midnight, when it has the least disruptive effect, mean solar time is taken as the *local hour angle of the mean sun* (LHAMS) (expressed in time) $\pm$ 12h. In other words, when the mean sun is on the meridian and its local hour angle is zero, the mean solar time is 12h. At midnight when the LHA is 12h, the mean solar time is 24h or 00h.

The *Local Mean Time* (LMT) is the mean time kept at any place on earth, when the LHAMS is measured from the meridian of that place. The LMT at any instant is the LHAMS (always measured westwards) $\pm$ 12h.

Greenwich Mean Time (GMT) is LMT on the Greenwich meridian. GMT at any instant is the *Greenwich hour angle of the mean sun* (GHAMS) $\pm$ 12h.

The earth revolves about its own axis at a constant rate, and completes a revolution of 360° in 24h, which is the same as 15° in 1h and 15′ in 1m. It is this fixed connection between longitude and time which provides a direct relationship between LMT and GMT. For instance, when the mean sun is on the meridian of 15°W, the LHAMS on that meridian is 0h, whereas an observer on the Greenwich meridian would say that the LHAMS is 1h, the sun having taken that hour to move from the Greenwich meridian to 15°W. The local mean time on the Greenwich meridian being Greenwich mean time, it follows that:

LMT + Long (W) (in time) = GMT

In the example quoted above, on the meridian of 15°W, LMT is 00h. This longitude of 15° is equivalent to 1h, so, on this meridian:

GMT = LMT + Long (W)
= 0h + 1h
GMT = 01h

Another example:

If the LMT in longitude 135°W is 04h, what is the GMT?

15° = 1h
135° = 9h
GMT = 04h + 9h

GMT = 13h

The converse is also true:

LMT — Long (E) (in time) = GMT

For example:

If the GMT is 16h, what is the LMT in longitude 75°E?

75° = 5h
LMT = GMT + Long (E)
= 16h + 5h
LMT = 21h

It is not very practicable for each place in the world to keep the same time, neither is it so for each to keep the time of its own meridian. What happens in practice is that areas in a given locality, often whole countries, keep a time based on a convenient local meridian, such that the local time differs from GMT by a whole number of hours. These times are known as Standard Times, and are listed under the names of the various countries in the *Nautical Almanac*.

In order to keep time at sea, where it is obviously impractical to work to the nearest meridian, which will be forever changing, the earth is divided into bands or zones of 15° of longitude, or 1h of time. The time kept in any particular zone is the LMT for the meridian at the centre of the zone.

The zone based on the Greenwich meridian is ZO (or just Z) and extends from $7\frac{1}{2}$°E to $7\frac{1}{2}$°W. The next zone westwards, extending from $7\frac{1}{2}$°W tp $22\frac{1}{2}$°W, is Z+1.
The time kept in ZO is GMT.
The time kept in Z+1 is 1h earlier than GMT.
The time kept in Z–2 ($22\frac{1}{2}$°E to $37\frac{1}{2}$°E) is 2h later than GMT.

So another rule emerges:

Zone Time + Zone Number = GMT

With these calculations, GMT is better called the *Greenwich Date* (GD) in order to allow for a change of day.

Examples:

1. If the Zone Time in Z+6 on 8th February is 11h 16m 36s, what is the Greenwich date?

ZT		08d 11h 16m 36s (February)
Z + 6	+	06h
GD		08d 17h 16m 36s (February)

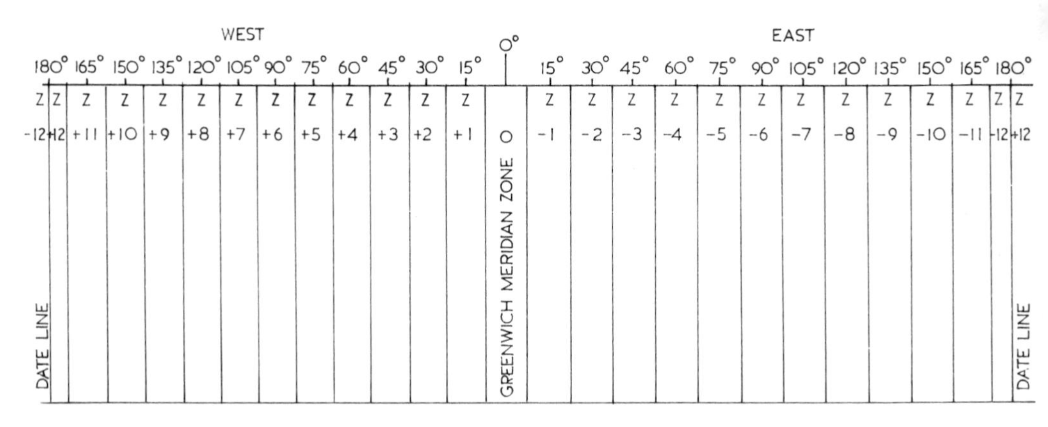

Fig 10

2. In Z–10, the Zone Time on 12th February is 06h 16m 37s. What is the Greenwich date?

ZT		12d	06h	16m	37s	(February)
Z − 10	−		10h			
GD		11d	20h	16m	37s	(February)

3. In Z+8 the Zone Time on 31st January is 19h 27m 54s. What is the Greenwich date?

ZT		31d	19h	27m	54s	(January)
Z + 8	+		08h			
GD		01d	03h	27m	54s	(February)

While at sea, if Zone Time is kept, it is important that this time should be entered in the ship's log above the time column, and changed as the appropriate meridians are crossed. The keeping of Zone Time is essential if the routine of the vessel is to bear any sensible relationship to night and day, and the 'domestic' clocks should be so set. However, the timings in the *Nautical Almanac* are all in GMT. It has already been said that the time of an observation is often needed to the nearest second. This means that the navigator needs constant reference to accurate GMT. The traditional way of achieving this is by the use of a chronometer–a timepiece, the greatest virtue of which is a constant rate of gain or loss regardless of climatic conditions, rather than an indication of the precise time. The constant rate of change makes it a relatively simple arithmetical calculation to deduce GMT, once the error for a particular time has been established by comparison of the chronometer with GMT, such as by the radio time signals. With the advent of the quartz-crystal watch and clock movements, the acquisition of good timepieces is not as expensive as it once was. None the less, these watches and clocks will still need frequent checking against time signals if one is to have confidence in them.

Whether one uses a chronometer or a quartz alarm clock (in future, the term 'deck watch' will be used to describe the timepiece), there is every chance that the indicated time will not be the exact GMT. The difference between *Deck Watch Time* (DWT) and the exact GMT is the *Deck Watch Error* (DWE) and must be applied to the timing of each observation.

A further complication in timekeeping is that most deck watches will keep to a 12h system whereas, because it is the easiest way of avoiding confusion between AM and PM, the 24h system is used for navigation. When away from the Greenwich meridian it is not always obvious whether the deck watch indication of 5h is 05h or 17h, particularly if lunch is being served! Uncertainty can be eliminated by deducing GMT, including the day, from the ship's clock and the Zone Time to which it is set.

Examples:

1. On 21st July an observation was made when the deck watch, which was 24s fast, indicated 1h 14m 17s. The ship's clock showed a time of 19h 10m and was set to Z+6. What was the Greenwich date of the observation?

ZT		21d	19h	10m	(July)
Z + 6	+		06h		
GD		22d	01h	10m	(July)

So the observation was actually made at about 01h 10m GMT on 22nd July, the exact time being:

DWT		1h	14m	17s
DWE (Fast)	−			24s
GMT		01h	13m	53s

NB The observation was made at this time on 22nd July, not 13h 13m 53s on 21st July.

2. On 7th August while in Z–10 and the ship's clock indicated 06h 16m, an observation was made when the deck watch indicated 8h 10m 34s. If the deck watch was 5m 18s slow, what was the Greenwich date of the observation?

ZT		07d	06h	16m	(August)
Z − 10	−		10h		
GD		06d	20h	16m	(August)

DWT		8h	10m	34s
DWE (Slow)	+		05m	18s
GMT		20h	15m	52s

NB The observation was made at this time on 6th August, not 08h 15m 52s on 7th August.

Exercises

1. LMT in longitude 120°W is 07h. What is GMT?
2. LMT in longitude 90°E is 17h. What is GMT?
3. GMT in longitude 147°W is 09h. What is LMT?
4. Zone Time in Z+6 on 18th January is 15h 37m 14s. What is the Greenwich date?

5. Zone Time in Z–12 on 12th September is 08h 16m 47s. What is the Greenwich date?

6. Zone Time in Z+11 on 30th June is 18h 56m 07s. What is the Greenwich date?

7. On 18th March when the DWT was 6h 14m 38s, an observation was made. The ship's time in Z+6 was 12h 05m. DWE 8m 17s fast. What was the Greenwich date of the observation?

8. On 15th July while in Z–8, the ship's clock indicated 06h 50m as an observation was made. DWT 10h 48m 39s. DWE 2m 18s slow. What was the Greenwich date of the observation?

9. On 18th August while in Z+11 and the ship's clock indicated 17h 07m, an observation was made. DWT 3h 53m 37s. DWE 10m 14s slow. What was the Greenwich date of the observation?

4 The Sextant

The previous chapters have begun to explain how, given the altitudes of heavenly bodies for specific times, one's position on the surface of the earth may be fixed. It is now time to consider how these altitudes–that is, the angles between the heavenly bodies and the horizon–are measured and also the instrument used for that purpose. Over the years a number of devices have been used, from the back-staff to the Al-Kemal, from the coconut shell to the octant, but the instrument to be considered here is the one which is probably most familiar, by name at least–the sextant.

Description

Basically there are two types of sextant: the 'micrometer' and the 'vernier'. The latter, though potentially just as accurate as the former, is much more difficult to read and has now fallen out of favour with both manufacturers and most navigators, so the micrometer sextant, as illustrated in Fig 11 (see overleaf, p24) is the one considered here.

The Frame. The 'backbone' of the sextant on which the rest of the component parts are mounted.

The Arc. The lower edge of the frame is marked in degrees, from right to left 0°–120°, known as degrees 'on' the arc, and from left to right 0°–5°, known as degrees 'off' the arc.

The Horizon Glass. Fixed at right angles to the frame, one half is clear through which the horizon is viewed, the other half being a mirror in which is seen a reflection of the heavenly body.

The Horizon Shades. A selection of coloured glasses to be turned up, as required, beyond the clear part of the horizon glass in order to clarify the view of the horizon.

The Index Bar. Pivoted at the top of the frame, the other end, with an arrow indicating by how much, moves along the arc.

The Index Glass. A mirror, fixed to the index bar such that it is at right angles to the frame, and located such that its centre of rotation is in line with the index bar pivot. When the arrow on the index bar points at 0′ on the arc, the index and horizon glasses should be parallel. In all other cases the arrow indicates the angle between the two glasses.

The Index Shades. A selection of coloured glasses, to be turned up as required, to modify the brightness of the heavenly body being observed.

The Telescope. With the more expensive sextants, a selection of telescopes are available enabling some observations to be made more easily or more accurately.

The Index Bar Clamp. While this is operated, a worm is disengaged from a rack, allowing the index bar to be moved freely. When moving the index bar in this way, make certain that this clamp is fully depressed, thus obviating any wear between the worm and the rack.

The Micrometer Drum. Small movements of the index bar–and during an actual observation the final ones–are made by turning this drum, which turns the worm which drives the index bar along the arc.

The Handle. This is not accessible while the sextant is in its case. The sextant should be removed from the case by grasping the frame (and nothing else) with the left hand, before transferring the sextant to the right hand when it should be held by the handle.

Fig 11

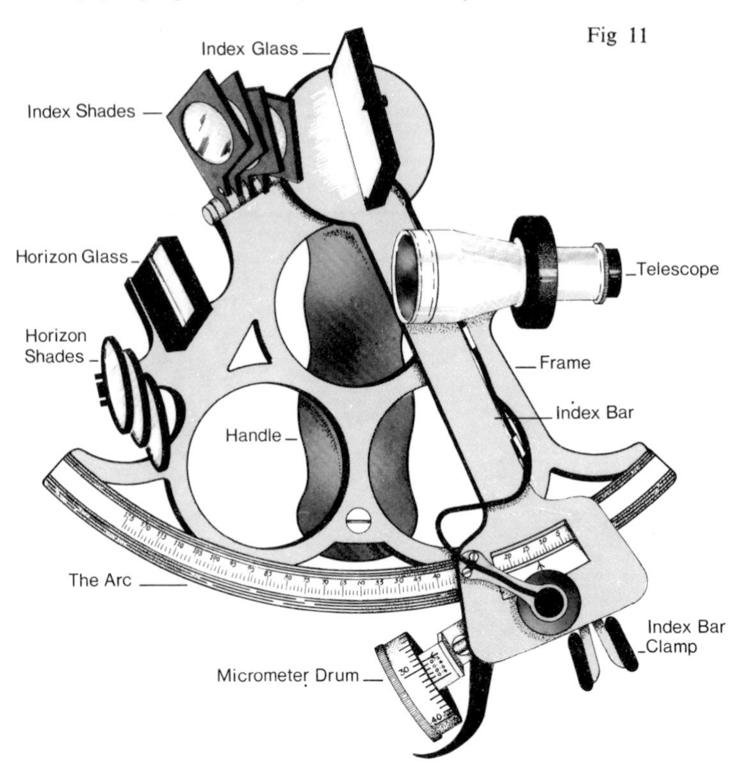

Care and Handling
The sextant, though often handled in atrocious conditions, must always be treated as a fragile, precise optical instrument, as indeed it is. One thoughtless move could result in the observer nursing an armful of scrap.

Before removing the sextant from its box, note the position of the shades and the index bar. There is every chance that the snug fit required means that the sextant will only fit into the box one way. Having made that mental note, remove the sextant from the box by the correct use of frame and handle. As mentioned earlier, the worm and rack must be fully disengaged by operating the clamp before moving the index bar. Other wear can be avoided by keeping the whole instrument–but particularly the moving parts–clean and lubricated. Sooner or later the sextant will get wet, and the only answer to that is to dry it as soon as possible, preferably with a chamois leather. Make a thorough job of the mirrors and the arc; with a little luck no harm will be done.

When replacing or changing the telescope, make sure the threads are not 'crossed'.

A final golden rule: the sextant should always be in a hand or in its box. There is virtually no excuse for it being anywhere else—even for a second. Before closing the lid on it, make sure the shades and index bar are in the right position.

The Principle
The sextant, more correctly called a mirror sextant, has an arc of a sixth part of a circle, or 60° hence its name, though it actually measures angles up to 120°. This apparent anomaly can be explained by two basic optical principles. The first is '*the angle of incidence equals the angle of reflection*'. This, quite simply, means that assuming a reflecting surface is flat (plane), a ray of light will be reflected from it at the same angle as that at which it hit the surface. This is illustrated in Fig 12.

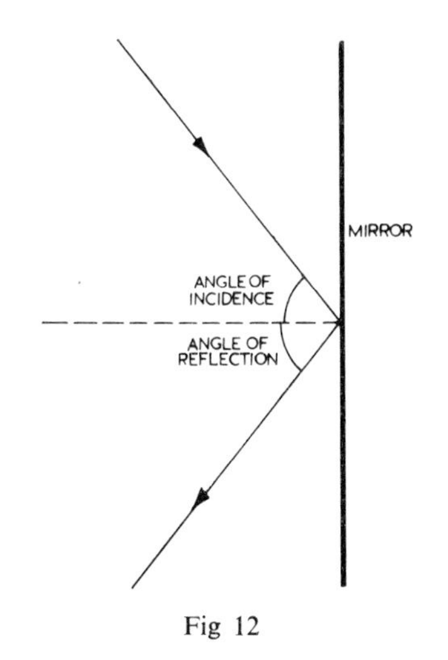

Fig 12

The second optical principle is '*if a ray of light is reflected twice in the same plane by two plane mirrors, the angle between the first and last directions of the ray is twice the angle between the reflecting surfaces of the mirrors*'. Fig 13 illustrates how this applies to the sextant.

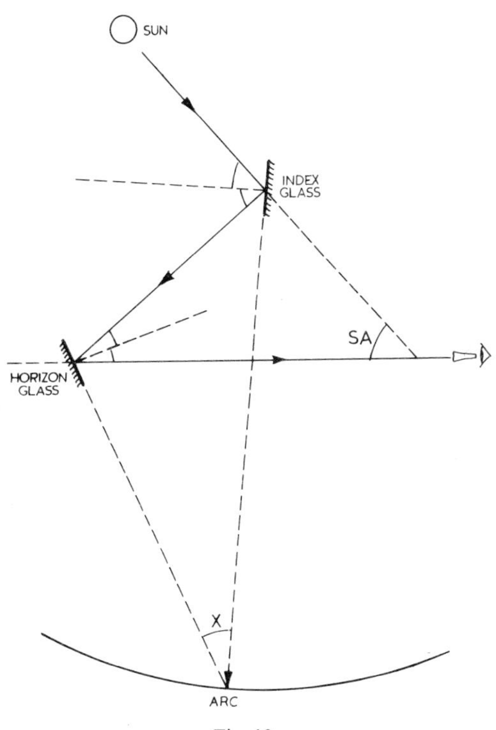

Fig 13

In all sextants the horizon glass and telescope are fixed so that a ray of light from the centre of the index glass will always be reflected through the telescope. As illustrated, by moving the index bar the index glass has been adjusted so that a ray of light from the sun has been reflected by it on to the horizon glass where, in turn, it has been reflected through the telescope to the observer's eye. Bearing in mind that the horizon glass is half clear and half mirror, the observer can now see through the left-hand half to the horizon, and in the right-hand half he can see the ray of light from the sun. If the index bar is adjusted so that the ray of light from the sun is coincident with the horizon, the angle SA is the altitude of that portion of the heavenly body from which the ray of light emanated.

All heavenly bodies except for the sun and the moon are taken to be a 'point source' of light, so the reflection of the whole of a star or planet is made coincident with the horizon. The sun and moon being of significant relative size, the reflection of one edge or '*limb*' is made to coincide with the horizon.

The actual angle between the two mirrors, X°, is half the angle SA°. To overcome this problem and enable the required angle to be read off directly, the arc of 60° is divided into 120 parts, and each part, though really a half degree, is graduated as a degree.

Reading the Sextant

It has already been said that the index bar has an arrow on it which points to the scale on the arc and indicates the number of degrees set on the sextant. To make an accurate observation, it is necessary to be able to read off the angle to decimals of a minute.

The micrometer drum with the worm and rack is geared so that one complete revolution of the drum will move the index bar through one complete (indicated) degree. The drum is thus divided into 60 parts, each equivalent to 1′. A second fixed arrow, adjacent to the drum, indicates the numer of minutes set on the sextant.

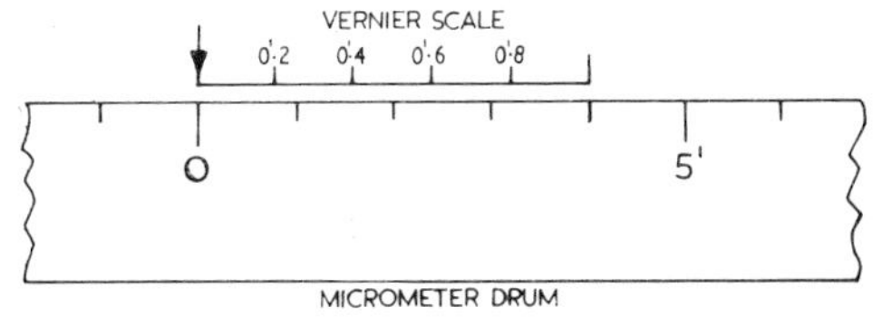

Fig 14

Also adjacent to the drum, and using the same second fixed arrow as a starting point, is inscribed a vernier scale to indicate the decimals of a minute, usually in units of two tenths.

Fig 14 shows a reading of X°00.′0 because the arrow on the vernier scale is in line with the zero.

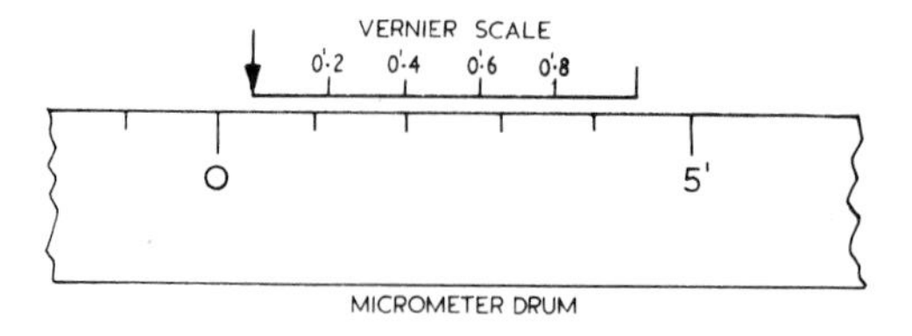

Fig 15

Fig 15 shows a reading of X°00.′4 because the arrow is between 00′ and 01′, and the 0.′4 line on the vernier scale is in line with a line on the micrometer drum.

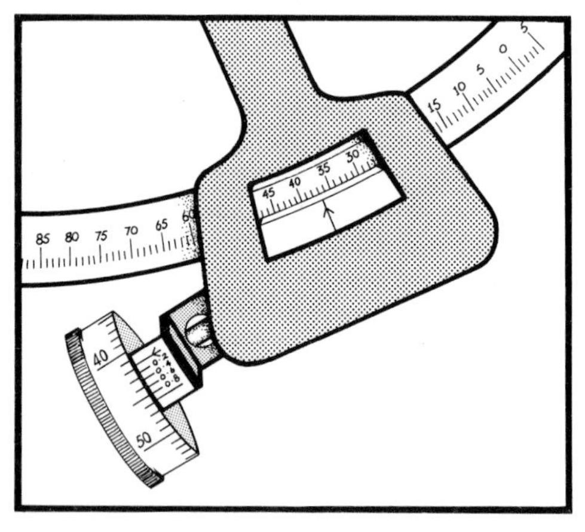

Fig 16

Fig 16 shows a complete reading of 36°41.′8.

When adjusting the sextant, it will sometimes be necessary to measure 'negative' angles. That is, the reading will be 'off' the arc. In this case, because the micrometer drum has been turned the 'wrong' way, the indicated minutes and decimals of minutes must be subtracted from 60′. The number of degrees will be indicated, as normal, by the arrow on the index bar, 'off' the arc.

The reading of the sextant should be practised at the earliest opportunity. Though not difficult, it requires a little experience to be sure of making quick and accurate readings.

Adjustments

In order to give accurate results, the sextant requires the following four conditions to be satisfied:

(1) The two surfaces of each mirror and each shade must be parallel.

(2) The arc, micrometer drum and vernier scale must be accurately graduated.

(3) The pivot of the index glass must be at the centre of the arc, and the axis of the index bar must be perpendicular to the plane of the instrument.

(4) The index and horizon glasses should be perpendicular, and the axis of the telescope parallel, to the plane of the instrument.

The first three conditions are attended to by the manufacturer, and any remaining errors are carefully checked with laboratory instruments and a certificate issued stating any discrepancies which should be allowed for. The fourth condition can be satisfied by 'on board' adjustments by the observer.

The errors listed below are named and explained in the only order in which they can be corrected.

Perpendicularity. This is the state of the index glass being perpendicular to the plane of the instrument. To check for perpendicularity, firstly the telescope must be removed, then the index bar set to a reading of about 40°. With the mirrors uppermost and the index glass nearest the eye, look across the sextant in such a way that the portion of the arc between the index bar and the index glass can be seen. In the index glass should also be seen a reflection of the 120° end of the arc. If this is not the case, adjust the index bar until it is.

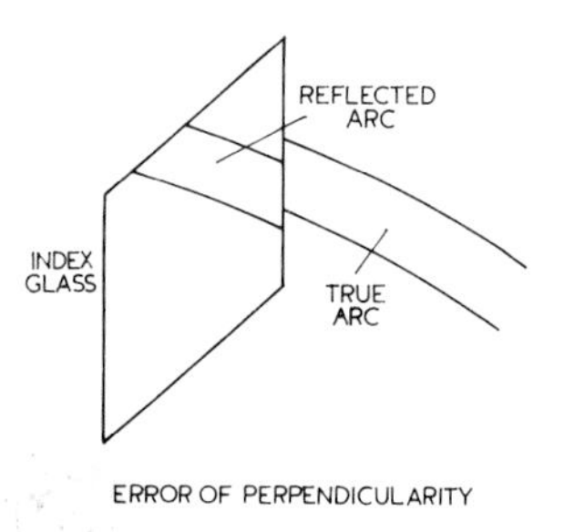

Fig 17

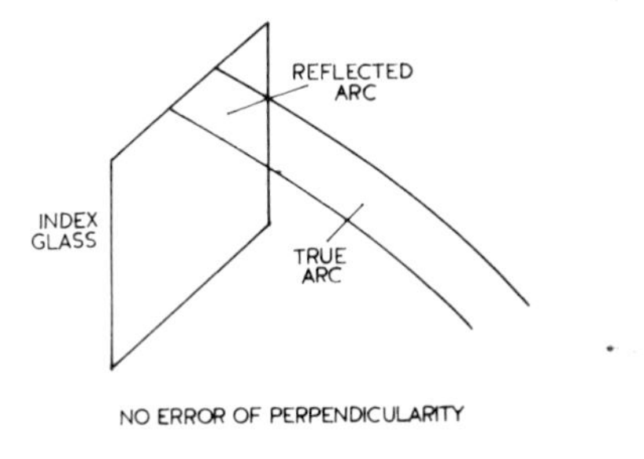

Fig 18

If the real arc and the reflected portion seen in the index mirror appear to be a continuous, unbroken line, the index mirror is perpendicular to the plane of the sextant and no error of perpendicularity exists. Should this not be the case, adjust the angle of the mirror very carefully by turning the screw at the back until the error is corrected. Finally, tap the side of the mirror gently to make sure it is 'settled', and check the angle once more. Make all adjustments as small and as gentle as possible. Too much adjustment might crack the glass.

Side error. The horizon glass must be perpendicular to the plane of the instrument, otherwise side error exists. In daylight the easiest way to check for and to adjust side error is to use the horizon. The telescope must be shipped and the index bar, micrometer drum and vernier set to zero. Turn the sextant on its side, mirrors uppermost, and look through the telescope at the horizon. In view should be the reflected horizon, and either side of the horizon glass the real horizon should be visible.

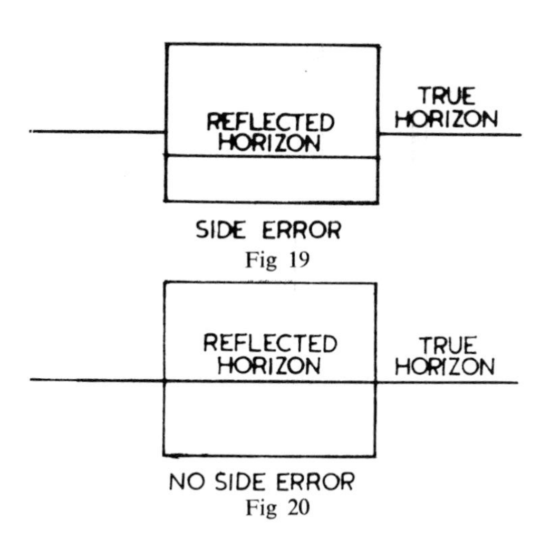

Fig 19

Fig 20

If the real and reflected horizons are not in line, the angle of the horizon glass must be adjusted by what is, for the moment, the upper screw at the back of the glass.

An alternative method of checking for and adjusting this error is to use a heavenly body. The sextant is used in its normal vertical position, and a heavenly body is observed–let's say it's a star. While moving the index bar across the zero on the arc, ensure that the reflected image of the star passes exactly over the real star as seen through the clear side of the horizon glass.

Index error. When the sextant reads zero, the index and horizon glasses should be parallel. If they are not, index error exists. To correct this error it is necessary to adjust a second screw on the back of the horizon glass. These two screws naturally enough interact to a certain extent, so by eliminating index error, the recently eliminated side error will be re-introduced. The secret is to 'juggle' with the two adjustments for a while, finally settling for no side error and a small amount of index error, perhaps less than 5′, which may be allowed for in the subsequent calculations.

There are, basically, three ways in which the index error may be checked, and they follow in ascending order of accuracy and descending order of ease. Which method is used is usually dictated by circumstance.

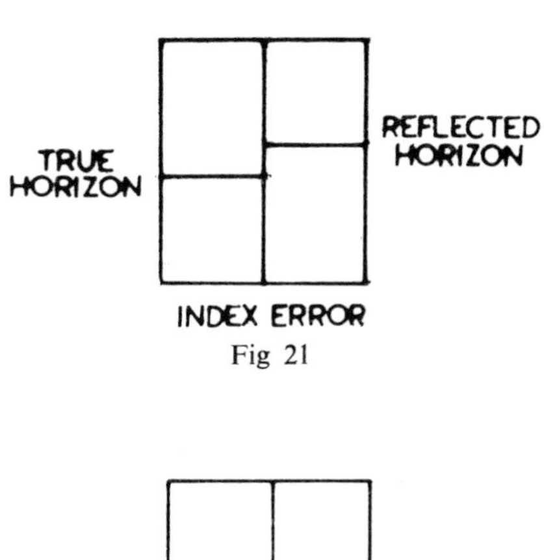

Fig 21

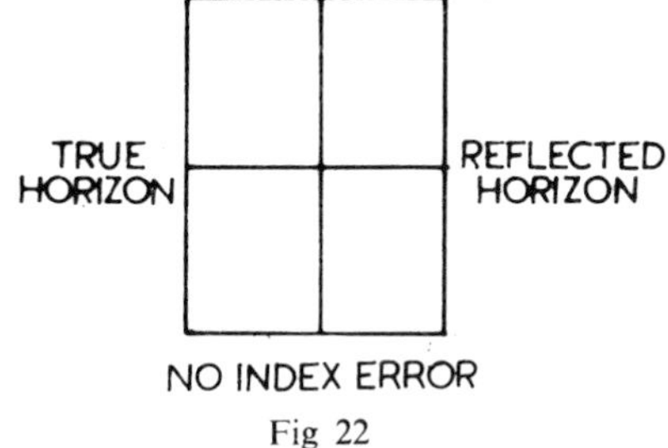

Fig 22

(1) *By observing the horizon*
Holding the sextant in its conventional upright position set the reading to zero; then, looking through the telescope to the horizon glass, view the true horizon and alongside it its reflected image.

If the true and reflected horizons do not make one continuous line, index error exists. By adjusting the micrometer drum until these two horizons are in line, the value of the index error will be indicated. Ideally, the circumstances of the two mirrors being parallel will occur when the instrument is reading zero. If this is the case, well and good. It is more likely that there will be index error as indicated by a reading. This reading will be either 'on' the arc or 'off' the arc.

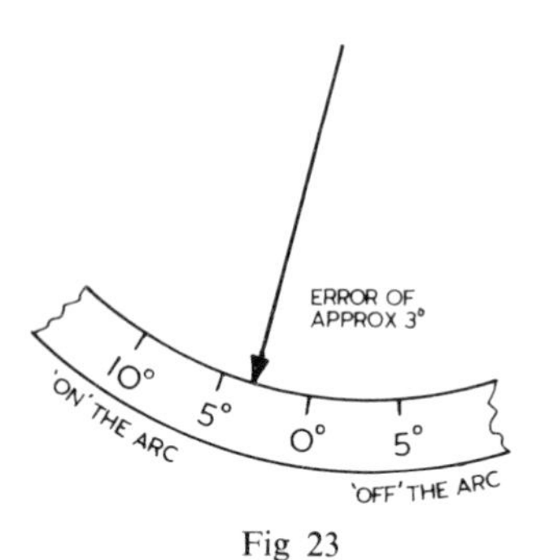

Fig 23

Fig 23 illustrates an unacceptably large index error of about 3° on the arc. If this instrument were used with no further adjustment, this index error would have to be subtracted from any further sextant readings in order to obtain the correct reading. To introduce the correct terminology, this index error would be subtracted from the *sextant altitude* to obtain the *observed altitude*. The reason for subtracting this index error, which is 'on' the arc, is simply that it is with this reading set on the instrument that the two mirrors are parallel, and it is from that starting point that all readings should be measured. Conversely, if the index error was found to be 'off' the arc, its value would have to be added to the sextant altitude to obtain the observed altitude.

The index error chosen above was a particularly large one, used merely to illustrate a point. In practice, by constantly adjusting the side error, then the index error, then the side error, etc, the moment should arrive when there is no side error and index error will be less than 5′. This is the time to cease the adjustments. The important point to be appreciated is that index error is the only one which can be allowed for arithmetically, so it is the only one which is acceptable. All other errors must be eliminated completely.

(2) *By observing a star*
Set the sextant to zero and point it directly at any star. Adjust the micrometer drum, if necessary, to make the reflected image of the star coincide with the true image. Once again, when this has been achieved, the resulting reading will be the index error, and will be either 'on' or 'off' the arc.

(3) *By observing the diameter of the sun*
Whenever observing the sun, care must be taken to avoid damage to the eyes by using the correct shades to reduce the glare.

To measure the diameter of the sun, the sextant is set to about zero, the correct selection of shades is made and then the instrument is pointed directly at the sun. The reflected image is made to 'sit' on top of the true image by adjusting the micrometer drum, when a reading 'off' the arc will be noted. The situation is then reversed, and the true image of the sun is made to sit on top of its reflected image. This time a reading 'on' the arc will be noted. Half the difference between these two readings is the index error, its sign (described as 'on' or 'off' the arc) being the same as the larger of the two readings obtained.

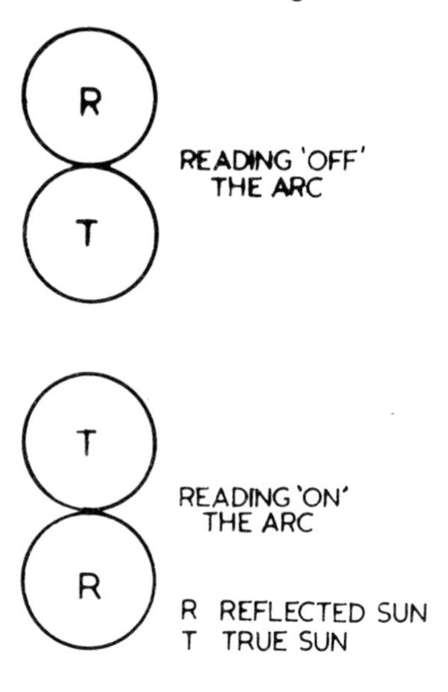

Figs 24 and 25 These are two representations of what is seen in the field of view of the sextant. In Fig 24 the reflected sun is 'sat' on top of the real sun; in Fig 25 the true sun is 'sat' upon the reflected image

The virtue of this method is that the accuracy of the observation can be checked quite easily. By adding the two readings together, the index error–which has appeared in both readings, but with opposite arithmetical signs–will cancel out, leaving a figure which represents two diameters of the sun. On the daily pages of the *Nautical Almanac*, at the bottom of the sun column, is an entry for SD (semi-diameter), the diameter of half the sun. When multiplied by 4, this figure should be the same as the sum of the two diameters just measured.

Example:
On the 20th June 1980 an observation of the sun was made to ascertain the index error of the sextant.

1st diameter of sun	33.′4	on the arc
2nd diameter of sun	29.′8	off the arc
Difference	3.′6	
Index error	1.′8	on the arc

On the daily page of the *Nautical Almanac* (App 3) for 20th June, at the bottom of the sun column, it is noted that the SD is 15.′8.

1st diameter of sun	33.′4
2nd diameter of sun	29.′8
Diameter of sun × 2	63.′2
Semi-diameter	15.′8
SD × 4	63.′2

Twice the diameter, as observed, equals 4 times the tabulated semi-diameter, therefore the observation is seen to be accurate.

Operation

If the sextant is not exactly vertical during an observation, the altitude measured will not be that above the point of the horizon immediately beneath the heavenly body, but that from a point to one side. The angle measured will be too great. If, during the observation, the sextant is '*rocked*' either side of the vertical, the reflection of the body will be seen to swing like a pendulum. It is when the body is at the lowest point of its swing that the sextant is vertical, and that is the reading which is required.

Summary

Always handle the sextant correctly and carefully. Each time it is used, it should be checked for the following errors in the order given: (1) Perpendicularity; (2) Side error; (3) Index error.

When observing the sun, be sure to use the correct shades to avoid eye damage.

If the index error is 'on' the arc, it must be subtracted from the sextant altitude to obtain the observed altitude. If the index error is 'off' the arc, it must be added to the sextant altitude to obtain the observed altitude. (If it's 'on', take it off, if it's 'off', add it on.)

Remember to 'rock' the sextant.

Conversion of sextant altitude to true altitude

The altitude as measured by the sextant requires five corrections to be applied before the *true altitude* is obtained. They are: (1) Index error; (2) Dip; (3) Refraction; (4) Semi-diameter; (5) Parallax. These corrections must be applied in the order given, for reasons which will become obvious.

INDEX ERROR

This is the error of the instrument itself and has already been discussed. All that need be said here is to repeat that if the index error is 'on' the arc it must (arithmetically) be taken off; if it is 'off' the arc it must be added on. The sextant altitude, when corrected for index error, becomes the *observed altitude*.

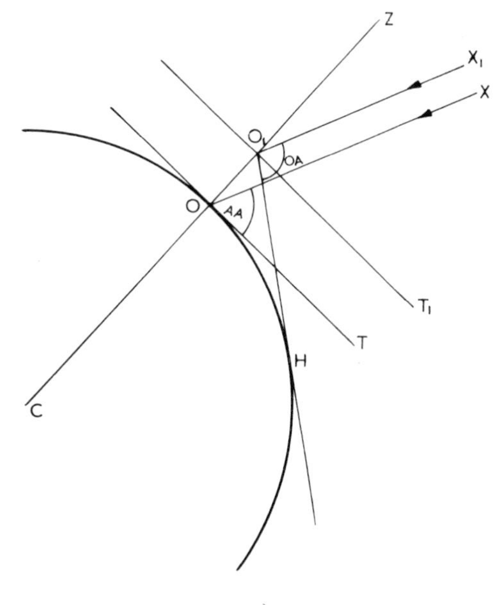

Fig 26

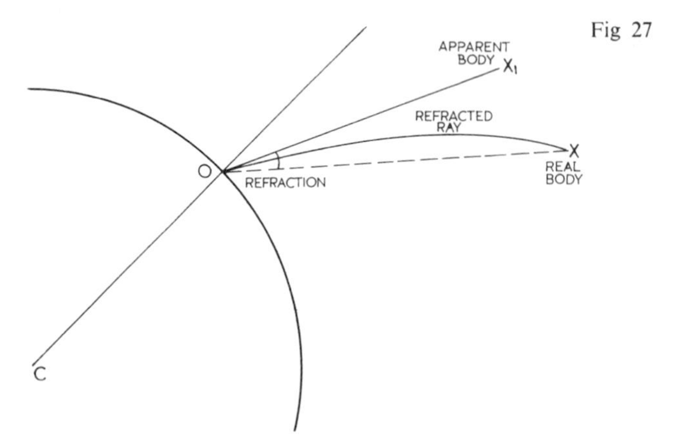

Fig 27

DIP

In Fig 26, 0_1 is the observer's eye, and 00_1 is the *height of eye*. H is the observer's visible sea horizon. OT is a tangent to the earth's surface, and O_1T_1 is parallel to that tangent. For the moment it is assumed that the heavenly body is so distant that X_1O_1 and XO, both rays of light from the same source, are parallel. This will be considered further under 'parallax'. $X_1\hat{O}_1H$ is the observed altitude.

$T_1\hat{O}_1H$ is known as the *angle of dip*, and when subtracted from the observed altitude, $X_1\hat{O}_1H$, leaves $X_1\hat{O}_1T_1$, which equals $X\hat{O}T$ and is known as the *apparent altitude*. It is worth noting that dip is always subtracted from the observed altitude to obtain the apparent altitude.

REFRACTION

When a ray of light passes from the rarefied atmosphere of 'space' into the relatively dense atmosphere of earth, it is refracted or bent in a curve, as illustrated in Fig 27.

The effect is that the body appears to be at point X_1 whereas in reality it is at point X. Consequently, the observer sees the body at a higher altitude than it really is. The 'extra' is the angle of refraction and is subtracted from the apparent altitude. This refraction varies from zero when the body is at the observer's zenith, to a maximum when the body is on the horizon.

SEMI-DIAMETER

Most of the heavenly bodies used for navigation are so distant, and apparently so small, that they may be considered as point sources of light. However, in the cases of the sun and the moon, this is not so.

When observing the sun, the observation is usually made of the lower edge or *lower limb*, denoted by LL or $\underline{O}$. The alternative, naturally, is to observe the *upper limb*, UL or $\overline{O}$. The position of all the heavenly bodies tabulated in the *Nautical Almanac* is that of the centres. If, therefore, an observation is made of one or other limb a correction equivalent to the half diameter must be applied to the observation. This semi-diameter correction is added if the lower limb has been

Fig 28

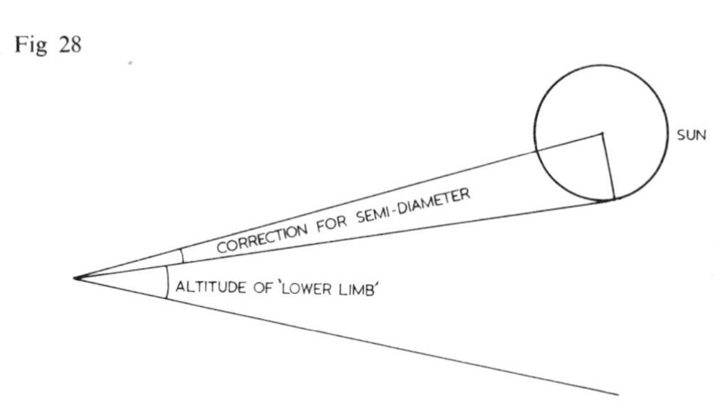

observed, and subtracted in the case of the upper limb.

When observing the moon one does not usually have a choice of limb, but the same principle applies.

PARALLAX

In Fig 29 OT is a tangent to the earth and CS is parallel to it. $X\hat{O}T$ is the *apparent altitude*. $X\hat{C}S$ is the *true altitude*. The true altitude is greater than the apparent altitude by an amount equal to the angle marked as parallax. Proof of that statement follows in a moment. When the body, X, is at the observer's zenith, Z, parallax is zero, and when the body is on the horizon, T, it is at a maximum. In this latter case it is known as *horizontal parallax*, and in all other cases as *parallax in altitude* or just simply *parallax*.

Now for the proof. Considering triangle COX and its external angle $Z\hat{O}X$:

$$
\begin{aligned}
Z\hat{O}X &= O\hat{C}X + O\hat{X}C \\
\text{or } O\hat{C}X &= Z\hat{O}X - \text{Parallax} \\
&= 90^\circ - \text{AA} - \text{Parallax} \\
X\hat{C}S &= 90^\circ - O\hat{C}X \\
\therefore \text{TA} &= 90^\circ - (90^\circ - \text{AA} - \text{Parallax}) \\
\text{TA} &= \text{AA} + \text{Parallax}
\end{aligned}
$$

In practice, some of these corrections are combined. For example, in the case of the sun, stars and planets, refraction, parallax and semi-diameter (where applicable) are combined in one correction known as an altitude correction. So, in practice, when converting the sextant altitude of either the sun, stars or planets to a true altitude, there are just three arithmetical corrections: (1) Index error; (2) Dip; (3) Altitude correction.

Because the moon is so close to the earth the effect of parallax is much greater, and consequently it requires special consideration and appears as a separate correction, making four arithmetical corrections necessary: (1) Index error; (2) Dip; (3) Altitude correction; (4) Parallax.

Each of these corrections, other than index error, is tabulated in the *Nautical Almanac*. App 1 is an extract entitled 'Altitude Correction Tables 10°–90° — Sun, Stars, Planets'. App 7 is a similar extract entitled 'Altitude Correction Tables for the Moon'. This particular extract is for altitudes 0°–35°.

The corrections are now considered in the order in which they must be applied to the sextant altitude.

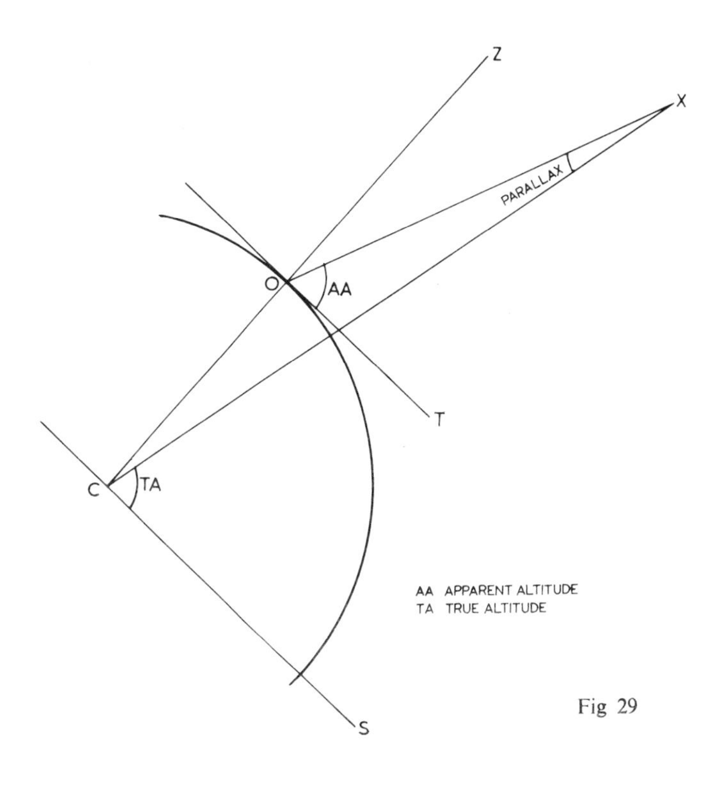

Fig 29

Index error. The value of index error is determined by adjustment of the sextant. The observed altitude is obtained by applying index error to the sextant altitude.

Dip. The value of dip is proportional to the height of the observer's eye and is tabulated in App 1, in the right-hand column. For example, the correction for a height of eye of 2.5m is –2.′8. That for a height of eye of 5.2m is –4.′0. If there is any apparent ambiguity, as in the case of the height of eye of 5.2m, choose the lower correction. The lower (1.0–3.0m) and higher (20–48m) heights of eye are on the extreme right of the table. The apparent altitude is obtained by subtracting dip from the observed altitude.

Altitude correction. The centre column of App 1 contains the combined corrections for refraction and parallax for both stars and planets. Entered with the apparent altitude, the correction extracted, always negative, is zero when the altitude is 90°, increasing as the altitude decreases. Additional corrections are included for Venus and Mars, but at this stage at least may safely be ignored. When considering the sun, an allowance must be made for its semi-diameter. The left-hand portion of App 1 contains the same corrections for refraction and parallax but with the sun's semi-diameter included. Due to the earth's elliptical orbit of the sun, the latter's apparent semi-diameter changes a little throughout the year, so the correction table must not only be entered with the correct limb observed (upper or lower), but also in the column appropriate to the month of the year (Oct–Mar or Apr–Sept).

The moon has its own, slightly more complicated altitude correction tables, an extract from which appears in App 7, with parallax tabulated as a separate correction. The argument with which it is determined is horizontal parallax (the parallax when the altitude is 0°), a quantity which is tabulated in the *Nautical Almanac* for each hour. As an additional convenience, the moon's correction table repeats most of the dip corrections.

The table is in two parts. The upper half is entered with the apparent altitude, each column covering a range of 5°, and, vertically, corrections are given for each 10′ of this apparent altitude. For intermediate angles it is necessary to interpolate. The lower half is entered with the value of the horizontal parallax. the correction being extracted from the same column as that used for the previous extraction. This second correctio has two figures, one for an observation of eac limb. Once again, interpolation may be necessar for an intermediate value of the horizonta parallax. Both corrections must be added to th apparent altitude. In the event of the observatio having been made of the upper limb, 30′ must b subtracted from the total. The true altitude i obtained when the altitude (and parallax correction has been applied to the apparen altitude.

Here are some examples to illustrate the use o the tables:

1. On 21st February 1980 the sextant altitude o the sun's lower limb was 29°47.′2. If the inde error was 2.′5 on the arc and the height of th observer's eye was 2m, what was the tru altitude?

Sextant altitude		29° 47.′2	
Index error (on)	–	2.′5	
Observed altitude		29° 44.′7	
Dip (Height of eye 2m)	–	2.′5	App 1
Apparent altitude		29° 42.′2	
Altitude correction	+	14.′6	App 1, Sun LL, Oct–Ma
True altitude		29° 56.′8	

2. If the sextant altitude of the moon's uppe limb was 27°18.′6 when the index error was 1.′ off the arc, the height of the observer's eye wa 3m and HP was 57.′0, what was the true altitude

SA		27° 18.′6	
IE	+	1.′7	
OA		27° 20.′3	
3m	–	3.′0	App 7 (Dip)
AA		27° 17.′3	
Corr	+	60.′0	App 7, 25°–29° column
HP 57.′0	+	3.′2	Same column, 'U'
		28° 20.′5	
UL	–	30.′0	Upper limb observed
TA		27° 50.′5	

Once again the chapter will close with som exercises. As before, *neatness* is essential. It i important that the conversion of sextant altitude to true altitudes is mastered, for it is somethin which has to be performed each time an ob servation is made.

Exercises

1. On 17th June 1980 an observation was made of the sun's lower limb. Sextant altitude 36°12.′4, index error 3.′0 off the arc, height of eye 2.5m. What was the true altitude?

2. The sextant altitude of Aldebaran was 48°37.′2. If the index error was 1.′5 on the arc and the height of eye was 2m, what was the true altitude?

3. An observation was made of the moon's lower limb. If the sextant altitude was 18°46.′7, the index error was 1.′2 off the arc, the height of eye was 3m and horizontal parallax was 59.′2, what was the true altitude?

5 Position Lines

In Chapter 1 it was suggested that subsequent to an observation the geographical position of the heavenly body could be plotted on a chart, and from that position the azimuth and zenith distance would determine the position of the observer. Whilst this might be so in theory, in practice the distances involved, often thousands of miles, usually make this apparently simple plotting impracticable. What is required is a way of utilising the azimuth and zenith distance in a practical manner.

For the moment, assume that the observer's position is known, and refer to Figs 7 (page 13) and 9 (page 15) as necessary:

The polar distance (PX) is known (90°–declination);
The co-latitude (PZ) is known (90°–latitude);
The LHA ($X\hat{P}Z$) is known (GHA ± longitude).

Knowing these three component parts of the PZX triangle enables the three remaining parts to be calculated. More particularly, the azimuth ($P\hat{Z}X$) and the zenith distance (XZ) can be calculated. But from the observer's real position it is possible to measure what the zenith distance really is. Of course, if the 'assumed position' happened to be the same as the true position this true zenith distance would be the same as the calculated zenith distance. The more likely case, however, is that the assumed position, often an estimated position (EP) will not be exact so there will be a *difference* between the two zenith *distances*.

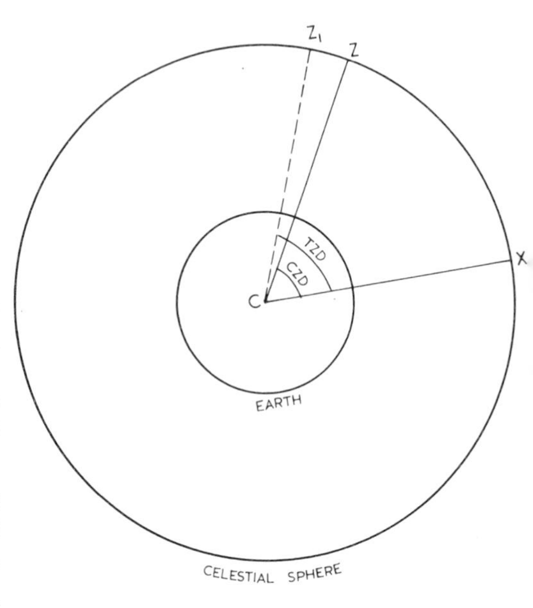

Fig 30

If Z is the zenith of the observer's assumed position, and Z_1 is the zenith of the true position of the observer, then Fig 30 represents a section through CZ_1 Z and X. Thus $Z\hat{C}X$ will be the calculated zenith distance (CZD) and $Z_1\hat{C}X$ will be the true zenith distance (TZD) as could be measured with a sextant. On the surface of the earth these angular distances equate to nautical miles, so the observer's true position is ($Z_1\hat{C}X$–$Z\hat{C}X$) miles from the assumed position. This distance is the *intercept*.

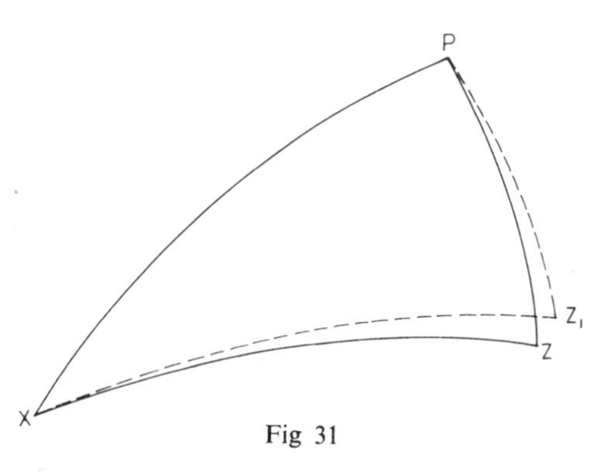

Fig 31

Now to return to the other quantity of interest, the azimuth–$P\hat{Z}X$ in Fig 31. If the assumed position of the observer is relatively close to the true position, then $P\hat{Z}X$ will not be significantly different from $P\hat{Z}_1X$. This being so, XZZ_1 can be taken as a straight line, as can the equivalent geographical positions–the assumed and true positions. If the assumed position were now plotted on a chart, the true position might be taken to be the distance of the intercept away, in the direction of the azimuth.

In reality, all that has been discovered with certainty is the zenith distance, and the observer's true position could be anywhere on the circumference of a circle whose centre is the geographical position of the heavenly body and the radius of which is the true zenith distance.

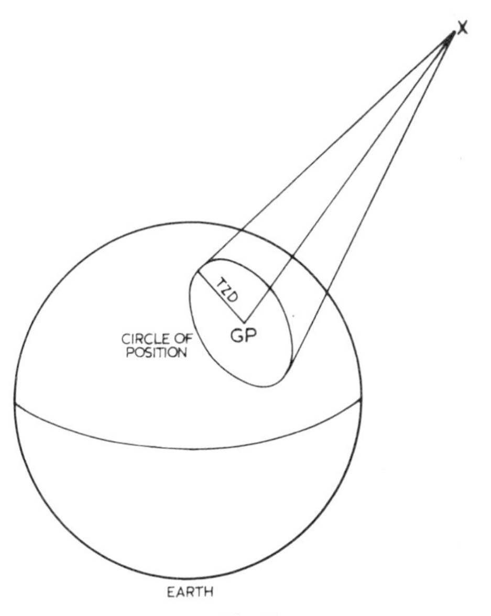

Fig 32

In practice yet another assumption is made, that the observer is somewhere near the assumed position, and that the arc of the circle of position in that immediate vicinity is a straight line at right-angles to the radius, or azimuth.

All this is probably best illustrated with figures and a drawing. From an assumed position it was calculated that the zenith distance should be 57°27′ and that the azimuth should be 050°. The true zenith distance was 57°37′. The intercept is the difference between the two zenith distances:

TZD	57° 37′
CZD	– 57° 27′
Intercept	10′

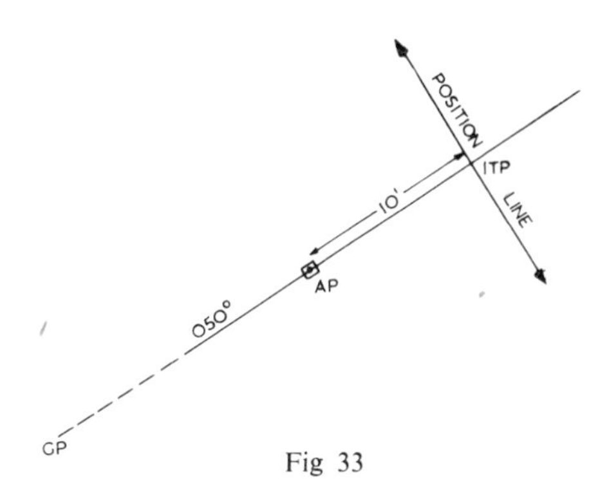

Fig 33

On an appropriate chart the assumed position (AP) is plotted and through it the azimuth of 050° is drawn. Along this azimuth is marked off the intercept of 10′. This position is the *intercept terminal position* (ITP). In this particular case the intercept terminal position has been plotted 'away' from the geographical position of the heavenly body because the true zenith distance is greater than the calculated zenith distance. Reference to Fig 30 should clarify why this is so and also why, when the calculated zenith distance is greater than the true zenith distance, the intercept terminal position is plotted 'towards' the geographical position.

Finally, to represent a very small arc of the circle of position, a line is drawn at right-angles to the azimuth through the intercept terminal position. This is the position line, and it is somewhere along this line that the true position of the observer lies.

It is of interest to note that in this case the radius of the circle of position is 57°37′ or 3,457′ (miles).

For a given set of conditions it is as easy to calculate an altitude as it is to calculate a zenith distance, so although the intercept has been described as the difference between the true and calculated zenith distances, it is now proposed to describe it as the difference between the true and calculated altitudes, for arithmetically it amounts to the same thing. The calculated altitude referred to is the altitude which it is calculated would be measured from the assumed position.

Sight reduction tables

The traditional method of calculating the zenith distance (or altitude) and azimuth was to use the EP as an 'assumed position' and conventional trigonometrical tables to solve the PZX triangle. The advantage of working from such first principles is that no special tables are required, and the degree of accuracy is determined only by the number of decimal points the observer is prepared to tolerate. The only serious disadvantage is that it takes even an experienced observer quite a long time to perform the calculations in which there are, relatively speaking, a large number of steps. In small vessels which are always moving in a most uncomfortable manner, it is easy to make simple mistakes, and the lower the number of arithmetical steps required, the greater the chances of completing the exercise without error.

A speedier method of solving the PZX triangle, with a minimum of arithmetical steps, is to use the *Sight Reduction Tables for Marine Navigation*, a British Hydrographic Department publication in six volumes. It contains the solutions to a large, but obviously finite, number of spherical triangles. The observer is required to adjust his EP in order that the resulting PZX triangle coincides with one contained within the tables. With correct use and sensible interpolation, the resulting position lines can be accurate to within one tenth of a mile.

Yet another method is to use a publication of Her Majesty's Stationery Office (or US Navy Hydrographic Office), the *Sight Reduction Tables for Air Navigation*. In three volumes, this publication also contains the solution to a large (though smaller than the marine version, yet still finite) number of spherical triangles. The *Air Tables* are comparatively compact and better suited to small-vessel navigation, though inevitably the degree of accuracy is less; this publication is, none the less, more than adequate for the great majority of cases. It is upon the *Air Tables* that this book is based, but should the reader wish to use the *Marine Tables* he will find the principles so similar as to present no problem in adaption.

The *Sight Reduction Tables for Air Navigation* (SRT) has two volumes devoted to general spherical triangles and a third devoted to stars only. The general volumes (Vols 2 and 3) contain the solutions to a number of spherical triangles which are defined by (1) latitude of a whole number of degrees; (2) local hour angle of a whole number of degrees; (3) declination not exceeding 30°. Condition (1) is satisfied by assuming a position, as close to the EP as possible, which is on a parallel of latitude of a whole number of degrees. Condition (2) is satisfied by assuming a longtitude, again as close to the EP as possible, such that when it is applied to the Greenwich hour angle, the resulting local hour angle is a whole number of degrees. Condition (3) is not very restricting because the sun, moon, those four planets used for navigation and quite a lot of the stars all have declinations of less than 30°. Those stars which do not have a declination of less than 30° are dealt with in a special way in Volume 1 of the *Sight Reduction Tables*, and further discussion of this appears in Chapter 10.

In practice, then, a position is assumed so that the assumed latitude is to the nearest whole number of degrees, and the assumed longitude is such that when applied to the Greenwich hour angle of the body observed, the resulting local hour angle is a whole number of degrees. Two examples should illustrate this point adequately:

1. While in EP 49°48′N 17°16′W an observation was made of a body whose GHA at the time was 52°34.′2. What should be the assumed position in order to use the *Sight Reduction Tables* (Vol 3)?

The estimated latitude of 49°48′N is 'rounded up' to 50°N.

The longitude is West, so it will be subtracted from the GHA to obtain the LHA. This being the case, the assumed longitude must have the same number of minutes as the GHA:

GHA	52° 34.′2	
Ass Long	− 17° 34.′2	W
LHA	35°	

So, in this case, the assumed position should be 50°N 17°34.′2W, and it is from that position that the azimuth and intercept should be plotted.

2. While in EP 50°27′S 164°38′E, an observation was made of the sun. If its GHA at that time was 336°18.′4, what should be the assumed position in order to use Volume 3 of the *Sight Reduction Tables?*

ASS LAT 50°S	GHA		336° 18.′4	
	Ass Long	+	164° 41.′6	E
	LHA		501°	
		−	360°	
	LHA		141°	

NB The longtitude, being East, is added to the GHA. 360° is subtracted from the LHA in order to reduce it below this figure.

USE OF THE SIGHT REDUCTION TABLES

Vol 1 of the *Sight Reduction Tables* deals with special stars and will be considered in another chapter; Vol 2 covers latitudes 0°–39°, while Vol 3 covers latitudes 40°–89°.

App 10 is an extract from Vol 3 of the pages covering latitude 50°. It will be noted that the extract is divided into two main parts, one covering declination 0°–14° while the other deals with declination 15°–29°. Each of these two parts is further divided into two sections: 'Declination Same Name as Latitude' and 'Declination Contrary Name to Latitude'.

The solutions of the spherical (PZX) triangles contained in the tables pay no regard to the hemisphere in which the triangle is situated, for this has little bearing on the arithmetic involved. The only extraction which needs to be 'corrected' for the hemisphere is 'Z'. This quantity 'Z' is the $P\hat{Z}X$, whereas the quantity required, the azimuth (Zn), is not necessarily the same thing. Rules for converting Z to Zn are given at the top of the page for observations in the northern hemisphere, and at the bottom of the page for those in the southern hemisphere. These will be considered in more detail shortly.

The only way in which the tables are aware of a 'hemisphere' is whether the triangle to be solved is completely in one hemisphere or whether it crosses the equator; ie whether latitude and declination are the same name (same hemisphere) or contrary name (opposite hemispheres).

For any given values of latitude, declination and LHA, the tables will give the Calculated Altitude of the body which would satisfy those conditions, and also 'Z', from which the azimuth of the body may be deduced. An example will illustrate a few points.

For a given set of circumstances the latitude of an observer was assumed to be 50°N, the declination

Fig 34

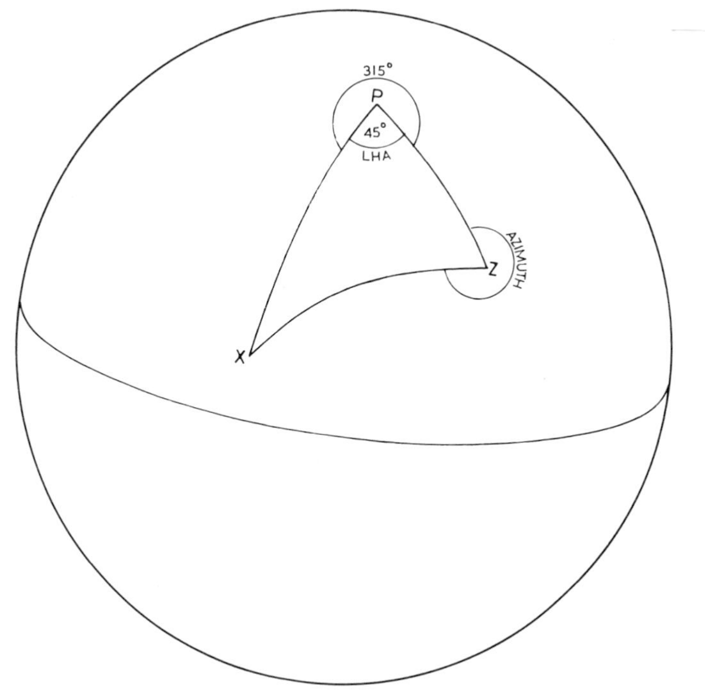

of the observed body was 12°N and the local hour angle was 45°. What was the calculated altitude and azimuth of the body?

Latitude and declination are both north and declination is 12°, so the section of the 50° latitude pages of the *Sight Reduction Tables* (App 10) required is headed 'Declination (0°–14°) Same Name as Latitude'. Using LHA as the vertical argument in the left-hand column, and declination 12° as the horizontal argument, the following information may be extracted:

Hc 37° 09′ d + 49′ Z 120°

Hc is the calculated altitude; 'd' is the rate of change of this altitude for a change of 60′ of declination; 'Z' is PẐX in Fig 34 (which is shown on page 37).

The true azimuth required is the external angle PẐX or 360°–Z. At the top (for northern hemisphere) of the page is the rule for this conversion:

LHA Greater than 180° Zn = Z
LHA Less than 180° Zn = 360° – Z

In the foregoing example, the observation was made in the northern hemisphere, and the LHA, 45°, was less than 180°. Using the above rule:

$$Zn = 360° - Z = 360° - 120° = 240°$$

Further examination of Fig 34 will show that the same PZX triangle could have been drawn for a local hour angle of 315°, but then Z and X would be transposed. This is the circumstance when the right-hand LHA column would be used. The same information would be extracted, and only the azimuth would be changed by the above rule.

One more example:

Latitude 50°S Declination 20°S LHA 265°

From App 10, Latitude 50°, Declination (15°–29°) Same Name as Latitude, using as arguments LHA 265° (found in the right-hand column) and Declination 20°, the following may be extracted:

Hc 12° 05′ d + 45′ Z 73°

This observation having been made in the southern hemisphere, the rule for converting Z to Zn is found at the bottom left-hand corner of the page:

LHA Greater than 180° Zn = 180° – Z
LHA Less than 180° Zn = 180° + Z

In this example, the LHA(265°) being greater than 180°:

$$Zn = 180° - Z = 180° - 73° = 107°$$

Fig 35

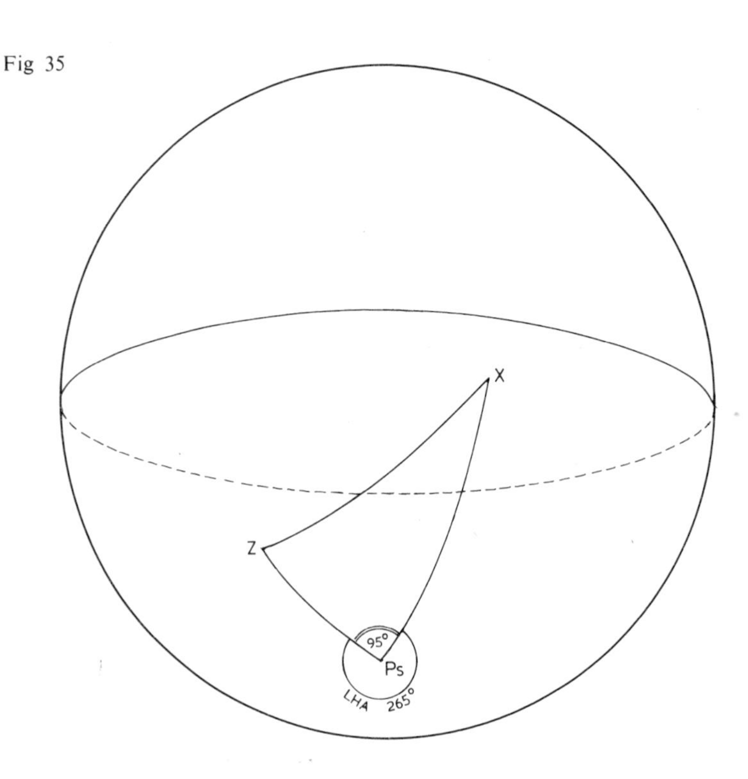

The third and final figure which is extracted from the tables is 'd'. This figure is the amount by which Hc would change if the declination changed by 60′. In the (likely) event of the declination not being a whole number of degrees, this 'd' figure, if divided by 60 and multiplied by the 'odd' minutes of declination, will give an increment to be applied to Hc. Note that the tables always give a sign (+ or −) for 'd'. As usual, to save arithmetical calculations, there is a table to do most of the work. In the *Sight Reduction Tables* it is Table 5. In this book, it is reproduced as App 11, and is entered with the arguments of 'd' and the minutes of declination.

If, for instance, in the last example the declination had not been exactly 20°S, but 20°17′.6S, this increase in declination would have had a negligible effect on the azimuth, but a quite considerable effect on the Tabulated Altitude (Hc). The tables would have been entered in exactly the same way as previously, using the whole number of degrees of declination, 20°. Among the extractions would be the 'd' figure of +45′, as noted above. Table 5 (App 11) would now be entered, using 45′ as the horizontal argument and 18′ (the 17.′6 of the declination 'rounded up') as the vertical argument. The increment found would be 14′. Because 'd' was found to be +45′, this increment would be added to Hc, the tabulated altitude:

Hc	12°	05′
Inc	+	14′
Hc	12°	19′

Now for a complete example of the use of the SRT:

Assumed Latitude 50°N Declination 16°23.′8N LHA 284°

Hc	21° 08′	(1)	d + 45′	Z	90°		
Inc	+ 18′	(2)		Zn	090°		(3)
Hc	21° 26′						

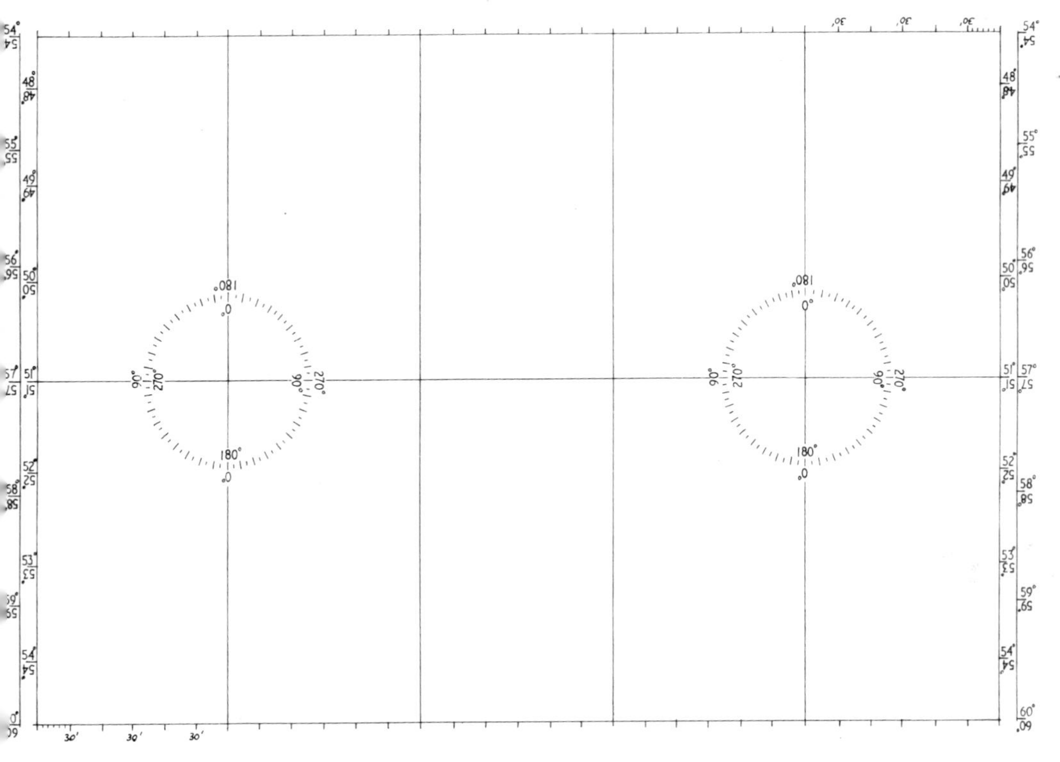

Fig 36 Diagrammatic redrawing of Admiralty One Million Plotting sheet 5333A (scale 1:1,000,000): this chart is too large to reproduce in legible form but this representation of it shows its main characteristics. Latitudes 48–60 are shown left and right and degrees of longitude are marked (not numbered) top and bottom. The instructions read: 'Select the East and West Latitude borders appropriate to the area of operations and rule the parallels of latitude to terminate at these borders. Longitude figures should be inserted as necessary in spaces provided.' The two circles represent True North bearings.

Notes:
(1) App 10, Latitude 50°, Declination (15°–29°) Same Name as Latitude.
Declination 16°, LHA 284° (right-hand column).
(2) App 11, d=45′, Declination 24′.
(3) Top left-hand corner App 10, LHA greater than 180°, Zn=Z.

PLOTTING

Having completed the observation and calculations, the final step is to plot the position line.

The scale of ocean charts is too small to allow for accurate plotting, so the navigator has to find an alternative. Several exist, such as using graph paper or even blank paper, both of which require a little arithmetical thought to get the relative latitude and longitude scales correct. Proprietary plotting charts are available, one of which–the Ocean Plotting Chart 5333A, published by the British Hydrographic Department–is that assumed for use with this book. Available from good chart agents, it costs about one tenth of a conventional chart. There is a series of such charts, each covering a selected range of latitudes. The one used for the examples in this book is illustrated in Fig 36 and covers the latitudes 48°–60°, both north and south, depending on the way in which the chart is viewed. Longitude scales are included, and all that the navigator has to do is to write his relevant longitudes in the spaces provided and he has a chart which may be used for any area in the world within the stated latitudes. The chart itself is completely blank apart from compass roses. The latitude is in two scales, 48°–54° and 54°–60°, so a little care is necessary to ensure that the right one is used.

The correct sequence of events leading to the plotting of a position line is as follows:
(a) Write the appropriate longitudes on the plotting chart;
(b) Note which scale of latitude to use (there are two, 48°–54° and 54°–60°);
(c) Plot the estimated position;
(d) Plot the assumed position;
(e) Through the assumed position, draw the azimuth;
(f) Measure along the azimuth line, from the assumed position to the intercept, taking care to ensure whether it should be 'towards' or 'away'. The position thus determined is the Intercept Terminal Position (ITP);
(g) Through the intercept terminal position, draw the position line at right-angles to the azimuth, putting a single arrow-head on each end;
(h) In the absence of any better information, drop a perpendicular from the EP to the position line. This is the Most Probable Position (MPP) and may be taken to be the new 'EP'.

6 Meridian Altitudes

So far only the most general form of the PZX has been considered, but there is a special case–when P and Z are on the same meridian.

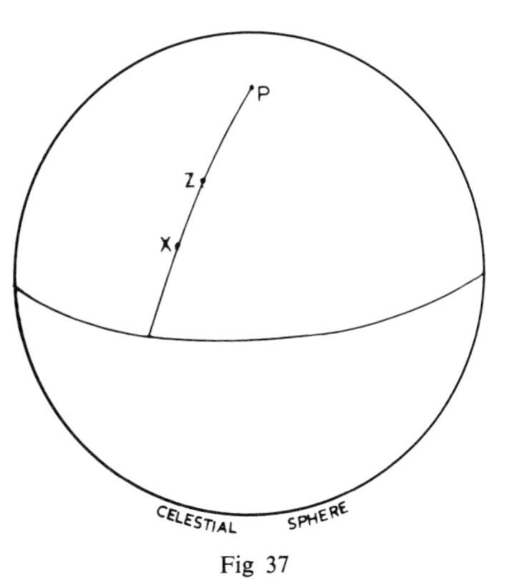

Fig 37

When a given heavenly body is 'on the meridian'–that is, on the same meridian as the observer–it must be either north or south of the observer. Since all position lines derived from observations of heavenly bodies are at right-angles to the azimuth of the observed body, an observation of a body on the meridian will produce a position line which lies east–west. It will be a parallel of latitude. During such an observation, the *meridian altitude* of the body is measured.

Comparison of Fig 38 (see p42) with Fig 29 will confirm that the true altitude is X$\hat{C}$S. The zenith distance is Z$\hat{C}$X. Thus:

$$ZD = 90° - TA$$

The true meridian altitude is named the same as the azimuth of the body, either north or south. The zenith distance takes the opposite name.

Examples:

1. If the true meridian altitude of the sun was 45°17.′6 and its azimuth was south, what was the zenith distance?

		90°	
TA	=	–45°	17.′6 S
ZD	=	44°	42.′4 N

2. If the true meridian altitude of the moon was 35°48.′1 and its azimuth was north, what was the zenith distance?

		90°	
TA	=	–35°	48.′1 N
ZD	=	54°	11.′9 S

Now to consider the particular case of a meridian altitude taken by an observer in the northern hemisphere when the declination of the heavenly body is southerly. Fig 39 is a great circle through P, Z and X. The heavenly body, X, being south of the observer, the azimuth is south, and consequently the true meridian altitude is named south. The zenith distance is thus named north.

Fig 38

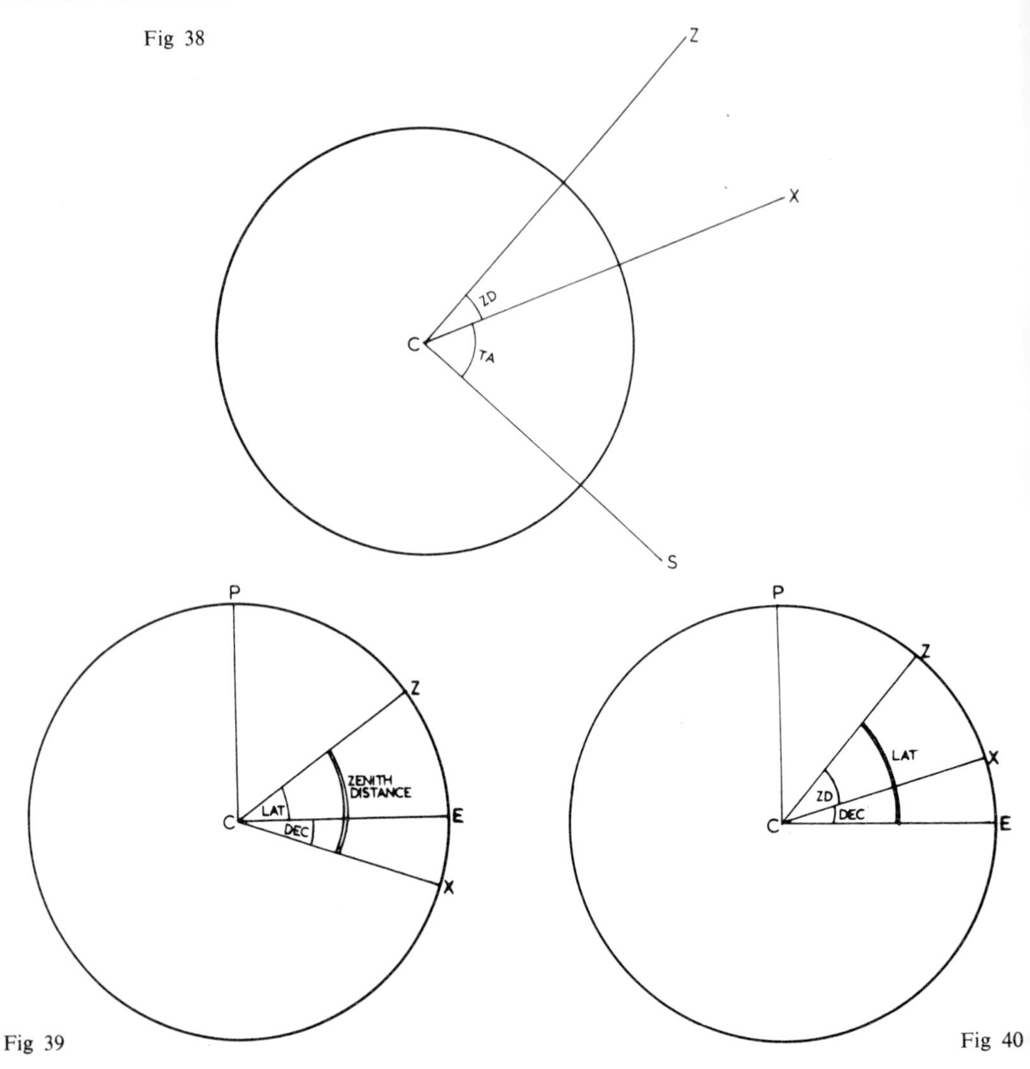

Fig 39

Fig 40

In this particular case the zenith distance (ZĈX) equals the sum of the observer's latitude (ZĈE) and the declination of the heavenly body (EĈX). This statement can be rearranged and the appropriate cardinal names added so that it appears in a more useful pattern:

$$\text{Lat (N)} = \text{ZD (N)} - \text{Dec (S)}$$

Another particular case is when the observer is in the northern hemisphere and the declination of the heavenly body is northerly.

In this case the meridian altitude is seen to be southerly, so the zenith distance will be named 'north'. The equation this time is:

$$\text{Lat (N)} = \text{ZD (N)} + \text{Dec (N)}$$

There are various combinations of the observer being in the northern or southern hemisphere, the declination being north or south, and the observed body being north or south of the observer. Each case could be examined individually, but there is a general rule for combining zenith distance and declination to deduce the latitude:
If the names of the zenith distance and the declination are the same, they should be added, if the names are different, they should be subtracted, the latitude taking the name of the larger quantity.

Examples:

1. If the true meridian altitude of the sun was 49°17.′6 S when the declination was 12°28.′6 S, what was the observed latitude?

TA	=	−49°	17.′6	S	
		+90°			
ZD	=	40°	42.′4	N	(Change the name)
Dec	=	12°	28.′6	S	
Lat	=	28°	13.′8	N	(Different names, subtract, lat named after the larger)

2. If the meridian altitude of the moon was 64°22.′8 S when the declination was 15°18.′6 N, what was the observed latitude?

TA	=	−64°	22.′8	S	
		+90°			
ZD	=	25°	37.′2	N	(Change the name)
Dec	=	15°	18.′6	N	
Lat	=	40°	55.′8	N	(Same names, add)

3. If the meridian altitude of the sun was 68°57.′6 S when its declination was 23°24.′7S, what was the observed latitude?

TA	=	−68°	57.′6	S	
		+90°			
ZD	=	21°	02.′4	N	(Change the name)
Dec	=	23°	24.′7	S	
Lat	=	2°	22.′3	S	(Different names, subtract, lat named after the larger)

So much for the theory; it is now time to consider the reality. The first step towards making a meridian altitude observation is to find out when a given heavenly body will be on the observer's meridian. This occurs twice in every complete revolution of the earth about its axis–that is, twice each day. For instance, the sun is on the Greenwich meridian at about midday each day, and on the meridian of 180° (strictly speaking, the same meridian as that of Greenwich) at about midnight each day. The former case, when the GHA is 0° or 00h, is known as the Upper Meridian Passage; the latter, when the GHA is 180° or 12h, is the Lower Meridian Passage. The lower meridian passage, generally speaking, is of little use to small-boat navigators, and consequently will be ignored for the rest of this book. Any further reference to a meridian passage will be taken as the upper meridian passage.

The times at which each of the navigational heavenly bodies crosses the Greenwich meridian are tabulated for each day of the year in the *Nautical Almanac* (see App 3 at the end of this book). The time of the meridian passage of the sun will be examined in detail, and the same principles can be applied to all the other heavenly bodies except the moon.

Fig 41 is an extract of the relevant part of the daily pages for 24th–26th February 1980.

DAY	SUN EQN OF TIME 00h		SUN EQN OF TIME 12h		MER PASS	
	m	s	m	s	h	m
24	13	26	13	22	12	13
25	13	18	13	13	12	13
26	13	09	13	04	12	13

Fig 41

The tabulated Equation of Time is, in minutes and seconds, the amount of time by which the meridian passages of the true and mean suns are separated. It is, of course, only the true sun which can be observed, so the tabulated meridian passage is, in GMT to the nearest minute, the time at which the true sun passes the Greenwich meridian. No significant error is introduced by taking this as the local mean time at which the sun will pass any other meridian.

In Chapter 3 the following rules were introduced for converting local mean time to Greenwich mean time:

$$GMT = LMT + Long\ (W) \quad \text{(in time)}$$
$$GMT = LMT - Long\ (E) \quad \text{(in time)}$$

The easiest way of converting the arc of longitude to time is to refer to the 'Conversion of Arc to Time' table, reproduced from the *Nautical Almanac* in App 5. The first six columns give the equivalents in time of the whole degrees 0°–359°. The last four columns give the equivalents in time of the angular minutes and quarter minutes. It is normally sufficient to consider only the whole minutes.

Examples:

1. On 24th February 1980, an observer in EP 49°17′ N 36°42′ W wanted to observe the sun on the meridian. At what time should he have expected the meridian passage?

From App 3 is extracted the time of meridian passage for 24th February. This is the local mean time of the meridian passage on any meridian. It is converted to the GMT of the meridian passage on the required meridian by applying the time correction proportional to the longitude, as extracted from App 5:

LMT MP			=	24d	12h	13m	
Long	36°		= +		2h	24m	
Long		42′ W	= +			2m	48s
GMT MP			=	24d	14h	39m	48s

NB The time equivalent to the longitude has been added because it was west. The timing is normally taken to the nearest minute, in this case 14h 40m. The reason for this approximation will be explained very shortly.

2. On 20th June 1980 while in EP 37°57′ S 148°17′ E, at what time will the sun be on the meridian?

LMT MP	=	20d	12h	02m
Long 148° 17′ E	= −		9h	53m
GMT MP	=	20d	02h	09m

The accuracy of this calculated time is limited by the accuracy of the EP, and that is why it is quite in order to take the timing to the nearest minute. In practice, the observer will be ready with his sextant some minutes before the appointed time in order that the actual meridian passage is not missed. It will be noticed that leading up to noon, the altitude will be increasing. The rate of increase of the altitude will decrease as noon approaches, until the sun is at its maximum altitude, where it will appear to hang suspended for a while prior to beginning its descent towards the western horizon, its altitude gradually decreasing. By constantly observing the altitude for some minutes before noon, and adjusting the sextant accordingly, the maximum altitude (which is the meridian altitude) will be readily noted without recourse to accurate timing.

Thus the meridian altitude observation has two great virtues. It is not necessary to make an accurate timing, and it gives a position line which is the latitude of the observer.

The time has now come to combine a few of the calculations already described into one sight reduction. All sights follow a predetermined format and in order to be helpful a blank format for the reduction of the meridian altitude of the sun is now offered in the hope that it will reduce the chances of omitting a stage and enable mistakes to be found more easily. This format is followed by two worked examples and three exercises.

Fig 42 Sun UL/LL Meridian Passage

EP

SA	°	′	N/S	LMT MP		d	h	m
IE On− Off+		′		° ′	E− W+		h	m
OA	°	′		GMT MP		d	h	m
m −		′						
AA	°	′						
Corr +/−		′						
TA −	°	′						
+	90°			Dec	h	°	′	N/S
ZD	°	′	S/N	d= ,	m +/−		′	
Dec	°	′	N/S	Dec		°	′	N/S
Lat	°	′	N/S					

1. On Sunday 24th February 1980 while in EP 48°17′N 18°42′W, at what time (GMT) will the sun be on the meridian?

The sun's lower limb was observed on the meridian at this time and the sextant altitude was 31°55.′6 S. If the index error was 2.′5 on the arc, and the height of eye was 1.5m, what was the observed latitude?

The correct sequence of events is in the same order as the explanatory notes.

Fig 43

24th Feb 1980 Sun UL/LL Meridian Passage

EP 48° 17′ N 18° 42′ W

SA	31° 55′.6 N/S	(6)	LMT MP		24d 12h 13m	(1)
IE On− Off+	2′.5		18° 42′	E− W+	01h 15m	(2)
OA	31° 53′.1		GMT MP		24d 13h 28m	(3)
1.5 m −	2′.2	(7)				
AA	31° 50′.9					
Corr +/−	14′.7	(8)				
TA −	32° 05′.6					
+	90°	(9)	Dec	13 h	9° 39′.0 N/S	(4)
ZD	57° 54′.4 S/N		d= 0.9, 28m	+/−	0′.4	(5)
Dec	9° 38′.6 N/S		Dec		9° 38′.6 N/S	
Lat	48° 15′.8 N/S	(10)				

Notes:

1. Daily pages, App 3, Mer Pass.
2. Conversion of Arc to Time, App 5.
3. GMT of the meridian passage in Long 18°42′W.
4. Daily pages, App 3, Dec of sun for 13h.
5. Daily pages, App 3, bottom of Dec column, d=0.′9 and is negative because the Dec for the following hour (14h) is less than that for 13h, App 6.
6. Sun was bearing south.
7. App 1, correction for a height of eye of 1.5m is −2.′2.
8. App 1, Oct–Mar, lower limb, correction for an apparent altitude of 31°50.′9 is +14.′7.
9. ZD=90°–TA, changing the sign from S to N.
10. Zenith distance and declination have different names so they are subtracted, the latitude taking the name of the larger, zenith distance.

2. On Saturday 21st June 1980, while in EP 17°52′S 130°14′W, at what time would the sun be on the meridian?

If the meridian altitude of the sun's lower limb at that time was 48°25.′5 N, index error was −2.′5 and the height of eye was 3m, what was the observed latitude?

Fig 44

21st June 1980 Sun UL/LL Meridian Passage

EP 17° 52′ S 130° 14′ W

SA		48° 25′.5 N/S
IE	On/Off −/+	2′.5
OA		48° 23′.0
3 m	−	3′.0
AA		48° 20′.0
Corr	−/+	15′.1
TA	−	48° 35′.1
	+	90°
ZD		41° 24′.9 S/N
Dec		23° 26′.3 N/S
Lat		17° 58′.6 N/S

LMT MP		21d	12h	02m
130° 14′	E−/W+		08h	41m
GMT MP		21d	20h	43m
Dec	20h			23° 26′.3 N/S
d= 0.47m	+/−			′.
Dec				23° 26′.3 N/S

Exercises

1. On 25th February 1980 it was estimated that at the approximate time of the sun's meridian passage the EP would be 17°18′N 34°48′W. At what time, GMT, should the sun be on the meridian?

If, at that time, the sun was on the meridian, and the sextant altitude of the sun's lower limb was 63°15.′7 bearing south, what was the observed latitude?

The height of eye was 2m and index error was 1.′5 off the arc.

2. On 22nd June 1980 the EP at the approximate time of the meridian passage of the sun was 48°37′N 158°12′E. At what GMT would the sun be on the meridian?

If at that time the sun was on the meridian and the sextant altitude of its lower limb was 64°26.′2 bearing south, what was the observed latitude?

The index error was 1.′5 off the arc and the height of eye was 3m.

3. On 21st September 1980, at what GMT would the sun be on the meridian in EP 12°14′S 38°52′W?

If the sun was on the meridian at that time and the sextant altitude of its lower limb was 77°06.′1 bearing north, what was the observed latitude?

The index error was 2.′5 on the arc and the height of eye was 2.5m.

7 The Sun

In this chapter, the most general sun sight will be considered. This will be followed by relating a meridian altitude observation to this general one to obtain an observed position.

Observation of the sun may be made at almost any time, but to avoid uncertain refraction it is preferable to limit sights to such times as when the altitude is greater than 10°.

In order to be able to compare an observation with the theoretical altitude, it is necessary to know the position of the heavenly body at the time of the observation. This, in turn, necessitates knowing the time of the observation, ideally to the nearest second.

Assuming that there is a deck watch available, and that it is set to GMT, and also that its error–if any–is known, there are then three options open to the navigator. The first is to make use of a reliable colleague who will note the *exact* time when the navigator says *now*. The second is for the navigator himself to use a stop-watch and make the necessary arithmetical calculations. The third–the one I favour, for it involves neither colleague nor calculation–is to count the seconds from the time of the observation until settled in front of the deck watch. Thousand one, thousand two, thousand three works for me, but undoubtedly there are other ways of counting. The only liability noticed with the counting method is that an inexperienced crew member, on seeing the navigator remove the sextant from his eye and clamber through the companionway muttering to himself, will inevitably attempt to strike up a conversation. The tolerance and tact of the navigator will decide whether such a crew member is foolish enough to make the same mistake twice.

The reduction of a sun sight now merely entails collecting together all the pieces of information already presented, but there is one more point to be made. When the principle of the intercept was introduced, whether it was named as being 'towards' or 'away' (from the geographical position) was determined by the relative sizes of the calculated and true zenith distances (Fig 30, page 34). The *Sight Reduction Tables* are arranged to present a calculated altitude rather than a zenith distance, which allows the navigator one less arithmetical step. He need only convert his sextant altitude to a true altitude. The arithmetical difference between the zenith distances is the same as between the altitudes. Whether the intercept is towards or away has to be decided in a different manner. Here are two *aide-mémoires*:

For those who favour mnemonics: GOAT—Greater Observed Angle Towards. (If the observed angle is greater than the calculated the intercept is towards.)

For those who favour logic, consider the following triangle, drawn through the heavenly body, its geographical position and the assumed position.

Fig 45

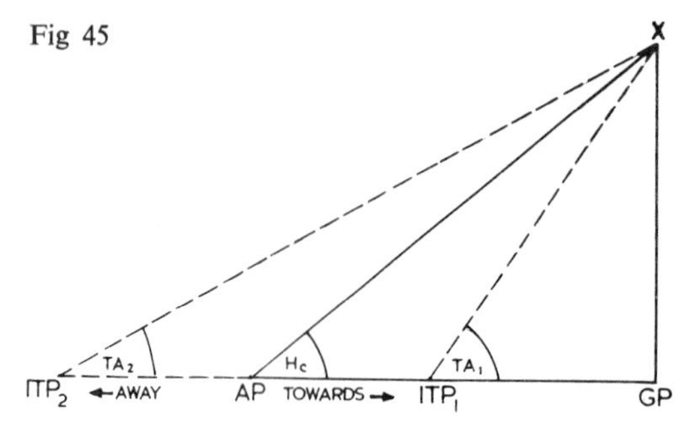

The calculated altitude (Hc) is the angle which would have been measured at the assumed position. If the true altitude is greater, the real position is towards (nearer) the geographical position; if smaller, the true position is away from the geographical position.

Again, in an attempt to maintain high standards of neatness another format is offered. Its use, or that of something similar, is highly recommended.

Fig 46

Sun UL/LL AM/PM

EP		Ass Lat °N/S
ZT d h m		DWT h m s
Z +/- h		DWE Fast - Slow + h m s
GD d h m		GMT h m s
SA ° '		GHA h ° '
IE On - Off + '		m s + ° '
OA ° '		GHA ° '
m - '		(+360°)
AA ° '		GHA ° '
Corr +/- '		Ass Long E + W - ° '
TA ° '		LHA °
		(-360°)
Dec h ° '		LHA °
d= +/- '		
Dec ° ' N/S		(180°)
		(360°)
Hc ° '	d= +/- '	Z +/- °
Inc +/- '		Zn °
Hc ° '		
TA ° '		
Intercept ' Towards/Away		

To minimise the page turning of the various volumes or appendices, it might be found useful to perform the extractions and calculations in the following order:

1. Calculate the Greenwich date.
2. Correct the deck watch time to GMT.
3. Convert the sextant altitude to the true altitude.
4. Extract the Greenwich hour angle, declination and 'd'.
5. Apply the increment and correction to the Greenwich hour angle and declination.
6. Calculate the assumed position and local hour angle.

7. Extract the calculated altitude, its 'd' figure and Z.
8 Convert Z to Zn.
9. Apply the 'd' increment to the calculated altitude.
10. Calculate the intercept.

And now for two examples:

1. At about 0930 ship's time in Z+1 on 24th February 1980, while in EP 50°10′N 12°37′W, an observation was made of the sun's lower limb when the deck watch, which was 37s slow, indicated 10h 27m 32s. The sextant altitude was 21°07.′0, the index error was 2.′5 on the arc and the height of eye was 2m. Calculate the assumed position, intercept and azimuth.

Fig 47 24th Feb 1980 Sun ~~UL~~/LL AM/~~PM~~

EP 50°10′N 12°37′W | Ass Lat 50°N/~~S~~

ZT	24d 09h 30m		DWT	10h 27m 32s
Z ⊕/+	01h		DWE ~~Fast −~~ Slow +	h m 37s
GD	24d 10h 30m		GMT	10h 28m 09s
SA	21° 07′.0		GHA 10h	326° 39′.3 (d)
IE On − ~~Off +~~	2′.5	(a)	28m 09s +	7° 02′.3 (f)
OA	21° 04′.5		GHA	333° 41′.6
Zm −	2′.5	(b)		(+360°)
AA	21° 02′.0		GHA	333° 41′.6
Corr ⊕/+	13′.8	(c)	Ass Long ~~E +~~ W −	12° 41′.6 (h)
TA	21° 15′.8		LHA	321°
				(−360°)
Dec 10h	9° 41′.8	(e)	LHA	321°
d= 0.9 +/⊖	0′.4	(g)		
Dec	9° 41′.4 ~~N~~/S			(~~180°~~)
				(~~360°~~)
Hc	21° 56′	(i)	d= +/⊖ 54′ (i)	Z +/−· 138° (i)
Inc +/⊖	37′	(k)	Zn	° (j)
Hc	21° 19′			
TA	21° 16′			
Intercept	3′ ~~Towards~~/Away	(l)		

Notes:
(a) Index Error is 'on', so it is substracted.
(b) App 1—Dip.
(c) App 1—Altitude Correction, Sun, Oct–Mar Lower Limb.
(d) App 3, daily pages.
(e) App 3, daily pages, 'd' at foot of Declination column.
(f) App 6—Minutes and seconds, Sun & Planets.
(g) App 6—'v' or 'd'.
(h) Longitude is west so it is subtracted.
(i) App 10—50°, Declination (0°—14°) Contrary Name to Latitude, Declination 9°, LHA 321°.
(j) Latitude is north, the rule for converting Z to Zn is at the top of the Sight Reduction Tables page.

LHA greater than 180°, Zn = Z.

(k) App 11, d = – 54′, declination = 41′.
(l) The calculated altitude is greater, so the intercept is away from the geographical position.

Fig 48 illustrates the plotting of the position line.

Fig 48

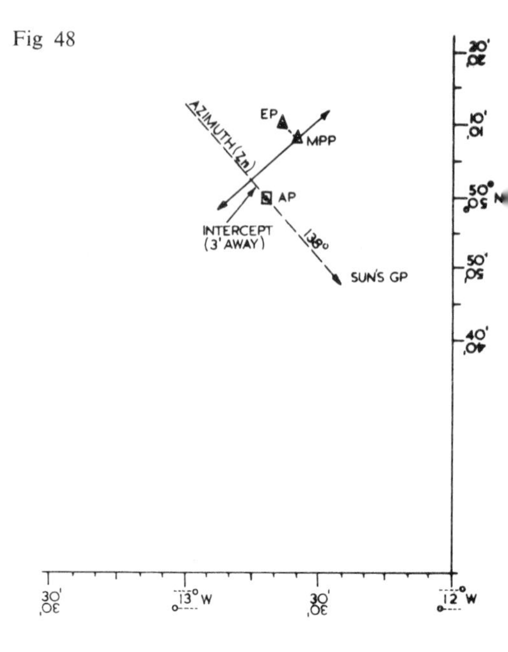

2. On Monday 22nd September 1980, while in EP 50°27′S 164°54′W, an observation was made of the sun's lower limb when the deck watch indicated 3h 32m 18s, and the time by the ship's clock, which was set to Z + 11, was 1630. Given the following information, calculate the assumed position, intercept and azimuth. Deck watch error 1m 20s fast; sextant altitude 12°38.′8; index error 3.′0 off the arc; height of eye 3m.

Note that in this example the calculation of the Greenwich date showed that the sight was taken on 23rd September at about 0330.

Fig 49

22nd Sep 1980 Sun ~~UL~~/LL ~~AM~~/PM

EP	50° 27′S 164° 54′W	Ass Lat	50° ~~N~~/S
ZT	22d 16h 30m	DWT	3h 32m 18s
Z (+)/–	11h	DWE Fast – ~~Slow +~~	h 01m 20s
GD	23d 03h 30m	GMT	03h 30m 58s
SA	12° 38′.8	GHA 03h	226° 53′.9
IE ~~On –~~ Off +	3′.0	30m 58s +	7° 44′.5
OA	12° 41′.8	GHA	234° 38′.4
3m –	3′.0		(+360°)
AA	12° 38′.8	GHA	234° 38′.4
Corr (+)/–	11′.8	Ass Long ~~E +~~ W –	164° 38′.4
TA	12° 50′.6	LHA	070°
			(–360°)
Dec 03h	0° 05′.7	LHA	070°
d=1.0 (+)/–	0′.5		
Dec	0° 06′.2 ~~N~~/S		(180°)
			~~(360°)~~

Hc	12° 42′	d= (+)/– 47′	Z (+)/– 106°
Inc (+)/–	5′		Zn 286°
Hc	12° 47′		
TA	12° 51′		
Intercept	4′ Towards/~~Away~~		

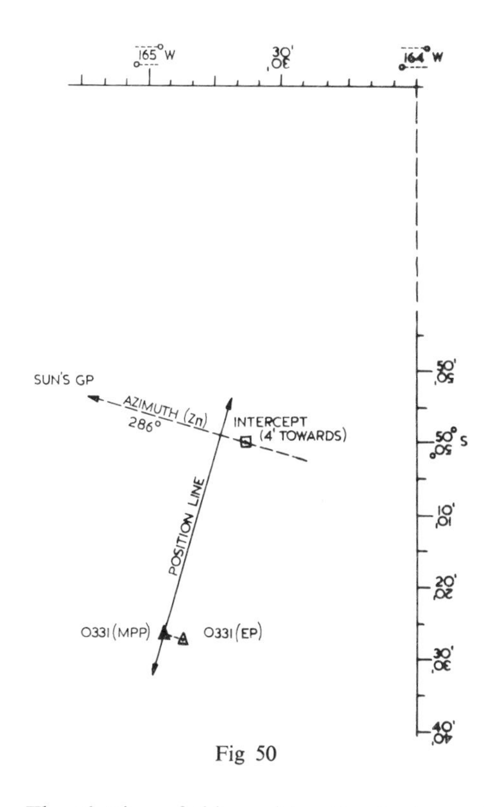

Fig 50

The plotting of this position line is shown in Fig 50.

During any particular voyage it is likely that sights will be taken regularly, in which case, when a position line has been plotted, the most recently 'out of date' position line will be 'run up' to that latest position line to produce an *Observed Position*. The 'running up' is done in much the same way as a terrestrial running fix, allowing for all the known factors such as current, tidal stream, leeway etc. Consequently, the accuracy of the observed position is limited by the accuracy of the 'run'.

A common practice is to run a morning position line derived from the sun to cross with the noon latitude, or, perhaps, to run the noon latitude up to cross with an afternoon sun position line.

For example, a morning sun sight had been taken while in EP 50°11′N 18°42′W at 0935 GMT, and the results were: assumed position 50°N 18°35′W, azimuth 127°, intercept 5′ away. The vessel made good a track of 239° and ran a distance of 22′ until the noon sight was made at 1218, when the observed latitude was 49°50′N. What was the observed position at 1218?

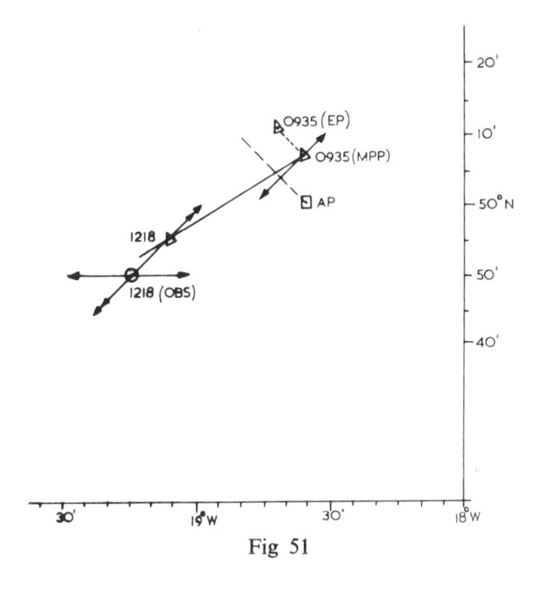

Fig 51

The sequence of plotting is as follows:

a. Plot the 0935 estimated position.
b. Plot the 0935 assumed position.
c. Draw the azimuth through the assumed position, away from the sun's geographical position.
d. Measure the intercept along the azimuth line to the intercept terminal position.
e. Draw the position line at right-angles to the azimuth.
f. Drop a perpendicular from the estimated position on to the position line. This is the most probable position for 0935.
g. From this most probable position draw in the track made good, 239°, and along it mark off the distance travelled between sights, 22′. This is the estimated position for 1218.
h. Through this 1218 EP draw a position line parallel to the 0935 position line, marking it with double arrow heads on each end. This is the transferred position line.
i. Draw in the latitude position line observed at 1218 with a single arrow head on each end.

The intersection of the transferred position line and the observed latitude position line is the observed 'noon' position, the actual time of which was 1218. The longitude of the observed position is then measured from the chart. In this example, the observed position was 49°50′N 19°15′W.

Exercises

1. On 25th February 1980 while in EP 49°37′N 16°14′W an observation was made of the sun's lower limb at a ship's time of 10.30 (Z + 1). SA 26°08.′4; DWT 11h 23m 29s; IE 2.′5 on the arc; HE 2m; DWE 5m 18s slow. What was the assumed position, intercept and azimuth?

2. On 21st June 1980 while in EP 50°07′N 145°18′W an observation was made of the sun's lower limb at about 1630 by the ship's clock which was set to Z + 10. SA 28°46.′5; DWT 2h 32m 11s; IE 3′ off the arc; HE 3m; DWE 1m 57s fast. What was the assumed position, intercept and azimuth?

3. On 22nd September 1980 while in EP 49°57′S 165°18′E an observation was made of the sun's upper limb at about 0930 ship's time (Z–11). SA 31°57.′1; DWT 10h 19m 53s; IE zero; HE $1\frac{1}{2}$m; DWE 12m 14s slow. What was the assumed position, intercept and azimuth?

4. At 0935 while in EP 50°18′N 27°14′W, an observation of the sun gave the following results: assumed position 50°N 27°38′W, azimuth 117°, intercept 6′ Towards.

During the rest of the forenoon the vessel made good a track of 240°T for a distance of 22′, at which time, 1235, a meridian altitude of the sun gave an observed latitude of 49°57′N. What was the observed position at 1235?

5. While in EP 49°37′S 125°18′W the observed latitude at the time of the meridian passage of the sun was 49°33′S.

The vessel proceeded to make good a track of 095°T for a distance of 27′ until at 0130 an observation of the sun gave the following assumed position 50°S 124°41′W; azimuth 285° intercept 5′ Away. What was the observed position at 0130?

6. At 1000 while in EP 49°05′N 16°52′W, log reading 482′, an observation of the sun gave the following: assumed position 49°N 17°01′W; azimuth 132°; intercept 8′ Towards.

Cloud obscured the sun at the time for the noon sight, but at 1540 the cloud cleared and an observation was made and the following results obtained: assumed position 49°N 17°48′W; azimuth 225°; intercept 17′ Towards.

If the track made good between the sights was 255°T, what was the observed position at 1540 if the log reading was then 524′?

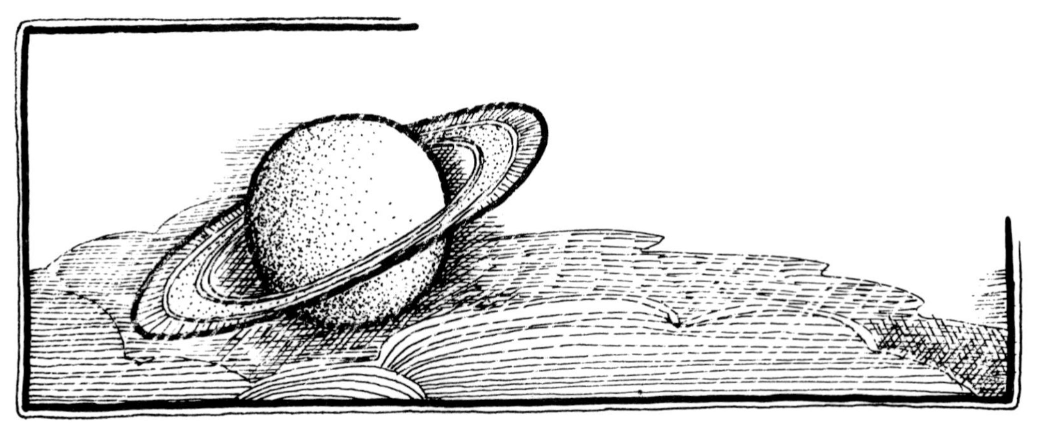

8 The Planets

Of the eight planets on which the terrestrial sailor is not situated, only four are sufficiently bright to be used for navigation. These four–Venus, Mars, Jupiter and Saturn–are all within the Zodiac, a band which extends about 8° either side of the ecliptic. This ensures that the declinations of these planets are always within the limits of the *Sight Reduction Tables*. Provided that they can be correctly identified they are eminently suitable for navigation.

The *Nautical Almanac* contains a Planet Diagram for each year and that for 1980 is reproduced as App 2. In graphical form, this diagram shows the local mean time of the meridian passages of the sun and five planets (the four navigational planets and Mercury which is always too close to the sun for observation). Each of the planets has a distinctive line linking the daily times of the meridian passages. Either side of a line joining the meridian passage times of the sun, is a shaded area. Whenever the line of a planet lies within the shaded area, the planet in question is too close to the sun for observation on that particular day.

Initially, at least, the small-vessel navigator will limit his observation of the planets (and, for that matter, the stars) to the periods of twilight at dusk and dawn when the horizon is clear and the sky is dark. Whether or not a particular planet will be visible during a given twilight is indicated by its position in the Planet Diagram. If in the lower half, the planet is a 'morning star', whereas when in the upper half it is an 'evening star'. If the meridian passage is between 00h and 02h the planet may be seen low in the west during morning twilight. On the other hand, if the meridian passage is just below the shaded area, it will be low in the east during morning twilight. Should the meridian passage be between 22h and 24h the planet will be low in the east during evening twilight, and if the meridian passage is just above the shaded area it will be low in the west during evening twilight. Mental interpolation between these extremes, using extra care when two planets are close together, should enable a positive identification to be made. In the *Nautical Almanac* additional help is given towards identification in the form of individual descriptions of both appearance and position.

As a result of the proximity of the planets to earth, the semi-diameters of all the planets is constantly changing, so it is essential that the centre of the planet should be observed.

Before embarking on the arithmetic involved in reducing planet sights, I would draw the reader's attention to one special point. If, after reducing a sight, an absurdity results–such as an enormous intercept–this will often be accounted for by an error in identification.

Twilight

The theoretical rising or setting of the sun occurs when its centre is on the observer's celestial horizon. That is when its true zenith distance is 90°. The actual timing of this event is of no practical value to the navigator.

Visible sunrise or sunset occurs when the upper limb appears on the visible horizon. Making due allowance for refraction and semi-diameter, this is when the centre of the sun is about 1° below the celestial horizon. Visible sunrise occurs before theoretical sunrise, and visible sunset occurs after theoretical sunset.

The period during which the sun is below the horizon, when the earth is still receiving light from it by reflection and scattering by the upper atmosphere, is known as *twilight* and is divided into three stages:

(a) *Civil twilight* begins or ends when the centre of the sun is 6° below the horizon.

(b) *Nautical twilight* begins or ends when the centre of the sun is 12° below the horizon.

(c) *Astronomical twilight* begins or ends when the centre of the sun is 18° below the horizon. This is the moment when absolute darkness begins or ends, at least as far as the sun is concerned.

Stars and planets become visible when the sun is 3° or more below the horizon, which becomes invisible when the sun is 9° or more below the horizon. These are the limits between which twilight observations must be made. The middle of this period is the time of civil twilight, which is tabulated, along with the times of nautical twilight, visible sunrise and visible sunset, in the *Nautical Almanac*. These times, given to the nearest minute are, strictly, the times in GMT of the event on the Greenwich meridian for the middle day of each three-day period, but may be taken to be the local mean time of the event on any other meridian for any of the three days. Great accuracy can be achieved by using the appropriate table to interpolate for latitude, but adequate accuracy is achieved much quicker by mental interpolation, assuming a linear rate of change.

The actual period during which observations should be possible is from approximately half way between nautical and civil twilights until about half way between civil twilight and sunrise. These periods can be estimated by inspection of the relevant times, but a good average in a latitude of 50°N is about twenty minutes either side of civil twilight. Thus the key to all planet and star observations is the prediction of the time of civil twilight (CT).

The prediction of the times of both twilights, sunrise and sunset are dealt with in the same way, but the following examples are for civil twilight only.

1. At what time is morning civil twilight in EP 50°37′N 16°07′W on 24th February 1980?

LMT CT 50° N		24d	06h	21m	(a)
LMT CT 52° N		24d	06h	22m	
LMT CT 50° 37′ N		24d	06h	21m	(b)
Long 16° 07′ W	+		1h	04m	(c)
GMT CT		24d	07h	25m	(d)

Notes:

(a) Local mean time of civil twilight for 50°N and 52°N are tabulated on the daily pages of the *Nautical Almanac* (App 3).

(b) Where necessary, interpolate between the two latitudes, assuming a linear rate of change.

(c) Convert the longitude to time (App 5) and add if west, subtract if east.

(d) This is the GMT of civil twilight at the EP, 50°37′N 16°07′W. Observations could probably begin at about twenty minutes before this time—0705 GMT.

2. At what time is evening civil twilight on 21st June 1980 in EP 49°31′N 167°45′E?

LMT CT 45° N		21d	20h	28m
LMT CT 50° N		21d	20h	58m
LMT CT 49° 31′ N		21d	20h	55m
Long 167° 45′ E	—		11h	11m
GMT CT		21d	09h	44m

Observations could probably begin at about 0924 GMT.

Planet sight reduction

The calculations involved in reducing planet sights are very similar to those employed with the sun. The small differences, such as they are, are readily appreciated if the recommended format is adhered to. Remember that, unlike all the other bodies, the hourly rate of change of the Greenwich hour angle of Venus may be less than that assumed in the increment table. Consequently, ‘v’ might be negative.

Fig 52 Venus/Mars/Jupiter/Saturn AM/PM

EP				
ZT	d	h	m	
Z +/-		h		
GD	d	h	m	
SA		°	'	
IE On - / Off +			'	
OA		°	'	
m -			'	
AA		°	'	
Corr -			'	
TA		°	'	
Dec	h	°	'	
d= +/-			'	
Dec		°	'	N/S

Ass Lat		°N/S		
DWT	h	m	s	
DWE Fast - / Slow +	h	m	s	
GMT	h	m	s	
GHA	h		°	'
m	s +		°	'
v=	+/-			'
GHA			°	'
		(+360°)		
GHA			°	'
Ass Long E + / W -			°	'
LHA			°	
		(-360°)		
LHA			°	

(180°)

(360°)

Hc	°	'	d= +/- '	Z +/-	°
Inc +/-		'		Zn	°
Hc	°	'			
TA	°	'			
Intercept		' Towards/Away			

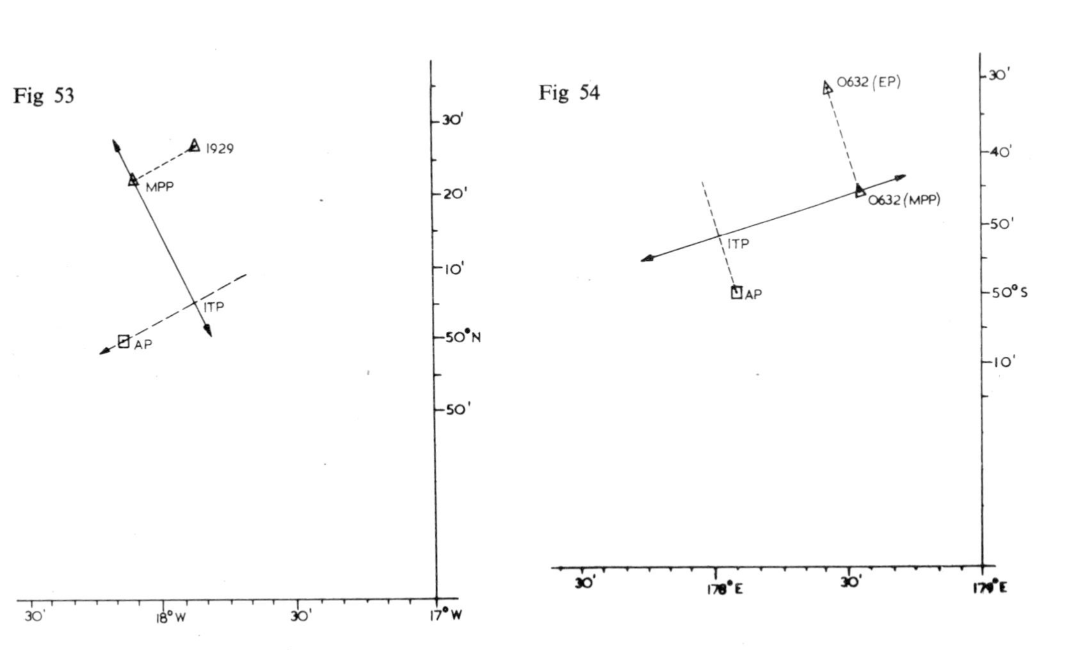

Fig 53

Fig 54

Now here are two worked examples.

1. On Sunday 24th February 1980 while in EP 50°27′N 17°58′W, at about 1830 by the ship's clock which was set to Z + 1, an observation was made of Venus when the deck watch, which was 5m 37s slow, indicated 7h 23m 47s. The sextant altitude was 29°04.′7, the index error 1.′5 off the arc and the height of eye 1.5m.

What was the assumed position, azimuth and intercept? By plotting, determine the intercept terminal position and most probable position.

Fig 55

24th Feb 1980 Venus/~~Mars/Jupiter/Saturn~~ ~~AM~~/PM

EP	50° 27′N 17° 58′W	Ass Lat	50°N/~~S~~
ZT	24d 18h 30m	DWT	7h 23m 47s
Z (+)/~~−~~	01h	DWE ~~Fast −~~ Slow +	h 05m 37s
GD	24d 19h 30m	GMT	19h 29m 24s
SA	29° 04′.7	GHA 19h	62° 53′.6
IE ~~On −~~ Off +	1′.5	29m 24s +	7° 21′.0
OA	29° 06′.2	v= 0.2 +/(−)	0′.1
1.5m −	2′.2	GHA	70° 14′.5
AA	29° 04′.0		(+360°)
Corr −	1′.7	GHA	70° 14′.5
TA	29° 02′.3	Ass Long ~~E +~~ W −	18° 14′.5
		LHA	052°
Dec 19h	7° 08′.9		(−360°)
d= 1.3 (+)/−	0′.6	LHA	052°
Dec	7° 09′.5 N/~~S~~		
			(~~180°~~)
			(360°)
Hc	29° 05′	d= (+)/− 49′	Z ~~+~~/E 117°
Inc (+)/−	8′		Zn 243°
Hc	29° 13′		
TA	29° 02′		
Intercept	11′ ~~Towards~~/Away		

By plotting, as in Fig 53, the intercept terminal position was found to be 50°05′N 17°59′W, and the most probable position 50°22′N 18°12′W.

2. On 21st June 1980 while in EP 49°31′S 178°25′E an observation was made of Mars when the ship's clock, set to Z− 12, showed the time as 1832. Given the following, determine the assumed position, intercept, azimuth and intercept terminal position: SA 33°52.′1; DWT 6h 44m 36s; DWE 12m 18s fast; IE 2.′ off the arc; HE 3m.

Fig 56

21st Jun 1980 ~~Venus~~/Mars/~~Jupiter/Saturn~~ AM/PM

EP	49° 31′S 178° 25′E	Ass Lat	50° N/S
ZT	21d 18h 32m	DWT	6h 44m 36s
Z +/−	12h	DWE Fast − ~~Slow +~~	h 12m 18s
GD	21d 06h 32m	GMT	06h 32m 18s
SA	33° 52′.1	GHA 06h	188° 50′.0
IE ~~On~~ Off +	2′.0	32m 18s +	8° 04′.5
OA	33° 54′.1	v= 1.3 +/−	0′.7
3 m −	3′.0	GHA	196° 55′.2
AA	33° 51′.1		(+360°)
Corr −	1′.4	GHA	196° 55′.2
TA	33° 49′.7	Ass Long E + ~~W −~~	178° 04′.8
		LHA	375°
Dec 06h	4° 47′.7		(−360°)
d=0.5 +/−	0′.3	LHA	015°
Dec	4° 47′.4 N/S		
			(180°)
			~~(360°)~~
Hc	34° 28′	d= +/− 59′	Z +/− 162°
Inc +/−	46′		Zn 342°
Hc	33° 42′		
TA	33° 50′		
Intercept	8′ Towards/~~Away~~		

By plotting, as in Fig 54, the intercept terminal position was found to be 49°52′S 178°01′E.

Exercises

1. On 22nd September 1980 while in EP 50°18′N 120°18′W an observation of Venus was made at about 1433 ship's time, the clock being set to Z+8. Given the following, determine the assumed position, azimuth, intercept and intercept terminal position: SA 17°43.′5; DWT 10h 31m 31s; DWE 1m 37s slow; IE 1.′5 on the arc; HE $1\frac{1}{2}$m.
2. On 20th June 1980 while in EP 50°27′S 155°49′E an observation was made of Jupiter at about 1928 by the ship's clock which was set to Z—10. Given the following, calculate the assumed position, azimuth and intercept, and determine the intercept terminal position by plotting: SA 15°08.′9; DWT 9h 40m 21s; IE nil; HE 3m; DWE 12m 07s fast.
3. On 24th February 1980 while in EP 49°45′S 74°55′W an observation was made of Saturn at about 2130 ship's time, the clock being set to Z+5. If the sextant altitude was 15°31.′0 at 2h 23m 29s by the deck watch, given that the deck watch was 9m 58s slow, the index error of the sextant was 3.′5 off the arc and the height of the observer's eye was 2m, determine the assumed position, azimuth, intercept and intercept terminal position.

9 The Stars

Observation of the stars is not only one of the most satisfying aspects of celestial navigation, but also one of the best ways of obtaining a position. A multi-sight observation, rarely possible with the other bodies, is quite possible twice each day with the stars. The size of the three-position line 'cocked hat' will also give an indication of the accuracy of the sights.

One fundamental requirement for any observation is that one must be able to see both the heavenly body and the horizon beneath it. As with planet sights, this requirement is satisfied during the two relatively short periods of twilight at about sunset and sunrise. There are other occasions when both body and horizon may be visible, but for the purposes of this exercise only sights during twilight will be considered.

Of course there is one other snag. Identifying the sun and the moon, and to a lesser extent the planets, is taken for granted, but one star does look very much like any other. Fortunately all the stars have a fixed relationship to each other, and quite a few of them appear in readily identifiable groups or *constellations*. It is by identifying the constellations and using them as 'stellar signposts' that individual stars may be identified.

Star identification

To the naked eye there are something like 4,000 stars visible, but fortunately not all are used for navigation. The *Nautical Almanac* tabulates on the daily pages (App 3) information concerning the 57 stars commonly used, and elsewhere is information concerning a further hundred or so of lesser importance. For the purposes of this book, this second group may be ignored.

Use of Vol 2 and 3 of the *Sight Reduction Tables* is limited to those heavenly bodies with declinations of less than 30′, so, for our immediate purpose, the number of stars available may be reduced from 57 to about the two dozen with the required declinations. The number may be reduced still further by eliminating those which are insufficiently bright to facilitate easy identification. This drastic pruning leaves twelve stars: namely, Aldebaran, Arcturus, Bellatrix, Betelgeuse, Polaris, Pollux, Procyon, Regulus, Rigel, Sirius and Spica. Polaris, otherwise known as the Pole Star, though not particularly bright, is included because of its special location very near the north celestial pole.

Figs 57 and 58 illustrate the northern and southern skies respectively. In the cause of simplicity, only those stars of immediate concern have been included.

There are four constellations to be identified:

The Plough is not, strictly speaking, a constellation. It is a group of seven stars in the shape of a plough, which form part of a large constellation, Ursa Major (The Great Bear).

Cassiopeia (a mythological queen, mother of Andromeda) comprises five main stars in the shape of a W or an M, depending on how it is viewed.

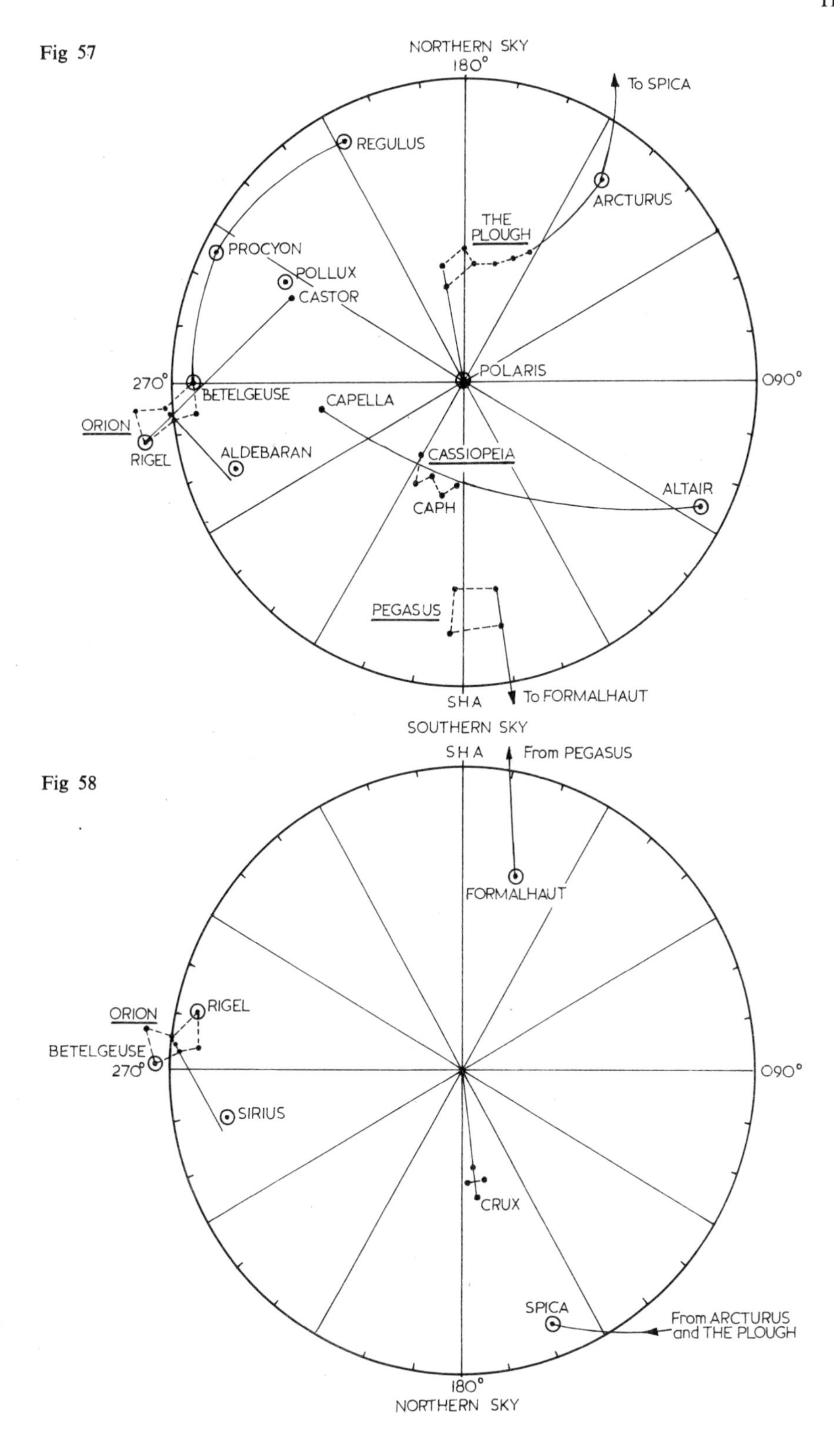
Fig 57
NORTHERN SKY
180°
To SPICA
REGULUS
ARCTURUS
THE PLOUGH
PROCYON
POLLUX
CASTOR
POLARIS
270°
090°
BETELGEUSE
CAPELLA
ORION
RIGEL
ALDEBARAN
CASSIOPEIA
CAPH
ALTAIR
PEGASUS
SHA
To FORMALHAUT
SOUTHERN SKY
SHA
From PEGASUS
Fig 58
FORMALHAUT
ORION
RIGEL
BETELGEUSE
270°
090°
SIRIUS
CRUX
SPICA
From ARCTURUS and THE PLOUGH
180°
NORTHERN SKY

Pegasus (The Flying Horse) is not particularly conspicuous at first. The four main stars form a very large square.

Orion (The Hunter) consists of seven main stars. Four form a quadrilateral, with three in the middle forming the 'Belt'.

The 'pointers' of the Plough point to *Polaris*, which is about 6½ times the distance between the pointers away (Figs 57 and 59). Following the curve of the tail of the Plough one will find *Arcturus* and then, a similar distance further on, *Spica* (Figs 57, 58 and 59).

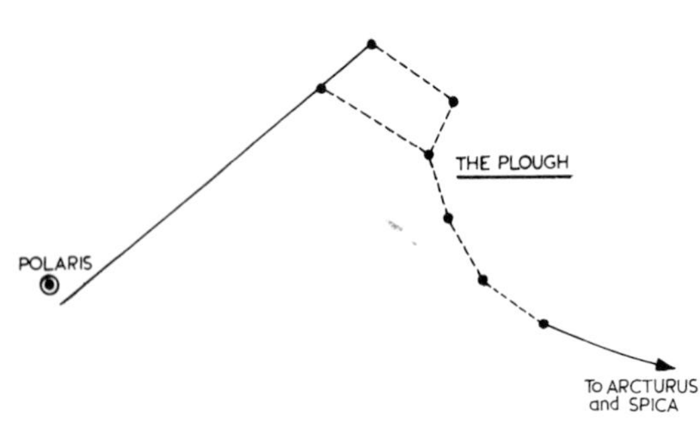

Fig 59

Fomalhaut is very nearly on a line projected from one side of Pegasus, away from Polaris (Figs 57 and 58). *Betelgeuse*, conspicuous for its reddish colour, is one of the three brighter corner stars of Orion. *Rigel* is another, diametrically opposed to Betelgeuse (Figs 57, 58 and 60).

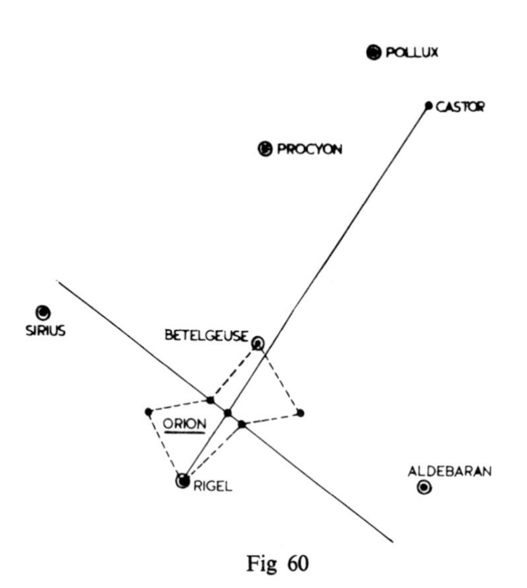

Fig 60

Orion's belt is about equidistant from *Sirius* and *Aldebaran*, and its line almost leads to both (Fig 60). Aldebaran is another star with a reddish tint, and Sirius is the brightest star. Aldebaran, Sirius and *Procyon* form an equilateral triangle (Fig 60).

The line of Rigel, through the middle star of Orion's belt, leads to *Castor* which is quite close to its twin, *Pollux* (Fig 60).

To find *Altair* it is first necessary to locate *Capella*, a very bright star which almost forms an equilateral triangle with Castor and Betelgeuse. Next identify *Caph*, at the top right of Cassiopeia's W (or is it the bottom left of the M?). The line through Capella and Caph leads to Altair (Fig 57).

The identification of the stars requires a little study, but it is a very pleasant way of whiling away the night watches.

As will be seen in the next chapter, there is a special way of using stars which is quite different to this method. However, the ability to readily identify the stars and reduce the observations of them by using Vol 2 and 3 of the *Sight Reduction Tables* will be found particularly useful during periods of partial cloud cover.

Before launching into the two worked examples, here is the recommended format for the reduction of star sights:

Fig 61 Star AM/PM

EP

Ass Lat °N/S

ZT d h m

Z +/- h

GD d h m

DWT h m s

DWE Fast - / Slow + h m s

GMT h m s

SA ° '.

IE On - / Off + '.

OA ° '.

m - '.

AA ° '.

Corr - '.

TA ° '.

Dec ° '. N/S

GHA ♈ h ° '.

m s + ° '.

SHA Star + ° '.

GHA Star ° '.

(+360°)

GHA Star ° '.

Ass Long E + / W - ° '.

LHA Star °

(-360°)

LHA Star °

(180°)

(360°)

Hc ° ' d= +/- ' Z +/- °

Inc +/- ' Zn °

Hc ° '

TA ° '

Intercept ' Towards/Away

Examples:

1. On 24th February 1980 while in EP 50°17′N 17°18′W, an observation was made of Sirius at the deck watch time of 7h 12m 09s. The ship's clock, set to Z+1, showed the time as 1830. Given the following, determine the assumed position, intercept, azimuth and intercept terminal position: SA 17°44.′8; IE 4.′5 off the arc; DWE 16m 32s slow; HE 3m.

Fig 62 — 24th Feb 1980 — Star Sirius — ~~AM~~/PM

EP 50°17′N 17°18′W		Ass Lat 50 °N/~~S~~	
ZT	24 d 18 h 30 m	DWT	7 h 12 m 09 s
Z+1 −	01 h	DWE ~~Fast −~~ Slow +	h 16 m 32 s
GD	24 d 19 h 30 m	GMT	19 h 28 m 41 s
SA	17° 44.′8	GHA ♈ 19 h	78° 49.′0 (b)
IE ~~On −~~ Off +	4.′5	28 m 41 s +	7° 11.′4 (d)
OA	17° 49.′3	SHA Star +	258° 55.′8 (c)
3 m −	3.′0	GHA Star	344° 56.′2
AA	17° 46.′3		(+360°)
Corr −	3.′0 (a)	GHA Star	344° 56.′2
TA	17° 43.′3	Ass Long ~~E +~~ W −	16° 56.′2
		LHA Star	328°
Dec	16° 41.′6 ~~N~~/S (c)		(−360°)
		LHA Star	328°

			(~~+~~180°)
			(~~+~~360°)
Hc	18° 14′	d= 40 56′	Z ~~+~~/= 148°
Inc 40	39′	Zn	148°
Hc	17° 35′		
TA	17° 43′		
Intercept	8′ Towards/~~Away~~		

Notes:

(a) App 1 — 'Stars and Planets'
(b) App 3 — Aries
(c) App 3 — Stars, Sirius
(d) App 6 — Aries

By plotting, the intercept terminal position was found to be 49°53′N 16°50′W.

2. On 21st June 1980 at 0730 zone time (Z−12) while in EP 50°17′S 176°43′E, an observation was made of Rigel at 7h 43m 20s by the deck watch. If the sextant altitude was 25°19.′2, the index error was 2.′5 on the arc, the height of eye was 1m and deck watch error was 12m 18s fast, what was the assumed position, intercept, azimuth and intercept terminal position?

Fig 63

21st Jun 1980 Star Rigel AM/~~PM~~

EP 50°17'S 176°43'E — Ass Lat 50° ~~N~~/S

ZT	21d 07h 30m	DWT	7h 43m 20s
Z ~~+~~/(−)	12h	DWE Fast − / ~~Slow +~~	h 12m 18s
GD	20d 19h 30m	GMT	19h 31m 02s

SA	25° 19'.2	GHA ♈ 19h	194° 08'.2
IE On − / ~~Off +~~	2'.5	31m 02s +	7° 46'.8
OA	25° 16'.7	SHA Star +	281° 36'.5
1 m −	1'.8	GHA Star	483° 31'.5
AA	25° 14'.9		(+360°)
Corr −	2'.0	GHA Star	483° 31'.5
TA	25° 12'.9	Ass Long E + / ~~W −~~	176° 28'.5
		LHA Star	660°
Dec	8° 13'.5 ~~N~~/S		(−360°)
		LHA Star	300°

			(180°)
			~~(360°)~~
Hc	25° 09'	d= (+)/− 47'	Z ~~+~~/(−) 109°
Inc (+)/−	11'		Zn 071°
Hc	25° 20'		
TA	25° 13'		
Intercept	7' ~~Towards~~/Away		

By plotting, the intercept terminal position was found to be 50°02′S 176°18′E.

Exercises

1. During morning twilight on 25th February 1980, while in EP 50°29′S 147°37′E, an observation was made of Spica at a ship's time of 0730 (Z−10). Given the following, determine the assumed position, intercept, azimuth and intercept terminal position: SA 25°21.′8; DWT 9h 34m 31s; IE 1.′5 on the arc; HE 2m; DWE 2m17s fast.
2. On 20th June 1980 while in EP 50°01′N 46°52′W, an observation was made of Arcturus during evening twilight at a zone time of 2135 (Z+3). Given the following, determine the assumed position, intercept, azimuth and intercept terminal position: SA 56°24.′2; DWT 12h 46m 42s; DWE 12m 04s fast; IE zero; HE 1½m.
3. On 22nd September 1980 while in EP 50°12′N 165°12′E an observation was made of Altair during evening twilight, at about 1830 ship's time. The ship's clock was set to Z−11. Given the following, determine the assumed position, intercept, azimuth and intercept terminal position: DWT 7h 28m 51s; DWE 1m 56s slow; SA 46°20.′7; IE 2.′0 off the arc; HE 3m.

10 Selected Stars

The two volumes of the *Sight Reduction Tables* discussed so far contain the solutions to a finite number of spherical triangles. In essence, from a number of assumed positions on earth, the altitudes and azimuths of almost any point on the celestial sphere is tabulated. The assumed positions more or less equate to all positions on the earth's surface. The points on the celestial sphere for which the altitudes and azimuths are tabulated are limited in that these points must have a declination of less than 30°. As seen in the previous chapter, this means that Vol 2 (and Vol 3) of the *Sight Reduction Tables* has a limited usage for stars, a large proportion of which have declinations in excess of 30°.

This apparent inconvenience is offset by the almost total lack of relative movement of the stars. What movement there is is virtually imperceptible, so the impression given is that each star has its own fixed point on the celestial sphere. This accounts for the regular patterns and constellations. In turn, this means that the position of each star is fixed relative to any one other.

In practice, rather than use a star, all the stars' positions are related to the First Point of Aries. By reference only to the Greenwich hour angle of Aries (it having no declination) it is possible to calculate the altitude and azimuth of any star when observed from any position on earth. However, to save the mortal navigator unnecessary work, this information has been built into Vol 1 of the *Sight Reduction Tables*. By reference to the hour angle of Aries and the position of the observer, the altitudes and azimuths of the various stars are tabulated.

In a manner similar to the use of the other volumes of the *Sight Reduction Tables*, the observer is required to assume a position so that both the latitude and the local hour angle of Aries are a whole number of degrees. In return, he is offered a choice not of fifty-seven stars, but seven, which have been carefully selected to give the best coverage of the sky. The full Vol 1 of the *Sight Reduction Tables* tabulates all latitudes from 89°S to 89°N. App 9 of this book is an extract for latitude 50°N. Fig 64 is a portion of that covering the range of local hour angle Aries from 0° to 14°.

The seven stars are arranged in ascending order of azimuth. Capella, Aldebaran, Altair and Vega are in capital letters signifying that they are of the first magnitude—the brightest. Capella, Alpheratz and Vega are identified with a small diamond indicating that the azimuths of these three make them best situated for a three-star fix. To obtain a good position it should normally be sufficient to observe just these three. For each star the altitude (to the nearest minute) and azimuth (to the nearest degree) is tabulated.

Precession and nutation

Albeit slowly, the stars do move and as a result, unlike Vol 2 and 3, Vol 1 of the *Sight Reduction Tables* has a limited life. The extract reproduced in App 9 is from the publication based on the

Fig 64

LAT 50°N

LHA ♈	Hc	Zn	Hc	Zn	Hc	Zn	Hc	Zn	Hc	Zn	Hc	Zn	Hc	Zn
	♦CAPELLA		ALDEBARAN		Hamal		♦Alpheratz		ALTAIR		♦VEGA		Kochab	
0	39 37	062	26 11	095	53 48	126	68 56	176	24 13	254	33 58	292	37 31	347
1	40 11	063	26 49	096	54 19	127	68 58	178	23 36	255	33 22	292	37 22	347
2	40 45	063	27 27	097	54 49	128	68 59	180	22 59	256	32 46	293	37 13	347
3	41 20	064	28 06	098	55 19	130	68 58	183	22 21	257	32 11	294	37 05	347
4	41 55	064	28 44	099	55 49	131	68 55	185	21 44	257	31 36	294	36 56	348
5	42 29	065	29 22	099	56 17	132	68 51	188	21 06	258	31 01	295	36 48	348
6	43 04	065	30 00	100	56 46	134	68 45	190	20 28	259	30 26	295	36 40	348
7	43 39	066	30 38	101	57 13	135	68 37	192	19 50	260	29 51	296	36 33	349
8	44 15	066	31 16	102	57 40	137	68 28	195	19 12	261	29 16	297	36 25	349
9	44 50	067	31 53	103	58 06	138	68 17	197	18 34	261	28 42	297	36 18	349
10	45 26	067	32 31	104	58 31	140	68 05	199	17 56	262	28 08	298	36 11	350
11	46 01	068	33 08	105	58 56	141	67 52	202	17 18	263	27 34	298	36 04	350
12	46 37	068	33 45	105	59 19	143	67 37	204	16 39	264	27 00	299	35 57	350
13	47 13	069	34 23	106	59 42	145	67 20	206	16 01	265	26 26	300	35 50	350
14	47 49	069	34 59	107	60 04	146	67 03	208	15 23	265	25 53	300	35 44	351
	♦CAPELLA		ALDEBARAN		Hamal		♦Diphda		Alpheratz		♦DENEB		Kochab	
15	48 25	070	35 36	108	60 25	148	21 48	184	66 44	210	47 25	290	35 38	351
[illegible]	[illegible]	[illegible]	36 13	109	[illegible]	[illegible]	21 44	185	[illegible]	[illegible]	[illegible]	[illegible]		

Epoch 1980, the year for which the position of the stars was used. For observations made in other years corrections must be applied. The 1980 volume is supplied with correction tables enabling accurate reductions to be made between 1977 and 1985.

The movement of the stars on the celestial sphere is slowly westwards, and the cumulative effect of this motion is known as Precession.

The earth 'wobbles' a little about its axis leading to fluctuations in the precessional movement and this is known as Nutation.

In Table 5 of Vol 1 of the *Sight Reduction Tables*, corrections for the combined effect of precession and nutation for the relevant years are given. Entered with the year, the latitude of the observer and the local hour angle of Aries, the correction extracted is a bearing and distance which may be applied to individual position lines or an observed position. For the years 1979 and 1980 no corrections were necessary.

Although initially intended for air navigation, acknowledgement is made of the use of these tables for navigation at sea by the inclusion of a loose-leaf version of Table 5 in which corrections are given to the nearest tenth of a mile.

Starsight planning

The nature of Vol 1 of the *Sight Reduction Tables* is such that it may be used in two distinct modes-one for the planning of observations, the other for reduction of observations.

When planning the observation of stars the first step is to predict the time of civil twilight (see Chapter 8) and use this time to extract from the *Nautical Almanac* the Greenwich hour angle of Aries. A position is then assumed, as close to the estimated position as possible, so that both latitude and the local hour angle of Aries are a whole number of degrees. Vol 1 of the *Sight Reduction Tables* is then entered, turning first to the page appropriate to the assumed latitude, on which, adjacent to the relevant local hour angle of Aries, will be found the seven selected stars, along with an altitude and azimuth for each.

At the appropriate time for the observations the altitude, with due allowance made for index error, dip and refraction, may be set on the sextant, and when looking in the right direction (azimuth), the brightest star in the field of view ought to be the selected star. If it is not, then either it is a planet or the calculations have gone wrong!

The selection of stars changes with each 15° of local hour angle of Aries (each hour approximately), so if the prediction is within the first or last two degrees (say ten minutes) of any particular block, care should be taken to choose for observation those stars which will appear in the block before or after, as appropriate, thus allowing for the observations to be made at a time slightly different to that planned.

Examples:

1. Which stars will be available for observation at dawn twilight on 24th February 1980 in EP 49°37′N 17°15′W?

LMT CT 45° N	24d	06h	17m	(App 3)
LMT CT 50° N	24d	06h	21m	(App 3)
LMT CT 49° 37′ N	24d	06h	21m	(Interpolate)
Long 17° 15′ W+		1h	09m	(App 5)
GMT CT	24d	07h	30m	

Although observations could probably begin at about 0710, it is better to plan for the time of civil twilight, the middle of the observation period.

GHA ♈	07h	258°	19.′4	(App 3)
Inc	30m+	7°	31.′2	(App 6—Aries)
GHA ♈		265°	50.′6	
Ass Long	−	16°	50.′6	W
LHA ♈		249°		
Ass Lat		50° N		

In Vol 1 of the *Sight Reduction Tables*, turning to the pages for 50°N (App 9), adjacent to local hour angle Aries 249° will be found the following seven stars with the stated altitudes and azimuths:

		Hc	Zn
◇	DENEB	49° 38′	072°
	ALTAIR	32° 36′	119°
	Rasalhague	50° 44′	157°
◇	ANTARES	13° 35′	182°
	ARCTURUS	48° 26′	235°
	Denebola	22° 44′	266°
◇	Dubhe	45° 16′	318°

In this case, the best stars to choose would be Deneb, Antares and Dubhe, those best situated for a three-star fix, as indicated by the diamonds. The remaining four will be available should any of the selected three be obscured by cloud. This local hour angle, 249°, is in the middle of a block, so there is little danger of the sights being taken sufficiently earlier or later as to change the local hour angle of Aries to a different block. However, it is worth noting that all three of the chosen stars appear in the earlier block, but only Deneb appears in the later block.

2. Which stars will be available for observation during evening twilight on 20th June 1980 in EP 50°17′N 157°34′E, assuming that it is intended to use Vol 1 of the *Sight Reduction Tables?*

LMT CT 50° N		20d	20h	58m
LMT CT 52° N		20d	21h	13m
LMT CT 50° 17′N		20d	21h	00m
Long 157° 34′ E	−		10h	30m
GMT CT		20d	10h	30m
Ass Lat 50° N				

GHA ♈ 10h		58°	46.′0	
Inc 30m	+	7°	31.′2	
GHA ♈		66°	17.′2	
Ass Long	+	157°	42.′8	E
LHA ♈		224°		

The stars available are:

		Hc	Zn
◇	DENEB	35° 01′	059°
	VEGA	50° 03′	085°
	Rasalhague	40° 36′	125°
◇	ARCTURUS	58° 12′	199°
	REGULUS	20° 39′	264°
◇	POLLUX	10° 41′	301°
	CAPELLA	10° 36′	336°

Ideally Deneb, Arcturus and Pollux would be used, but every effort should be made to get the sights early, for a five-minute delay will mean that Pollux will no longer be available (in the tables!).

Starsight reduction

After the planning, the next stage is to 'shoot' the chosen three stars (assuming the sky to be free of cloud) and reduce the sights.

Each sight must be timed and reduced individually. Once again, but perhaps with even more purpose, a planned format is recommended. The one illustrated in Fig 65 allows for both planning and reduction.

The following two examples are the logical extensions of the previous two. The planning stages are included for the sake of completeness.

Fig 65

Stars AM/PM

EP				Ass Lat		°N/S	
LMT CT	°		d h m	GHA ♈	h	°	'.
LMT CT	°		d h m	Inc	m +	°	'.
LMT CT	°	'	d h m	GHA ♈		°	'.
Long	°	' E − W +	h m			(+360°)	
GMT CT			d h m	GHA ♈		°	'.
Available:	Hc		Zn	Ass Long	E + W −	°	'.
	° '		°	LHA ♈		°	
	° '		°			(−360°)	
	° '		°	LHA ♈		°	

	1.	2.	3.
DWT	h m s	h m s	h m s
DWE Fast − Slow +	h m s	h m s	h m s
GMT	h m s	h m s	h m s
GHA ♈ h	° '.	° '.	° '.
m s +	° '.	° '.	° '.
GHA ♈	° '.	° '.	° '.
	(+360°)	(+360°)	(+360°)
GHA ♈	° '.	° '.	° '.
Ass Long E + W −	° '.	° '.	° '.
LHA ♈	°	°	°
	(−360°)	(−360°)	(−360°)
LHA ♈	°	°	°
SA	° '.	° '.	° '.
IE On − Off +	'.	'.	'.
OA	° '.	° '.	° '.
m −	'.	'.	'.
AA	° '.	° '.	° '.
Corr −	'.	'.	'.
TA	° '.	° '.	° '.
Hc	° '	° '	° '
Intercept	'T/A	'T/A	'T/A
Zn	°	°	°

1. During morning twilight on 24th February 1980, while in EP 49°37′N 17°15′W, which stars would be available for observation and reduction using Vol 1 of the *Sight Reduction Tables?* Which of those would you use, and why?

The following three stars were observed to have these sextant altitudes at the deck watch times indicated:

	SA	DWT
Deneb	49° 20.′1	7h 25m 37s
Antares	13° 55.′7	7h 27m 08s
Dubhe	45° 11.′3	7h 28m 42s

Given the following, calculate the three assumed positions, intercepts and azimuths: IE 2.′5 on; HE 2m; DWE 3m 17s slow.

Fig 66

24th Feb 1980 Stars AM/~~PM~~

EP 49° 37′N 17° 15′W Ass Lat 50 °N/~~S~~

LMT CT 50 °N	24d06h21m	GHA ♈ 07h	258°	19′.4
LMT CT 45 °N	24d06h17m	Inc 30 m +	7°	31′.2
LMT CT 49° 37′N	24d06h21m	GHA ♈	265°	50′.6
Long 17° 15′ ~~E~~ W +	01h09m		(+360°)	
GMT CT	24d07h30m	GHA ♈	265°	50′.6
Available: Hc	Zn	Ass Long ~~E +~~ W −	16°	50′.6
DENEB 49° 38′	072°	LHA ♈	249°	
ANTARES 13° 35′	182°		(−360°)	
DUBHE 45° 16′	318°	LHA ♈	249°	

	1. DENEB	2. ANTARES	3. DUBHE
DWT	7h 25m 37s	7h 27m 08s	7h 28m 42s
DWE ~~Fast −~~ Slow +	h 03m 17s	h 03m 17s	h 03m 17s
GMT	07h 28m 54s	07h 30m 25s	07h 31m 59s
GHA ♈ 07h	258° 19′.4	258° 19′.4	258° 19′.4
m s +	7° 14′.7	7° 37′.5	8° 01′.1
GHA ♈	265° 34′.1	265° 56′.9	266° 20′.5
	(+360°)	(+360°)	(+360°)
GHA ♈	265° 34′.1	265° 56′.9	266° 20′.5
Ass Long ~~E +~~ W −	17° 34′.1	16° 56′.9	17° 20′.5
LHA ♈	248°	249°	249°
	(−360°)	(−360°)	(−360°)
LHA ♈	248°	249°	249°
SA	49° 20′.1	13° 55′.7	45° 11′.3
IE On − ~~Off +~~	2′.5	2′.5	2′.5
OA	49° 17′.6	13° 53′.2	45° 08′.8
2 m −	2′.5	2′.5	2′.5
AA	49° 15′.1	13° 50′.7	45° 06′.3
Corr −	0′.8	3′.9	1′.0
TA	49° 14′.3	13° 46′.8	45° 05′.3
Hc	49° 01′	13° 35′	45° 16′
Intercept	13′ T/~~A~~	12′ T/~~A~~	11′ ~~T~~/A
Zn	072°	182°	318°

Of the seven stars available (see the earlier example), Deneb, Antares and Dubhe would be used by choice, because they are best situated for a three-star fix.

2. Assuming that it was required to use Vol 1 of the *Sight Reduction Tables*, which stars would be available for observation during evening twilight on 20th June 1980, while in EP 50°17′N 157°34′E? Of the seven, which would you use and why?

Given the following, calculate the three assumed positions, intercepts and azimuths: IE 3.′5 off; HE 3m; DWE 6m 18s fast.

	SA	DWT
Deneb	34° 53.′7	10h 34m 25s
Arcturus	57° 53.′8	10h 36m 08s
Pollux	10° 51.′6	10h 37m 42s

Fig 67

20th June 1980 Stars ~~AM~~/PM

EP 56°17′N 157°34′E — Ass Lat 56 °N/~~S~~

LMT CT 52°	20d21h13m	GHA ♈ 10h	58°	46′.0
LMT CT 50°	20d20h58m	Inc 30m +	7°	31′.2
LMT CT 50°17′N	20d21h00m	GHA ♈	66°	17′.2
Long 157°34′ E − (~~W +~~)	10h30m		(+360°)	
GMT CT	20d10h30m	GHA ♈	66°	17′.2
Available: Hc Zn		Ass Long E + (~~W −~~)	157°	42′.8
DENEB 35°01′	059°	LHA ♈	224°	
ARCTURUS 58°12′	199°		(−360°)	
POLLUX 10°41′	301°	LHA ♈	224°	

	1. DENEB	2. ARCTURUS	3. POLLUX
DWT	10h34m25s	10h36m08s	10h37m42s
DWE Fast − (~~Slow +~~)	h06m18s	h06m18s	h06m18s
GMT	10h28m07s	10h29m50s	10h31m24s
GHA ♈ 10 h	58°46′.0	58°46′.0	58°46′.0
m s +	7°02′.9	7°28′.7	7°52′.3
GHA ♈	65°48′.9	66°14′.7	66°38′.3
	(+360°)	(+360°)	(+360°)
GHA ♈	65°48′.9	66°14′.7	66°38′.3
Ass Long E + (~~W −~~)	157°11′.1	157°45′.3	157°21′.7
LHA ♈	223°	224°	224°
	(−360°)	(−360°)	(−360°)
LHA ♈	223°	224°	224°
SA	34°53′.7	57°53′.8	10°51′.6
IE (~~On −~~) Off +	3′.5	3′.5	3′.5
OA	34°57′.2	57°57′.3	10°55′.1
3 m −	3′.0	3′.0	3′.0
AA	34°54′.2	57°54′.3	10°52′.1
Corr −	1′.4	0′.6	4′.9
TA	34°52′.8	57°53′.7	10°47′.2
Hc	34°28′	58°12′	10°41′
Intercept	25′ T/~~A~~	18′ ~~T~~/A	6′ T/~~A~~
Zn	059°	199°	301°

Of the seven stars available (see the earlier example) Deneb, Arcturus and Pollux are best situated for a three-star fix. However, a delay of five minutes beyond the predicted 'shooting' time would mean that Pollux would no longer be tabulated (because its altitude would be too low). In addition, neither Regulus nor Capella is tabulated for a local hour angle of Aries of 225°, so the final choice for a third star rests between Vega and Rasalhague. Each has an azimuth which differs from its neighbouring star by only 26°, so there is no difference in that respect. Therefore the final choice must be Vega, the brighter of the two.

For the purposes of this last example, the theoretically 'correct' stars were used.

Plotting

The final step is to plot the position lines and the observed position. The assumed latitude will be the same for all three stars, but all three longitudes will be different.

The method to be adopted is as follows:

(a) Write the appropriate longitudes on the chart.
(b) Note the scale of latitude to be used.
(c) Plot the assumed positions numbering them 1–3 to correspond with the numbers of the stars on the reduction format.
(d) Plot the estimated position.
(e) Through each assumed position, draw each azimuth.
(f) Mark off each intercept along each azimuth ('towards' or 'away'), to each intercept terminal position.
(g) Through these intercept terminal positions draw the position lines at right-angles to the azimuths.
(h) The observed position will be within the 'cocked hat', and may be adjusted for precession and nutation if necessary.

NB The size of the 'cocked hat' gives a good indication of the accuracy of the observations.

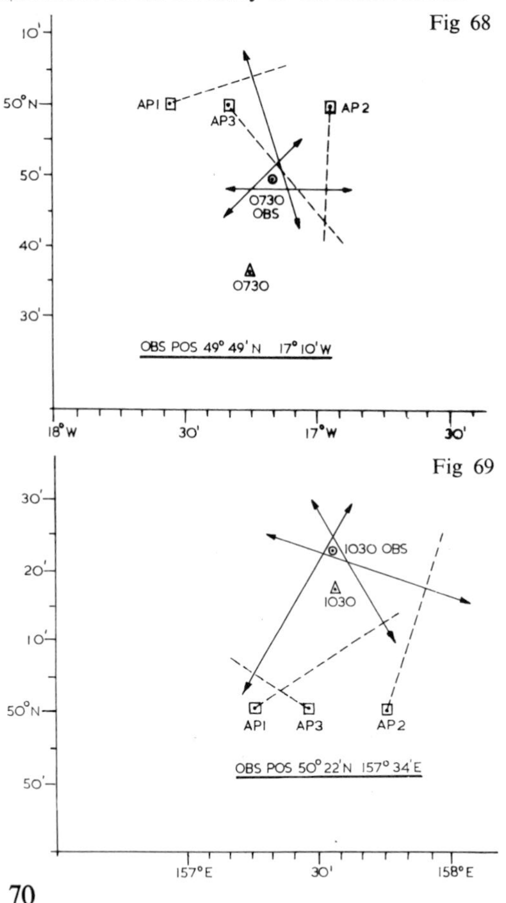

Fig 68

Fig 69

Figs 68 and 69 illustrate the plotting of the two examples just worked. The azimuths are drawn as dotted lines and each position line has a single arrowhead at each end. No adjustment for precession and nutation was necessary during 1980.

Exercises

All three of these exercises are intended to be completed with the aid of Vol 1 of the *Sight Reduction Tables.*

1. On 25th February 1980, while in EP 50°05′N 20°47′W, it was required to observe stars during evening twilight. State which stars, with tabulated altitudes and azimuths, are available. Of those, which would you have used, and why?

During that evening twilight, the following three stars were observed to have these sextant altitudes at the deck watch times indicated.

	SA	DWT
Dubhe	39° 02.′4	7h 35m 30s
Rigel	30° 45.′3	7h 37m 04s
Alpheratz	37° 17.′9	7h 38m 40s

The index error was 1.′5 off the arc, the deck watch error was 5m 12s fast and the height of eye was 2m. What was the observed position? State the GMT of the observation.

2. While in EP 49°37′N 53°00′W on 21st June 1980, it was planned to 'shoot' the stars during evening twilight. Which stars were available, and what were the tabulated altitudes and azimuths? Of these, which would be used, by choice?

	SA	DWT
Vega	50° 17.′0	12h 14m 43s
Arcturus	58° 24.′5	12h 16m 07s
Dubhe	56° 04.′1	12h 17m 40s

Given the following, determine the observed position, stating the GMT (including the day): IE—2.′5; DWE 13m 18s slow; HE 3m.

3. On 22nd September 1980 it was estimated that the ship's position during morning twilight would be 49°31′N 146°15′E. Which stars were available for observation, and what were the tabulated altitudes and azimuths?

Three stars were observed, the following being noted:

	SA	DWT
Dubhe	43° 52.′1	7h 39m 42s
Sirius	21° 12.′5	7h 41m 15s
Hamal	43° 55.′6	7h 42m 51s

Given the following information, determine the observed position and the time (GMT) the observation was made: IE+2.′0; HE 2.5m; DWE 8m 03s fast.

11 Polaris

Polaris, or the Pole Star, is so named because it is almost directly above the north pole, and as such (for those in the northern hemisphere) provides a quick and easy reference to 'north'. It also has another navigational advantage in that it provides a relatively quick and easy way of determining latitude.

Imagine for the moment that Polaris is exactly above the north pole. In other words, its declination is 90°00.′0 N.

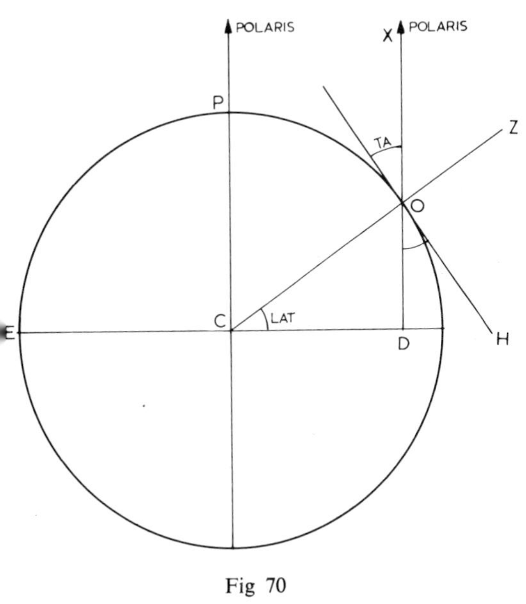

Fig 70

The true altitude of Polaris, TA, is equal to DÔH (Fig 70).

$$
\begin{aligned}
\text{But } & C\hat{O}H = C\hat{D}O = 90^\circ \\
\therefore\ & C\hat{O}D = 90^\circ - D\hat{O}H = 90^\circ - TA \\
\text{But } & \text{Lat} = 90^\circ - C\hat{O}D \\
\therefore\ & \text{Lat} = TA
\end{aligned}
$$

Thus the latitude of the observer is the same as the true altitude of Polaris. (The true altitude being the sextant altitude corrected for index error, dip and refraction.)

If Polaris were exactly situated as described, an observer could obtain his latitude, with no reference to time, simply with one observation. Though not quite that simple, the problem is none the less relatively easily solved.

Subsequent to an observation, the sextant altitude is converted to a true altitude in the same way, using the same altitude correction tables, as for any other star. To convert this true altitude to a latitude, corrections are applied to allow for the declination of Polaris being a little less than 90°N.

The corrections are contained in the 'Polaris (Pole Star) Tables' in the *Nautical Almanac*. App 4 is an extract from the complete tables. The table is entered with the local hour angle of Aries, the approximate latitude of the observer, and the month of the year. The correction is extracted in three parts, named a_o, a_1 and a_2. In order that each of these three corrections is always positive, each contains a constant. The sum of these three constants is 1°, so the total correction to be applied to the true altitude is: $+a_0 + a_1 + a_2 - 1°$.

a_0 is determined by the local hour angle of Aries, but its rate of change is such that it is sufficiently accurate to know this local hour angle to the nearest degree. Consequently, the timing of this sight is not critical; to the nearest minute is quite adequate. a_1, is determined by the latitude of the observer, but, once again, a very approximate latitude is sufficiently accurate. a_2 is determined by the month of the year.

The same vertical column must be used for all three extractions. Each covers a range of local hour angle of Aries of 10°, and this is the deciding factor. Once in the correct column, a_0 is determined by reference to the units of degrees of the local hour angle.

As with all celestial observations, the position line should be taken as being at right-angles to the azimuth. However, Polaris is always within 2° of the pole, so it is quite in order to assume that the position line is a parallel of latitude.

Fig 71 is the proposed format for reducing Polaris observations. It includes a provision for twilight calculations, for–as with the other stars–this is the best time to observe it.

Fig 71

Polaris AM/PM

EP

LMT CT	°N		d	h	m
LMT CT	°N		d	h	m
LMT CT	°	'N	d	h	m
Long	°	'E − / W +		h	m
GMT CT			d	h	m

SA		°	'	DWT		h	m	s
IE	On − / Off +		'	DWE	Fast − / Slow +	h	m	s
OA		°	'	GMT		h	m	s
m	−		'					
AA		°	'	GHA ♈	h	°	'	
Corr	−		'	m	s +	°	'	
TA		°	'	GHA ♈		°	'	
a_0	+		'			(+360°)		
a_1	+		'	GHA ♈		°	'	
a_2	+		'	Long	E + / W −	°	'	
		°	'	LHA ♈		°	'	
	−	1°				(−360°)		
Lat		°	' N	LHA ♈		°	'	

Examples:

1. On 21st June 1980 an observation was made of Polaris during evening twilight. The estimated position at the time was 50°25'N 113°15'W. Given the following, calculate the observer's latitude: SA 49°36.'1; IE 5.'1 off; HE 2.5m; DWT 4h 33m 15s; DWE 1m 02s slow.

Fig 72 — 21st June 1980 Polaris ~~AM~~/PM

EP 50° 25′N 113° 15′W

LMT CT	52 °N	21 d	21 h	13 m
LMT CT	50 °N	21 d	20 h	58 m
LMT CT	50 ° 25 ′N	21 d	21 h	01 m
Long	113 ° 15 ′ ~~E~~ W +		07 h	33 m
GMT CT		22 d	04 h	34 m (a)

SA	49 ° 36′.1		DWT	4 h 33 m 15 s
IE ~~On~~ Off +	5′.1		DWE ~~Fast~~ Slow +	h 01 m 02 s
OA	49 ° 41′.2		GMT	04 h 34 m 17 s
2.5 m −	2′.8			
AA	49 ° 38′.4		GHA ♈ 04h	330 ° 29′.5
Corr −	0′.8		34 m 17 s +	8 ° 35′.7
TA	49 ° 37′.6		GHA ♈	339 ° 05′.2
a_0 +	1° 47′.1	(b)		(+360°)
a_1 +	0′.6	(c)	GHA ♈	339 ° 05′.2
a_2 +	0′.9	(d)	Long ~~E +~~ W −	113 ° 15′
	51 ° 26′.2		LHA ♈	225 ° 50′.2
−	1°	(e)		(−360°)
Lat	50 ° 26′.2 N		LHA ♈	225 ° 50′.2

Notes:

(a) Observation made on 22nd (GMT).

(b) Polaris Tables (App 4), 220°–229° column, 5°50.′2 in the vertical column. (Interpolate if necessary.)

(c) Same table, same column, Latitude 50°.

(d) Same table, same column, June.

(e) Always subtract 1°.

It is sometimes useful to set the approximate altitude of Polaris on the sextant before observation in order that this not very bright star –perhaps, during evening twilight– may be seen through the sextant telescope before it is visible to the naked eye. To obtain the setting for the sextant, a_0 should be subtracted from the EP latitude and 1° added. Allowance should then be made for index error and dip.

In the case of the first example above, having predicted the time of civil twilight the local hour angle of Aries at this time would be calculated thus:

GHA ♈ 22d	04h		330° 29.′5
Inc	34m		8° 31.′4
GHA ♈			339° 00.′9
Long		—	113° 15′ W
LHA ♈			225° 45.′9

Entering the Polaris Tables (App 4) with this local hour angle of Aries, it is found that a_0 is 1°47.′1. The index error is 5.′1 off the arc and dip is −2.′8, the two combining to a correction of +2.′3.

EP latitude		50° 25.′	
a_0	—	1° 47.′1	
		48° 37.′9	
	+	1°	
		49° 37.′9	
IE and dip	—	2.′3	(Sign reversed)
Sextant setting		49° 35.′6	

If the observer had set the sextant to 49°35.′6 and 'swept' the northern horizon, he would have found Polaris in the field of view, whereupon adjustment would have been made to measure the altitude accurately.

2. While in EP 49°37′N 07°14′W an observation was made of Polaris during evening twilight on 20th June 1980. Given the following, calculate the observed latitude: SA48°59.′7; IE 2.′5 on the arc; HE 2m; DWT 9h 24m 58s; DWE 3m 17s slow.

Fig 73

20th June 1980 Polaris ~~AM~~/PM

EP 49° 37′N 07° 14′W

LMT CT	50 °N	20 d	20 h	58 m
LMT CT	45 °N	20 d	20 h	28 m
LMT CT	49 ° 37 ′N	20 d	20 h	56 m
Long	07 ° 14 ′ ~~E~~ W +		h	29 m
GMT CT		20 d	21 h	25 m

SA		48 ° 59′.7
IE On ~~Off~~	− ~~+~~	2′.5
OA		48 ° 57′.2
2 m	−	2′.5
AA		48 ° 54′.7
Corr	−	0′.8
TA		48 ° 53′.9
a_0	+	1 ° 47′.4
a_1	+	0′.6
a_2	+	0′.9
		50 ° 42′.8
	−	1°
Lat		49 ° 42′.8 N

DWT	9 h	24 m	58 s
DWE ~~Fast~~ Slow +	h	03 m	17 s
GMT	21 h	28 m	15 s
GHA ♈ 21 h	224°		13′.1
28 m 15 s +	7°		04′.9
GHA ♈	231°		18′.0
	(+360°)		
GHA ♈	231 °		18′.0
Long ~~E +~~ W −	7°		14′
LHA ♈	224°		04′.0
	(−360°)		
LHA ♈	224 °		04′.0

NB Add 12h to the deck watch time.

Exercises:

1. During the evening twilight on 20th June 1980 while in EP 50°05′N 07°14′E an observation was made of Polaris, the sextant altitude being 49°15.′6. Given the following information, calculate the observed latitude: DWT 8h 37m 18s; DWE 2m 37s fast; IE 3.′5 on; HE 3m.
2. On 20th June 1980 while in EP 27°30′N 165°30′W, an observation was made of Polaris during evening twilight. Given the following information, calculate the observed latitude: SA 26°50.′6; IE 2.′5 on; HE 2m; DWT 6h 22m 24s; DWE 5m 53s slow.
3. While in EP 32°15′N 166°15′E on 22nd June 1980, an observation was made of Polaris during evening twilight. Given the following information, calculate the observed latitude: SA 31°24.′9; IE 1.′5 off; HE 3m; DWT 8h 34m 17s; DWE 12s slow.

12 The Moon

In spite of its nocturnal romantic connotations, the moon is of greatest value to the navigator when it is visible during daylight. Then, the vessel's position can be 'fixed' at the intersection of the two position lines obtained by simultaneous (or nearly so) observation of both sun and moon, thus obviating the waiting time (and effort?) involved in 'running up' the position lines obtained from the sun alone.

Unlike all the other heavenly bodies used for navigation which revolve around the sun, the moon is in orbit around the earth. It is also a lot closer to earth (about 250,000 miles) than the next nearest, Venus (about 25,000,000 miles at its closest). The moon's proximity leads to a relative high speed and, consequently, large and rapid changes in both hour angle and declination. The Increment & Correction tables assume an hourly rate of change of hour angle for the moon as 14°19.′0, whereas inspection of the tabulated 'v' figure shows that the actual change from hour to hour can be 14°34.′0 or even higher (that is v = 15.′0 or more). Compared with that for other bodies, the hourly rate of change of declination is also very high, the tabulated 'd' figure often being 12.′0 or more. The nearness of the moon also leads to parallax way in excess of that found with the other bodies. Indeed, the correction for parallax is dealt with in a unique way in the Altitude Correction Table for the Moon (App 6), using a figure for Horizontal Parallax which is tabulated hourly in the *Nautical Almanac* (see Chapter 3). These large and rapid changes mean that great care is necessary in the timing of an observation, and in the extraction and interpolation of the corrections.

A final complication is that it is but rarely that the moon is full. The usual case is that we see either a gibbous (more than half) or crescent (less than half) moon. On these occasions neither navigator nor cloud can determine which limb is to be observed. The take-it-or-leave-it decision has already been made. If there is any doubt about which is the complete limb, remember it is the one nearer the sun.

By all means use the Dip table in Appendix 1 if that in Appendix 6 has not tabulated the relevant height of eye, and remember to subtract 30′ from the altitude if the upper limb has been observed.

In spite of its complications, the moon has one great virtue—it is easy to identify!

Fig 74 is a format which may be of use to reduce the sights.

Fig 74

Moon UL/LL AM/PM

EP				Ass Lat			°N/S
ZT	d	h	m	DWT	h	m	s
Z +/-		h		DWE Fast – Slow +	h	m	s
GD	d	h	m	GMT	h	m	s
SA		°	'.	GHA h		°	'.
IE On – Off +			'.	m s +		°	'.
OA		°	'.	v= +			'.
m –			'.	GHA		°	'.
AA		°	'.		(+360°)		
Corr +			'.	GHA		°	'.
HP= +			'.	Ass Long E + W –		°	'.
UL (–		30'.0)		LHA		°	
TA		°	'.		(–360°)		
				LHA		°	
Dec h		°	'. N/S				
d= +/-			'.				
Dec		°	'. N/S		(180°)		
					(360°)		
Hc		°	'	d= +/- '	Z +/-	°	
Inc +/-			'		Zn	°	
Hc		°	'				
TA		°	'				
Intercept			' Towards/Away				

Examples:

1. On 24th February 1980 while in EP 50°12′N 48°58′W an observation was made of the moon's lower limb when the ship's clock, set to Z+3, showed the time as 1528. Given the following information, calculate the assumed position, azimuth and intercept: SA 29°23.′7; IE 1.′5 off; HE 2.′5; DWT 6h 23m 48s; DWE 4m 18s slow.

Fig 75 — 24th Feb 1980 Moon ~~UL~~/LL ~~AM~~/PM

EP	50°12′N 48°58′W	Ass Lat	50° N/~~S~~
ZT	24d 15h 28m	DWT	6h 23m 48s
Z (+)/–	03h	DWE ~~Fast –~~ Slow +	h 04m 18s
GD	24d 18h 28m	GMT	18h 28m 06s

SA	29° 23′.7		GHA 18h	337° 28′.7
IE ~~On –~~ Off +	1′.5		28m 06s +	6° 42′.3
OA	29° 25′.2		v= 9.6 +	4′.6 (a)
2.5 m –	2′.8		GHA	344° 15′.6
AA	29° 22′.4			(+360°)
Corr +	59′.2	(b)	GHA	344° 15′.6
HP= 56.5 +	3′.6	(c)	Ass Long ~~E +~~ W –	49° 15′.6
UL	~~(– 30′.0)~~		LHA	295°
TA	30° 25′.2			(–360°)
			LHA	295°

Dec 18h	18° 40′.7 N/~~S~~
d=2.1 (+)/–	1′.0
Dec	18° 41′.7 N/~~S~~

				~~(180°)~~
				~~(360°)~~
Hc	29° 41′	d= (+)/– 44′	Z ~~+/–~~	97°
Inc (+)/–	31′		Zn	097°
Hc	30° 12′			
TA	30° 25′			
Intercept	13′ Towards/~~Away~~			

Notes:

(a) 'v' from App 3, correction from App 6, always positive.

(b) App 7, 25°–29° column, always positive.

(c) Horizontal Parallax (HP) from App 3; correction from App 7, same column as for (b): 'L' and HP 56.5 (interpolated), always positive.

2. On 23rd September 1980 while in EP 49°48′S 10°17′E, an observation was made of the moon's upper limb when the ship's clock indicated a time of 0435, and was set to Z–1. Given the following information, determine the assumed position, intercept and azimuth: SA 10°57.′6; DWT 3h 50m 10s; DWE 15m 17s fast; IE 1.′0 on; HE 3m.

Fig 76

23rd Sept 1980 Moon UL/~~LL~~ AM/~~PM~~

EP 49° 48'S 10°17'E — Ass Lat 50° ~~N~~/S

ZT	23d 04h 35m	DWT	3h 50m 10s
Z +/(-)	01h	DWE Fast − ~~Slow +~~	h 15m 17s
GD	23d 03h 35m	GMT	03h 34m 53s
SA	10° 57'.6	GHA 03h	64° 08'.0
IE On − ~~Off +~~	1'.0	34m 53s +	8° 19'.4
OA	10° 56'.6	v= 7.4 +	4'.3
3 m −	3'.0	GHA	72° 31'.7
AA	10° 53'.6		(+360°)
Corr +	62'.4	GHA	72° 31'.7
HP=60.7 +	5'.8	Ass Long E + ~~W −~~	10° 28'.3
UL (−	30'.0) (a)	LHA	83°
TA	11° 31'.8		(−360°)
		LHA	83°
Dec 03 h	9° 15'.1 ~~N~~/S		
d= 11.3 +/(-)	6'.5		
Dec	9° 08'.6 ~~N~~/S		(180°)
			~~(360°)~~
Hc	11° 22'	d= (+)/− 46'	Z (+)/− 90°
Inc (+)/−	7'	Zn	270°
Hc	11° 29'		
TA	11° 32'		
Intercept	3' Towards/~~Away~~		

NB (a) Upper limb observed, subtract 30′.

Exercises:

1. In EP 50°23′N 159°20′W on 25th February 1980 at 1530 ship's time, clock set to Z+11, an observation of the moon's lower limb was made at 2h 46m 25s by the deck watch which was 16m 07s fast. If the sextant altitude was 25°13.′2, the index error 1.′5 off the arc and the height of eye 3m, calculate the assumed position, intercept and azimuth, then plot them to find the intercept terminal position.

2. While in EP 49°48′S 152°36′W, at 1433 in Z+10 on 21st June 1980, an observation was made of the moon's upper limb at a time by the deck watch of 12h 32m 02s. If the sextant altitude was 13°39.′5, index error 0.′7 on the arc, height of eye 1m and the deck watch error 1m 12s slow, what was the assumed position, intercept, azimuth and intercept terminal position?

3. At a ship's time of 0334 on 22nd September 1980 while in EP 50°04′S 83°18′E, an observation was made of the moon's lower limb at a deck watch time of 9h 15m 05s. The ship's clock was set to Z–6, the sextant altitude was 15°10.′5, the index error 2.′3 off the arc, height of eye 2.5m and the error of the deck watch 18m 57s slow. What was the assumed position, azimuth, intercept and intercept terminal position?

13 Compass Checking

So far the azimuth–the true bearing–of an observed heavenly body has been used only for plotting a position line, but if at the time of the observation a bearing of the body were taken with the steering compass, the deviation of that compass on that heading could be checked.

In practice it is often easier to make the checking of the compass a completely separate operation, performed once each day while on passage and soon after each course alteration.

The type of compass with a vertical pin in the centre of the card frequently has a shadow cast across the card allowing for easy reading of the reciprocal of the sun's bearing (azimuth). Other types of compass might necessitate the use of an azimuth ring or a pelorus, but whatever the method involved in taking bearings with the steering compass, the checking of the deviation of that compass remains the same.

If, at the time of taking or noting the azimuth of the sun the time were also noted, it is then possible to make an 'abbreviated' reduction of the observation with the intention of extracting only the azimuth.

Examples:

1. On 24th February 1980 while in EP 49°37′N 18°45′W the bearing of the sun, taken with the steering compass, was found to be 163°C. If the time was 11h 32m 40s GMT and the variation was 17°W, what was the deviation of the compass?

GHA 11h		341° 39.′4	Dec 11h	9° 40.′8	S
32m 40s	+	8° 10.′0	d=0.′9, −	0.′5	
GHA		349° 49.′4	Dec	9° 40.′3	S
Ass Long	−	18° 49.′4			
LHA		331°			

Local hour angle and declination are extracted from the *Nautical Almanac* (App 3) as normal, then the *Sight Reduction Tables* (App 10) are entered, but only Z is extracted. In this case Zn=Z and is 148°.

Z = Zn	148°T
Compass bearing	163°C
Compass error	15°W
Variation	17°W
Deviation	2°E

2. On 22nd September 1980 while in EP 50°29′S 175°57′E the bearing of the sun was found to be 017°C. If the ship's time was 1032 (Z–12), deck watch time was 10h 32m 18s, deck watch error was 28s fast, variation 17°E, what was the deviation of the compass used for the observation?

ZT	22d	10h	32m	DWT	10h	32m	18s
Z	—	12h		DWE	—		28s
GD	21d	22h	32m	GMT	22h	31m	50s

GHA 21d 22h	151° 47.′6	Dec 22h	0° 22.′5 N
31m 50s +	7° 57.′5	d=1.′0, —	0.′5
GHA	159° 45.′1	Dec	0° 22.′0 N
Ass Long	+ 176° 14.′9		
LHA	336°	Ass Lat 50°S	

	180°
Z	−150°
Zn	030°T
Compass bearing	017°C
Compass error	13°E
Variation	17°E
Deviation	4°W

Note that with all observations it is vital to compare the zone time with the zone number to deduce the correct Greenwich Date before entering the *Nautical Almanac*.

This method of checking the deviation of the compass may be used with any of the navigational heavenly bodies, but the sun has many advantages, not the least of which is the good working light it provides.

Amplitudes

The arc of the horizon between the rising or setting sun and the pole is its *amplitude*.

Theoretical sunrise or sunset occurs when the centre of the sun is on the horizon. As a result of refraction, this occurs when the sun's lower limb appears to be about half a diameter above the horizon.

Various forms of amplitude tables appear in various publications, a convenient one being found in Reed's *Nautical Almanac*. By kind permission of the publishers, part of this table is reproduced here as App 8.

With recourse, then, to neither sextant nor chronometer, but simply taking a compass bearing of the sun when it appears to be about half a diameter above the horizon, entering amplitude tables with the sun's declination and the latitude of the observer, and then comparing the results, the deviation of the compass may be checked.

Examples:

1. In latitude 50°N when the sun's declination was 9°S, the compass bearing of the setting sun was 284°C. If the variation was 25°W, what was the deviation of the compass?

Entering the table with a declination of 9° and a latitude of 50°, a figure of 75.9 is extracted. This is rounded up to 76 and named according to the rules at the foot of the page, S, after the declination, and W, because the sun is setting.

Zn	S76°W
or	256°T
Compass bearing	284°C
Compass error	28°W
Variation	25°W
Deviation	3°W

2. In latitude 50°S when the declination was 5°S the sun rose bearing 089°C. If the variation was 12°E, what was the deviation of the compass?

Zn	S82.2°E
or	098°T
Compass bearing	089°C
Compass error	9°E
Variation	12°E
Deviation	3°W

Exercises:

1. While in latitude 47°N the sun rose bearing 102°C. If the declination of the sun was 2°N and the variation was 12°W, what was the deviation of the compass?
2. While in latitude 15°S, the sun, whose declination was 8°S, set bearing 255°C. If the variation was 14°E what was the deviation of the compass?
3. While in latitude 5°N and the declination of the sun was 11°N, it rose bearing 093°C. If the variation was 17°W, what was the deviation of the compass?

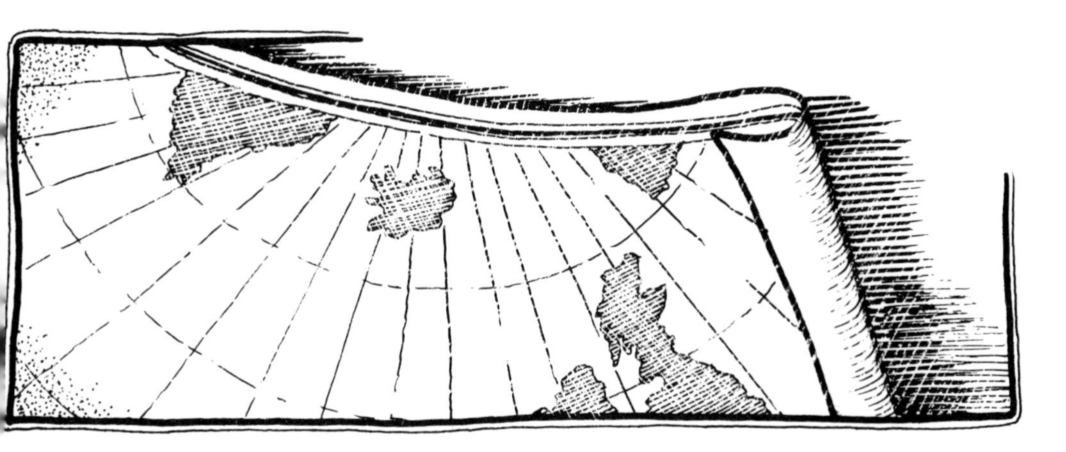

14 Great Circle Sailing

The shortest distance between two points on the surface of a sphere is the lesser arc of the Great Circle through those two points.

With the exception of such circumstances as land being in the way, or perhaps the weather patterns dictating alternative routes, the 'proper' track for which the navigator should aim during long passages of more than about 500 miles is the great-circle track. This is not only the shortest but also the track which would be followed if it were possible to see the destination and steer straight for it. The problem in trying to follow a great-circle track is that it is a curve, and to follow it exactly would necessitate continually changing the course of the vessel. That is not only impracticable but virtually impossible. What *is* practicable is to determine the great-circle track and note the latitudes at which it cuts the 5° meridians, and then steer rhumb lines between these numerous points.

A *gnomonic* chart is used to determine the great-circle track. The special feature of this projection is that a straight line on it is, in fact, a great circle. Fig 77 shows such a straight line drawn between Bishop Rock Light and Cape Race Light on a reproduction of a gnomonic chart (5095) published by the British Hydrographic Department.

The latitudes at which this great-circle track cuts each of the 5° meridians could be noted and these positions subsequently plotted on a mercator chart. If these points were then joined in a series of straight lines (rhumb lines), one would then have a track, close to the ideal of a great circle, but actually made up of a series of rhumb lines. Fig 78 is a diagrammatic illustration of such a series of rhumb lines 'around' a great circle.

On a mercator chart, Fig 79 shows both the great circle 'legs' and the rhumb line between Bishop Rock Light and Cape Race Light.

The distance along each 'leg' of the great circle may now be measured and the total compared with the distance along the rhumb line. In this particular case, the two distances are 1,842 and 1,871 miles, the great circle being shorter. The difference between great circle and rhumb line

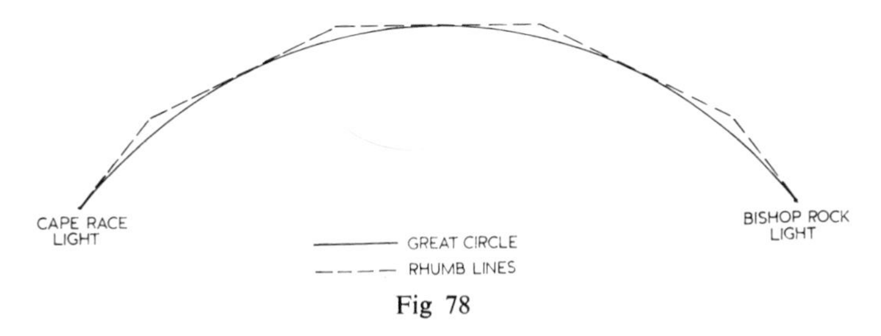

Fig 78

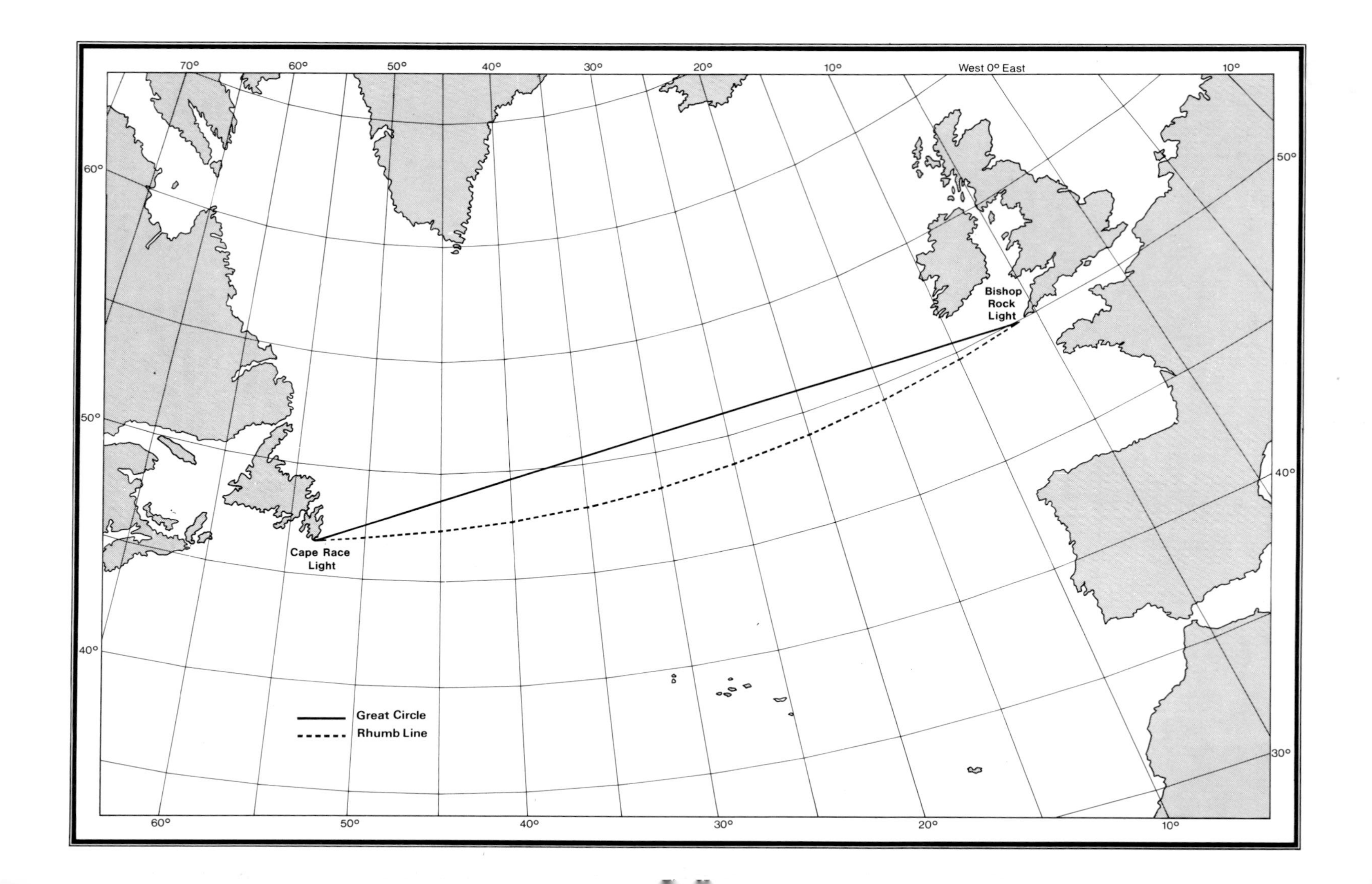
70°
60°
50°
40°
30°
20°
10°
West 0° East
10°
60°
50°
40°
30°
Bishop
Rock
Light
Cape Race
Light
Great Circle
Rhumb Line
60°
50°
40°
30°
20°
10°

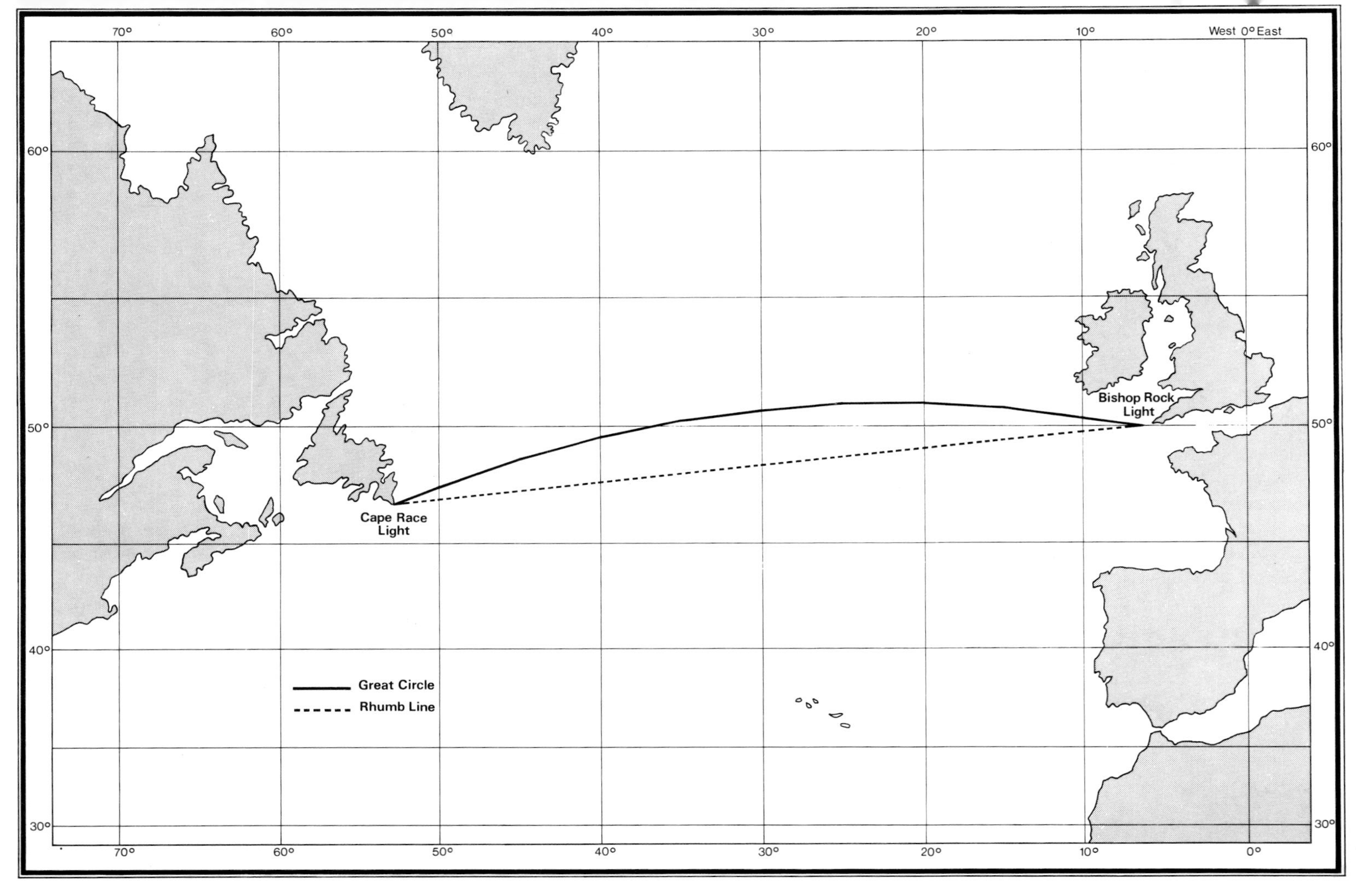
70°
60°
50°
40°
30°
20°
10°
West 0° East
Bishop Rock
Light
Cape Race
Light
Great Circle
Rhumb Line

Fig 79

distances is greater in higher latitudes, and also at the greatest when the course is east–west.

If one wished to follow this great-circle course, one would initially set the course as measured on the first leg. Each subsequent leg would have its own course, necessitating these course alterations at the predetermined points.

A power-driven vessel might well be able to steer the courses required to make good this track, but the chances of a sailing vessel doing so are less certain. That being the case, instead of trying to stay on the planned great-circle track, it is better to plot the noon position on the gnomonic chart each day, and draw a new straight line to the destination. From this track choose a position on it about one day's sailing away, transfer that position to the mercator chart, and make that the immediate destination, if at all possible.

Referring once more to Fig 79, it will be noted that the great-circle track curves towards the pole. The point of the curve in the highest latitude (that is nearest the pole) is the *vertex*, and at this point the track lies east–west. It has already been said that there are often good reasons for not following a great-circle track implicitly, and one is that it might stray into a region of ice. This being the case, a limiting latitude will be chosen and a great-circle track utilised from the point of departure to the required latitude, which is then followed until the vertex of the next great-circle track from that latitude to the destination is reached. This is a *composite track*.

The composite track is not simply the basic great-circle track interrupted by a parallel of latitude, but is made up of two new tracks and a rhumb line on the parallel of latitude. Each of the two new tracks has its vertex on the required parallel. The great circles are tangential to the parallels of latitude.

Fig 80 is a Polar Gnomonic Chart, used to illustrate a composite track. A and B are the departure and destination points respectively. AB is the great-circle track. ACDB is the composite track, with vertices C and D on the limiting latitude of 70°N.

For comparison, the same two tracks are shown on a mercator chart in Fig 81.

By far the easiest way for the yachtsman to deal with great-circle sailing is to use a graphic method, transferring tracks and positions between gnomonic and mercator charts. However, great-

Fig 80 A polar gnomonic chart

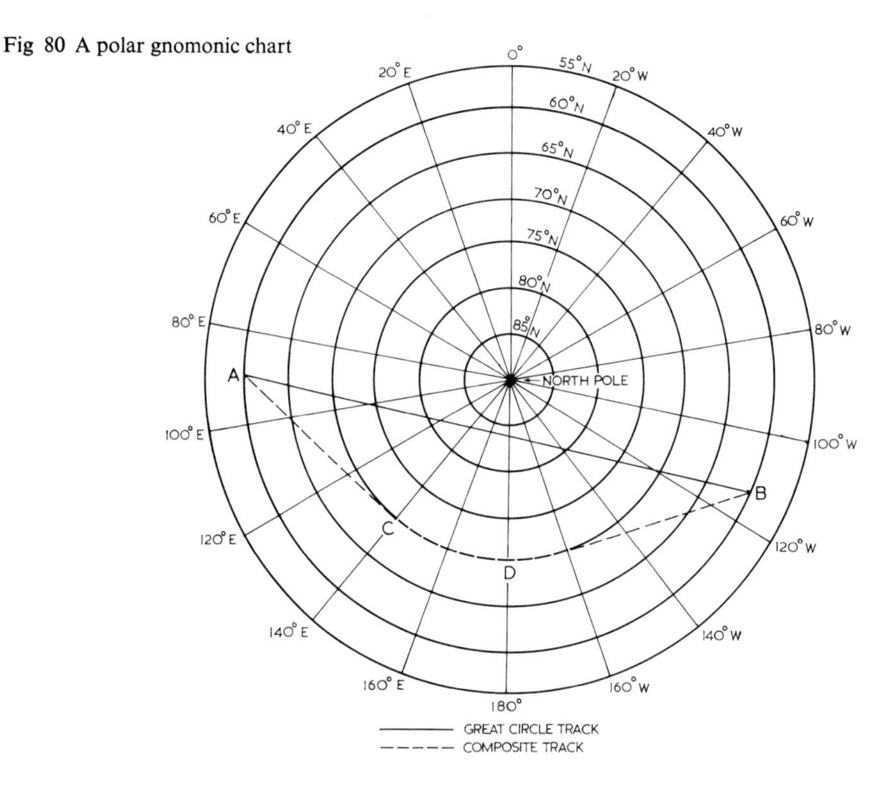

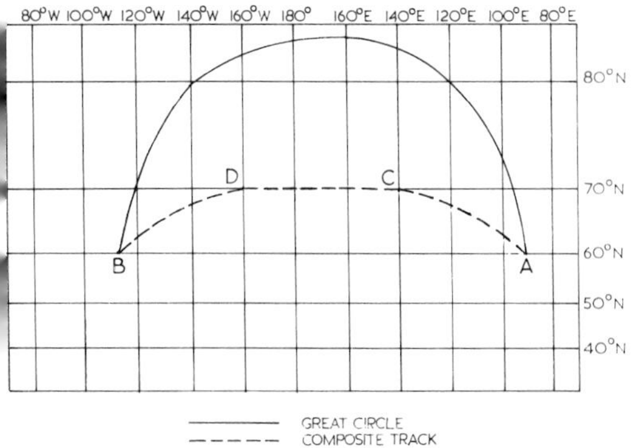

Fig 81 A Mercator chart

circle sailing can be dealt with arithmetically, for it is once again the solving of a spherical triangle which is the key to the problem. The composite track difficulty is a special case requiring the solution of two right-angled spherical triangles.

The solving of spherical triangles by basic trigonometry or the use of the ABC tables is beyond the scope of this book. It is considered worth noting, however, that the *Sight Reduction Tables* may be used to solve a limited number of the problems. After all, the tables are merely solutions to a number of spherical triangles. The most restricting limitation is that either the point of departure or the destination must have a latitude of less than 30°.

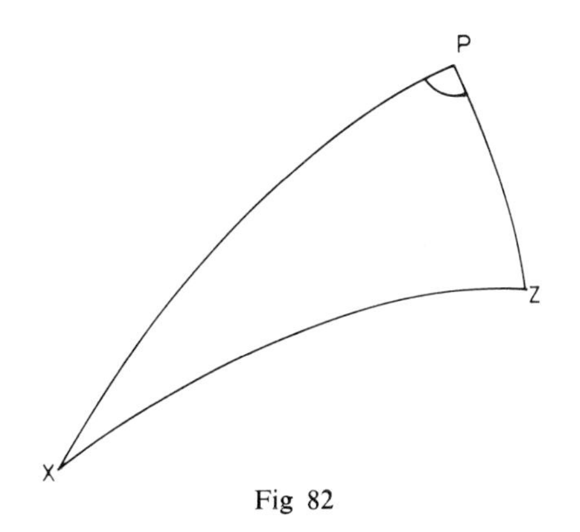

Fig 82

The *Sight Reduction Tables* are used to solve the spherical triangle PZX illustrated in Fig 82. For normal use, X is taken to be the heavenly body and Z is taken to be the observer's zenith. For use in solving great-circle problems, X and Z are taken to be the points of departure and destination, which being which usually dictated by the one with the latitude less than 30°.

The 'LHA' used to enter the tables is the difference in longitude between the two places. The 'latitude' used to enter the tables is the latitude of one of the places. The 'declination' used to enter the tables is the latitude of the second place.

Zn, as extracted from the tables, is the initial great-circle course from Z to X. (If the course from X to Z is required, it is but a matter of simple arithmetic.) XZ is the 'zenith distance', whereas the tabulated quantity, Hc, is the 'altitude'. Thus: XZ = 90° − Hc. XZ, in angular minutes, is the great-circle distance between X and Z.

Example:

1. What is the initial great-circle course and distance from Bishop Rock Light (49°52′N 06°27′W) to Elbow Clay Light (26°35′N 76°56′W)?

In this case, Bishop Rock is taken to be Z, and Elbow Clay is taken to be X.

The *Sight Reduction Tables* are entered with:
Latitude (of Bishop Rock Light) 50°N (49°52′ rounded up).
Declination (latitude of Elbow Clay Light) 26°35′N.
LHA (difference of longitude) 76°56′ — 06°27′ = 70°29′ (70°).
Declination same name as latitude.

The solution to this triangle is extracted from the tables:

Hc	32° 14′	d + 42′		360°
			Z	− 87°
Corr	+ 24′		Zn	273°
Hc	32° 38′			

XZ = 90° — 32° 38′ = 57° 22′ = 3,442′

Initial GC course 273°

GC distance 3,442′

Greater accuracy could be achieved by finding the solution with a latitude of 49° and interpolating for 49°52′, and then doing a similar thing with an LHA of 71° and interpolating for 70°29′.

15 Meteorology

Once again it must be stressed that this book assumes a knowledge up to the standard of RYA Yachtmaster (Offshore), and this chapter deals only with world-wide meteorology, assuming that the detail of local phenomena has been studied elsewhere.

Ocean meteorology is in two distinct parts. The first deals with the general pressure distribution throughout the world and the resultant winds and currents. The second deals with tropical revolving storms.

General pressure and wind distribution

If the surface of the earth were uniform, the bands of pressure and resulting winds would be something like those illustrated in Fig 83.

This idealised, theoretical distribution is the *Planetary System* of pressure and wind.

In reality the surface of the earth is not uniform. It is encumbered with land masses of various areas and heights. A further meteorological complication is that the heat received by any particular zone varies with the season, and this in-

Fig 83

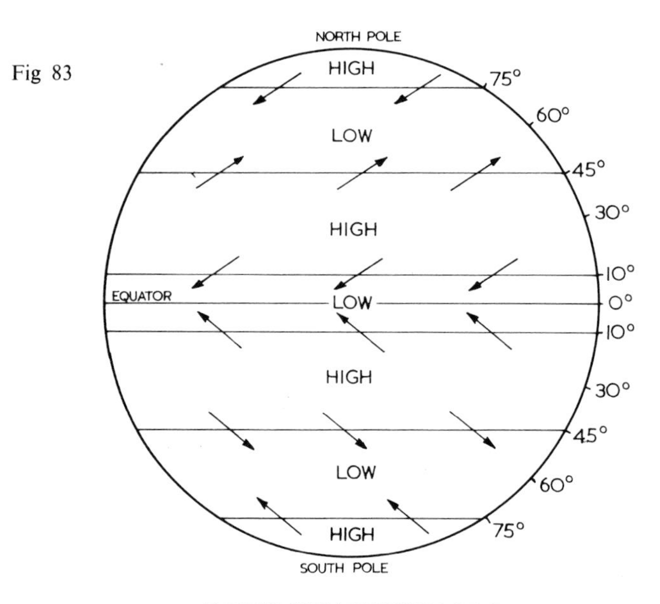

PLANETARY SYSTEM OF PRESSURE AND WIND

turn has an effect on the pressure distribution.

The belts of pressure tend to follow the sun, moving a little north during the northern summer and a little south during the southern summer. The movement, about 4° of latitude in each direction, lags behind the declination of the sun by about 6–8 weeks, making the system at its most northerly in July or August, and at its most southerly in January or February. The result of these variations is two distinct pictures, one for the northern summer and one for the southern summer.

The winds caused by these pressure patterns are illustrated in Figs 86 and 87. Some have become so much a part of life that they have names.

The Westerlies. On the polar sides of the oceanic highs in both hemispheres, the wind direction is mainly westerly. These winds are not constant enough to be described as trade winds, for they are subject to constant interruptions by the passage of depressions moving from west to east. The result of these is a relatively high precipitation and frequent gales, particularly in winter. In the northern hemisphere this band is broken up by the continents of North America and Asia, and this effectively breaks up the weather pattern. In the southern hemisphere, however, there is virtually no land mass at all to interrupt the pattern, so the wind speeds generally are higher. In this southern hemisphere, these westerlies are named the *Roaring Forties*, after the latitude in which they flourish.

The Variables. In the areas covered by the oceanic highs, between the trade winds and the westerlies, as is only to be expected the winds are light and variable and there is very little rainfall. Yesteryear this led to a likely shortage of water at the end of a passage to Europe, and the story goes that at such a time, in an attempt to conserve whatever fresh water was available, the horses were thrown overboard. Whether that is true or false is almost immaterial, but this area of the North Atlantic is still known as the *Horse Latitudes*.

Trades. On the equatorial side of the oceanic highs, with no interrupting depressions, the winds are both permanent and steady. On average about force 3–4, in the northern hemisphere they are the *NE Trades* and in the southern hemisphere they are the *SE Trades*. One exception is the North Indian Ocean and the western part of the Pacific, where the Trades are replaced by the *monsoons*. One other exception is that during certain seasons these Trades may be interrupted by tropical revolving storms.

Doldrums. In the equatorial trough between the two trade winds is an area which has given its name to a human state of depression. This area, on average about 200 miles wide but often much more or less, is plagued with calms and light and variable winds alternating with squalls accompanied by heavy rain or thunderstorms. When the Trades are light the Doldrums are bad; when the Trades are strong, the Doldrums are worse.

Monsoons. These affect the North Indian Ocean and the western Pacific. During the northern summer, the vast land mass of southern Asia is greatly heated by the sun, and that in turn leads to the formation of a large area of low pressure centred just about over north-west India. The winds revolving anti-clockwise around this area draw the SE Trades across the equator, where they join in this cyclonic circulation. This *SW Monsoon* is felt in (a) the Arabian Sea, where the wind strength is fresh to strong, occasionally reaching gale force; (b) the Bay of Bengal, with similar strengths; (c) the China Sea, where the winds are light; (d) the western part of the north Pacific, where the winds are also light. The season for this SW Monsoon is during the months May to September.

In the northern winter Asia cools quite considerably, resulting in an area of high pressure over Mongolia. This anti-cyclonic circulation of wind sets up the *NE Monsoon* which is felt in (a) the western part of the north Pacific as a fresh to strong wind; (b) the Bay of Bengal, as a light wind; (c) the Arabian Sea, also as a light wind. This wind eventually crosses the equator, whence it is deflected to the left to become the *NW* or *Cross Monsoon*. In the western part of the south Pacific these W–NW winds are felt as far south as 12°–15°. The season of the NE Monsoon is October to March; that of the NW Monsoon from November to March.

Currents

After about 48 hours of constant wind, the surface water moves at about 1/50th of the wind speed. If the wind persists, this current will increase. It is not surprising then that wherever constant winds blow, currents will also flow in about the same direction. These 'trade' currents are illustrated and named in Fig 88.

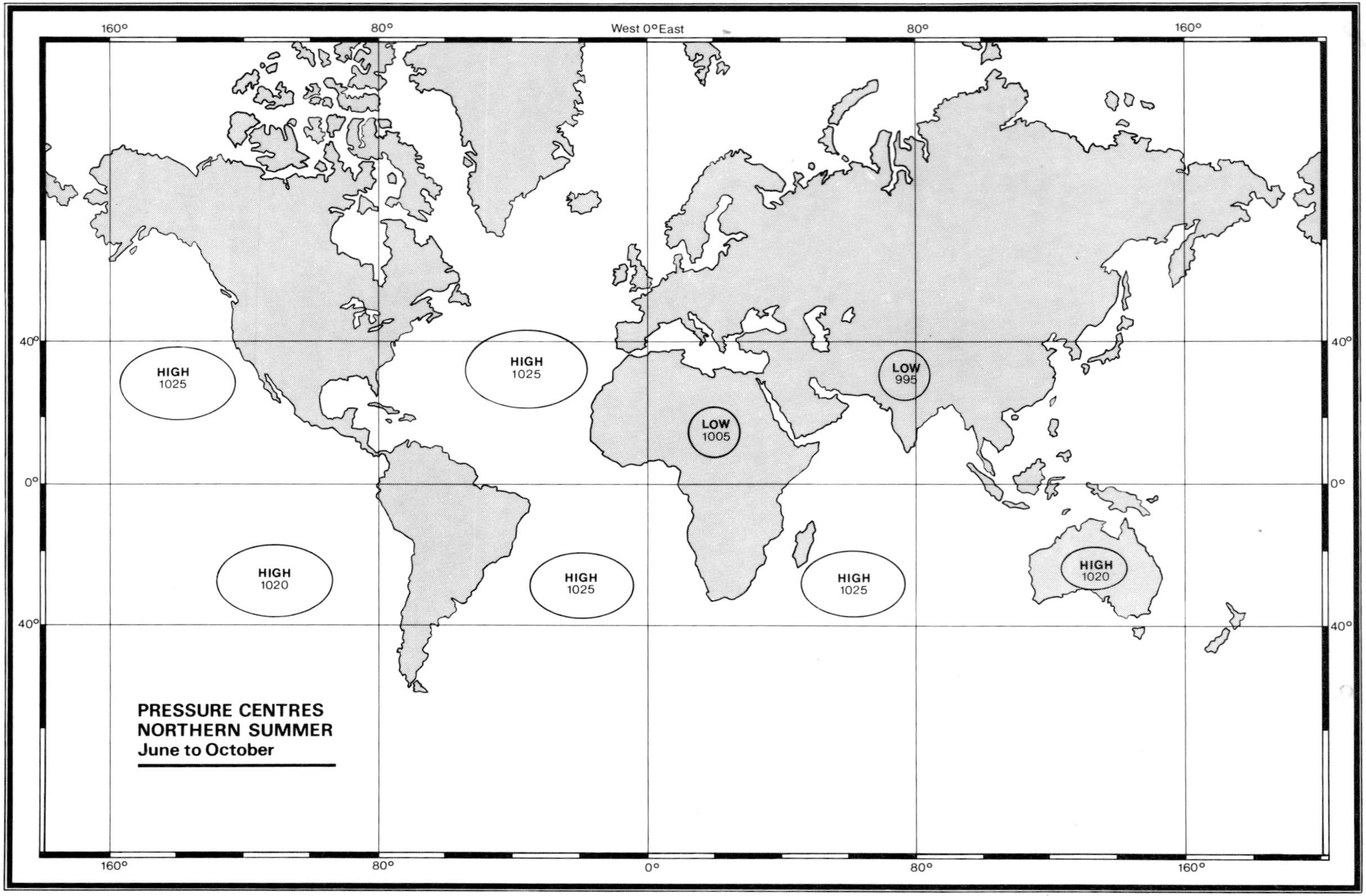

PRESSURE CENTRES
NORTHERN SUMMER
June to October

160° 80° West 0° East 80° 160°

40° 0° 40°

HIGH 1025
HIGH 1025
LOW 1005
LOW 995
HIGH 1020
HIGH 1025
HIGH 1025
HIGH 1020

160° 80° 0° 80° 160°

Fig. 84

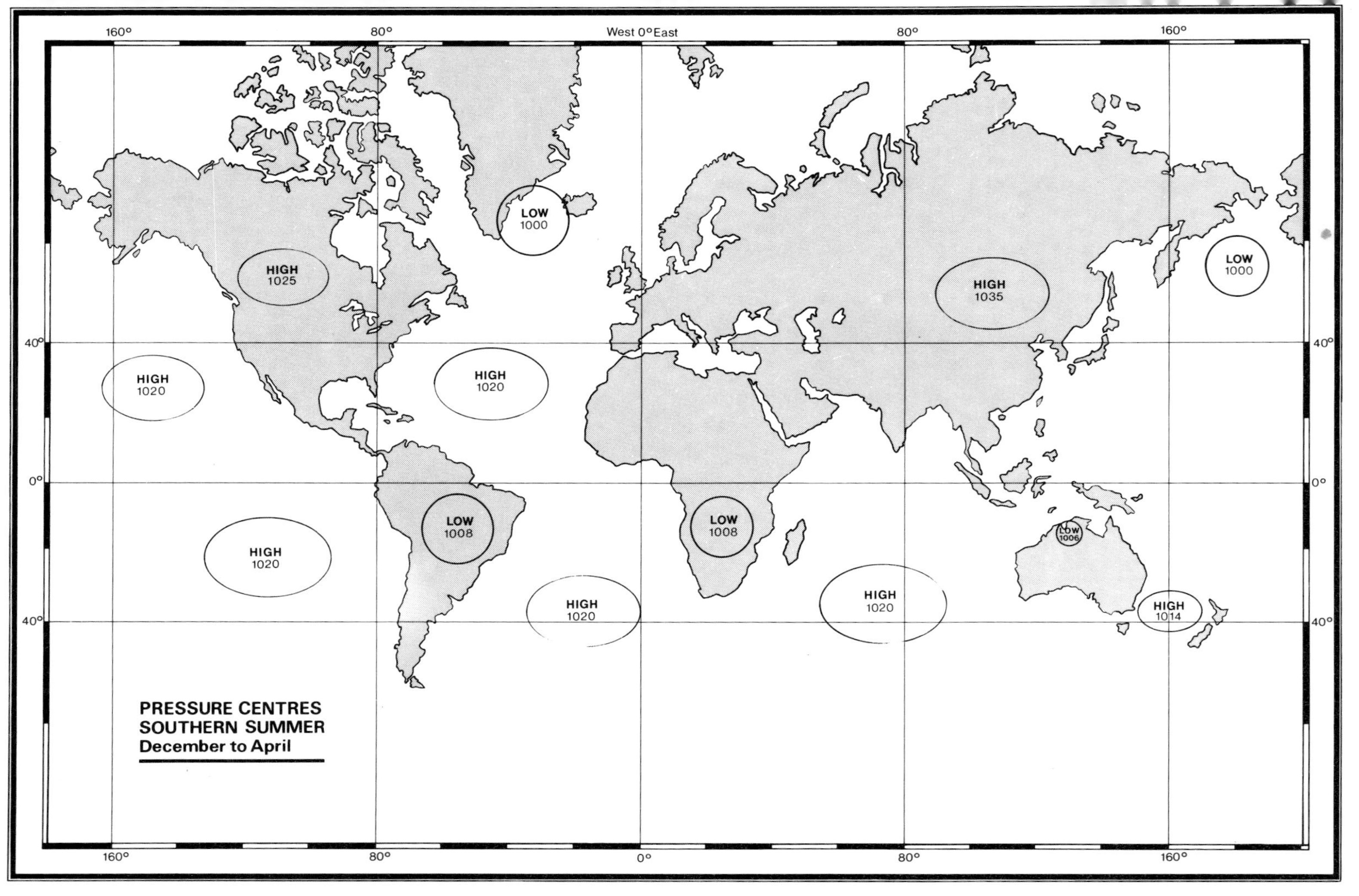
PRESSURE CENTRES
SOUTHERN SUMMER
December to April
West 0° East
160°
80°
80°
160°
40°
0°
40°
HIGH 1025
LOW 1000
HIGH 1035
LOW 1000
HIGH 1020
HIGH 1020
LOW 1008
LOW 1008
LOW 1006
HIGH 1020
HIGH 1020
HIGH 1020
HIGH 1014

Fig 85

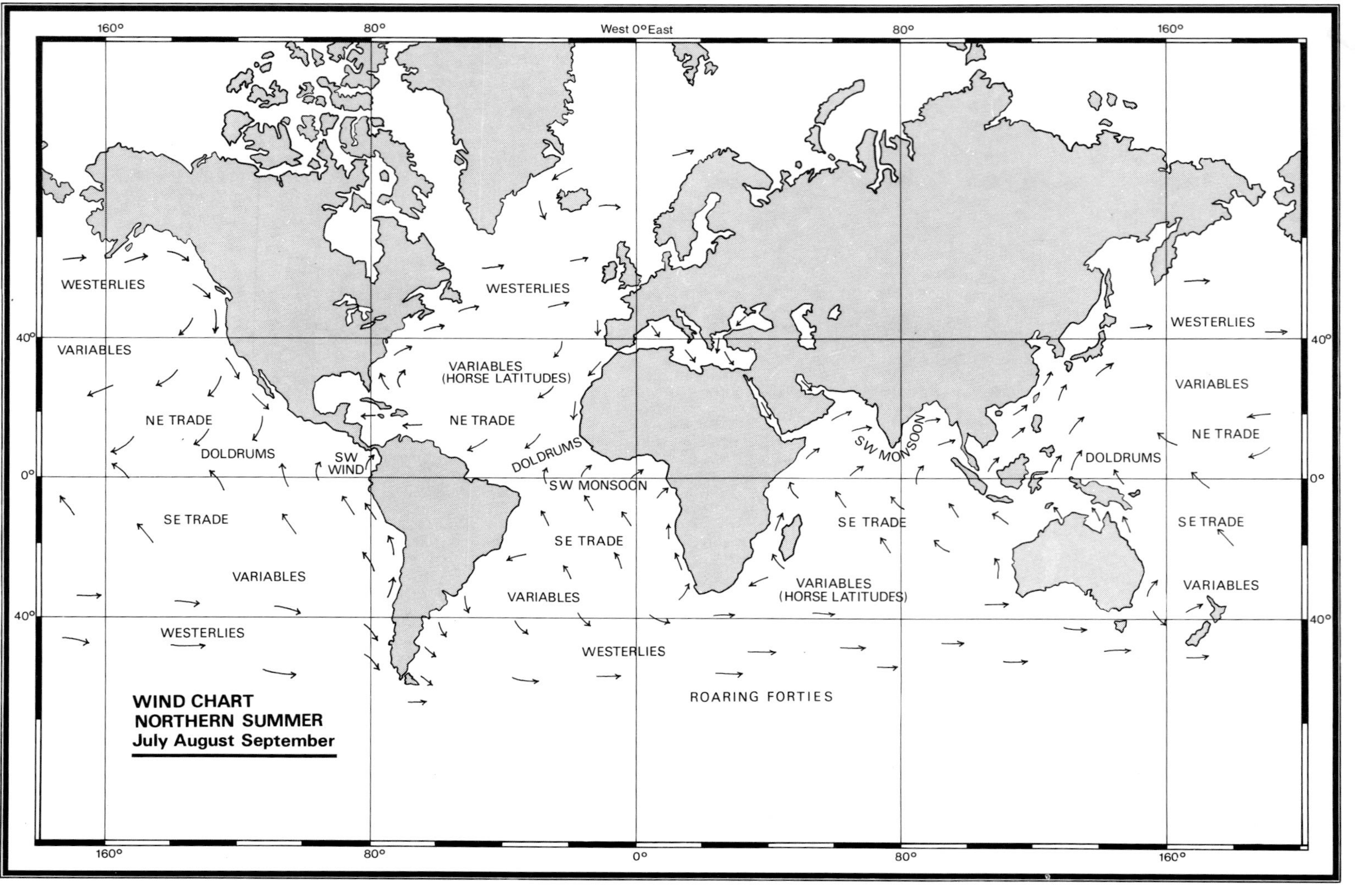
WIND CHART
NORTHERN SUMMER
July August September
160°
80°
West 0° East
80°
160°
40°
0°
40°
WESTERLIES
VARIABLES
NE TRADE
DOLDRUMS
SW
WIND
SE TRADE
VARIABLES
WESTERLIES
WESTERLIES
VARIABLES
(HORSE LATITUDES)
NE TRADE
DOLDRUMS
SW MONSOON
SE TRADE
VARIABLES
WESTERLIES
ROARING FORTIES
SW MONSOON
SE TRADE
VARIABLES
(HORSE LATITUDES)
DOLDRUMS
WESTERLIES
VARIABLES
NE TRADE
SE TRADE
VARIABLES

Fig. 86

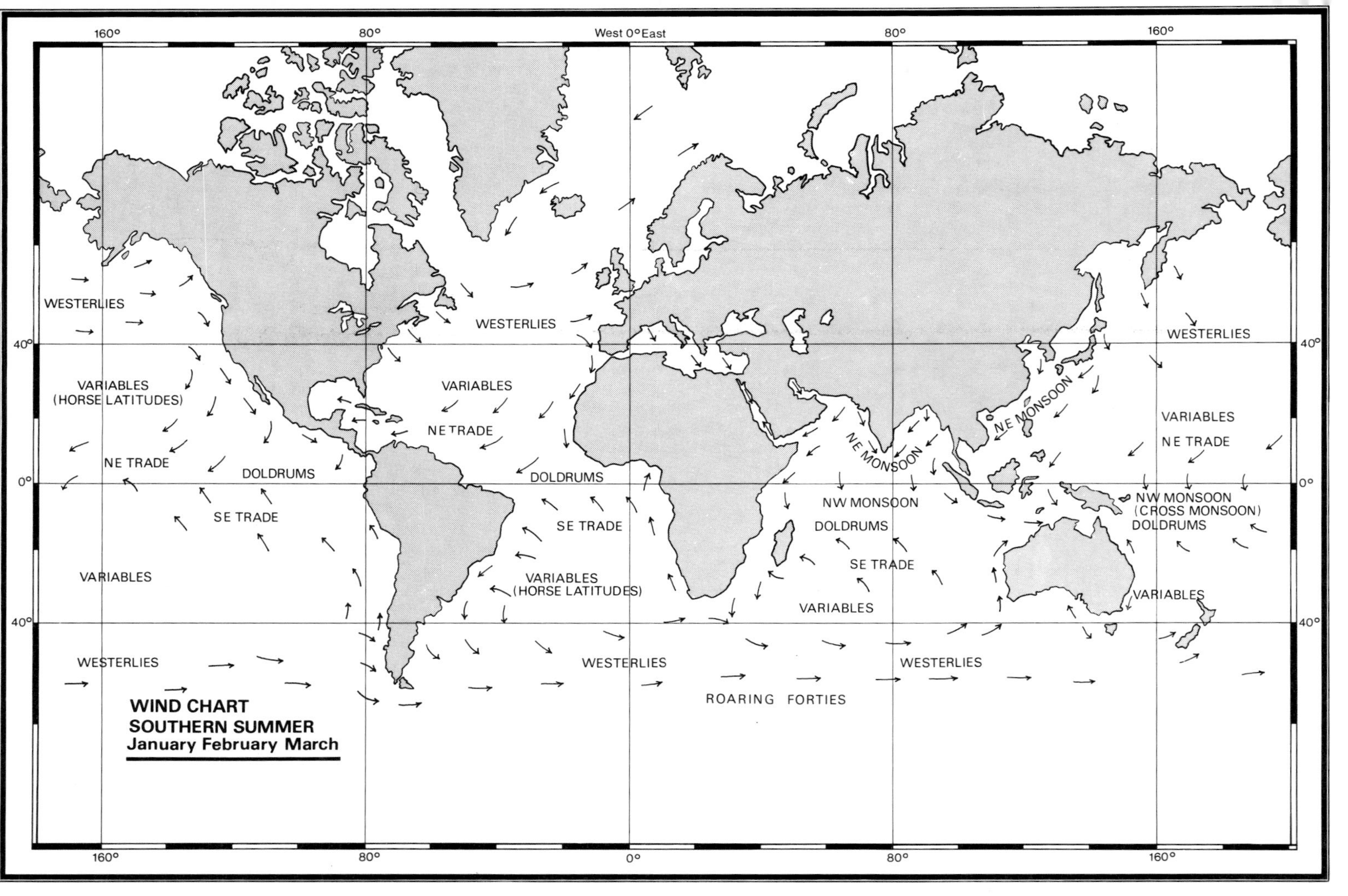
WIND CHART
SOUTHERN SUMMER
January February March
160°
80°
West 0° East
80°
160°
40°
0°
40°
WESTERLIES
VARIABLES
(HORSE LATITUDES)
NE TRADE
DOLDRUMS
SE TRADE
VARIABLES
WESTERLIES
WESTERLIES
VARIABLES
NE TRADE
DOLDRUMS
SE TRADE
VARIABLES
(HORSE LATITUDES)
WESTERLIES
ROARING FORTIES
NE MONSOON
NE MONSOON
NW MONSOON
DOLDRUMS
SE TRADE
VARIABLES
WESTERLIES
WESTERLIES
VARIABLES
NE TRADE
NW MONSOON
(CROSS MONSOON)
DOLDRUMS
VARIABLES
160°
80°
0°
80°
160°

Fig 87

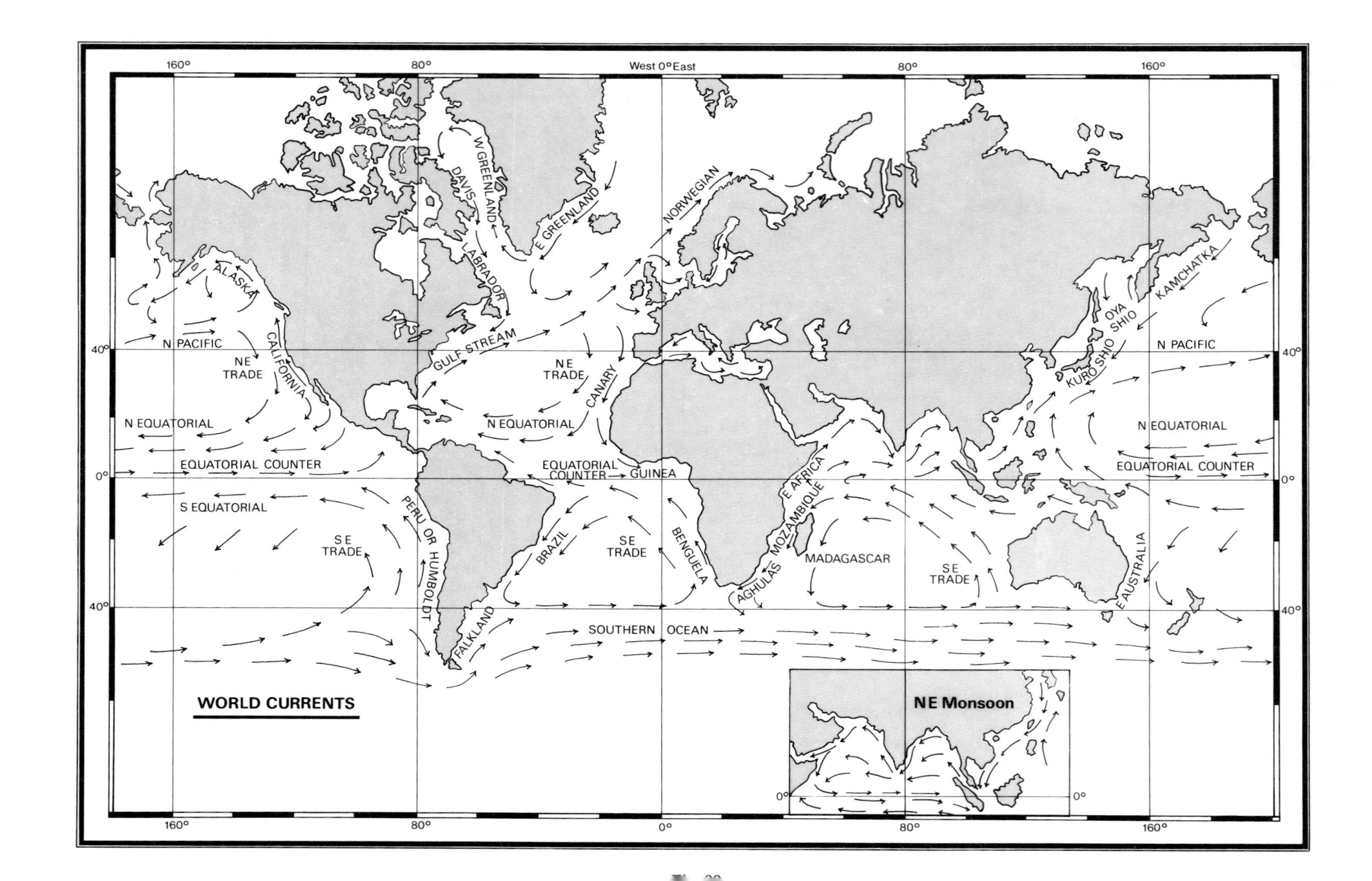
WORLD CURRENTS
West 0° East
160°
80°
40°
0°
N PACIFIC
ALASKA
NE TRADE
CALIFORNIA
N EQUATORIAL
EQUATORIAL COUNTER
S EQUATORIAL
SE TRADE
PERU OR HUMBOLDT
W GREENLAND
DAVIS
LABRADOR
E GREENLAND
GULF STREAM
NORWEGIAN
CANARY
N EQUATORIAL
EQUATORIAL COUNTER
GUINEA
BRAZIL
BENGUELA
FALKLAND
SOUTHERN OCEAN
E AFRICA
MOZAMBIQUE
MADAGASCAR
AGHULAS
OYA SHIO
KURO SHIO
KAMCHATKA
E AUSTRALIA
NE Monsoon

Although wind friction is one of the main causes of ocean currents, it is by no means the only motivating force. A substantial contribution is made by the internal effects of temperature and salinity, for example. Cooler water, or water of greater density, will tend to sink. The converse is also true, leading to *Gradient Currents.*

Whatever the cause of an ocean current, the rotation of the earth causes it to be deflected to the right of the motivating force in the northern hemisphere, and to the left in the southern hemisphere. Currents are also affected by a change in the sea bed such as islands, shoals and deeps.

Ocean currents often result in a transference of water over thousands of miles, taking water of one temperature into an area with a quite different temperature, with the result that the weather of adjacent coasts may be affected. For instance in Fig 88 it can be seen that the Labrador Current takes cold polar water south to the relatively warm waters off Newfoundland. The warm air over the sea is cooled by this water, resulting in extensive fog over the Newfoundland Banks. Another example is the Gulf Stream which conveys warm water from the Gulf of Mexico all the way to Europe, where it is credited with improving the climate of quite a few places, for instance the Isles of Scilly.

A good knowledge of ocean currents can sometimes help the navigator to plan a passage in a way to give an extra 12 miles a day — not a consideration to be ignored lightly.

Tropical revolving storms

The following passage is taken from the *Admiralty Manual of Navigation*, Vol 1, reproduced by permission of the Controller of Her Majesty's Stationery Office.

"In December 1944, vessels of the United States Pacific Fleet, operating to the east of the Philippines, were caught near the centre of a typhoon of extreme violence. Three destroyers capsized and went down with practically all hands. Serious damage was sustained by a light cruiser, three small carriers, three escort carriers and three destroyers. Lesser damage was sustained by at least 19 other vessels, from heavy cruisers down to escort vessels. Fires occurred in three aircraft carriers when planes were smashed in their hangars; some 146 aircraft were damaged beyond repair by fires, by being smashed up, or by being washed overboard. About 790 officers and men were lost or killed. Several surviving destroyers reported rolling 70° or more. The following conditions were typical during this storm:

1. Visibility zero to one thousand yards.
2. Ships not merely rolling but heeled over continually by the force of the wind, thus leaving them very little margin for further rolling to leeward.
3. Water being shipped in quantity through ventilators, blower intakes and every upper deck opening.
4. Switchboards and electrical machinery of all kinds short-circuited and flooded; fires resulted from short circuits.
5. Loss of steering control, failure of power and lighting and stoppage of main engines; loss of radar and all communications facilities.
6. Free water up to two or three feet over engines or engine-room deck plates and in many other compartments.
7. Wind speeds and seas which carried away masts, funnels, boats, davits and deck structures generally and made it impossible for men to secure gear which had gone adrift, or to jettison or strike below topside weights when the necessity had become paramount. Men could not even stay up where they would have a chance of getting clear of the ship.
8. Ships lost took a long roll to leeward, varying from 50° to 80°, hung there for a little while and then capsized, floating for only a short time before sinking.

These conditions are typical of all fully developed tropical revolving storms, irrespective of the area in which they are encountered. They are a major hazard to seamen and consequently merit a special study."

The tropical revolving storm, for convenience hereafter referred to simply as a storm, is so named because it originates in tropical oceanic areas, and the associated winds blow around the low pressure at its centre. As with all other low-pressure systems, in the northern hemisphere the winds blow in an anti-clockwise direction, not concentrically but inclined across the isobars towards the centre. In the southern hemisphere, the converse is so–the winds blowing in a clockwise direction, inclined across the isobars away from the centre.

Though far less extensive than the depressions of higher latitudes, within about 100 miles of the centre gale-force winds rise rapidly until within 50 miles of the centre when wind speeds of 150 kts are common, and stronger gusts have been observed. The accompanying seas, of course, are potentially disastrous for any size of vessel.

The first pattern of the storm to emerge is that it is a seasonal phenomena. Thus the first step towards avoiding them is to stay away from the tropical areas concerned during the 'bad' season. These storms generally occur during the late summer and early autumn. Fig 89 is a table giving the number of such storms observed in a given area during a ten-year period, the local name, and the season when the storms are most common.

The 'safe' season during which the storms are comparatively rare is from mid-November to mid-June in the northern hemisphere, and from mid-May to November in the southern hemisphere. However, it is as well to appreciate that the storm may rear its ugly head at any time, so even if it is the 'safe' season when you venture into tropical waters, it would be as well to keep a weather eye.

Origins

The Doldrums, that meteorologically disturbed area near the equator, is the breeding ground for the storms. They would normally start life in the western third of the ocean, though there are exceptions. For example, in the northern Atlantic occasionally a storm will start near the Cape Verde Islands during August or September.

What follows is a description of the movement of a tropical revolving storm in the northern hemisphere. For the southern hemisphere a 'mirror image' must be imagined.

Originating in a latitude between 7°N and 15°N, the storm usually moves off in a direction between 275° and 350°, but most frequently between 275° and 300°. The initial speed of the storm will be about 10 kts, gradually increasing to about 15 kts. In latitude 25°N or thereabouts, the storm 'recurves' away from the equator until by about 30°N it is tracking about NE. The speed will then increase to 20–25 kts, or perhaps even 40 kts.

It is possible that the direction of movement of the storm will be different from the average quoted above, but if that is so, it is unlikely that the speed will exceed 10 kts.

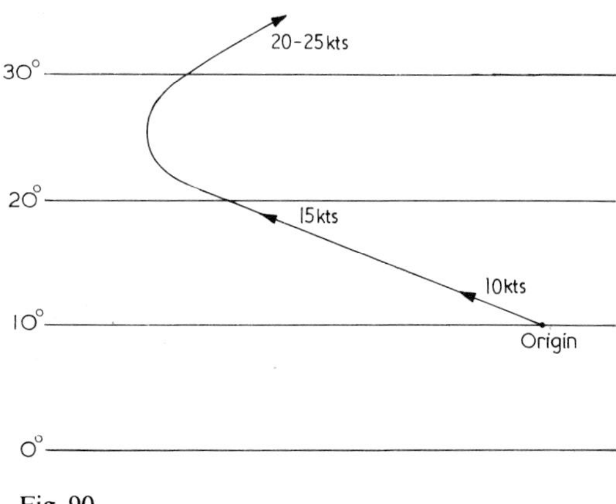

Fig 90

AREA (No IN 10 YEARS)		NAME	SEASON
N ATLANTIC (W)	50	HURRICANE	JUNE – NOVEMBER
N PACIFIC (E)	30	HURRICANE OR CORDONAZO	JUNE – NOVEMBER
N PACIFIC (W)	250	TYPHOON OR BAGUIOS	ALL YEAR ROUND BUT MOSTLY JUNE – NOVEMBER
S PACIFIC (W)	30	HURRICANE	DECEMBER – APRIL
S INDIAN OCEAN (E) (W)	60	WILLY-WILLY CYCLONE	DECEMBER – APRIL
BAY OF BENGAL ARABIAN SEA	20 10	CYCLONE	AT THE CHANGE OF MONSOON — OCTOBER-NOVEMBER AND MAY-JUNE

Fig 89 Incidence of tropical revolving storms

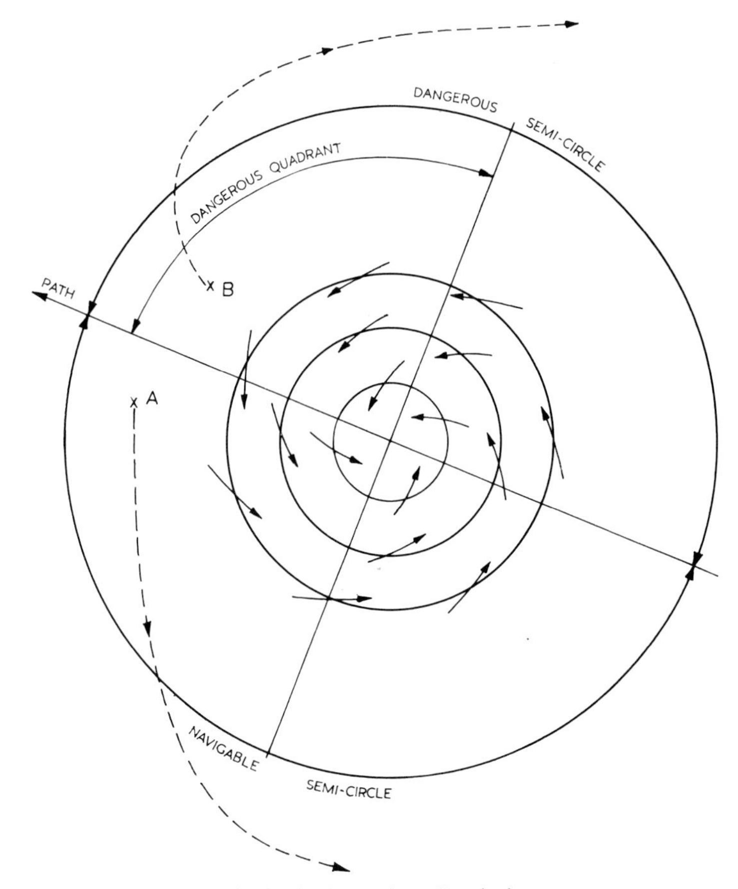

Fig 91 TRS Northern Hemisphere

The extent of the storms vary considerably, but generally speaking winds of force 7 are unlikely until within 200 miles of the centre, with marginally stronger winds manifesting themselves on the polar side. As the centre is approached, the winds rapidly increase in strength with an associated loss of visibility due to torrential rain and spray. Within about 10 miles of the centre the wind moderates to about force 4–5; the sky often clears, but there is always a mountainous sea. This comparatively quiet spot is the 'eye' of the storm.

If in the vicinity of a storm one must use all the speed available to make the best of a potentially bad situation. To enable the correct decisions to be made, it is necessary to consider in detail the direction in which the storm is moving (its 'path') and the direction of its winds. Fig 91 illustrates a storm with a path of about WNW before recurving.

The arrows indicate the approximate wind direction to be expected.

The left-hand semicircle is known as the navigable semicircle for two reasons:

(i) A vessel anywhere within this semicircle will have a 'free' wind to get away from the storm centre.
(ii) Recurvature, when it happens, will take the centre away from the vessel.

The other half is the dangerous semicircle with a particularly hazardous quadrant, for three reasons:

(i) The winds on this polar side are a little stronger.
(ii) To get away from the storm a vessel will have to experience head winds.
(iii) Recurvature, when it happens, will take the centre towards the vessel.

Any vessel in the vicinity of a storm will be in one or other semicircle, or in its path.

A vessel in the navigable semicircle, whether sail or power, should make full speed with the wind on the starboard quarter, following a track similar to vessel A in Fig 91, hauling round to port as the wind permits.

If in the dangerous semicircle, a sailing vessel should go close hauled on a starboard tack until overwhelmed by the conditions, when she should heave-to on a starboard tack. A power-driven vessel should steer with the wind on the starboard bow. Both power and sail should haul round to starboard as the wind permits, in an attempt to follow a track similar to vessel B in Fig 91.

If in the path of the storm, a vessel should behave as though she were in the navigable semicircle.

The rules for the required action are simple enough–provided that it is known which semicircle one is in–so naturally it is as well to assimilate all the available information as soon as one is aware of the proximity of a storm. There are two ways in which the awareness of such a storm will come: either from a radio warning or from the navigator's own observations. We will deal with the radio warnings first, but in reality there will be an overlap of the two types of information.

The radio warnings of storms (transmitted by coastguard stations, etc) will normally include three facts:

1. Storm centre in latitude and longitude for a stated time.
2. Diameter of the storm.
3. Forecast path and speed.

Best use will be made of this information if the following plot is made on whichever chart is in use, in order that the relative positions of the vessel and the storm may be appreciated.

1. Plot the storm centre.
2. Draw the storm diameter.
3. Draw tangential lines at 40° to the forecast path.
4. From the storm centre, describe two arcs between the two tangential lines, representing 24hr and 48hr of forecast movement.

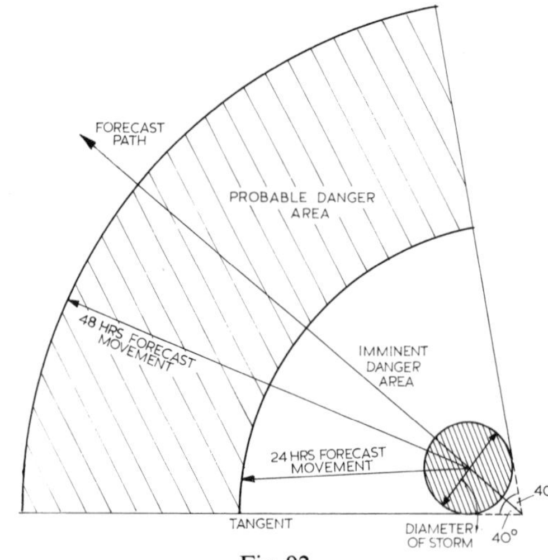

Fig 92

If the plot is remade each time a new radio report is received, the progressive relative positions of storm and vessel will give a good indication of whether or not a confrontation is to take place. If the vessel is ever in either the probable or imminent danger area, immediate action should be taken to vacate the area.

In this context, at least, radio warnings are of inestimable value, and maximum use should be made of them. However, some storms may be both very intense and particularly small and, as such, unknown to the powers that be. Local observation is the only means of becoming aware of such a storm, and should be practised meticulously whenever in the region of storms whatever the season.

WARNING SIGNS

The proximity of a storm will be indicated in four ways, other than by radio.

Barometer. The barometric pressure in the tropical areas where the storms abound varies hardly at all except for the diurnal variation. Sailing directions or pilot charts will give the mean pressure and diurnal variation for any given area, and any pressure which is at all different from that predicted should be regarded with suspicion.

When the barometer is 3mb below 'normal' (allowing for diurnal variation) a storm is possible.

When the barometer is 5mb below normal, not only is a storm a certainty but it is probable that it is within 200 miles.

Within 20° of the equator the barometer is by

far the best indication of an approaching storm· As the centre approaches the following may be noted:

(a) When 500–120 miles from the centre, the pressure will fall slowly and the diurnal variation will still be obvious.
(b) When 120–60 miles from the centre, the fall will become steeper and the diurnal variation will no longer be apparent.
(c) When 60–10 miles from the centre, the fall is rapid.
(d) At the centre, the pressure is usually 60–70mb below normal.

Swell. At more than 200 miles from the centre of a storm, the swell–which travels faster than the storm itself–will give an early indication, appearing straight from the centre—just like the ripples emanating from a stone thrown in a pond. At this stage, though there is no indication of the distance of the storm, the indication of direction is very good. Any 'new' swell should be regarded with suspicion.

Wind. Any sudden appreciable change in either direction or strength of wind may indicate the presence of or formation of a storm.

Sky. A storm is often preceded by a very clear day with excellent visibility. At the edge of a storm will be found cirrus cloud, often V-shaped, pointing towards the centre. As the centre approaches this will gradually give way to altostratus, then nimbostratus and finally very low, rapidly moving 'scud'.

The above four features together will give a good indication of the presence of a storm. What is required next, before any action can be taken, is to know:

(a) The bearing of the centre of the storm.
(b) Its path.
(c) Which semicircle the observer is in.

We will deal with each of these points individually.

(a) An early indication of the bearing of the centre may have been noted from the swell. Later, a slightly modified Buys-Ballot's Law will give a very good indication. When facing the wind the low pressure, or storm centre, will be on the right hand. The closer one is to the centre, the nearer the angle on the right hand gets to a right angle:

When the barometer is 5mb below normal the centre should be about 12 points (135°) on the right hand. When the barometer has fallen to about 10mb below normal the centre should be about 10 points (112½°) on the right hand. When the barometer is 20mb below normal the centre should be about 8 points (90°) on the right hand.

(b) A series of bearings of the storm centre, even such approximate ones as those above, should enable its position to be plotted, and, ultimately, its path determined.

Useful rules at this stage are: (i) the path is unlikely to be towards the equator; (ii) in latitudes of less than 20°, the path is most unlikely to have an easterly component; (iii) in the event of either (i) or (ii) not being the case, the storm will almost certainly be moving very slowly.

(c) If the wind direction remains steady, the observer is in the path of the storm. A backing wind indicates that the observer is in the navigable semicircle. A veering wind indicates that the observer is in the dangerous semicircle.

Once one knows which semicircle one is in, one should react according to the rules already stated but worth repeating:

1. In the path of a storm, act as if in the navigable semicircle.
2. In the navigable semicircle, make maximum speed with the wind on the starboard quarter, altering course to port as the wind permits.
3. In the dangerous semicircle, make to windward with the wind on the starboard bow, or heave-to on a starboard tack. Alter course to starboard as the wind permits.

16 Passage Planning

Generally speaking, yachtsmen do not suddenly drop everything and embark on an ocean voyage. Of course there is a breed of professional yachtsmen such as delivery and charter crews who often make long voyages at short notice, but for most that is not the case. By far the great majority of yachtsmen start a long voyage in an armchair with a winter storm rattling the windows. The inspiration might come from a book, a television programme or simply a long-felt ambition. From whatever source the seed is sown, germinate it will, and it is from that point that good planning will reap good rewards, be it many years later.

In this chapter, primary consideration will be given to British publications, but it should be borne in mind that most countries will have their own equivalent publications. Indeed, it is often the case that 'local' publications, particularly charts, are either the only ones available or the ones best suited to yacht navigation.

The planning navigator will do a lot worse than make his first acquisition *Ocean Passages for the World*, published by the British Hydrographic Department. It is the author's opinion that the second edition (1950) is of greater interest to small boat and sailing navigators than the more recent publication. However, both contain a wealth of information which is virtually indispensable to the ocean voyager. The book is made up of three sections: the first considers in detail ocean winds, weather, ice and currents; the second section details steamship routes between all the major ports in the world and makes particular reference to local meteorological phenomena; the third section contains the recommended sailing-ship routes between all the major ports in the world, with particular emphasis on taking advantage of the prevailing conditions. When considering these routes bear in mind the introductory remark 'that the routes described in this third section are for large sailing-vessels able to stand up to, and take advantage of, the heavy weather to be expected on many of the passages.' This section also contains some average ship passage times. Finally, in a wallet at the end of the book there is a series of charts illustrating climate, currents, steamship routes and sailing-ship routes.

Perhaps the next most important publication is a good world-wide chart catalogue. The British Hydrographic Department publication NP 131–*Catalogue of Admiralty Charts and other Hydrographic Publications*–is an excellent guide. By assisting the navigator to make exactly the right choice of publications for his purpose, it will pay for itself several times over. This chart catalogue, as the name implies, includes much more than just chart numbers. World-wide charts of all scales and types are included–mercator, gnomonic, plotting, also sailing directions (pilots), tide tables, lists of radio signals, lists of lights etc. From this catalogue a selection of large-scale charts covering the projected voyage may be made, along with the relevant gnomonic charts and routeing charts. The large-scale charts will be essential for obtaining an overall 'picture' of the projected voyage, and the gnomonic charts will be necessary for calculating great-circle courses and distances as discussed in Chapter 14.

Routeing charts are published for each ocean, for each month of the year, and contain the most comprehensive information of interest to the mariner. Each chart is divided into rectangles, each of 5° of latitude and 5° of longitude. Within each rectangle is a wind rose, and on the rest of the chart is contained other information, all best summarised as follows:

(1) Wind roses: direction, force, frequency, number of observations, percentages of variables, percentages of calms.
(2) Currents: predominant direction, consistency, rate.
(3) Storms: Percentage frequency of winds over force 7, selected tracks of tropical revolving storms.
(4) Ice: pack and iceberg limits.
(5) Mean sea temperature and dew point temperature.
(6) Mean air temperature and mean air pressure.
(7) Low visibility: percentage frequency of visibility less than 5 miles, percentage frequency of fog, when visibility is less than 1 mile.
(8) Steamer tracks and distances.

With all the information contained within *Ocean Passages for the World*, the large-scale charts, gnomonic and routeing charts, it is possible to select a route appropriate to the expected weather conditions, estimate passage time and, consequently, to consider the ship's victuals.

Much pleasure will have been derived from planning a voyage thus far, but undoubtedly even greater pleasure will be derived from the next logical step–that is, the detailed planning. For this, reference is made once more to the chart catalogue to select:

(a) *Sailing Directions;*
(b) More detailed charts;
(c) *Admiralty List of Radio Signals;*
(d) *Admiralty List of Lights;*
(e) *Admiralty Tide Tables.*

The appropriate *Sailing Directions* will give very detailed information of everything of concern to the mariner when within 20 miles of land or in harbour, including weather, currents, winds etc. In addition they include more 'domestic' information such as the type of government, languages spoken, currency, population etc. All this is in addition to describing every known rock, headland, cove and harbour on the coast.

Having read the *Sailing Directions* a decision can be made about which harbours are likely to be of interest, and the numbers of the appropriate larger-scale charts extracted from the chart catalogue. At this stage it is as well to give a reminder about the many 'Yachting Pilots' available, many of which give charts of small harbours and anchorages beyond the scope of the British Hydrographic Department. They vary in quality from first class to the other extreme. It is as well to examine such books very carefully before purchasing.

The next item of interest is the *Admiralty List of Radio Signals*, in six volumes, containing the following information:

Vol 1: Coast Radio Stations.
Vol 2: Radio Beacons.
Vol 3: Meteorological Services and Codes.
Vol 4: Meteorological Observation Stations.
Vol 5: Time Signals and Radio Position Fixing Systems.
Vol 6: Port Operations.

Which of these will be of interest or use will be determined partly by the radio equipment to be carried and partly by the interest of the navigator, but Vol 3 and 5, listing all the weather forecasts and time signals available, anywhere in the world, will almost certainly be considered essential.

The *Admiralty List of Lights* is another publication in a number of volumes (twelve this time), each covering a different geographical area and containing a list of all lights (but not light buoys) and fog signals in the selected area. The information given for any particular light is its latitude and longitude, characteristic, intensity, elevation, range, height and a description of the structure. It is a very comprehensive publication, and useful even in daylight.

The final item on the list is the *Admiralty Tide Tables*, once again a multi-volume publication, but this time there are only three to cover the world.

One big advantage of all the Admiralty publications is that each contains full instructions and explanations of its use. A further advantage, which is a bit of a mixed blessing when it comes to the work involved, is that all these publications can be kept up to date by utilising the corrections promulgated in the *Weekly Notices to Mariners*.

17 Landfall

This final chapter is a simulation of the last three days of a hypothetical passage from North America to the United Kingdom. In it the reader is offered all the kinds of information which would have been available to him had he been the navigator involved. For the purposes of the exercise as much variety as possible has been introduced at the expense of making it a little more complicated than it might have been in reality. If the tyro navigator completes this exercise satisfactorily he will have enough theoretical knowledge to navigate at sea. All that remains is to set sail and prove it.

Our hypothetical yacht set sail from Plymouth, Massachusetts early on Saturday 1st June 1980, bound for Plymouth, Devon. After a reasonably uneventful passage for most of the way, the yacht met with a westerly gale with accompanying cloud and rain, and by 19th June the navigator was becoming impatient to fix his position. Four days without a sight and about 350 miles from Plymouth, Devon, and he felt that it was time he had a better idea of his whereabouts than a gale-buffeted EP.

At this time the ship's clock was set to Z+1. The deck watch was losing at a regular rate of 2 sec each day. The navigator was in the habit of taking his sights from the cockpit where his height of eye was 2m. The index error of his sextant had been constant at 2.′5 on the arc for the whole voyage.

Just after dawn on 20th June, at ship's time 0535, he caught a glimpse of Venus through a break in the cloud just long enough for a quick sight. As a result, he made the following notes in his log: SA 18°01.′8; DWT 6h 34m 00s; DWE 19×2=38s slow; Log 2,435.

A happier man now, he settled at the chart table and worked up an EP for the time of the sight of 50°27′N 13°54′W. Having reduced the observation and then plotted it, he made a note in his log of the MPP for 0635 (GMT).

(a) What was it?

During the remainder of the forenoon the sky continued to clear and an even happier navigator looked forward to a noon sight. He estimated that by the time the sun was on the meridian they would have made good 48 miles on a track of 100°T, since the Venus sight.

(b) What was the EP at the time of the sun's meridian passage?

(c) At what time (GMT) did the navigator calculate the noon sight?

At the appropriate time the navigator was in the cockpit with his sextant, and measured the meridian altitude (sextant reading) as 63°42.′8 bearing south, log reading 2,483. An awkwardly placed little cloud had made it necessary to observe the sun's upper limb.

(d) What was the observed noon position?

The sky remained clear all afternoon as the yacht continued to make good a track of 100°T at a little over 5kt. At 1630 ship's time, the navigator took advantage of the clear sky, particularly as thick, dark cloud was rolling in from the west once more, to 'shoot' the sun

again. He made his customary notes: DWT 5h 29m 09s; SA 29°53.′0; LL; Log 2,508.
(e) At what time, GMT, was the sun observed?
(f) What was the EP at that time?
(g) What was the observed position?

Even though the sky was soon completely overcast, the navigator was confident that the present course would take them some 20 miles south of the Scillies, and at the present speed they should be south of Bishop Rock light at about midnight on the 21st.

In damp but relatively comfortable conditions, all the crew had a fair share of sleep, and the navigator, up to view a grey and dismal dawn, volunteered to cook breakfast for there was not much else he would be doing for a while.

As the day wore on it seemed that sights were going to be out of the question, until just after the sun had set at about 2030 ship's time, the clouds parted, albeit temporarily, and the alert navigator managed two rapid sights. His notes were: Rasalhague SA 41°34.′9; DWT 9h 27m 56s. Moon SA 31°24.′9 LL; DWT 9h 28m 57s; Log 2,668.

As the yacht sailed on, the navigator announced that, whereas technically the ship's clock should be altered from Z+1 to Z at midnight, he proposed leaving it set as it was, which was the same as the time kept in Britain, anyway. He then set about reducing and plotting the sights.
(h) What was the EP at the time of the sights?
(i) What was the GMT of the sight of Rasalhague?
(j) What was the observed position?

At this stage the Scillies were about 40 miles away, and the navigator asked for an alteration of course to take them about 15 miles south of Bishop Rock, hoping to raise the light at about 0230 on the 22nd. Unfortunately he was out of luck and the visibility was just not good enough, and remained moderate all through the night and well into the next day. Towards the end of the day our intrepid navigator, assessing the visibility as sufficient for a good horizon, took advantage of the clearing skies and planned for the evening stars.

The yacht was now making good a track of 080°, and it was estimated that the run up to the evening stars, from the previous evening's sights, would be 103 miles.
(k) What was the EP at the time of the proposed sights?
(l) What was the GMT of civil twilight?
(m) Assuming that Vol 1 of the *Sight Reduction Tables*, was available, which stars do you think the navigator should have used, theoretically?
(n) Why do you think he chose to use Deneb, Rasalhague and Arcturus?

Having observed these stars, he had the following notes in his log book:

	SA	DWT
Deneb	37°40.′5	9h 27m 29s
Rasalhague	43°21.′8	9h 29m 04s
Arcturus	57°04.′3	9h 30m 29s

(o) What was the observed position? (State the GMT.)
(p) What was the bearing and distance from Eddystone Light (50°11′N 04°16′W)?

NB The increment of GHA Aries for 16min is 4°00.′7.

Answers to Exercises

Chapter 2

1. GHA 52°34.′2 Declination 23°26.′0 N
2. GHA 190°11.′6 Declination 7°19.′6 N
3. GHA 357°28.′7 Declination 16°41.′5 S
4. GHA 200°28.′5 Declination 18°15.′4 N

Chapter 3

1. 15h
2. 11h
3. 23h 12m the previous day
4. 18th January, 21h 37m 14s
5. 11th September, 20h 16m 47s
6. 1st July, 05h 56m 07s
7. 18th March, 18h 06m 21s
8. 14th July, 22h 50m 57s
9. 19th August, 04h 03m 51s

Chapter 4

1. 36°27.′3
2. 48°32.′3
3. 19°54.′1

Chapter 6

1. 17°14.′2 N
2. 48°46.′1 N
3. 12°13.′7 S

Chapter 7

1. AP 50°N 15°53.′4W
   Intercept 6′ Towards
   Azimuth 150°
2. AP 50°N 145°05.′5W
   Intercept 7′ Away
   Azimuth 272°
   (GD 22d 02h 30m 14s)
3. AP 50°S 165° 10.′6E
   Intercept 12′ Towards
   Azimuth 042°
   (GD 21d 22h 32m 07s)
4. 49°57′N 27°51′W
5. 49°36′S 124°23′W
6. 48°41′N 17°56′W

Chapter 8

1. AP 50°N 120°32.′7W
   Intercept 12′ Towards
   Azimuth 273°
   ITP 50°01′N 120°51′W
2. AP 50°S 155°55.′2E
   Intercept 4′ Away
   Azimuth 308°
   ITP 50°03′S 156°00′E
3. AP 50°S 75°06.′4W
   Intercept 27′ Away
   Azimuth 063°
   ITP 50°13′S 75°45′W

Chapter 9

1. AP 50°S 148°03.′6E
   Intercept 12′ Towards
   Azimuth 283°
   ITP 49°57′S 147°45′E
   (GD 24d 21h 32m 14s)
2. AP 50°N 47°19.′9W
   Intercept 5′ Away
   Azimuth 210°
   ITP 50°04′N 47°16′W
   (GD 21d 00h 34m 38s)
3. AP 50°N 165°26.′9E
   Intercept 8′ Towards
   Azimuth 154°
   ITP 49°53′N 165°32′E
   (GD 22d 07h 30m 47s)

Chapter 10

1. Stars available:

		Hc	Zn
◇	Dubhe	39°03′	037°
	POLLUX	47°05′	102°
	SIRIUS	16°52′	146°
◇	Rigel	30°56′	167°
	Hamal	51°39′	239°
◇	Alpheratz	37°24′	272°
	DENEB	19°50′	318°

NB GD CT 25d 19h 30m; LHA ♈ 67°

By choice Dubhe, Rigel and Alpheratz would be used because they are best situated for a three-star fix.
Observed position 50°12′N 20°58′W at 1932 on 25th February.
NB It was necessary to add 12h to the DWT

2. Available stars:

		Hc	Zn
◇	DENEB	35°01′	059°
	VEGA	50°03′	085°
	Rasalhague	40°36′	125°
◇	ARCTURUS	58°12′	199°
	REGULUS	20°39′	264°
◇	POLLUX	10°41′	301°
	CAPELLA	10°36′	336°

NB GD CT 22d 00h 28m; LHA ♈ 224°

Theoretically Deneb, Arcturus and Pollux, those best situated for a three-star fix would be used, but to allow for the possibility of a delay in starting the sights, such as caused by partial cloud cover, it would be better to plan for Deneb, Vega, Rasalhague and Arcturus. Three of these would be available during the whole of the likely observation period.
Observed position 49°47′N 53°07′W at 0029 On 22nd June.
NB It was necessary to add 12h to the DWT

3. Stars available:

		Hc	Zn
◇	Dubhe	43°54′	041°
	REGULUS	20°14′	095°
	PROCYON	36°14′	134°
◇	SIRIUS	20°32′	157°
	RIGEL	31°46′	181°
◇	Hamal	44°38′	252°
	DENEB	15°03′	325°

NB GD CT 21d 19h 29m; LHA ♈ 79°

By choice the three to use would be Dubhe, Sirius and Hamal, those best situated for a three-star fix.
Observed position 49°36′N 145°51′E at 1933 on 21st September.
NB It was necessary to add 12h to the DWT

Chapter 11

1. Observed latitude 49°57.′1N
   (20d 20h 34m 41s GMT)
2. Observed latitude 27°32.′3N
   (21d 06h 28m 17s GMT)
3. Observed latitude 32°11.′3N
   (22d 08h 34m 29s GMT)

Chapter 12

1. AP 50°N 159°14.′4W
   Intercept 18′ Away
   Azimuth 093°
   ITP 50°01′N 159°42′W
   (26d 02h 30m 18s GMT)
2. AP 50°S 152°16.′2W
   Intercept 5′ Away
   Azimuth 076°
   ITP 50°01′S 152°24′W
   (22d 00h 33m 14s GMT)
3. AP 50°S 82°50.′7E
   Intercept 25′ Towards
   Azimuth 267°
   ITP 50°01′S 82°12′E
   (21d 21h 34m 02s)

Chapter 13

1. 3°W
2. 7°W
3. 3°E

Chapter 17

a. 20d 06h 34m 38s GMT
   MPP 50°30′N 13°28′W
   (AP 50°N 13°35′W; Int 10′ Towards; Zn 079°)
b. Noon EP 50°22′N 12°15′W
c. GMT MP 20d 12h 51m
d. Observed noon position 50°05′N 12°10′W
e. 20d 17h 29m 48s GMT
f. EP 50°01′N 11°32′W
g. Observed position 50°01′N 11°27′W
   (AP 50°N 11°03.′5W; Int 15′ Towards; Zn 271°)
h. EP 49°33′N 07°24′W
i. 21d 21h 28m 37s GMT
j. Observed position 49°31′N 07°16′W
   (Rasalhague AP 50°N 07°52.′1W; Int 36′ Towards; Zn 126°. Moon AP 50°N 07°40.′3W; Int 15′ Towards; Zn 215°)
k. EP 49°50′N 04°39′W
l. GMT CT 22d 21h 16m

m.

	Hc	Zn
Vega	51°20′	086°
Arcturus	57°45′	202°
Dubhe	55°37′	313°

n. The navigator decided to plan for Deneb, Rasalhague and Arcturus to allow for the possibility of needing to start the sights a little earlier than planned.

o. Observed position at 22d 21h 30m GMT was 49°50′N 04°35′W.

p. The yacht's position is 210° and 24′ from the Eddystone light.

Appendices

ALTITUDE CORRECTION TABLES 10°-90°—SUN, STARS, PLANETS

SUN

App. Alt. (Oct.—Mar.)	Lower Limb	Upper Limb	App. Alt. (Apr.—Sept.)	Lower Limb	Upper Limb
° ′	′	′	° ′	′	′
9 34	+10·8	−21·5	9 39	+10·6	−21·2
9 45	+10·9	−21·4	9 51	+10·7	−21·1
9 56	+11·0	−21·3	10 03	+10·8	−21·0
10 08	+11·1	−21·2	10 15	+10·9	−20·9
10 21	+11·2	−21·1	10 27	+11·0	−20·8
10 34	+11·3	−21·0	10 40	+11·1	−20·7
10 47	+11·4	−20·9	10 54	+11·2	−20·6
11 01	+11·5	−20·8	11 08	+11·3	−20·5
11 15	+11·6	−20·7	11 23	+11·4	−20·4
11 30	+11·7	−20·6	11 38	+11·5	−20·3
11 46	+11·8	−20·5	11 54	+11·6	−20·2
12 02	+11·9	−20·4	12 10	+11·7	−20·1
12 19	+12·0	−20·3	12 28	+11·8	−20·0
12 37	+12·1	−20·2	12 46	+11·9	−19·9
12 55	+12·2	−20·1	13 05	+12·0	−19·8
13 14	+12·3	−20·0	13 24	+12·1	−19·7
13 35	+12·4	−19·9	13 45	+12·2	−19·6
13 56	+12·5	−19·8	14 07	+12·3	−19·5
14 18	+12·6	−19·7	14 30	+12·4	−19·4
14 42	+12·7	−19·6	14 54	+12·5	−19·3
15 06	+12·8	−19·5	15 19	+12·6	−19·2
15 32	+12·9	−19·4	15 46	+12·7	−19·1
15 59	+13·0	−19·3	16 14	+12·8	−19·0
16 28	+13·1	−19·2	16 44	+12·9	−18·9
16 59	+13·2	−19·1	17 15	+13·0	−18·8
17 32	+13·3	−19·0	17 48	+13·1	−18·7
18 06	+13·4	−18·9	18 24	+13·2	−18·6
18 42	+13·5	−18·8	19 01	+13·3	−18·5
19 21	+13·6	−18·7	19 42	+13·4	−18·4
20 03	+13·7	−18·6	20 25	+13·5	−18·3
20 48	+13·8	−18·5	21 11	+13·6	−18·2
21 35	+13·9	−18·4	22 00	+13·7	−18·1
22 26	+14·0	−18·3	22 54	+13·8	−18·0
23 22	+14·1	−18·2	23 51	+13·9	−17·9
24 21	+14·2	−18·1	24 53	+14·0	−17·8
25 26	+14·3	−18·0	26 00	+14·1	−17·7
26 36	+14·4	−17·9	27 13	+14·2	−17·6
27 52	+14·5	−17·8	28 33	+14·3	−17·5
29 15	+14·6	−17·7	30 00	+14·4	−17·4
30 46	+14·7	−17·6	31 35	+14·5	−17·3
32 26	+14·8	−17·5	33 20	+14·6	−17·2
34 17	+14·9	−17·4	35 17	+14·7	−17·1
36 20	+15·0	−17·3	37 26	+14·8	−17·0
38 36	+15·1	−17·2	39 50	+14·9	−16·9
41 08	+15·2	−17·1	42 31	+15·0	−16·8
43 59	+15·3	−17·0	45 31	+15·1	−16·7
47 10	+15·4	−16·9	48 55	+15·2	−16·6
50 46	+15·5	−16·8	52 44	+15·3	−16·5
54 49	+15·6	−16·7	57 02	+15·4	−16·4
59 23	+15·7	−16·6	61 51	+15·5	−16·3
64 30	+15·8	−16·5	67 17	+15·6	−16·2
70 12	+15·9	−16·4	73 16	+15·7	−16·1
76 26	+16·0	−16·3	79 43	+15·8	−16·0
83 05	+16·1	−16·2	86 32	+15·9	−15·9
90 00			90 00		

STARS AND PLANETS

App. Alt.	Corr^n
° ′	′
9 56	−5·3
10 08	−5·2
10 20	−5·1
10 33	−5·0
10 46	−4·9
11 00	−4·8
11 14	−4·7
11 29	−4·6
11 45	−4·5
12 01	−4·4
12 18	−4·3
12 35	−4·2
12 54	−4·1
13 13	−4·0
13 33	−3·9
13 54	−3·8
14 16	−3·7
14 40	−3·6
15 04	−3·5
15 30	−3·4
15 57	−3·3
16 26	−3·2
16 56	−3·1
17 28	−3·0
18 02	−2·9
18 38	−2·8
19 17	−2·7
19 58	−2·6
20 42	−2·5
21 28	−2·4
22 19	−2·3
23 13	−2·2
24 11	−2·1
25 14	−2·0
26 22	−1·9
27 36	−1·8
28 56	−1·7
30 24	−1·6
32 00	−1·5
33 45	−1·4
35 40	−1·3
37 48	−1·2
40 08	−1·1
42 44	−1·0
45 36	−0·9
48 47	−0·8
52 18	−0·7
56 11	−0·6
60 28	−0·5
65 08	−0·4
70 11	−0·3
75 34	−0·2
81 13	−0·1
87 03	0·0
90 00	

App. Alt. — Additional Corr^n

1980

VENUS

Jan. 1-Feb. 26: 0°–42°: + 0′·1

Feb. 27-Apr. 13: 0°–47°: + 0′·2

Apr. 14-May 9: 0°–46°: + 0′·3

May 10-May 25: 0°–11°: + 0′·4; 11°–41°: + 0·5

May 26-June 3: 0°–6°: + 0′·5; 6°–20°: + 0·6; 20°–31°: + 0·7

June 4-June 26: 0°–4°: + 0′·6; 4°–12°: + 0·7; 12°–22°: + 0·8

June 27-July 6: 0°–6°: + 0′·5; 6°–20°: + 0·6; 20°–31°: + 0·7

July 7-July 21: 0°–11°: + 0′·4; 11°–41°: + 0·5

July 22-Aug. 17: 0°–46°: + 0′·3

Aug. 18-Oct. 2: 0°–47°: + 0′·2

Oct. 3-Dec. 31: 0°–42°: + 0′·1

MARS

Jan. 1-Apr. 28: 0°–41°: + 0′·2; 41°–75°: + 0·1

Apr. 29-Dec. 31: 0°–60°: + 0′·1

DIP

Ht. of Eye (m)	Corr^n	Ht. of Eye (ft.)
2·4	−2·8	8·0
2·6	−2·9	8·6
2·8	−3·0	9·2
3·0	−3·1	9·8
3·2	−3·2	10·5
3·4	−3·3	11·2
3·6	−3·4	11·9
3·8	−3·5	12·6
4·0	−3·6	13·3
4·3	−3·7	14·1
4·5	−3·8	14·9
4·7	−3·9	15·7
5·0	−4·0	16·5
5·2	−4·1	17·4
5·5	−4·2	18·3
5·8	−4·3	19·1
6·1	−4·4	20·1
6·3	−4·5	21·0
6·6	−4·6	22·0
6·9	−4·7	22·9
7·2	−4·8	23·9
7·5	−4·9	24·9
7·9	−5·0	26·0
8·2	−5·1	27·1
8·5	−5·2	28·1
8·8	−5·3	29·2
9·2	−5·4	30·4
9·5	−5·5	31·5
9·9	−5·6	32·7
10·3	−5·7	33·9
10·6	−5·8	35·1
11·0	−5·9	36·3
11·4	−6·0	37·6
11·8	−6·1	38·9
12·2	−6·2	40·1
12·6	−6·3	41·5
13·0	−6·4	42·8
13·4	−6·5	44·2
13·8	−6·6	45·5
14·2	−6·7	46·9
14·7	−6·8	48·4
15·1	−6·9	49·8
15·5	−7·0	51·3
16·0	−7·1	52·8
16·5	−7·2	54·3
16·9	−7·3	55·8
17·4	−7·4	57·4
17·9	−7·5	58·9
18·4	−7·6	60·5
18·8	−7·7	62·1
19·3	−7·8	63·8
19·8	−7·9	65·4
20·4	−8·0	67·1
20·9	−8·1	68·8
21·4		70·5

Ht. of Eye	Corr^n
m	
1·0	1·8
1·5	2·2
2·0	2·5
2·5	2·8
3·0	3·0
See table ←	
m	
20	7·9
22	8·3
24	8·6
26	9·0
28	9·3
30	9·6
32	10·0
34	10·3
36	10·6
38	10·8
40	11·1
42	11·4
44	11·7
46	11·9
48	12·2
ft.	
2	1·4
4	1·9
6	2·4
8	2·7
10	3·1
See table ←	
ft.	
70	8·1
75	8·4
80	8·7
85	8·9
90	9·2
95	9·5
100	9·7
105	9·9
110	10·2
115	10·4
120	10·6
125	10·8
130	11·1
135	11·3
140	11·5
145	11·7
150	11·9
155	12·1

App. Alt. = Apparent altitude = Sextant altitude corrected for index error and dip.

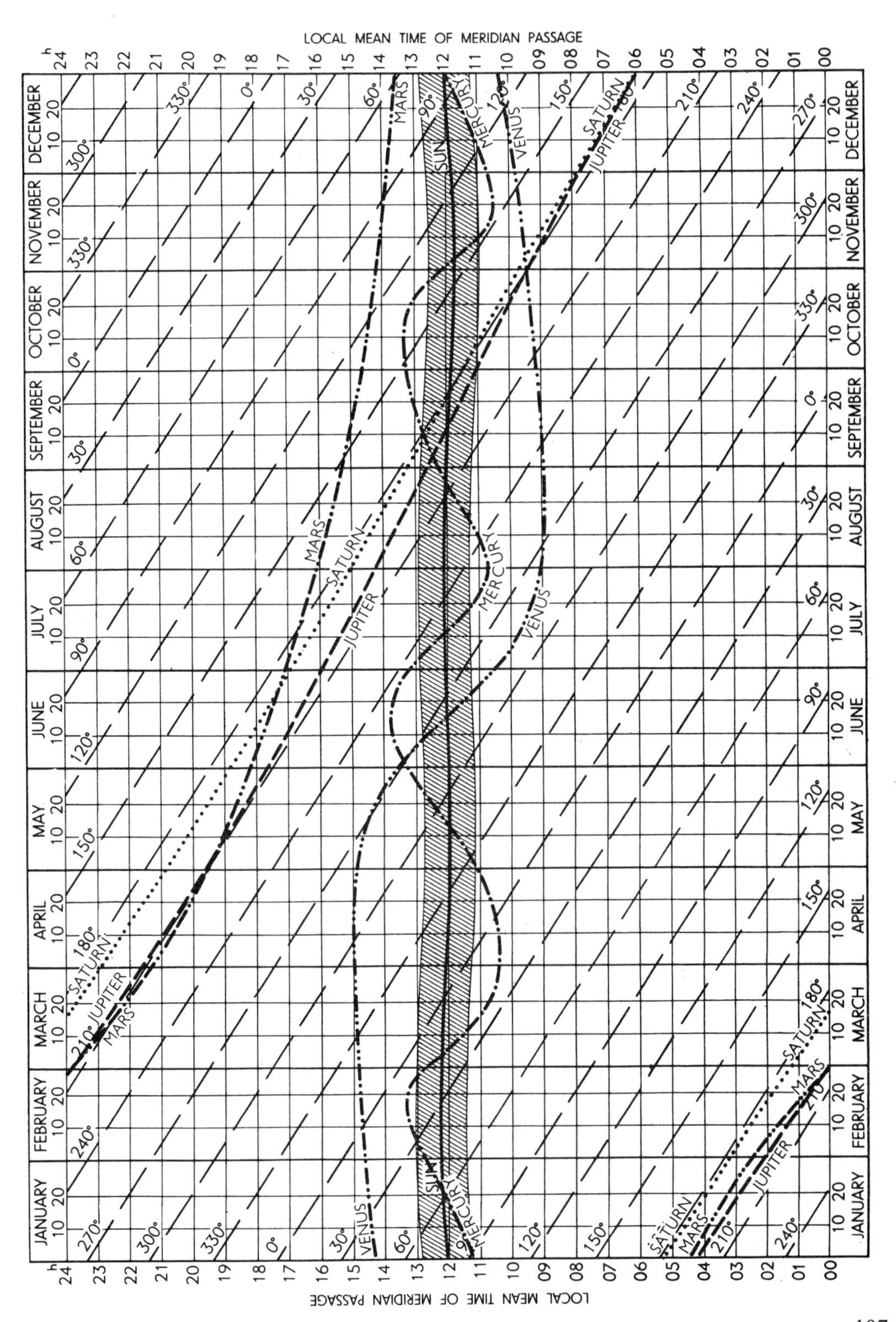
LOCAL MEAN TIME OF MERIDIAN PASSAGE
JANUARY
FEBRUARY
MARCH
APRIL
MAY
JUNE
JULY
AUGUST
SEPTEMBER
OCTOBER
NOVEMBER
DECEMBER
SUN
MERCURY
VENUS
MARS
JUPITER
SATURN

NAUTICAL ALMANAC 1980

1980 FEBRUARY 24, 25, 26 (SUN., MON., TUES.)

G.M.T.	ARIES	VENUS −3.7		MARS −1.0		JUPITER −2.1		SATURN +0.9	
d h	G.H.A. ° ′	G.H.A. ° ′	Dec. ° ′	G.H.A. ° ′	Dec. ° ′	G.H.A. ° ′	Dec. ° ′	G.H.A. ° ′	Dec. ° ′
24 00	153 02.2	137 56.8	N 6 44.7	353 20.6	N13 16.5	355 20.6	N10 45.2	336 34.8	N 4 07.5
01	168 04.6	152 56.6	46.0	8 24.0	16.9	10 23.4	45.4	351 37.4	07.6
02	183 07.1	167 56.5	47.3	23 27.4	17.2	25 26.2	45.5	6 40.1	07.7
03	198 09.6	182 56.3	·· 48.5	38 30.9	·· 17.6	40 29.0	·· 45.6	21 42.7	·· 07.7
04	213 12.0	197 56.1	49.8	53 34.3	17.9	55 31.7	45.7	36 45.3	07.8
05	228 14.5	212 55.9	51.1	68 37.7	18.3	70 34.5	45.9	51 47.9	07.9
06	243 17.0	227 55.8	N 6 52.4	83 41.1	N13 18.6	85 37.3	N10 46.0	66 50.6	N 4 08.0
07	258 19.4	242 55.6	53.6	98 44.5	19.0	100 40.1	46.1	81 53.2	08.0
08	273 21.9	257 55.4	54.9	113 47.9	19.4	115 42.8	46.2	96 55.8	08.1
S 09	288 24.4	272 55.3	·· 56.2	128 51.3	·· 19.7	130 45.6	·· 46.4	111 58.4	·· 08.2
U 10	303 26.8	287 55.1	57.5	143 54.8	20.1	145 48.4	46.5	127 01.1	08.3
N 11	318 29.3	302 54.9	6 58.7	158 58.2	20.4	160 51.1	46.6	142 03.7	08.4
D 12	333 31.7	317 54.8	N 7 00.0	174 01.6	N13 20.8	175 53.9	N10 46.7	157 06.3	N 4 08.4
A 13	348 34.2	332 54.6	01.3	189 05.0	21.1	190 56.7	46.9	172 09.0	08.5
Y 14	3 36.7	347 54.4	02.5	204 08.4	21.5	205 59.5	47.0	187 11.6	08.6
15	18 39.1	2 54.3	·· 03.8	219 11.8	·· 21.8	221 02.2	·· 47.1	202 14.2	·· 08.7
16	33 41.6	17 54.1	05.1	234 15.2	22.2	236 05.0	47.2	217 16.8	08.7
17	48 44.1	32 53.9	06.4	249 18.7	22.5	251 07.8	47.4	232 19.5	08.8
18	63 46.5	47 53.7	N 7 07.6	264 22.1	N13 22.9	266 10.6	N10 47.5	247 22.1	N 4 08.9
19	78 49.0	62 53.6	08.9	279 25.5	23.2	281 13.3	47.6	262 24.7	09.0
20	93 51.5	77 53.4	10.2	294 28.9	23.6	296 16.1	47.7	277 27.3	09.0
21	108 53.9	92 53.2	·· 11.4	309 32.3	·· 24.0	311 18.9	·· 47.8	292 30.0	·· 09.1
22	123 56.4	107 53.1	12.7	324 35.7	24.3	326 21.7	48.0	307 32.6	09.2
23	138 58.9	122 52.9	14.0	339 39.2	24.7	341 24.4	48.1	322 35.2	09.3
25 00	154 01.3	137 52.7	N 7 15.2	354 42.6	N13 25.0	356 27.2	N10 48.2	337 37.8	N 4 09.4
01	169 03.8	152 52.6	16.5	9 46.0	25.4	11 30.0	48.3	352 40.5	09.4
02	184 06.2	167 52.4	17.8	24 49.4	25.7	26 32.8	48.5	7 43.1	09.5
03	199 08.7	182 52.2	·· 19.0	39 52.8	·· 26.1	41 35.5	·· 48.6	22 45.7	·· 09.6
04	214 11.2	197 52.1	20.3	54 56.2	26.4	56 38.3	48.7	37 48.4	09.7
05	229 13.6	212 51.9	21.6	69 59.7	26.8	71 41.1	48.8	52 51.0	09.7
06	244 16.1	227 51.7	N 7 22.8	85 03.1	N13 27.1	86 43.9	N10 49.0	67 53.6	N 4 09.8
07	259 18.6	242 51.5	24.1	100 06.5	27.5	101 46.6	49.1	82 56.2	09.9
08	274 21.0	257 51.4	25.4	115 09.9	27.8	116 49.4	49.2	97 58.9	10.0
M 09	289 23.5	272 51.2	·· 26.6	130 13.3	·· 28.2	131 52.2	·· 49.3	113 01.5	·· 10.1
O 10	304 26.0	287 51.0	27.9	145 16.7	28.5	146 55.0	49.5	128 04.1	10.1
N 11	319 28.4	302 50.9	29.2	160 20.2	28.9	161 57.7	49.6	143 06.8	10.2
D 12	334 30.9	317 50.7	N 7 30.4	175 23.6	N13 29.2	177 00.5	N10 49.7	158 09.4	N 4 10.3
A 13	349 33.4	332 50.5	31.7	190 27.0	29.6	192 03.3	49.8	173 12.0	10.4
Y 14	4 35.8	347 50.4	33.0	205 30.4	29.9	207 06.1	50.0	188 14.6	10.4
15	19 38.3	2 50.2	·· 34.2	220 33.8	·· 30.3	222 08.8	·· 50.1	203 17.3	·· 10.5
16	34 40.7	17 50.0	35.5	235 37.2	30.6	237 11.6	50.2	218 19.9	10.6
17	49 43.2	32 49.9	36.8	250 40.7	31.0	252 14.4	50.3	233 22.5	10.7
18	64 45.7	47 49.7	N 7 38.0	265 44.1	N13 31.3	267 17.1	N10 50.4	248 25.1	N 4 10.8
19	79 48.1	62 49.5	39.3	280 47.5	31.7	282 19.9	50.6	263 27.8	10.8
20	94 50.6	77 49.4	40.6	295 50.9	32.0	297 22.7	50.7	278 30.4	10.9
21	109 53.1	92 49.2	·· 41.8	310 54.3	·· 32.3	312 25.5	·· 50.8	293 33.0	·· 11.0
22	124 55.5	107 49.0	43.1	325 57.8	32.7	327 28.2	50.9	308 35.7	11.1
23	139 58.0	122 48.9	44.3	341 01.2	33.0	342 31.0	51.1	323 38.3	11.1
26 00	155 00.5	137 48.7	N 7 45.6	356 04.6	N13 33.4	357 33.8	N10 51.2	338 40.9	N 4 11.2
01	170 02.9	152 48.5	46.9	11 08.0	33.7	12 36.6	51.3	353 43.6	11.3
02	185 05.4	167 48.4	48.1	26 11.4	34.1	27 39.3	51.4	8 46.2	11.4
03	200 07.8	182 48.2	·· 49.4	41 14.9	·· 34.4	42 42.1	·· 51.6	23 48.8	·· 11.5
04	215 10.3	197 48.0	50.6	56 18.3	34.8	57 44.9	51.7	38 51.4	11.5
05	230 12.8	212 47.8	51.9	71 21.7	35.1	72 47.7	51.8	53 54.1	11.6
06	245 15.2	227 47.7	N 7 53.2	86 25.1	N13 35.5	87 50.4	N10 51.9	68 56.7	N 4 11.7
07	260 17.7	242 47.5	54.4	101 28.5	35.8	102 53.2	52.1	83 59.3	11.8
T 08	275 20.2	257 47.3	55.7	116 31.9	36.2	117 56.0	52.2	99 02.0	11.8
U 09	290 22.6	272 47.2	·· 56.9	131 35.4	·· 36.5	132 58.8	·· 52.3	114 04.6	·· 11.9
E 10	305 25.1	287 47.0	58.2	146 38.8	36.8	148 01.5	52.4	129 07.2	12.0
S 11	320 27.6	302 46.8	7 59.5	161 42.2	37.2	163 04.3	52.5	144 09.8	12.1
D 12	335 30.0	317 46.7	N 8 00.7	176 45.6	N13 37.5	178 07.1	N10 52.7	159 12.5	N 4 12.2
A 13	350 32.5	332 46.5	02.0	191 49.0	37.9	193 09.9	52.8	174 15.1	12.2
Y 14	5 35.0	347 46.3	03.2	206 52.5	38.2	208 12.6	52.9	189 17.7	12.3
15	20 37.4	2 46.2	·· 04.5	221 55.9	·· 38.6	223 15.4	·· 53.0	204 20.4	·· 12.4
16	35 39.9	17 46.0	05.7	236 59.3	38.9	238 18.2	53.2	219 23.0	12.5
17	50 42.3	32 45.8	07.0	252 02.7	39.2	253 21.0	53.3	234 25.6	12.5
18	65 44.8	47 45.7	N 8 08.3	267 06.1	N13 39.6	268 23.7	N10 53.4	249 28.3	N 4 12.6
19	80 47.3	62 45.5	09.5	282 09.6	39.9	283 26.5	53.5	264 30.9	12.7
20	95 49.7	77 45.3	10.8	297 13.0	40.3	298 29.3	53.7	279 33.5	12.8
21	110 52.2	92 45.2	·· 12.0	312 16.4	·· 40.6	313 32.0	·· 53.8	294 36.1	·· 12.9
22	125 54.7	107 45.0	13.3	327 19.8	41.0	328 34.8	53.9	309 38.8	12.9
23	140 57.1	122 44.8	14.5	342 23.2	41.3	343 37.6	54.0	324 41.4	13.0
Mer. Pass.	h m 13 41.7	*v* −0.2	*d* 1.3	*v* 3.4	*d* 0.3	*v* 2.8	*d* 0.1	*v* 2.6	*d* 0.1

STARS

Name	S.H.A. ° ′	Dec. ° ′
Acamar	315 37.7	S40 23.4
Achernar	335 46.0	S57 20.6
Acrux	173 37.0	S62 59.2
Adhara	255 32.2	S28 57.0
Aldebaran	291 18.4	N16 28.1
Alioth	166 42.5	N56 03.9
Alkaid	153 18.6	N49 24.6
Al Na'ir	28 15.9	S47 03.5
Alnilam	276 11.9	S 1 13.1
Alphard	218 20.6	S 8 34.5
Alphecca	126 32.4	N26 46.7
Alpheratz	358 10.0	N28 58.8
Altair	62 33.2	N 8 48.8
Ankaa	353 41.0	S42 25.1
Antares	112 57.3	S26 23.2
Arcturus	146 18.7	N19 17.0
Atria	108 22.0	S68 59.2
Avior	234 27.8	S59 27.0
Bellatrix	278 59.1	N 6 19.7
Betelgeuse	271 28.6	N 7 24.1
Canopus	264 07.1	S52 41.5
Capella	281 11.7	N45 58.8
Deneb	49 49.1	N45 12.4
Denebola	182 59.1	N14 40.9
Diphda	349 21.5	S18 06.0
Dubhe	194 22.0	N61 51.4
Elnath	278 44.5	N28 35.4
Eltanin	90 58.1	N51 29.3
Enif	34 12.3	N 9 46.9
Fomalhaut	15 52.2	S29 43.8
Gacrux	172 28.6	S57 00.0
Gienah	176 18.1	S17 25.9
Hadar	149 23.5	S60 16.4
Hamal	328 29.5	N23 22.0
Kaus Aust.	84 17.6	S34 23.5
Kochab	137 18.7	N74 14.0
Markab	14 03.9	N15 05.8
Menkar	314 41.6	N 4 00.5
Menkent	148 37.2	S36 16.2
Miaplacidus	221 44.1	S69 38.3
Mirfak	309 16.7	N49 47.5
Nunki	76 29.9	S26 19.2
Peacock	53 59.5	S56 47.9
Pollux	243 58.4	N28 04.4
Procyon	245 25.9	N 5 16.4
Rasalhague	96 30.1	N12 34.4
Regulus	208 10.1	N12 03.8
Rigel	281 36.3	S 8 13.7
Rigil Kent.	140 26.0	S60 44.9
Sabik	102 41.6	S15 42.0
Schedar.	350 09.8	N56 25.7
Shaula	96 56.4	S37 05.2
Sirius	258 55.8	S16 41.6
Spica	158 57.7	S11 03.5
Suhail	223 10.6	S43 21.3
Vega	80 56.3	N38 45.7
Zuben'ubi	137 33.3	S15 57.5

	S.H.A. ° ′	Mer. Pass. h m
Venus	343 51.4	14 49
Mars	200 41.3	0 21
Jupiter	202 25.9	0 14
Saturn	183 36.5	1 29

1980 FEBRUARY 24, 25, 26 (SUN., MON., TUES.)

Day	G.M.T. d h	SUN G.H.A. ° ′	SUN Dec. ° ′	MOON G.H.A. ° ′	MOON *v* ′	MOON Dec. ° ′	MOON *d* ′	MOON H.P. ′
SUNDAY	24 00	176 38.4	S 9 50.9	76 56.2	9.3	N17 44.6	4.0	57.0
	01	191 38.5	50.0	91 24.5	9.4	17 48.6	3.9	57.0
	02	206 38.6	49.1	105 52.9	9.4	17 52.5	3.8	57.0
	03	221 38.7	48.2	120 21.3	9.4	17 56.3	3.7	56.9
	04	236 38.8	47.3	134 49.7	9.4	18 00.0	3.5	56.9
	05	251 38.9	46.3	149 18.1	9.5	18 03.5	3.5	56.9
	06	266 38.9	S 9 45.4	163 46.6	9.4	N18 07.0	3.4	56.8
	07	281 39.0	44.5	178 15.0	9.4	18 10.4	3.3	56.8
	08	296 39.1	43.6	192 43.4	9.5	18 13.7	3.1	56.8
	09	311 39.2	42.7	207 11.9	9.5	18 16.8	3.1	56.8
	10	326 39.3	41.8	221 40.4	9.5	18 19.9	3.0	56.7
	11	341 39.4	40.8	236 08.9	9.5	18 22.9	2.8	56.7
	12	356 39.5	S 9 39.9	250 37.4	9.5	N18 25.7	2.8	56.7
	13	11 39.6	39.0	265 05.9	9.5	18 28.5	2.6	56.6
	14	26 39.7	38.1	279 34.4	9.6	18 31.1	2.6	56.6
	15	41 39.7	37.1	294 03.0	9.5	18 33.7	2.4	56.6
	16	56 39.8	36.2	308 31.5	9.6	18 36.1	2.3	56.6
	17	71 39.9	35.3	323 00.1	9.6	18 38.4	2.3	56.5
	18	86 40.0	S 9 34.4	337 28.7	9.6	N18 40.7	2.1	56.5
	19	101 40.1	33.5	351 57.3	9.6	18 42.8	2.0	56.5
	20	116 40.2	32.5	6 25.9	9.7	18 44.8	2.0	56.4
	21	131 40.3	31.6	20 54.6	9.7	18 46.8	1.8	56.4
	22	146 40.4	30.7	35 23.3	9.6	18 48.6	1.7	56.4
	23	161 40.5	29.8	49 51.9	9.7	18 50.3	1.6	56.4
MONDAY	25 00	176 40.6	S 9 28.9	64 20.6	9.8	N18 51.9	1.5	56.3
	01	191 40.7	27.9	78 49.4	9.7	18 53.4	1.5	56.3
	02	206 40.8	27.0	93 18.1	9.8	18 54.9	1.3	56.3
	03	221 40.8	26.1	107 46.9	9.8	18 56.2	1.2	56.2
	04	236 40.9	25.2	122 15.7	9.8	18 57.4	1.1	56.2
	05	251 41.0	24.2	136 44.5	9.8	18 58.5	1.0	56.2
	06	266 41.1	S 9 23.3	151 13.3	9.9	N18 59.5	0.9	56.2
	07	281 41.2	22.4	165 42.2	9.8	19 00.4	0.8	56.1
	08	296 41.3	21.5	180 11.0	9.9	19 01.2	0.7	56.1
	09	311 41.4	20.5	194 39.9	10.0	19 01.9	0.6	56.1
	10	326 41.5	19.6	209 08.9	9.9	19 02.5	0.5	56.1
	11	341 41.6	18.7	223 37.8	10.0	19 03.0	0.4	56.0
	12	356 41.7	S 9 17.8	238 06.8	10.0	N19 03.4	0.3	56.0
	13	11 41.8	16.8	252 35.8	10.0	19 03.7	0.2	56.0
	14	26 41.9	15.9	267 04.8	10.1	19 03.9	0.0	56.0
	15	41 42.0	15.0	281 33.9	10.0	19 03.9	0.0	55.9
	16	56 42.1	14.0	296 02.9	10.1	19 03.9	0.1	55.9
	17	71 42.2	13.1	310 32.0	10.2	19 03.8	0.2	55.9
	18	86 42.3	S 9 12.2	325 01.2	10.1	N19 03.6	0.3	55.9
	19	101 42.4	11.3	339 30.3	10.2	19 03.3	0.4	55.8
	20	116 42.5	10.3	353 59.5	10.2	19 02.9	0.5	55.8
	21	131 42.6	09.4	8 28.7	10.3	19 02.4	0.6	55.8
	22	146 42.7	08.5	22 58.0	10.3	19 01.8	0.7	55.8
	23	161 42.8	07.6	37 27.3	10.3	19 01.1	0.8	55.8
TUESDAY	26 00	176 42.9	S 9 06.6	51 56.6	10.3	N19 00.3	0.9	55.7
	01	191 43.0	05.7	66 25.9	10.4	18 59.4	1.0	55.7
	02	206 43.1	04.8	80 55.3	10.4	18 58.4	1.1	55.7
	03	221 43.2	03.8	95 24.7	10.4	18 57.3	1.2	55.7
	04	236 43.3	02.9	109 54.1	10.4	18 56.1	1.3	55.6
	05	251 43.4	02.0	124 23.5	10.5	18 54.8	1.4	55.6
	06	266 43.5	S 9 01.0	138 53.0	10.6	N18 53.4	1.4	55.6
	07	281 43.6	9 00.1	153 22.6	10.5	18 52.0	1.6	55.6
	08	296 43.7	8 59.2	167 52.1	10.6	18 50.4	1.7	55.5
	09	311 43.8	58.3	182 21.7	10.6	18 48.7	1.8	55.5
	10	326 43.9	57.3	196 51.3	10.7	18 46.9	1.8	55.5
	11	341 44.0	56.4	211 21.0	10.7	18 45.1	2.0	55.5
	12	356 44.1	S 8 55.5	225 50.7	10.7	N18 43.1	2.0	55.5
	13	11 44.2	54.5	240 20.4	10.8	18 41.1	2.2	55.4
	14	26 44.3	53.6	254 50.2	10.8	18 38.9	2.2	55.4
	15	41 44.4	52.7	269 20.0	10.8	18 36.7	2.3	55.4
	16	56 44.5	51.7	283 49.8	10.9	18 34.4	2.4	55.4
	17	71 44.6	50.8	298 19.7	10.9	18 32.0	2.5	55.4
	18	86 44.7	S 8 49.9	312 49.6	11.0	N18 29.5	2.6	55.3
	19	101 44.8	48.9	327 19.6	10.9	18 26.9	2.7	55.3
	20	116 44.9	48.0	341 49.5	11.1	18 24.2	2.8	55.3
	21	131 45.0	47.1	356 19.6	11.0	18 21.4	2.9	55.3
	22	146 45.1	46.1	10 49.6	11.1	18 18.5	2.9	55.3
	23	161 45.2	45.2	25 19.7	11.2	18 15.6	3.1	55.2
		S.D. 16.2	*d* 0.9	S.D. 15.4		15.3		15.1

Lat. °	Twilight Naut. h m	Twilight Civil h m	Sunrise h m	Moonrise 24 h m	Moonrise 25 h m	Moonrise 26 h m	Moonrise 27 h m
N 72	05 33	06 51	08 03	▭	▭	▭	10 39
N 70	05 36	06 46	07 50	08 54	09 21	10 21	11 46
68	05 38	06 42	07 40	09 35	10 12	11 09	12 22
66	05 40	06 39	07 31	10 03	10 43	11 39	12 48
64	05 41	06 36	07 24	10 24	11 07	12 02	13 08
62	05 42	06 33	07 18	10 42	11 26	12 20	13 24
60	05 42	06 30	07 13	10 56	11 41	12 35	13 37
N 58	05 43	06 28	07 08	11 08	11 54	12 48	13 49
56	05 43	06 26	07 04	11 19	12 06	12 59	13 59
54	05 43	06 24	07 00	11 28	12 15	13 09	14 08
52	05 43	06 22	06 56	11 37	12 24	13 18	14 15
50	05 43	06 21	06 53	11 44	12 32	13 25	14 22
45	05 43	06 17	06 46	12 00	12 49	13 42	14 38
N 40	05 42	06 13	06 41	12 14	13 03	13 55	14 50
35	05 41	06 10	06 36	12 25	13 15	14 07	15 00
30	05 39	06 07	06 31	12 35	13 25	14 17	15 10
20	05 35	06 01	06 23	12 52	13 43	14 34	15 26
N 10	05 31	05 55	06 17	13 07	13 58	14 49	15 39
0	05 25	05 49	06 10	13 21	14 13	15 03	15 52
S 10	05 17	05 42	06 03	13 35	14 27	15 17	16 05
20	05 07	05 33	05 56	13 50	14 43	15 32	16 19
30	04 54	05 23	05 47	14 07	15 00	15 50	16 35
35	04 46	05 16	05 43	14 17	15 11	16 00	16 44
40	04 35	05 09	05 37	14 29	15 23	16 11	16 54
45	04 23	05 00	05 30	14 42	15 37	16 25	17 07
S 50	04 06	04 48	05 22	14 59	15 54	16 41	17 22
52	03 59	04 43	05 19	15 07	16 02	16 49	17 28
54	03 50	04 37	05 15	15 15	16 11	16 57	17 36
56	03 39	04 30	05 10	15 25	16 21	17 07	17 45
58	03 27	04 22	05 05	15 36	16 32	17 18	17 54
S 60	03 13	04 13	04 59	15 49	16 46	17 31	18 06

Lat. °	Sunset h m	Twilight Civil h m	Twilight Naut. h m	Moonset 24 h m	Moonset 25 h m	Moonset 26 h m	Moonset 27 h m
N 72	16 26	17 37	18 56	▭	▭	▭	08 48
N 70	16 38	17 42	18 53	05 15	06 37	07 23	07 40
68	16 48	17 46	18 50	04 34	05 46	06 35	07 03
66	16 57	17 49	18 49	04 07	05 14	06 04	06 37
64	17 04	17 52	18 47	03 46	04 50	05 41	06 17
62	17 10	17 55	18 46	03 29	04 32	05 22	06 01
60	17 15	17 57	18 46	03 14	04 16	05 07	05 47
N 58	17 20	18 00	18 45	03 02	04 03	04 54	05 35
56	17 24	18 02	18 45	02 52	03 52	04 43	05 25
54	17 27	18 03	18 44	02 43	03 42	04 33	05 16
52	17 31	18 05	18 44	02 35	03 33	04 25	05 08
50	17 34	18 07	18 44	02 27	03 26	04 17	05 01
45	17 41	18 10	18 44	02 11	03 09	04 00	04 45
N 40	17 46	18 14	18 45	01 59	02 55	03 46	04 32
35	17 51	18 17	18 46	01 48	02 43	03 35	04 21
30	17 56	18 20	18 48	01 38	02 33	03 24	04 12
20	18 03	18 26	18 51	01 21	02 15	03 07	03 55
N 10	18 10	18 31	18 56	01 07	02 00	02 51	03 41
0	18 17	18 37	19 02	00 54	01 46	02 37	03 27
S 10	18 23	18 44	19 09	00 40	01 31	02 23	03 13
20	18 30	18 53	19 19	00 26	01 16	02 07	02 59
30	18 39	19 03	19 32	00 09	00 59	01 50	02 42
35	18 43	19 09	19 40	00 00	00 48	01 39	02 32
40	18 49	19 17	19 50	24 37	00 37	01 27	02 21
45	18 55	19 26	20 03	24 23	00 23	01 14	02 08
S 50	19 03	19 37	20 18	24 06	00 06	00 57	01 52
52	19 07	19 42	20 26	23 58	24 48	00 48	01 44
54	19 11	19 48	20 35	23 49	24 40	00 40	01 36
56	19 15	19 55	20 45	23 39	24 30	00 30	01 26
58	19 20	20 02	20 57	23 28	24 18	00 18	01 16
S 60	19 25	20 11	21 11	23 15	24 05	00 05	01 03

Day	SUN Eqn. of Time 00ʰ m s	SUN Eqn. of Time 12ʰ m s	SUN Mer. Pass. h m	MOON Mer. Pass. Upper h m	MOON Mer. Pass. Lower h m	MOON Age d	MOON Phase
24	13 26	13 22	12 13	19 33	07 07	08	
25	13 18	13 13	12 13	20 25	07 59	09	◐
26	13 09	13 04	12 13	21 15	08 50	10	

1980 SEPTEMBER 21, 22, 23 (SUN., MON., TUES.)

G.M.T.	ARIES	VENUS −3.7		MARS +1.5		JUPITER −1.2		SATURN +1.2	
	G.H.A.	G.H.A.	Dec.	G.H.A.	Dec.	G.H.A.	Dec.	G.H.A.	Dec.
d h	° ′	° ′	° ′	° ′	° ′	° ′	° ′	° ′	° ′
21 00	0 01.3	223 31.5	N15 48.2	137 30.1	S16 57.3	186 35.4	N 3 58.5	179 15.1	N 1 55.0
01	15 03.7	238 31.2	47.6	152 30.8	57.8	201 37.3	58.3	194 17.3	54.9
02	30 06.2	253 30.8	47.0	167 31.6	58.3	216 39.3	58.1	209 19.4	54.7
03	45 08.7	268 30.5	·· 46.4	182 32.3	·· 58.8	231 41.3	·· 57.9	224 21.6	·· 54.6
04	60 11.1	283 30.2	45.8	197 33.1	59.4	246 43.2	57.7	239 23.8	54.5
05	75 13.6	298 29.8	45.2	212 33.9	16 59.9	261 45.2	57.5	254 26.0	54.4
06	90 16.1	313 29.5	N15 44.5	227 34.6	S17 00.4	276 47.2	N 3 57.2	269 28.2	N 1 54.2
07	105 18.5	328 29.1	43.9	242 35.4	00.9	291 49.1	57.0	284 30.3	54.1
08	120 21.0	343 28.8	43.3	257 36.2	01.5	306 51.1	56.8	299 32.5	54.0
S 09	135 23.5	358 28.5	·· 42.7	272 36.9	·· 02.0	321 53.1	·· 56.6	314 34.7	·· 53.9
U 10	150 25.9	13 28.1	42.1	287 37.7	02.5	336 55.0	56.4	329 36.9	53.8
N 11	165 28.4	28 27.8	41.5	302 38.5	03.0	351 57.0	56.2	344 39.1	53.6
D 12	180 30.8	43 27.4	N15 40.9	317 39.2	S17 03.6	6 59.0	N 3 56.0	359 41.2	N 1 53.5
A 13	195 33.3	58 27.1	40.2	332 40.0	04.1	22 00.9	55.8	14 43.4	53.4
Y 14	210 35.8	73 26.8	39.6	347 40.7	04.6	37 02.9	55.6	29 45.6	53.3
15	225 38.2	88 26.4	·· 39.0	2 41.5	·· 05.1	52 04.9	·· 55.3	44 47.8	·· 53.1
16	240 40.7	103 26.1	38.4	17 42.3	05.6	67 06.8	55.1	59 49.9	53.0
17	255 43.2	118 25.7	37.8	32 43.0	06.2	82 08.8	54.9	74 52.1	52.9
18	270 45.6	133 25.4	N15 37.1	47 43.8	S17 06.7	97 10.8	N 3 54.7	89 54.3	N 1 52.8
19	285 48.1	148 25.1	36.5	62 44.5	07.2	112 12.7	54.5	104 56.5	52.7
20	300 50.6	163 24.7	35.9	77 45.3	07.7	127 14.7	54.3	119 58.7	52.5
21	315 53.0	178 24.4	·· 35.3	92 46.1	·· 08.3	142 16.7	·· 54.1	135 00.8	·· 52.4
22	330 55.5	193 24.0	34.6	107 46.8	08.8	157 18.6	53.9	150 03.0	52.3
23	345 58.0	208 23.7	34.0	122 47.6	09.3	172 20.6	53.6	165 05.2	52.2
22 00	1 00.4	223 23.4	N15 33.4	137 48.3	S17 09.8	187 22.6	N 3 53.4	180 07.4	N 1 52.0
01	16 02.9	238 23.0	32.8	152 49.1	10.3	202 24.5	53.2	195 09.6	51.9
02	31 05.3	253 22.7	32.1	167 49.9	10.9	217 26.5	53.0	210 11.7	51.8
03	46 07.8	268 22.3	·· 31.5	182 50.6	·· 11.4	232 28.4	·· 52.8	225 13.9	·· 51.7
04	61 10.3	283 22.0	30.9	197 51.4	11.9	247 30.4	52.6	240 16.1	51.6
05	76 12.7	298 21.7	30.2	212 52.1	12.4	262 32.4	52.4	255 18.3	51.4
06	91 15.2	313 21.3	N15 29.6	227 52.9	S17 12.9	277 34.3	N 3 52.2	270 20.5	N 1 51.3
07	106 17.7	328 21.0	29.0	242 53.6	13.5	292 36.3	52.0	285 22.6	51.2
08	121 20.1	343 20.6	28.3	257 54.4	14.0	307 38.3	51.7	300 24.8	51.1
M 09	136 22.6	358 20.3	·· 27.7	272 55.1	·· 14.5	322 40.2	·· 51.5	315 27.0	·· 50.9
O 10	151 25.1	13 20.0	27.1	287 55.9	15.0	337 42.2	51.3	330 29.2	50.8
N 11	166 27.5	28 19.6	26.4	302 56.7	15.5	352 44.2	51.1	345 31.3	50.7
D 12	181 30.0	43 19.3	N15 25.8	317 57.4	S17 16.0	7 46.1	N 3 50.9	0 33.5	N 1 50.6
A 13	196 32.5	58 18.9	25.2	332 58.2	16.6	22 48.1	50.7	15 35.7	50.5
Y 14	211 34.9	73 18.6	24.5	347 58.9	17.1	37 50.1	50.5	30 37.9	50.3
15	226 37.4	88 18.2	·· 23.9	2 59.7	·· 17.6	52 52.1	·· 50.3	45 40.1	·· 50.2
16	241 39.8	103 17.9	23.2	18 00.4	18.1	67 54.0	50.1	60 42.2	50.1
17	256 42.3	118 17.6	22.6	33 01.2	18.6	82 56.0	49.8	75 44.4	50.0
18	271 44.8	133 17.2	N15 22.0	48 01.9	S17 19.2	97 58.0	N 3 49.6	90 46.6	N 1 49.8
19	286 47.2	148 16.9	21.3	63 02.7	19.7	112 59.9	49.4	105 48.8	49.7
20	301 49.7	163 16.5	20.7	78 03.4	20.2	128 01.9	49.2	120 51.0	49.6
21	316 52.2	178 16.2	·· 20.0	93 04.2	·· 20.7	143 03.9	·· 49.0	135 53.1	·· 49.5
22	331 54.6	193 15.9	19.4	108 04.9	21.2	158 05.8	48.8	150 55.3	49.4
23	346 57.1	208 15.5	18.7	123 05.7	21.7	173 07.8	48.6	165 57.5	49.2
23 00	1 59.6	223 15.2	N15 18.1	138 06.4	S17 22.3	188 09.8	N 3 48.4	180 59.7	N 1 49.1
01	17 02.0	238 14.8	17.4	153 07.2	22.8	203 11.7	48.1	196 01.9	49.0
02	32 04.5	253 14.5	16.8	168 07.9	23.3	218 13.7	47.9	211 04.0	48.9
03	47 06.9	268 14.1	·· 16.2	183 08.7	·· 23.8	233 15.7	·· 47.7	226 06.2	·· 48.8
04	62 09.4	283 13.8	15.5	198 09.5	24.3	248 17.6	47.5	241 08.4	48.6
05	77 11.9	298 13.5	14.9	213 10.2	24.8	263 19.6	47.3	256 10.6	48.5
06	92 14.3	313 13.1	N15 14.2	228 10.9	S17 25.3	278 21.6	N 3 47.1	271 12.7	N 1 48.4
07	107 16.8	328 12.8	13.5	243 11.7	25.9	293 23.5	46.9	286 14.9	48.3
T 08	122 19.3	343 12.4	12.9	258 12.4	26.4	308 25.5	46.7	301 17.1	48.1
U 09	137 21.7	358 12.1	·· 12.2	273 13.2	·· 26.9	323 27.5	·· 46.5	316 19.3	·· 48.0
E 10	152 24.2	13 11.7	11.6	288 13.9	27.4	338 29.4	46.2	331 21.5	47.9
S 11	167 26.7	28 11.4	10.9	303 14.7	27.9	353 31.4	46.0	346 23.6	47.8
D 12	182 29.1	43 11.1	N15 10.3	318 15.4	S17 28.4	8 33.4	N 3 45.8	1 25.8	N 1 47.7
A 13	197 31.6	58 10.7	09.6	333 16.2	28.9	23 35.3	45.6	16 28.0	47.5
Y 14	212 34.1	73 10.4	09.0	348 16.9	29.5	38 37.3	45.4	31 30.2	47.4
15	227 36.5	88 10.0	·· 08.3	3 17.7	·· 30.0	53 39.3	·· 45.2	46 32.4	·· 47.3
16	242 39.0	103 09.7	07.6	18 18.4	30.5	68 41.2	45.0	61 34.5	47.2
17	257 41.4	118 09.3	07.0	33 19.2	31.0	83 43.2	44.8	76 36.7	47.0
18	272 43.9	133 09.0	N15 06.3	48 19.9	S17 31.5	98 45.2	N 3 44.6	91 38.9	N 1 46.9
19	287 46.4	148 08.7	05.7	63 20.7	32.0	113 47.1	44.3	106 41.1	46.8
20	302 48.8	163 08.3	05.0	78 21.4	32.5	128 49.1	44.1	121 43.2	46.7
21	317 51.3	178 08.0	·· 04.3	93 22.2	·· 33.0	143 51.1	·· 43.9	136 45.4	·· 46.6
22	332 53.8	193 07.6	03.7	108 22.9	33.5	158 53.0	43.7	151 47.6	46.4
23	347 56.2	208 07.3	03.0	123 23.6	34.1	173 55.0	43.5	166 49.8	46.3
Mer. Pass. (h m)	23 52.1	v −0.3	d 0.6	v 0.8	d 0.5	v 2.0	d 0.2	v 2.2	d 0.1

STARS		
Name	S.H.A.	Dec.
	° ′	° ′
Acamar	315 37.0	S40 22.8
Achernar	335 44.8	S57 20.0
Acrux	173 37.9	S62 59.4
Adhara	255 32.2	S28 56.5
Aldebaran	291 17.9	N16 28.2
Alioth	166 43.1	N56 04.1
Alkaid	153 19.0	N49 24.9
Al Na'ir	28 14.6	S47 03.3
Alnilam	276 11.6	S 1 12.8
Alphard	218 20.8	S 8 34.3
Alphecca	126 32.3	N26 47.1
Alpheratz	358 09.0	N28 59.1
Altair	62 32.4	N 8 49.2
Ankaa	353 39.8	S42 24.6
Antares	112 57.0	S26 23.3
Arcturus	146 18.8	N19 17.2
Atria	108 21.4	S68 59.8
Avior	234 28.5	S59 26.6
Bellatrix	278 58.7	N 6 20.0
Betelgeuse	271 28.3	N 7 24.3
Canopus	264 07.3	S52 40.8
Capella	281 11.2	N45 58.5
Deneb	49 48.2	N45 13.0
Denebola	182 59.4	N14 41.0
Diphda	349 20.6	S18 05.5
Dubhe	194 22.8	N61 51.4
Elnath	278 44.1	N28 35.4
Eltanin	90 57.7	N51 29.9
Enif	34 11.3	N 9 47.3
Fomalhaut	15 51.1	S29 43.5
Gacrux	172 29.3	S57 00.2
Gienah	176 18.3	S17 25.9
Hadar	149 23.9	S60 16.8
Hamal	328 28.6	N23 22.3
Kaus Aust.	84 16.8	S34 23.7
Kochab	137 19.9	N74 14.4
Markab	14 02.9	N15 06.2
Menkar	314 40.9	N 4 00.9
Menkent	148 37.3	S36 16.4
Miaplacidus	221 45.6	S69 38.0
Mirfak	309 15.8	N49 47.4
Nunki	76 29.1	S26 19.2
Peacock	53 58.1	S56 48.0
Pollux	243 58.3	N28 04.4
Procyon	245 25.9	N 5 16.6
Rasalhague	96 29.6	N12 34.7
Regulus	208 10.3	N12 03.8
Rigel	281 36.0	S 8 13.3
Rigil Kent.	140 26.3	S60 45.3
Sabik	102 41.2	S15 42.0
Schedar	350 08.4	N56 25.8
Shaula	96 55.8	S37 05.4
Sirius	258 55.8	S16 41.2
Spica	158 57.8	S11 03.4
Suhail	223 11.1	S43 21.0
Vega	80 55.8	N38 46.3
Zuben'ubi	137 33.3	S15 57.5

	S.H.A.	Mer. Pass.
	° ′	h m
Venus	222 22.9	9 07
Mars	136 47.9	14 48
Jupiter	186 22.1	11 29
Saturn	179 07.0	11 58

1980 JUNE 20, 21, 22 (FRI., SAT., SUN.)

G.M.T.	SUN G.H.A.	SUN Dec.	MOON G.H.A.	v	MOON Dec.	d	H.P.
d h	° ′	° ′	° ′	′	° ′	′	′
20 00	179 38.8	N23 26.1	93 36.3	15.2	N 5 12.0	9.7	54.4
01	194 38.6	26.1	108 10.5	15.2	5 02.3	9.7	54.4
02	209 38.5	26.1	122 44.7	15.3	4 52.6	9.7	54.4
03	224 38.4	·· 26.1	137 19.0	15.3	4 42.9	9.8	54.4
04	239 38.2	26.1	151 53.3	15.3	4 33.1	9.7	54.3
05	254 38.1	26.2	166 27.6	15.4	4 23.4	9.8	54.3
06	269 38.0	N23 26.2	181 02.0	15.3	N 4 13.6	9.8	54.3
07	284 37.8	26.2	195 36.3	15.4	4 03.8	9.8	54.3
08	299 37.7	26.2	210 10.7	15.4	3 54.0	9.8	54.3
F 09	314 37.6	·· 26.2	224 45.1	15.4	3 44.2	9.8	54.3
R 10	329 37.4	26.2	239 19.5	15.5	3 34.4	9.8	54.3
I 11	344 37.3	26.3	253 54.0	15.4	3 24.6	9.9	54.3
D 12	359 37.1	N23 26.3	268 28.4	15.5	N 3 14.7	9.8	54.3
A 13	14 37.0	26.3	283 02.9	15.4	3 04.9	9.9	54.3
Y 14	29 36.9	26.3	297 37.3	15.5	2 55.0	9.9	54.3
15	44 36.7	·· 26.3	312 11.8	15.5	2 45.1	9.8	54.3
16	59 36.6	26.3	326 46.3	15.5	2 35.3	9.9	54.3
17	74 36.5	26.3	341 20.8	15.5	2 25.4	9.9	54.3
18	89 36.3	N23 26.3	355 55.3	15.6	N 2 15.5	9.9	54.3
19	104 36.2	26.3	10 29.9	15.5	2 05.6	10.0	54.3
20	119 36.1	26.4	25 04.4	15.5	1 55.6	9.9	54.3
21	134 35.9	·· 26.4	39 38.9	15.6	1 45.7	9.9	54.3
22	149 35.8	26.4	54 13.5	15.6	1 35.8	10.0	54.3
23	164 35.7	26.4	68 48.1	15.5	1 25.8	9.9	54.3
21 00	179 35.5	N23 26.4	83 22.6	15.6	N 1 15.9	9.9	54.3
01	194 35.4	26.4	97 57.2	15.6	1 06.0	10.0	54.3
02	209 35.2	26.4	112 31.8	15.5	0 56.0	9.9	54.3
03	224 35.1	·· 26.4	127 06.3	15.6	0 46.1	10.0	54.3
04	239 35.0	26.4	141 40.9	15.6	0 36.1	10.0	54.3
05	254 34.8	26.4	156 15.5	15.6	0 26.1	9.9	54.3
06	269 34.7	N23 26.4	170 50.1	15.6	N 0 16.2	10.0	54.3
07	284 34.6	26.4	185 24.7	15.6	N 0 06.2	9.9	54.3
S 08	299 34.4	26.4	199 59.3	15.5	S 0 03.7	10.0	54.3
A 09	314 34.3	·· 26.4	214 33.8	15.6	0 13.7	10.0	54.3
T 10	329 34.2	26.4	229 08.4	15.6	0 23.7	9.9	54.3
U 11	344 34.0	26.4	243 43.0	15.6	0 33.6	10.0	54.3
R 12	359 33.9	N23 26.4	258 17.6	15.5	S 0 43.6	9.9	54.3
D 13	14 33.7	26.4	272 52.1	15.6	0 53.5	10.0	54.3
A 14	29 33.6	26.4	287 26.7	15.5	1 03.5	10.0	54.3
Y 15	44 33.5	·· 26.4	302 01.2	15.6	1 13.5	9.9	54.3
16	59 33.3	26.4	316 35.8	15.5	1 23.4	10.0	54.3
17	74 33.2	26.3	331 10.3	15.5	1 33.4	9.9	54.3
18	89 33.1	N23 26.3	345 44.8	15.6	S 1 43.3	9.9	54.3
19	104 32.9	26.3	0 19.4	15.5	1 53.2	10.0	54.3
20	119 32.8	26.3	14 53.9	15.5	2 03.2	9.9	54.3
21	134 32.6	·· 26.3	29 28.4	15.5	2 13.1	9.9	54.3
22	149 32.5	26.3	44 02.9	15.4	2 23.0	9.9	54.3
23	164 32.4	26.3	58 37.3	15.5	2 32.9	9.9	54.3
22 00	179 32.2	N23 26.3	73 11.8	15.4	S 2 42.8	9.9	54.3
01	194 32.1	26.3	87 46.2	15.5	2 52.7	9.9	54.3
02	209 32.0	26.2	102 20.7	15.4	3 02.6	9.9	54.3
03	224 31.8	·· 26.2	116 55.1	15.4	3 12.5	9.8	54.3
04	239 31.7	26.2	131 29.5	15.3	3 22.3	9.9	54.3
05	254 31.6	26.2	146 03.8	15.4	3 32.2	9.8	54.3
06	269 31.4	N23 26.2	160 38.2	15.3	S 3 42.0	9.9	54.3
07	284 31.3	26.2	175 12.5	15.4	3 51.9	9.8	54.3
08	299 31.2	26.1	189 46.9	15.3	4 01.7	9.8	54.4
S 09	314 31.0	·· 26.1	204 21.2	15.2	4 11.5	9.8	54.4
U 10	329 30.9	26.1	218 55.4	15.3	4 21.3	9.8	54.4
N 11	344 30.8	26.1	233 29.7	15.2	4 31.1	9.8	54.4
D 12	359 30.6	N23 26.1	248 03.9	15.2	S 4 40.9	9.7	54.4
A 13	14 30.5	26.0	262 38.1	15.2	4 50.6	9.7	54.4
Y 14	29 30.4	26.0	277 12.3	15.2	5 00.3	9.8	54.4
15	44 30.2	·· 26.0	291 46.5	15.1	5 10.1	9.7	54.4
16	59 30.1	26.0	306 20.6	15.1	5 19.8	9.7	54.4
17	74 30.0	25.9	320 54.7	15.1	5 29.5	9.6	54.4
18	89 29.8	N23 25.9	335 28.8	15.1	S 5 39.1	9.7	54.4
19	104 29.7	25.9	350 02.9	15.0	5 48.8	9.6	54.5
20	119 29.6	25.9	4 36.9	15.0	5 58.4	9.6	54.5
21	134 29.4	·· 25.8	19 10.9	14.9	6 08.0	9.6	54.5
22	149 29.3	25.8	33 44.8	15.0	6 17.6	9.6	54.5
23	164 29.2	25.8	48 18.8	14.9	6 27.2	9.5	54.5
	S.D. 15.8	d 0.0	S.D.	14.8	14.8		14.8

Lat.	Twilight Naut.	Twilight Civil	Sunrise	Moonrise 20	Moonrise 21	Moonrise 22	Moonrise 23
°	h m	h m	h m	h m	h m	h m	h m
N 72	□	□	□	11 25	13 01	14 37	16 17
N 70	□	□	□	11 30	12 59	14 30	16 03
68	□	□	□	11 33	12 58	14 24	15 51
66	□	□	□	11 36	12 57	14 18	15 41
64	////	////	01 31	11 39	12 57	14 14	15 33
62	////	////	02 09	11 41	12 56	14 10	15 26
60	////	00 49	02 36	11 44	12 55	14 07	15 20
N 58	////	01 40	02 56	11 45	12 55	14 04	15 15
56	////	02 10	03 13	11 47	12 54	14 02	15 10
54	00 45	02 33	03 27	11 48	12 54	13 59	15 06
52	01 32	02 51	03 40	11 50	12 53	13 57	15 02
50	02 00	03 06	03 51	11 51	12 53	13 56	14 59
45	02 46	03 36	04 13	11 53	12 52	13 51	14 51
N 40	03 17	03 58	04 31	11 56	12 52	13 48	14 45
35	03 40	04 17	04 46	11 57	12 51	13 45	14 40
30	03 58	04 32	04 59	11 59	12 51	13 43	14 35
20	04 28	04 57	05 21	12 02	12 50	13 38	14 27
N 10	04 50	05 17	05 40	12 04	12 49	13 34	14 20
0	05 09	05 36	05 58	12 07	12 49	13 31	14 14
S 10	05 26	05 53	06 16	12 09	12 48	13 27	14 07
20	05 43	06 10	06 34	12 12	12 47	13 23	14 01
30	05 59	06 29	06 55	12 14	12 47	13 19	13 53
35	06 08	06 40	07 08	12 16	12 46	13 17	13 48
40	06 17	06 51	07 22	12 18	12 46	13 14	13 43
45	06 28	07 05	07 39	12 20	12 45	13 11	13 38
S 50	06 39	07 21	08 00	12 23	12 45	13 07	13 31
52	06 45	07 29	08 10	12 24	12 44	13 05	13 28
54	06 50	07 37	08 21	12 25	12 44	13 03	13 24
56	06 57	07 46	08 33	12 26	12 44	13 01	13 20
58	07 03	07 56	08 48	12 28	12 43	12 59	13 16
S 60	07 11	08 08	09 06	12 30	12 43	12 56	13 11

Lat.	Sunset	Twilight Civil	Twilight Naut.	Moonset 20	Moonset 21	Moonset 22	Moonset 23
°	h m	h m	h m	h m	h m	h m	h m
N 72	□	□	□	00 49	00 41	00 32	00 23
N 70	□	□	□	00 42	00 39	00 36	00 33
68	□	□	□	00 37	00 38	00 39	00 41
66	□	□	□	00 32	00 37	00 42	00 47
64	22 33	////	////	00 28	00 36	00 44	00 53
62	21 54	////	////	00 24	00 36	00 46	00 58
60	21 28	23 15	////	00 21	00 35	00 48	01 02
N 58	21 07	22 23	////	00 19	00 34	00 50	01 06
56	20 50	21 53	////	00 16	00 34	00 51	01 09
54	20 36	21 31	23 19	00 14	00 33	00 52	01 12
52	20 24	21 13	22 31	00 12	00 33	00 53	01 15
50	20 13	20 58	22 03	00 10	00 32	00 55	01 17
45	19 50	20 28	21 18	00 06	00 32	00 57	01 23
N 40	19 32	20 05	20 47	00 03	00 31	00 59	01 27
35	19 17	19 47	20 24	00 00	00 30	01 00	01 31
30	19 04	19 32	20 05	24 30	00 30	01 02	01 35
20	18 42	19 07	19 36	24 29	00 29	01 04	01 41
N 10	18 23	18 46	19 13	24 28	00 28	01 07	01 46
0	18 05	18 28	18 54	24 27	00 27	01 09	01 51
S 10	17 48	18 11	18 37	24 26	00 26	01 11	01 56
20	17 29	17 53	18 21	24 25	00 25	01 13	02 02
30	17 08	17 35	18 04	24 24	00 24	01 16	02 08
35	16 56	17 24	17 56	24 23	00 23	01 17	02 11
40	16 42	17 12	17 46	24 23	00 23	01 19	02 15
45	16 25	16 59	17 36	24 22	00 22	01 21	02 20
S 50	16 04	16 42	17 24	24 21	00 21	01 23	02 26
52	15 54	16 35	17 19	24 20	00 20	01 24	02 28
54	15 43	16 27	17 13	24 20	00 20	01 25	02 31
56	15 30	16 18	17 07	24 19	00 19	01 27	02 34
58	15 15	16 07	17 00	24 19	00 19	01 28	02 38
S 60	14 58	15 56	16 53	24 18	00 18	01 30	02 42

Day	SUN Eqn. of Time 00ʰ	SUN Eqn. of Time 12ʰ	SUN Mer. Pass.	MOON Mer. Pass. Upper	MOON Mer. Pass. Lower	Age	Phase
	m s	m s	h m	h m	h m	d	
20	01 25	01 31	12 02	18 17	05 56	08	◐
21	01 38	01 44	12 02	18 59	06 38	09	
22	01 51	01 57	12 02	19 41	07 20	10	

APPENDIX 3

1980 JUNE 20, 21, 22 (FRI., SAT., SUN.)

	G.M.T.	ARIES	VENUS −3.2		MARS +1.1		JUPITER −1.5		SATURN +1.3	
d	h	G.H.A. ° ′	G.H.A. ° ′	Dec. ° ′	G.H.A. ° ′	Dec. ° ′	G.H.A. ° ′	Dec. ° ′	G.H.A. ° ′	Dec. ° ′
20	00	268 21.4	187 29.4	N20 56.8	98 10.4	N 5 03.9	111 41.1	N10 55.7	95 51.9	N 5 38.5
	01	283 23.9	202 33.4	56.2	113 11.7	03.4	126 43.2	55.6	110 54.2	38.4
	02	298 26.3	217 37.4	55.6	128 13.0	02.9	141 45.4	55.4	125 56.6	38.4
	03	313 28.8	232 41.3	·· 55.0	143 14.4	·· 02.3	156 47.5	·· 55.3	140 58.9	·· 38.3
	04	328 31.3	247 45.3	54.3	158 15.7	01.8	171 49.6	55.2	156 01.3	38.3
	05	343 33.7	262 49.3	53.7	173 17.0	01.2	186 51.7	55.0	171 03.6	38.2
	06	358 36.2	277 53.3	N20 53.1	188 18.3	N 5 00.7	201 53.9	N10 54.9	186 06.0	N 5 38.2
	07	13 38.6	292 57.2	52.5	203 19.7	5 00.2	216 56.0	54.8	201 08.4	38.1
	08	28 41.1	308 01.2	51.8	218 21.0	4 59.6	231 58.1	54.6	216 10.7	38.1
F	09	43 43.6	323 05.2	·· 51.2	233 22.3	·· 59.1	247 00.3	·· 54.5	231 13.1	·· 38.0
R	10	58 46.0	338 09.1	50.6	248 23.6	58.5	262 02.4	54.4	246 15.4	38.0
I	11	73 48.5	353 13.1	50.0	263 24.9	58.0	277 04.5	54.2	261 17.8	37.9
D	12	88 51.0	8 17.1	N20 49.4	278 26.3	N 4 57.5	292 06.7	N10 54.1	276 20.1	N 5 37.9
A	13	103 53.4	23 21.0	48.7	293 27.6	56.9	307 08.8	54.0	291 22.5	37.8
Y	14	118 55.9	38 25.0	48.1	308 28.9	56.4	322 10.9	53.8	306 24.9	37.7
	15	133 58.4	53 28.9	·· 47.5	323 30.2	·· 55.8	337 13.1	·· 53.7	321 27.2	·· 37.7
	16	149 00.8	68 32.9	46.9	338 31.6	55.3	352 15.2	53.5	336 29.6	37.6
	17	164 03.3	83 36.8	46.3	353 32.9	54.8	7 17.3	53.4	351 31.9	37.6
	18	179 05.7	98 40.8	N20 45.6	8 34.2	N 4 54.2	22 19.5	N10 53.3	6 34.3	N 5 37.5
	19	194 08.2	113 44.7	45.0	23 35.5	53.7	37 21.6	53.1	21 36.6	37.5
	20	209 10.7	128 48.7	44.4	38 36.8	53.1	52 23.7	53.0	36 39.0	37.4
	21	224 13.1	143 52.6	·· 43.8	53 38.2	·· 52.6	67 25.8	·· 52.9	51 41.3	·· 37.4
	22	239 15.6	158 56.5	43.2	68 39.5	52.0	82 28.0	52.7	66 43.7	37.3
	23	254 18.1	174 00.5	42.6	83 40.8	51.5	97 30.1	52.6	81 46.0	37.3
21	00	269 20.5	189 04.4	N20 42.0	98 42.1	N 4 51.0	112 32.2	N10 52.5	96 48.4	N 5 37.2
	01	284 23.0	204 08.3	41.3	113 43.4	50.4	127 34.4	52.3	111 50.8	37.1
	02	299 25.5	219 12.3	40.7	128 44.7	49.9	142 36.5	52.2	126 53.1	37.1
	03	314 27.9	234 16.2	·· 40.1	143 46.1	·· 49.3	157 38.6	·· 52.1	141 55.5	·· 37.0
	04	329 30.4	249 20.1	39.5	158 47.4	48.8	172 40.7	51.9	156 57.8	37.0
	05	344 32.9	264 24.0	38.9	173 48.7	48.2	187 42.9	51.8	172 00.2	36.9
	06	359 35.3	279 27.9	N20 38.3	188 50.0	N 4 47.7	202 45.0	N10 51.7	187 02.5	N 5 36.9
	07	14 37.8	294 31.9	37.7	203 51.3	47.2	217 47.1	51.5	202 04.9	36.8
S	08	29 40.2	309 35.8	37.1	218 52.7	46.6	232 49.2	51.4	217 07.2	36.8
A	09	44 42.7	324 39.7	·· 36.5	233 54.0	·· 46.1	247 51.4	·· 51.3	232 09.6	·· 36.7
T	10	59 45.2	339 43.6	35.9	248 55.3	45.5	262 53.5	51.1	247 11.9	36.6
U	11	74 47.6	354 47.5	35.3	263 56.6	45.0	277 55.6	51.0	262 14.3	36.6
R	12	89 50.1	9 51.4	N20 34.6	278 57.9	N 4 44.4	292 57.8	N10 50.8	277 16.6	N 5 36.5
D	13	104 52.6	24 55.3	34.0	293 59.2	43.9	307 59.9	50.7	292 19.0	36.5
A	14	119 55.0	39 59.2	33.4	309 00.5	43.3	323 02.0	50.6	307 21.4	36.4
Y	15	134 57.5	55 03.1	·· 32.8	324 01.9	·· 42.8	338 04.1	·· 50.4	322 23.7	·· 36.4
	16	150 00.0	70 07.0	32.2	339 03.2	42.3	353 06.3	50.3	337 26.1	36.3
	17	165 02.4	85 10.8	31.6	354 04.5	41.7	8 08.4	50.2	352 28.4	36.3
	18	180 04.9	100 14.7	N20 31.0	9 05.8	N 4 41.2	23 10.5	N10 50.0	7 30.8	N 5 36.2
	19	195 07.4	115 18.6	30.4	24 07.1	40.6	38 12.6	49.9	22 33.1	36.1
	20	210 09.8	130 22.5	29.8	39 08.4	40.1	53 14.8	49.8	37 35.5	36.1
	21	225 12.3	145 26.4	·· 29.2	54 09.7	·· 39.5	68 16.9	·· 49.6	52 37.8	·· 36.0
	22	240 14.7	160 30.2	28.6	69 11.0	39.0	83 19.0	49.5	67 40.2	36.0
	23	255 17.2	175 34.1	28.0	84 12.4	38.4	98 21.1	49.3	82 42.5	35.9
22	00	270 19.7	190 38.0	N20 27.4	99 13.7	N 4 37.9	113 23.3	N10 49.2	97 44.9	N 5 35.9
	01	285 22.1	205 41.8	26.8	114 15.0	37.4	128 25.4	49.1	112 47.2	35.8
	02	300 24.6	220 45.7	26.2	129 16.3	36.8	143 27.5	49.0	127 49.6	35.7
	03	315 27.1	235 49.6	·· 25.6	144 17.6	·· 36.3	158 29.6	·· 48.8	142 51.9	·· 35.7
	04	330 29.5	250 53.4	25.0	159 18.9	35.7	173 31.8	48.7	157 54.3	35.6
	05	345 32.0	265 57.3	24.4	174 20.2	35.2	188 33.9	48.5	172 56.6	35.6
	06	0 34.5	281 01.1	N20 23.9	189 21.6	N 4 34.6	203 36.0	N10 48.4	187 59.0	N 5 35.5
	07	15 36.9	296 05.0	23.3	204 22.9	34.1	218 38.1	48.3	203 01.3	35.5
	08	30 39.4	311 08.8	22.7	219 24.2	33.5	233 40.3	48.1	218 03.7	35.4
S	09	45 41.8	326 12.7	·· 22.1	234 25.5	·· 33.0	248 42.4	·· 48.0	233 06.0	·· 35.3
U	10	60 44.3	341 16.5	21.5	249 26.8	32.4	263 44.5	47.9	248 08.4	35.3
N	11	75 46.8	356 20.3	20.9	264 28.1	31.9	278 46.6	47.7	263 10.7	35.2
D	12	90 49.2	11 24.2	N20 20.3	279 29.4	N 4 31.3	293 48.7	N10 47.6	278 13.1	N 5 35.2
A	13	105 51.7	26 28.0	19.7	294 30.7	30.8	308 50.9	47.5	293 15.4	35.1
Y	14	120 54.2	41 31.8	19.2	309 32.0	30.3	323 53.0	47.3	308 17.8	35.1
	15	135 56.6	56 35.6	·· 18.6	324 33.3	·· 29.7	338 55.1	·· 47.2	323 20.1	·· 35.0
	16	150 59.1	71 39.5	18.0	339 34.7	29.2	353 57.2	47.0	338 22.5	34.9
	17	166 01.6	86 43.3	17.4	354 36.0	28.6	8 59.4	46.9	353 24.8	34.9
	18	181 04.0	101 47.1	N20 16.8	9 37.3	N 4 28.1	24 01.5	N10 46.8	8 27.2	N 5 34.8
	19	196 06.5	116 50.9	16.2	24 38.6	27.5	39 03.6	46.6	23 29.5	34.8
	20	211 09.0	131 54.7	15.7	39 39.9	27.0	54 05.7	46.5	38 31.9	34.7
	21	226 11.4	146 58.5	·· 15.1	54 41.2	·· 26.4	69 07.8	·· 46.3	53 34.2	·· 34.7
	22	241 13.9	162 02.3	14.5	69 42.5	25.9	84 10.0	46.2	68 36.6	34.6
	23	256 16.3	177 06.1	13.9	84 43.8	25.3	99 12.1	46.1	83 38.9	34.5
Mer. Pass.		h m 6 01.6	v 3.9	d 0.6	v 1.3	d 0.5	v 2.1	d 0.1	v 2.4	d 0.1

STARS		
Name	S.H.A. ° ′	Dec. ° ′
Acamar	315 37.7	S40 22.9
Achernar	335 45.7	S57 20.0
Acrux	173 37.3	S62 59.7
Adhara	255 32.6	S28 56.8
Aldebaran	291 18.5	N16 28.1
Alioth	166 42.6	N56 04.3
Alkaid	153 18.5	N49 25.0
Al Na'ir	28 15.0	S47 03.2
Alnilam	276 12.2	S 1 12.9
Alphard	218 21.0	S 8 34.5
Alphecca	126 32.0	N26 47.0
Alpheratz	358 09.5	N28 58.7
Altair	62 32.4	N 8 49.0
Ankaa	353 40.5	S42 24.6
Antares	112 56.7	S26 23.3
Arcturus	146 18.5	N19 17.2
Atria	108 20.5	S68 59.6
Avior	234 28.8	S59 27.0
Bellatrix	278 59.3	N 6 19.8
Betelgeuse	271 28.8	N 7 24.1
Canopus	264 07.8	S52 41.2
Capella	281 12.0	N45 58.6
Deneb	49 48.2	N45 12.5
Denebola	182 59.3	N14 41.0
Diphda	349 21.1	S18 05.6
Dubhe	194 22.6	N61 51.7
Elnath	278 44.7	N28 35.4
Eltanin	90 57.3	N51 29.6
Enif	34 11.6	N 9 47.1
Fomalhaut	15 51.5	S29 43.4
Gacrux	172 28.8	S57 00.4
Gienah	176 18.1	S17 26.0
Hadar	149 23.2	S60 16.9
Hamal	328 29.3	N23 22.0
Kaus Aust.	84 16.7	S34 23.6
Kochab	137 18.3	N74 14.5
Markab	14 03.2	N15 05.9
Menkar	314 41.6	N 4 00.7
Menkent	148 37.0	S36 16.5
Miaplacidus	221 45.5	S69 38.5
Mirfak	309 16.7	N49 47.3
Nunki	76 29.0	S26 19.2
Peacock	53 58.2	S56 47.7
Pollux	243 58.7	N28 04.4
Procyon	245 26.3	N 5 16.5
Rasalhague	96 29.4	N12 34.5
Regulus	208 10.4	N12 03.9
Rigel	281 36.5	S 8 13.5
Rigil Kent.	140 25.6	S60 45.4
Sabik	102 41.0	S15 42.0
Schedar	350 09.2	N56 25.5
Shaula	96 55.6	S37 05.3
Sirius	258 56.2	S16 41.5
Spica	158 57.6	S11 03.5
Suhail	223 11.2	S43 21.4
Vega	80 55.5	N38 46.0
Zuben'ubi	137 33.0	S15 57.6

	S.H.A. ° ′	Mer. Pass. h m
Venus	279 43.9	11 21
Mars	189 21.6	17 24
Jupiter	203 11.7	16 28
Saturn	187 27.9	17 30

1980 SEPTEMBER 21, 22, 23 (SUN., MON., TUES.)

G.M.T.		SUN G.H.A.	SUN Dec.	MOON G.H.A.	v	MOON Dec.	d	H.P.
d	h	° ′	° ′	° ′	′	° ′	′	′
21	00	181 42.7	N 0 43.9	47 45.2	7.4	S16 53.3	6.4	59.0
	01	196 42.9	42.9	62 11.6	7.4	16 46.9	6.5	59.0
	02	211 43.1	42.0	76 38.0	7.3	16 40.4	6.7	59.0
	03	226 43.4	· · 41.0	91 04.3	7.4	16 33.7	6.7	59.1
	04	241 43.6	40.0	105 30.7	7.3	16 27.0	6.8	59.1
	05	256 43.8	39.1	119 57.0	7.4	16 20.2	7.0	59.2
	06	271 44.0	N 0 38.1	134 23.4	7.3	S16 13.2	7.1	59.2
	07	286 44.2	37.1	148 49.7	7.3	16 06.1	7.2	59.2
	08	301 44.5	36.1	163 16.0	7.4	15 58.9	7.3	59.3
S	09	316 44.7	· · 35.2	177 42.4	7.3	15 51.6	7.4	59.3
U	10	331 44.9	34.2	192 08.7	7.3	15 44.2	7.5	59.4
N	11	346 45.1	33.2	206 35.0	7.3	15 36.7	7.6	59.4
D	12	1 45.3	N 0 32.2	221 01.3	7.3	S15 29.1	7.7	59.4
A	13	16 45.6	31.3	235 27.6	7.3	15 21.4	7.9	59.5
Y	14	31 45.8	30.3	249 53.9	7.3	15 13.5	7.9	59.5
	15	46 46.0	· · 29.3	264 20.2	7.3	15 05.6	8.1	59.5
	16	61 46.2	28.4	278 46.5	7.3	14 57.5	8.1	59.6
	17	76 46.5	27.4	293 12.8	7.3	14 49.4	8.3	59.6
	18	91 46.7	N 0 26.4	307 39.1	7.3	S14 41.1	8.4	59.7
	19	106 46.9	25.4	322 05.4	7.2	14 32.7	8.4	59.7
	20	121 47.1	24.5	336 31.6	7.3	14 24.3	8.6	59.7
	21	136 47.3	· · 23.5	350 57.9	7.3	14 15.7	8.7	59.8
	22	151 47.6	22.5	5 24.2	7.3	14 07.0	8.8	59.8
	23	166 47.8	21.5	19 50.5	7.3	13 58.2	8.9	59.8
22	00	181 48.0	N 0 20.6	34 16.8	7.3	S13 49.3	8.9	59.9
	01	196 48.2	19.6	48 43.1	7.3	13 40.4	9.1	59.9
	02	211 48.4	18.6	63 09.4	7.3	13 31.3	9.2	59.9
	03	226 48.7	· · 17.7	77 35.7	7.3	13 22.1	9.3	60.0
	04	241 48.9	16.7	92 02.0	7.3	13 12.8	9.3	60.0
	05	256 49.1	15.7	106 28.3	7.3	13 03.5	9.5	60.1
	06	271 49.3	N 0 14.7	120 54.6	7.3	S12 54.0	9.6	60.1
	07	286 49.5	13.8	135 20.9	7.3	12 44.4	9.6	60.1
	08	301 49.8	12.8	149 47.2	7.3	12 34.8	9.8	60.2
M	09	316 50.0	· · 11.8	164 13.5	7.3	12 25.0	9.8	60.2
O	10	331 50.2	10.8	178 39.8	7.3	12 15.2	9.9	60.2
N	11	346 50.4	09.9	193 06.1	7.3	12 05.3	10.0	60.2
D	12	1 50.6	N 0 08.9	207 32.4	7.4	S11 55.3	10.1	60.3
A	13	16 50.9	07.9	221 58.8	7.3	11 45.2	10.2	60.3
Y	14	31 51.1	07.0	236 25.1	7.3	11 35.0	10.3	60.3
	15	46 51.3	· · 06.0	250 51.4	7.4	11 24.7	10.4	60.4
	16	61 51.5	05.0	265 17.8	7.3	11 14.3	10.4	60.4
	17	76 51.7	04.0	279 44.1	7.4	11 03.9	10.6	60.4
	18	91 52.0	N 0 03.1	294 10.5	7.3	S10 53.3	10.6	60.5
	19	106 52.2	02.1	308 36.8	7.4	10 42.7	10.7	60.5
	20	121 52.4	01.1	323 03.2	7.4	10 32.0	10.7	60.5
	21	136 52.6	N 0 00.1	337 29.6	7.4	10 21.3	10.9	60.6
	22	151 52.8	S 0 00.8	351 56.0	7.4	10 10.4	10.9	60.6
	23	166 53.1	01.8	6 22.4	7.3	9 59.5	11.0	60.6
23	00	181 53.3	S 0 02.8	20 48.7	7.4	S 9 48.5	11.1	60.6
	01	196 53.5	03.8	35 15.1	7.4	9 37.4	11.1	60.7
	02	211 53.7	04.7	49 41.5	7.5	9 26.3	11.2	60.7
	03	226 53.9	· · 05.7	64 08.0	7.4	9 15.1	11.3	60.7
	04	241 54.2	06.7	78 34.4	7.4	9 03.8	11.4	60.7
	05	256 54.4	07.6	93 00.8	7.4	8 52.4	11.4	60.8
	06	271 54.6	S 0 08.6	107 27.2	7.5	S 8 41.0	11.5	60.8
	07	286 54.8	09.6	121 53.7	7.4	8 29.5	11.5	60.8
	08	301 55.0	10.6	136 20.1	7.5	8 18.0	11.7	60.8
T	09	316 55.3	· · 11.5	150 46.6	7.4	8 06.3	11.6	60.9
U	10	331 55.5	12.5	165 13.0	7.5	7 54.7	11.8	60.9
E	11	346 55.7	13.5	179 39.5	7.4	7 42.9	11.8	60.9
S	12	1 55.9	S 0 14.5	194 05.9	7.5	S 7 31.1	11.8	60.9
D	13	16 56.1	15.4	208 32.4	7.5	7 19.3	12.0	60.9
A	14	31 56.4	16.4	222 58.9	7.5	7 07.3	11.9	61.0
Y	15	46 56.6	· · 17.4	237 25.4	7.5	6 55.4	12.1	61.0
	16	61 56.8	18.4	251 51.9	7.5	6 43.3	12.0	61.0
	17	76 57.0	19.3	266 18.4	7.5	6 31.3	12.2	61.0
	18	91 57.2	S 0 20.3	280 44.9	7.5	S 6 19.1	12.1	61.0
	19	106 57.4	21.3	295 11.4	7.5	6 07.0	12.3	61.1
	20	121 57.7	22.3	309 37.9	7.5	5 54.7	12.2	61.1
	21	136 57.9	· · 23.2	324 04.4	7.6	5 42.5	12.3	61.1
	22	151 58.1	24.2	338 31.0	7.5	5 30.2	12.4	61.1
	23	166 58.3	25.2	352 57.5	7.5	5 17.8	12.4	61.1
		S.D. 16.0	*d* 1.0	S.D.		16.2	16.4	16.6

Lat.	Twilight Naut.	Twilight Civil	Sunrise	Moonrise 21	Moonrise 22	Moonrise 23	Moonrise 24
°	h m	h m	h m	h m	h m	h m	h m
N 72	02 59	04 30	05 39	19 07	18 51	18 39	18 28
N 70	03 19	04 38	05 40	18 36	18 33	18 30	18 27
68	03 34	04 45	05 41	18 14	18 19	18 23	18 25
66	03 47	04 51	05 42	17 56	18 08	18 16	18 24
64	03 57	04 55	05 43	17 41	17 58	18 11	18 23
62	04 05	04 59	05 44	17 29	17 50	18 07	18 22
60	04 12	05 03	05 44	17 18	17 42	18 03	18 21
N 58	04 18	05 06	05 45	17 09	17 36	17 59	18 20
56	04 24	05 08	05 45	17 01	17 30	17 56	18 20
54	04 28	05 10	05 46	16 54	17 25	17 53	18 19
52	04 32	05 12	05 46	16 47	17 21	17 51	18 19
50	04 36	05 14	05 46	16 41	17 16	17 48	18 18
45	04 43	05 18	05 47	16 29	17 07	17 43	18 17
N 40	04 49	05 20	05 48	16 18	17 00	17 39	18 16
35	04 53	05 23	05 48	16 09	16 53	17 35	18 15
30	04 57	05 24	05 48	16 01	16 47	17 32	18 15
20	05 01	05 27	05 49	15 47	16 37	17 26	18 14
N 10	05 04	05 28	05 49	15 35	16 29	17 21	18 13
0	05 05	05 29	05 49	15 24	16 20	17 16	18 12
S 10	05 04	05 29	05 50	15 13	16 12	17 11	18 11
20	05 02	05 28	05 50	15 01	16 03	17 06	18 10
30	04 58	05 26	05 49	14 47	15 53	17 00	18 09
35	04 55	05 24	05 49	14 39	15 47	16 57	18 08
40	04 51	05 22	05 49	14 30	15 40	16 53	18 07
45	04 45	05 20	05 49	14 19	15 33	16 49	18 07
S 50	04 39	05 17	05 49	14 06	15 23	16 44	18 06
52	04 35	05 15	05 49	14 00	15 19	16 41	18 05
54	04 31	05 13	05 48	13 53	15 14	16 39	18 05
56	04 27	05 11	05 48	13 46	15 09	16 36	18 04
58	04 22	05 09	05 48	13 37	15 03	16 32	18 04
S 60	04 17	05 06	05 48	13 28	14 56	16 29	18 03

Lat.	Sunset	Twilight Civil	Twilight Naut.	Moonset 21	Moonset 22	Moonset 23	Moonset 24
°	h m	h m	h m	h m	h m	h m	h m
N 72	18 04	19 12	20 42	24 25	00 25	02 39	04 48
N 70	18 03	19 04	20 22	24 54	00 54	02 54	04 54
68	18 02	18 58	20 08	25 16	01 16	03 07	04 59
66	18 01	18 52	19 56	25 33	01 33	03 17	05 03
64	18 01	18 48	19 46	00 14	01 47	03 25	05 07
62	18 00	18 44	19 38	00 30	01 58	03 33	05 10
60	18 00	18 41	19 31	00 43	02 08	03 39	05 13
N 58	17 59	18 38	19 25	00 54	02 16	03 44	05 15
56	17 59	18 36	19 20	01 04	02 24	03 49	05 17
54	17 58	18 34	19 16	01 13	02 30	03 53	05 19
52	17 58	18 32	19 12	01 20	02 36	03 57	05 21
50	17 58	18 30	19 08	01 27	02 42	04 01	05 22
45	17 57	18 27	19 01	01 42	02 53	04 08	05 26
N 40	17 57	18 24	18 56	01 54	03 03	04 15	05 28
35	17 57	18 22	18 51	02 04	03 11	04 20	05 31
30	17 57	18 20	18 48	02 13	03 18	04 25	05 33
20	17 56	18 18	18 44	02 29	03 30	04 33	05 36
N 10	17 56	18 17	18 41	02 42	03 41	04 40	05 40
0	17 56	18 17	18 41	02 55	03 51	04 47	05 42
S 10	17 56	18 17	18 41	03 07	04 01	04 53	05 45
20	17 56	18 18	18 44	03 21	04 11	05 00	05 48
30	17 56	18 20	18 48	03 36	04 23	05 08	05 52
35	17 56	18 22	18 51	03 44	04 30	05 13	05 54
40	17 57	18 24	18 55	03 54	04 37	05 18	05 56
45	17 57	18 26	19 01	04 06	04 46	05 23	05 58
S 50	17 57	18 30	19 08	04 20	04 57	05 30	06 01
52	17 58	18 31	19 11	04 26	05 02	05 34	06 02
54	17 58	18 33	19 15	04 34	05 08	05 37	06 04
56	17 58	18 35	19 20	04 42	05 14	05 41	06 05
58	17 59	18 38	19 25	04 51	05 20	05 45	06 07
S 60	17 59	18 41	19 31	05 01	05 28	05 50	06 09

Day	SUN Eqn. of Time 00ʰ	SUN Eqn. of Time 12ʰ	SUN Mer. Pass.	MOON Mer. Pass. Upper	MOON Mer. Pass. Lower	Age	Phase
	m s	m s	h m	h m	h m	d	
21	06 50	07 01	11 53	21 38	09 10	12	
22	07 12	07 22	11 53	22 34	10 06	13	○
23	07 33	07 43	11 52	23 29	11 01	14	

APPENDIX 4

POLARIS (POLE STAR) TABLES, 1980

FOR DETERMINING LATITUDE FROM SEXTANT ALTITUDE AND FOR AZIMUTH

L.H.A. ARIES	120°–129°	130°–139°	140°–149°	150°–159°	160°–169°	170°–179°	180°–189°	190°–199°	200°–209°	210°–219°	220°–229°	230°–239°
	a_0	a_0	a_0	a_0	a_0	a_0	a_0	a_0	a_0	a_0	a_0	a_0
°	° ′	° ′	° ′	° ′	° ′	° ′	° ′	° ′	° ′	° ′	° ′	° ′
0	0 56·5	1 05·1	1 13·6	1 21·5	1 28·8	1 35·1	1 40·4	1 44·4	1 47·0	1 48·2	1 48·0	1 46·2
1	57·4	06·0	14·4	22·3	29·4	35·7	40·8	44·7	47·2	48·3	47·8	46·0
2	58·2	06·8	15·2	23·0	30·1	36·3	41·3	45·0	47·4	48·3	47·7	45·7
3	0 59·1	07·7	16·0	23·8	30·8	36·8	41·7	45·3	47·5	48·3	47·6	45·4
4	1 00·0	08·5	16·8	24·5	31·4	37·4	42·1	45·6	47·7	48·3	47·4	45·1
5	1 00·8	1 09·4	1 17·6	1 25·2	1 32·1	1 37·9	1 42·5	1 45·9	1 47·8	1 48·3	1 47·3	1 44·8
6	01·7	10·2	18·4	26·0	32·7	38·4	42·9	46·1	47·9	48·2	47·1	44·5
7	02·6	11·1	19·2	26·7	33·3	38·9	43·3	46·4	48·0	48·2	46·9	44·1
8	03·4	11·9	20·0	27·4	33·9	39·4	43·7	46·6	48·1	48·1	46·7	43·8
9	04·3	12·7	20·7	28·1	34·5	39·9	44·0	46·8	48·2	48·0	46·4	43·4
10	1 05·1	1 13·6	1 21·5	1 28·8	1 35·1	1 40·4	1 44·4	1 47·0	1 48·2	1 48·0	1 46·2	1 43·0
Lat.	a_1	a_1	a_1	a_1	a_1	a_1	a_1	a_1	a_1	a_1	a_1	a_1
°	′	′	′	′	′	′	′	′	′	′	′	′
0	0·2	0·2	0·2	0·3	0·4	0·4	0·5	0·6	0·6	0·6	0·6	0·5
10	·2	·3	·3	·3	·4	·5	·5	·6	·6	·6	·6	·5
20	·3	·3	·3	·4	·4	·5	·5	·6	·6	·6	·6	·6
30	·4	·4	·4	·4	·5	·5	·6	·6	·6	·6	·6	·6
40	0·5	0·5	0·5	0·5	0·5	0·6	0·6	0·6	0·6	0·6	0·6	0·6
45	·5	·5	·5	·6	·6	·6	·6	·6	·6	·6	·6	·6
50	·6	·6	·6	·6	·6	·6	·6	·6	·6	·6	·6	·6
55	·7	·7	·7	·7	·6	·6	·6	·6	·6	·6	·6	·6
60	·8	·8	·8	·7	·7	·7	·6	·6	·6	·6	·6	·6
62	0·8	0·8	0·8	0·8	0·7	0·7	0·7	0·6	0·6	0·6	0·6	0·6
64	0·9	0·9	·9	·8	·8	·7	·7	·6	·6	·6	·6	·6
66	1·0	1·0	0·9	·9	·8	·7	·7	·6	·6	·6	·6	·7
68	1·1	1·0	1·0	0·9	0·9	0·8	0·7	0·6	0·6	0·6	0·6	0·7
Month	a_2	a_2	a_2	a_2	a_2	a_2	a_2	a_2	a_2	a_2	a_2	a_2
	′	′	′	′	′	′	′	′	′	′	′	′
Jan.	0·6	0·6	0·6	0·5	0·5	0·5	0·5	0·5	0·5	0·5	0·5	0·5
Feb.	·8	·7	·7	·7	·6	·6	·6	·5	·5	·5	·5	·4
Mar.	0·9	0·9	0·9	0·8	·8	·8	·7	·7	·6	·6	·5	·5
Apr.	1·0	1·0	1·0	1·0	0·9	0·9	0·9	0·8	0·8	0·7	0·6	0·6
May	0·9	1·0	1·0	1·0	1·0	1·0	1·0	0·9	0·9	0·8	·8	·7
June	·8	0·9	0·9	1·0	1·0	1·0	1·0	1·0	1·0	1·0	0·9	·9
July	0·7	0·7	0·8	0·8	0·9	0·9	1·0	1·0	1·0	1·0	1·0	0·9
Aug.	·5	·6	·6	·7	·7	·8	0·8	0·9	0·9	0·9	1·0	1·0
Sept.	·4	·4	·4	·5	·6	·6	·7	·7	·8	·8	0·9	0·9
Oct.	0·3	0·3	0·3	0·3	0·4	0·4	0·5	0·5	0·6	0·7	0·7	0·8
Nov.	·2	·2	·2	·2	·2	·3	·3	·4	·4	·5	·5	·6
Dec.	0·3	0·3	0·2	0·2	0·2	0·2	0·2	0·2	0·3	0·3	0·4	0·4
Lat.	AZIMUTH											
°	°	°	°	°	°	°	°	°	°	°	°	°
0	359·2	359·2	359·2	359·3	359·4	359·5	359·6	359·7	359·9	0·0	0·2	0·3
20	359·1	359·1	359·2	359·3	359·3	359·5	359·6	359·7	359·9	0·0	0·2	0·3
40	358·9	358·9	359·0	359·1	359·2	359·3	359·5	359·7	359·8	0·0	0·2	0·4
50	358·7	358·7	358·8	358·9	359·1	359·2	359·4	359·6	359·8	0·0	0·3	0·5
55	358·6	358·6	358·7	358·8	358·9	359·1	359·3	359·6	359·8	0·0	0·3	0·5
60	358·4	358·4	358·5	358·6	358·8	359·0	359·2	359·5	359·8	0·1	0·3	0·6
65	358·1	358·1	358·2	358·4	358·6	358·8	359·1	359·4	359·7	0·1	0·4	0·7

ILLUSTRATION

On 1980 April 21 at G.M.T. $23^h\ 18^m\ 56^s$ in longitude W. 37° 14′ the apparent altitude (corrected for refraction), *Ho*, of *Polaris* was 49° 31′·6.

From the daily pages:	° ′
G.H.A. Aries (23^h)	195 09·8
Increment ($18^m\ 56^s$)	4 44·8
Longitude (west)	−37 14
L.H.A. Aries	162 41

	° ′
Ho	49 31·6
a_0 (argument 162° 41′)	1 30·6
a_1 (lat. 50° approx.)	0·6
a_2 (April)	0·9
Sum −1° = Lat. =	50 03·7

CONVERSION OF ARC TO TIME

0°–59°		60°–119°		120°–179°		180°–239°		240°–299°		300°–359°			0′·00	0′·25	0′·50	0′·75
°	h m	°	h m	°	h m	°	h m	°	h m	°	h m	′	m s	m s	m s	m s
0	0 00	60	4 00	120	8 00	180	12 00	240	16 00	300	20 00	0	0 00	0 01	0 02	0 03
1	0 04	61	4 04	121	8 04	181	12 04	241	16 04	301	20 04	1	0 04	0 05	0 06	0 07
2	0 08	62	4 08	122	8 08	182	12 08	242	16 08	302	20 08	2	0 08	0 09	0 10	0 11
3	0 12	63	4 12	123	8 12	183	12 12	243	16 12	303	20 12	3	0 12	0 13	0 14	0 15
4	0 16	64	4 16	124	8 16	184	12 16	244	16 16	304	20 16	4	0 16	0 17	0 18	0 19
5	0 20	65	4 20	125	8 20	185	12 20	245	16 20	305	20 20	5	0 20	0 21	0 22	0 23
6	0 24	66	4 24	126	8 24	186	12 24	246	16 24	306	20 24	6	0 24	0 25	0 26	0 27
7	0 28	67	4 28	127	8 28	187	12 28	247	16 28	307	20 28	7	0 28	0 29	0 30	0 31
8	0 32	68	4 32	128	8 32	188	12 32	248	16 32	308	20 32	8	0 32	0 33	0 34	0 35
9	0 36	69	4 36	129	8 36	189	12 36	249	16 36	309	20 36	9	0 36	0 37	0 38	0 39
10	0 40	70	4 40	130	8 40	190	12 40	250	16 40	310	20 40	10	0 40	0 41	0 42	0 43
11	0 44	71	4 44	131	8 44	191	12 44	251	16 44	311	20 44	11	0 44	0 45	0 46	0 47
12	0 48	72	4 48	132	8 48	192	12 48	252	16 48	312	20 48	12	0 48	0 49	0 50	0 51
13	0 52	73	4 52	133	8 52	193	12 52	253	16 52	313	20 52	13	0 52	0 53	0 54	0 55
14	0 56	74	4 56	134	8 56	194	12 56	254	16 56	314	20 56	14	0 56	0 57	0 58	0 59
15	1 00	75	5 00	135	9 00	195	13 00	255	17 00	315	21 00	15	1 00	1 01	1 02	1 03
16	1 04	76	5 04	136	9 04	196	13 04	256	17 04	316	21 04	16	1 04	1 05	1 06	1 07
17	1 08	77	5 08	137	9 08	197	13 08	257	17 08	317	21 08	17	1 08	1 09	1 10	1 11
18	1 12	78	5 12	138	9 12	198	13 12	258	17 12	318	21 12	18	1 12	1 13	1 14	1 15
19	1 16	79	5 16	139	9 16	199	13 16	259	17 16	319	21 16	19	1 16	1 17	1 18	1 19
20	1 20	80	5 20	140	9 20	200	13 20	260	17 20	320	21 20	20	1 20	1 21	1 22	1 23
21	1 24	81	5 24	141	9 24	201	13 24	261	17 24	321	21 24	21	1 24	1 25	1 26	1 27
22	1 28	82	5 28	142	9 28	202	13 28	262	17 28	322	21 28	22	1 28	1 29	1 30	1 31
23	1 32	83	5 32	143	9 32	203	13 32	263	17 32	323	21 32	23	1 32	1 33	1 34	1 35
24	1 36	84	5 36	144	9 36	204	13 36	264	17 36	324	21 36	24	1 36	1 37	1 38	1 39
25	1 40	85	5 40	145	9 40	205	13 40	265	17 40	325	21 40	25	1 40	1 41	1 42	1 43
26	1 44	86	5 44	146	9 44	206	13 44	266	17 44	326	21 44	26	1 44	1 45	1 46	1 47
27	1 48	87	5 48	147	9 48	207	13 48	267	17 48	327	21 48	27	1 48	1 49	1 50	1 51
28	1 52	88	5 52	148	9 52	208	13 52	268	17 52	328	21 52	28	1 52	1 53	1 54	1 55
29	1 56	89	5 56	149	9 56	209	13 56	269	17 56	329	21 56	29	1 56	1 57	1 58	1 59
30	2 00	90	6 00	150	10 00	210	14 00	270	18 00	330	22 00	30	2 00	2 01	2 02	2 03
31	2 04	91	6 04	151	10 04	211	14 04	271	18 04	331	22 04	31	2 04	2 05	2 06	2 07
32	2 08	92	6 08	152	10 08	212	14 08	272	18 08	332	22 08	32	2 08	2 09	2 10	2 11
33	2 12	93	6 12	153	10 12	213	14 12	273	18 12	333	22 12	33	2 12	2 13	2 14	2 15
34	2 16	94	6 16	154	10 16	214	14 16	274	18 16	334	22 16	34	2 16	2 17	2 18	2 19
35	2 20	95	6 20	155	10 20	215	14 20	275	18 20	335	22 20	35	2 20	2 21	2 22	2 23
36	2 24	96	6 24	156	10 24	216	14 24	276	18 24	336	22 24	36	2 24	2 25	2 26	2 27
37	2 28	97	6 28	157	10 28	217	14 28	277	18 28	337	22 28	37	2 28	2 29	2 30	2 31
38	2 32	98	6 32	158	10 32	218	14 32	278	18 32	338	22 32	38	2 32	2 33	2 34	2 35
39	2 36	99	6 36	159	10 36	219	14 36	279	18 36	339	22 36	39	2 36	2 37	2 38	2 39
40	2 40	100	6 40	160	10 40	220	14 40	280	18 40	340	22 40	40	2 40	2 41	2 42	2 43
41	2 44	101	6 44	161	10 44	221	14 44	281	18 44	341	22 44	41	2 44	2 45	2 46	2 47
42	2 48	102	6 48	162	10 48	222	14 48	282	18 48	342	22 48	42	2 48	2 49	2 50	2 51
43	2 52	103	6 52	163	10 52	223	14 52	283	18 52	343	22 52	43	2 52	2 53	2 54	2 55
44	2 56	104	6 56	164	10 56	224	14 56	284	18 56	344	22 56	44	2 56	2 57	2 58	2 59
45	3 00	105	7 00	165	11 00	225	15 00	285	19 00	345	23 00	45	3 00	3 01	3 02	3 03
46	3 04	106	7 04	166	11 04	226	15 04	286	19 04	346	23 04	46	3 04	3 05	3 06	3 07
47	3 08	107	7 08	167	11 08	227	15 08	287	19 08	347	23 08	47	3 08	3 09	3 10	3 11
48	3 12	108	7 12	168	11 12	228	15 12	288	19 12	348	23 12	48	3 12	3 13	3 14	3 15
49	3 16	109	7 16	169	11 16	229	15 16	289	19 16	349	23 16	49	3 16	3 17	3 18	3 19
50	3 20	110	7 20	170	11 20	230	15 20	290	19 20	350	23 20	50	3 20	3 21	3 22	3 23
51	3 24	111	7 24	171	11 24	231	15 24	291	19 24	351	23 24	51	3 24	3 25	3 26	3 27
52	3 28	112	7 28	172	11 28	232	15 28	292	19 28	352	23 28	52	3 28	3 29	3 30	3 31
53	3 32	113	7 32	173	11 32	233	15 32	293	19 32	353	23 32	53	3 32	3 33	3 34	3 35
54	3 36	114	7 36	174	11 36	234	15 36	294	19 36	354	23 36	54	3 36	3 37	3 38	3 39
55	3 40	115	7 40	175	11 40	235	15 40	295	19 40	355	23 40	55	3 40	3 41	3 42	3 43
56	3 44	116	7 44	176	11 44	236	15 44	296	19 44	356	23 44	56	3 44	3 45	3 46	3 47
57	3 48	117	7 48	177	11 48	237	15 48	297	19 48	357	23 48	57	3 48	3 49	3 50	3 51
58	3 52	118	7 52	178	11 52	238	15 52	298	19 52	358	23 52	58	3 52	3 53	3 54	3 55
59	3 56	119	7 56	179	11 56	239	15 56	299	19 56	359	23 56	59	3 56	3 57	3 58	3 59

The above table is for converting expressions in arc to their equivalent in time ; its main use in this Almanac is for the conversion of longitude for application to L.M.T. (*added* if *west*, *subtracted* if *east*) to give G.M.T. or vice

28^m INCREMENTS AND CORRECTIONS 29^m

28^m	SUN PLANETS	ARIES	MOON	v or d	Corr^n	v or d	Corr^n	v or d	Corr^n
s	° ′	° ′	° ′	′	′	′	′	′	′
00	7 00·0	7 01·1	6 40·9	0·0	0·0	6·0	2·9	12·0	5·7
01	7 00·3	7 01·4	6 41·1	0·1	0·0	6·1	2·9	12·1	5·7
02	7 00·5	7 01·7	6 41·3	0·2	0·1	6·2	2·9	12·2	5·8
03	7 00·8	7 01·9	6 41·6	0·3	0·1	6·3	3·0	12·3	5·8
04	7 01·0	7 02·2	6 41·8	0·4	0·2	6·4	3·0	12·4	5·9
05	7 01·3	7 02·4	6 42·1	0·5	0·2	6·5	3·1	12·5	5·9
06	7 01·5	7 02·7	6 42·3	0·6	0·3	6·6	3·1	12·6	6·0
07	7 01·8	7 02·9	6 42·5	0·7	0·3	6·7	3·2	12·7	6·0
08	7 02·0	7 03·2	6 42·8	0·8	0·4	6·8	3·2	12·8	6·1
09	7 02·3	7 03·4	6 43·0	0·9	0·4	6·9	3·3	12·9	6·1
10	7 02·5	7 03·7	6 43·3	1·0	0·5	7·0	3·3	13·0	6·2
11	7 02·8	7 03·9	6 43·5	1·1	0·5	7·1	3·4	13·1	6·2
12	7 03·0	7 04·2	6 43·7	1·2	0·6	7·2	3·4	13·2	6·3
13	7 03·3	7 04·4	6 44·0	1·3	0·6	7·3	3·5	13·3	6·3
14	7 03·5	7 04·7	6 44·2	1·4	0·7	7·4	3·5	13·4	6·4
15	7 03·8	7 04·9	6 44·4	1·5	0·7	7·5	3·6	13·5	6·4
16	7 04·0	7 05·2	6 44·7	1·6	0·8	7·6	3·6	13·6	6·5
17	7 04·3	7 05·4	6 44·9	1·7	0·8	7·7	3·7	13·7	6·5
18	7 04·5	7 05·7	6 45·2	1·8	0·9	7·8	3·7	13·8	6·6
19	7 04·8	7 05·9	6 45·4	1·9	0·9	7·9	3·8	13·9	6·6
20	7 05·0	7 06·2	6 45·6	2·0	1·0	8·0	3·8	14·0	6·7
21	7 05·3	7 06·4	6 45·9	2·1	1·0	8·1	3·8	14·1	6·7
22	7 05·5	7 06·7	6 46·1	2·2	1·0	8·2	3·9	14·2	6·7
23	7 05·8	7 06·9	6 46·4	2·3	1·1	8·3	3·9	14·3	6·8
24	7 06·0	7 07·2	6 46·6	2·4	1·1	8·4	4·0	14·4	6·8
25	7 06·3	7 07·4	6 46·8	2·5	1·2	8·5	4·0	14·5	6·9
26	7 06·5	7 07·7	6 47·1	2·6	1·2	8·6	4·1	14·6	6·9
27	7 06·8	7 07·9	6 47·3	2·7	1·3	8·7	4·1	14·7	7·0
28	7 07·0	7 08·2	6 47·5	2·8	1·3	8·8	4·2	14·8	7·0
29	7 07·3	7 08·4	6 47·8	2·9	1·4	8·9	4·2	14·9	7·1
30	7 07·5	7 08·7	6 48·0	3·0	1·4	9·0	4·3	15·0	7·1
31	7 07·8	7 08·9	6 48·3	3·1	1·5	9·1	4·3	15·1	7·2
32	7 08·0	7 09·2	6 48·5	3·2	1·5	9·2	4·4	15·2	7·2
33	7 08·3	7 09·4	6 48·7	3·3	1·6	9·3	4·4	15·3	7·3
34	7 08·5	7 09·7	6 49·0	3·4	1·6	9·4	4·5	15·4	7·3
35	7 08·8	7 09·9	6 49·2	3·5	1·7	9·5	4·5	15·5	7·4
36	7 09·0	7 10·2	6 49·5	3·6	1·7	9·6	4·6	15·6	7·4
37	7 09·3	7 10·4	6 49·7	3·7	1·8	9·7	4·6	15·7	7·5
38	7 09·5	7 10·7	6 49·9	3·8	1·8	9·8	4·7	15·8	7·5
39	7 09·8	7 10·9	6 50·2	3·9	1·9	9·9	4·7	15·9	7·6
40	7 10·0	7 11·2	6 50·4	4·0	1·9	10·0	4·8	16·0	7·6
41	7 10·3	7 11·4	6 50·6	4·1	1·9	10·1	4·8	16·1	7·6
42	7 10·5	7 11·7	6 50·9	4·2	2·0	10·2	4·8	16·2	7·7
43	7 10·8	7 11·9	6 51·1	4·3	2·0	10·3	4·9	16·3	7·7
44	7 11·0	7 12·2	6 51·4	4·4	2·1	10·4	4·9	16·4	7·8
45	7 11·3	7 12·4	6 51·6	4·5	2·1	10·5	5·0	16·5	7·8
46	7 11·5	7 12·7	6 51·8	4·6	2·2	10·6	5·0	16·6	7·9
47	7 11·8	7 12·9	6 52·1	4·7	2·2	10·7	5·1	16·7	7·9
48	7 12·0	7 13·2	6 52·3	4·8	2·3	10·8	5·1	16·8	8·0
49	7 12·3	7 13·4	6 52·6	4·9	2·3	10·9	5·2	16·9	8·0
50	7 12·5	7 13·7	6 52·8	5·0	2·4	11·0	5·2	17·0	8·1
51	7 12·8	7 13·9	6 53·0	5·1	2·4	11·1	5·3	17·1	8·1
52	7 13·0	7 14·2	6 53·3	5·2	2·5	11·2	5·3	17·2	8·2
53	7 13·3	7 14·4	6 53·5	5·3	2·5	11·3	5·4	17·3	8·2
54	7 13·5	7 14·7	6 53·8	5·4	2·6	11·4	5·4	17·4	8·3
55	7 13·8	7 14·9	6 54·0	5·5	2·6	11·5	5·5	17·5	8·3
56	7 14·0	7 15·2	6 54·2	5·6	2·7	11·6	5·5	17·6	8·4
57	7 14·3	7 15·4	6 54·5	5·7	2·7	11·7	5·6	17·7	8·4
58	7 14·5	7 15·7	6 54·7	5·8	2·8	11·8	5·6	17·8	8·5
59	7 14·8	7 15·9	6 54·9	5·9	2·8	11·9	5·7	17·9	8·5
60	7 15·0	7 16·2	6 55·2	6·0	2·9	12·0	5·7	18·0	8·6

29^m	SUN PLANETS	ARIES	MOON	v or d	Corr^n	v or d	Corr^n	v or d	Corr^n
s	° ′	° ′	° ′	′	′	′	′	′	′
00	7 15·0	7 16·2	6 55·2	0·0	0·0	6·0	3·0	12·0	5·9
01	7 15·3	7 16·4	6 55·4	0·1	0·0	6·1	3·0	12·1	5·9
02	7 15·5	7 16·7	6 55·7	0·2	0·1	6·2	3·0	12·2	6·0
03	7 15·8	7 16·9	6 55·9	0·3	0·1	6·3	3·1	12·3	6·0
04	7 16·0	7 17·2	6 56·1	0·4	0·2	6·4	3·1	12·4	6·1
05	7 16·3	7 17·4	6 56·4	0·5	0·2	6·5	3·2	12·5	6·1
06	7 16·5	7 17·7	6 56·6	0·6	0·3	6·6	3·2	12·6	6·2
07	7 16·8	7 17·9	6 56·9	0·7	0·3	6·7	3·3	12·7	6·2
08	7 17·0	7 18·2	6 57·1	0·8	0·4	6·8	3·3	12·8	6·3
09	7 17·3	7 18·4	6 57·3	0·9	0·4	6·9	3·4	12·9	6·3
10	7 17·5	7 18·7	6 57·6	1·0	0·5	7·0	3·4	13·0	6·4
11	7 17·8	7 18·9	6 57·8	1·1	0·5	7·1	3·5	13·1	6·4
12	7 18·0	7 19·2	6 58·0	1·2	0·6	7·2	3·5	13·2	6·5
13	7 18·3	7 19·4	6 58·3	1·3	0·6	7·3	3·6	13·3	6·5
14	7 18·5	7 19·7	6 58·5	1·4	0·7	7·4	3·6	13·4	6·6
15	7 18·8	7 20·0	6 58·8	1·5	0·7	7·5	3·7	13·5	6·6
16	7 19·0	7 20·2	6 59·0	1·6	0·8	7·6	3·7	13·6	6·7
17	7 19·3	7 20·5	6 59·2	1·7	0·8	7·7	3·8	13·7	6·7
18	7 19·5	7 20·7	6 59·5	1·8	0·9	7·8	3·8	13·8	6·8
19	7 19·8	7 21·0	6 59·7	1·9	0·9	7·9	3·9	13·9	6·8
20	7 20·0	7 21·2	7 00·0	2·0	1·0	8·0	3·9	14·0	6·9
21	7 20·3	7 21·5	7 00·2	2·1	1·0	8·1	4·0	14·1	6·9
22	7 20·5	7 21·7	7 00·4	2·2	1·1	8·2	4·0	14·2	7·0
23	7 20·8	7 22·0	7 00·7	2·3	1·1	8·3	4·1	14·3	7·0
24	7 21·0	7 22·2	7 00·9	2·4	1·2	8·4	4·1	14·4	7·1
25	7 21·3	7 22·5	7 01·1	2·5	1·2	8·5	4·2	14·5	7·1
26	7 21·5	7 22·7	7 01·4	2·6	1·3	8·6	4·2	14·6	7·2
27	7 21·8	7 23·0	7 01·6	2·7	1·3	8·7	4·3	14·7	7·2
28	7 22·0	7 23·2	7 01·9	2·8	1·4	8·8	4·3	14·8	7·3
29	7 22·3	7 23·5	7 02·1	2·9	1·4	8·9	4·4	14·9	7·3
30	7 22·5	7 23·7	7 02·3	3·0	1·5	9·0	4·4	15·0	7·4
31	7 22·8	7 24·0	7 02·6	3·1	1·5	9·1	4·5	15·1	7·4
32	7 23·0	7 24·2	7 02·8	3·2	1·6	9·2	4·5	15·2	7·5
33	7 23·3	7 24·5	7 03·1	3·3	1·6	9·3	4·6	15·3	7·5
34	7 23·5	7 24·7	7 03·3	3·4	1·7	9·4	4·6	15·4	7·6
35	7 23·8	7 25·0	7 03·5	3·5	1·7	9·5	4·7	15·5	7·6
36	7 24·0	7 25·2	7 03·8	3·6	1·8	9·6	4·7	15·6	7·7
37	7 24·3	7 25·5	7 04·0	3·7	1·8	9·7	4·8	15·7	7·7
38	7 24·5	7 25·7	7 04·3	3·8	1·9	9·8	4·8	15·8	7·8
39	7 24·8	7 26·0	7 04·5	3·9	1·9	9·9	4·9	15·9	7·8
40	7 25·0	7 26·2	7 04·7	4·0	2·0	10·0	4·9	16·0	7·9
41	7 25·3	7 26·5	7 05·0	4·1	2·0	10·1	5·0	16·1	7·9
42	7 25·5	7 26·7	7 05·2	4·2	2·1	10·2	5·0	16·2	8·0
43	7 25·8	7 27·0	7 05·4	4·3	2·1	10·3	5·1	16·3	8·0
44	7 26·0	7 27·2	7 05·7	4·4	2·2	10·4	5·1	16·4	8·1
45	7 26·3	7 27·5	7 05·9	4·5	2·2	10·5	5·2	16·5	8·1
46	7 26·5	7 27·7	7 06·2	4·6	2·3	10·6	5·2	16·6	8·2
47	7 26·8	7 28·0	7 06·4	4·7	2·3	10·7	5·3	16·7	8·2
48	7 27·0	7 28·2	7 06·6	4·8	2·4	10·8	5·3	16·8	8·3
49	7 27·3	7 28·5	7 06·9	4·9	2·4	10·9	5·4	16·9	8·3
50	7 27·5	7 28·7	7 07·1	5·0	2·5	11·0	5·4	17·0	8·4
51	7 27·8	7 29·0	7 07·4	5·1	2·5	11·1	5·5	17·1	8·4
52	7 28·0	7 29·2	7 07·6	5·2	2·6	11·2	5·5	17·2	8·5
53	7 28·3	7 29·5	7 07·8	5·3	2·6	11·3	5·6	17·3	8·5
54	7 28·5	7 29·7	7 08·1	5·4	2·7	11·4	5·6	17·4	8·6
55	7 28·8	7 30·0	7 08·3	5·5	2·7	11·5	5·7	17·5	8·6
56	7 29·0	7 30·2	7 08·5	5·6	2·8	11·6	5·7	17·6	8·7
57	7 29·3	7 30·5	7 08·8	5·7	2·8	11·7	5·8	17·7	8·7
58	7 29·5	7 30·7	7 09·0	5·8	2·9	11·8	5·8	17·8	8·8
59	7 29·8	7 31·0	7 09·3	5·9	2·9	11·9	5·9	17·9	8·8
60	7 30·0	7 31·2	7 09·5	6·0	3·0	12·0	5·9	18·0	8·9

30^m INCREMENTS AND CORRECTIONS 31^m

30^m	SUN PLANETS	ARIES	MOON	v or d	Corr^n	v or d	Corr^n	v or d	Corr^n
s	° ′	° ′	° ′	′	′	′	′	′	′
00	7 30·0	7 31·2	7 09·5	0·0	0·0	6·0	3·1	12·0	6·1
01	7 30·3	7 31·5	7 09·7	0·1	0·1	6·1	3·1	12·1	6·2
02	7 30·5	7 31·7	7 10·0	0·2	0·1	6·2	3·2	12·2	6·2
03	7 30·8	7 32·0	7 10·2	0·3	0·2	6·3	3·2	12·3	6·3
04	7 31·0	7 32·2	7 10·5	0·4	0·2	6·4	3·3	12·4	6·3
05	7 31·3	7 32·5	7 10·7	0·5	0·3	6·5	3·3	12·5	6·4
06	7 31·5	7 32·7	7 10·9	0·6	0·3	6·6	3·4	12·6	6·4
07	7 31·8	7 33·0	7 11·2	0·7	0·4	6·7	3·4	12·7	6·5
08	7 32·0	7 33·2	7 11·4	0·8	0·4	6·8	3·5	12·8	6·5
09	7 32·3	7 33·5	7 11·6	0·9	0·5	6·9	3·5	12·9	6·6
10	7 32·5	7 33·7	7 11·9	1·0	0·5	7·0	3·6	13·0	6·6
11	7 32·8	7 34·0	7 12·1	1·1	0·6	7·1	3·6	13·1	6·7
12	7 33·0	7 34·2	7 12·4	1·2	0·6	7·2	3·7	13·2	6·7
13	7 33·3	7 34·5	7 12·6	1·3	0·7	7·3	3·7	13·3	6·8
14	7 33·5	7 34·7	7 12·8	1·4	0·7	7·4	3·8	13·4	6·8
15	7 33·8	7 35·0	7 13·1	1·5	0·8	7·5	3·8	13·5	6·9
16	7 34·0	7 35·2	7 13·3	1·6	0·8	7·6	3·9	13·6	6·9
17	7 34·3	7 35·5	7 13·6	1·7	0·9	7·7	3·9	13·7	7·0
18	7 34·5	7 35·7	7 13·8	1·8	0·9	7·8	4·0	13·8	7·0
19	7 34·8	7 36·0	7 14·0	1·9	1·0	7·9	4·0	13·9	7·1
20	7 35·0	7 36·2	7 14·3	2·0	1·0	8·0	4·1	14·0	7·1
21	7 35·3	7 36·5	7 14·5	2·1	1·1	8·1	4·1	14·1	7·2
22	7 35·5	7 36·7	7 14·7	2·2	1·1	8·2	4·2	14·2	7·2
23	7 35·8	7 37·0	7 15·0	2·3	1·2	8·3	4·2	14·3	7·3
24	7 36·0	7 37·2	7 15·2	2·4	1·2	8·4	4·3	14·4	7·3
25	7 36·3	7 37·5	7 15·5	2·5	1·3	8·5	4·3	14·5	7·4
26	7 36·5	7 37·7	7 15·7	2·6	1·3	8·6	4·4	14·6	7·4
27	7 36·8	7 38·0	7 15·9	2·7	1·4	8·7	4·4	14·7	7·5
28	7 37·0	7 38·3	7 16·2	2·8	1·4	8·8	4·5	14·8	7·5
29	7 37·3	7 38·5	7 16·4	2·9	1·5	8·9	4·5	14·9	7·6
30	7 37·5	7 38·8	7 16·7	3·0	1·5	9·0	4·6	15·0	7·6
31	7 37·8	7 39·0	7 16·9	3·1	1·6	9·1	4·6	15·1	7·7
32	7 38·0	7 39·3	7 17·1	3·2	1·6	9·2	4·7	15·2	7·7
33	7 38·3	7 39·5	7 17·4	3·3	1·7	9·3	4·7	15·3	7·8
34	7 38·5	7 39·8	7 17·6	3·4	1·7	9·4	4·8	15·4	7·8
35	7 38·8	7 40·0	7 17·9	3·5	1·8	9·5	4·8	15·5	7·9
36	7 39·0	7 40·3	7 18·1	3·6	1·8	9·6	4·9	15·6	7·9
37	7 39·3	7 40·5	7 18·3	3·7	1·9	9·7	4·9	15·7	8·0
38	7 39·5	7 40·8	7 18·6	3·8	1·9	9·8	5·0	15·8	8·0
39	7 39·8	7 41·0	7 18·8	3·9	2·0	9·9	5·0	15·9	8·1
40	7 40·0	7 41·3	7 19·0	4·0	2·0	10·0	5·1	16·0	8·1
41	7 40·3	7 41·5	7 19·3	4·1	2·1	10·1	5·1	16·1	8·2
42	7 40·5	7 41·8	7 19·5	4·2	2·1	10·2	5·2	16·2	8·2
43	7 40·8	7 42·0	7 19·8	4·3	2·2	10·3	5·2	16·3	8·3
44	7 41·0	7 42·3	7 20·0	4·4	2·2	10·4	5·3	16·4	8·3
45	7 41·3	7 42·5	7 20·2	4·5	2·3	10·5	5·3	16·5	8·4
46	7 41·5	7 42·8	7 20·5	4·6	2·3	10·6	5·4	16·6	8·4
47	7 41·8	7 43·0	7 20·7	4·7	2·4	10·7	5·4	16·7	8·5
48	7 42·0	7 43·3	7 21·0	4·8	2·4	10·8	5·5	16·8	8·5
49	7 42·3	7 43·5	7 21·2	4·9	2·5	10·9	5·5	16·9	8·6
50	7 42·5	7 43·8	7 21·4	5·0	2·5	11·0	5·6	17·0	8·6
51	7 42·8	7 44·0	7 21·7	5·1	2·6	11·1	5·6	17·1	8·7
52	7 43·0	7 44·3	7 21·9	5·2	2·6	11·2	5·7	17·2	8·7
53	7 43·3	7 44·5	7 22·1	5·3	2·7	11·3	5·7	17·3	8·8
54	7 43·5	7 44·8	7 22·4	5·4	2·7	11·4	5·8	17·4	8·8
55	7 43·8	7 45·0	7 22·6	5·5	2·8	11·5	5·8	17·5	8·9
56	7 44·0	7 45·3	7 22·9	5·6	2·8	11·6	5·9	17·6	8·9
57	7 44·3	7 45·5	7 23·1	5·7	2·9	11·7	5·9	17·7	9·0
58	7 44·5	7 45·8	7 23·3	5·8	2·9	11·8	6·0	17·8	9·0
59	7 44·8	7 46·0	7 23·6	5·9	3·0	11·9	6·0	17·9	9·1
60	7 45·0	7 46·3	7 23·8	6·0	3·1	12·0	6·1	18·0	9·2

31^m	SUN PLANETS	ARIES	MOON	v or d	Corr^n	v or d	Corr^n	v or d	Corr^n
s	° ′	° ′	° ′	′	′	′	′	′	′
00	7 45·0	7 46·3	7 23·8	0·0	0·0	6·0	3·2	12·0	6·3
01	7 45·3	7 46·5	7 24·1	0·1	0·1	6·1	3·2	12·1	6·4
02	7 45·5	7 46·8	7 24·3	0·2	0·1	6·2	3·3	12·2	6·4
03	7 45·8	7 47·0	7 24·5	0·3	0·2	6·3	3·3	12·3	6·5
04	7 46·0	7 47·3	7 24·8	0·4	0·2	6·4	3·4	12·4	6·5
05	7 46·3	7 47·5	7 25·0	0·5	0·3	6·5	3·4	12·5	6·6
06	7 46·5	7 47·8	7 25·2	0·6	0·3	6·6	3·5	12·6	6·6
07	7 46·8	7 48·0	7 25·5	0·7	0·4	6·7	3·5	12·7	6·7
08	7 47·0	7 48·3	7 25·7	0·8	0·4	6·8	3·6	12·8	6·7
09	7 47·3	7 48·5	7 26·0	0·9	0·5	6·9	3·6	12·9	6·8
10	7 47·5	7 48·8	7 26·2	1·0	0·5	7·0	3·7	13·0	6·8
11	7 47·8	7 49·0	7 26·4	1·1	0·6	7·1	3·7	13·1	6·9
12	7 48·0	7 49·3	7 26·7	1·2	0·6	7·2	3·8	13·2	6·9
13	7 48·3	7 49·5	7 26·9	1·3	0·7	7·3	3·8	13·3	7·0
14	7 48·5	7 49·8	7 27·2	1·4	0·7	7·4	3·9	13·4	7·0
15	7 48·8	7 50·0	7 27·4	1·5	0·8	7·5	3·9	13·5	7·1
16	7 49·0	7 50·3	7 27·6	1·6	0·8	7·6	4·0	13·6	7·1
17	7 49·3	7 50·5	7 27·9	1·7	0·9	7·7	4·0	13·7	7·2
18	7 49·5	7 50·8	7 28·1	1·8	0·9	7·8	4·1	13·8	7·2
19	7 49·8	7 51·0	7 28·4	1·9	1·0	7·9	4·1	13·9	7·3
20	7 50·0	7 51·3	7 28·6	2·0	1·1	8·0	4·2	14·0	7·4
21	7 50·3	7 51·5	7 28·8	2·1	1·1	8·1	4·3	14·1	7·4
22	7 50·5	7 51·8	7 29·1	2·2	1·2	8·2	4·3	14·2	7·5
23	7 50·8	7 52·0	7 29·3	2·3	1·2	8·3	4·4	14·3	7·5
24	7 51·0	7 52·3	7 29·5	2·4	1·3	8·4	4·4	14·4	7·6
25	7 51·3	7 52·5	7 29·8	2·5	1·3	8·5	4·5	14·5	7·6
26	7 51·5	7 52·8	7 30·0	2·6	1·4	8·6	4·5	14·6	7·7
27	7 51·8	7 53·0	7 30·3	2·7	1·4	8·7	4·6	14·7	7·7
28	7 52·0	7 53·3	7 30·5	2·8	1·5	8·8	4·6	14·8	7·8
29	7 52·3	7 53·5	7 30·7	2·9	1·5	8·9	4·7	14·9	7·8
30	7 52·5	7 53·8	7 31·0	3·0	1·6	9·0	4·7	15·0	7·9
31	7 52·8	7 54·0	7 31·2	3·1	1·6	9·1	4·8	15·1	7·9
32	7 53·0	7 54·3	7 31·5	3·2	1·7	9·2	4·8	15·2	8·0
33	7 53·3	7 54·5	7 31·7	3·3	1·7	9·3	4·9	15·3	8·0
34	7 53·5	7 54·8	7 31·9	3·4	1·8	9·4	4·9	15·4	8·1
35	7 53·8	7 55·0	7 32·2	3·5	1·8	9·5	5·0	15·5	8·1
36	7 54·0	7 55·3	7 32·4	3·6	1·9	9·6	5·0	15·6	8·2
37	7 54·3	7 55·5	7 32·6	3·7	1·9	9·7	5·1	15·7	8·2
38	7 54·5	7 55·8	7 32·9	3·8	2·0	9·8	5·1	15·8	8·3
39	7 54·8	7 56·0	7 33·1	3·9	2·0	9·9	5·2	15·9	8·3
40	7 55·0	7 56·3	7 33·4	4·0	2·1	10·0	5·3	16·0	8·4
41	7 55·3	7 56·6	7 33·6	4·1	2·2	10·1	5·3	16·1	8·5
42	7 55·5	7 56·8	7 33·8	4·2	2·2	10·2	5·4	16·2	8·5
43	7 55·8	7 57·1	7 34·1	4·3	2·3	10·3	5·4	16·3	8·6
44	7 56·0	7 57·3	7 34·3	4·4	2·3	10·4	5·5	16·4	8·6
45	7 56·3	7 57·6	7 34·6	4·5	2·4	10·5	5·5	16·5	8·7
46	7 56·5	7 57·8	7 34·8	4·6	2·4	10·6	5·6	16·6	8·7
47	7 56·8	7 58·1	7 35·0	4·7	2·5	10·7	5·6	16·7	8·8
48	7 57·0	7 58·3	7 35·3	4·8	2·5	10·8	5·7	16·8	8·8
49	7 57·3	7 58·6	7 35·5	4·9	2·6	10·9	5·7	16·9	8·9
50	7 57·5	7 58·8	7 35·7	5·0	2·6	11·0	5·8	17·0	8·9
51	7 57·8	7 59·1	7 36·0	5·1	2·7	11·1	5·8	17·1	9·0
52	7 58·0	7 59·3	7 36·2	5·2	2·7	11·2	5·9	17·2	9·0
53	7 58·3	7 59·6	7 36·5	5·3	2·8	11·3	5·9	17·3	9·1
54	7 58·5	7 59·8	7 36·7	5·4	2·8	11·4	6·0	17·4	9·1
55	7 58·8	8 00·1	7 36·9	5·5	2·9	11·5	6·0	17·5	9·2
56	7 59·0	8 00·3	7 37·2	5·6	2·9	11·6	6·1	17·6	9·2
57	7 59·3	8 00·6	7 37·4	5·7	3·0	11·7	6·1	17·7	9·3
58	7 59·5	8 00·8	7 37·7	5·8	3·0	11·8	6·2	17·8	9·3
59	7 59·8	8 01·1	7 37·9	5·9	3·1	11·9	6·2	17·9	9·4
60	8 00·0	8 01·3	7 38·1	6·0	3·2	12·0	6·3	18·0	9·5

32ᵐ INCREMENTS AND CORRECTIONS 33ᵐ

32ᵐ s	SUN PLANETS ° ′	ARIES ° ′	MOON ° ′	v or d ′	Corrⁿ ′	v or d ′	Corrⁿ ′	v or d ′	Corrⁿ ′
00	8 00·0	8 01·3	7 38·1	0·0	0·0	6·0	3·3	12·0	6·5
01	8 00·3	8 01·6	7 38·4	0·1	0·1	6·1	3·3	12·1	6·6
02	8 00·5	8 01·8	7 38·6	0·2	0·1	6·2	3·4	12·2	6·6
03	8 00·8	8 02·1	7 38·8	0·3	0·2	6·3	3·4	12·3	6·7
04	8 01·0	8 02·3	7 39·1	0·4	0·2	6·4	3·5	12·4	6·7
05	8 01·3	8 02·6	7 39·3	0·5	0·3	6·5	3·5	12·5	6·8
06	8 01·5	8 02·8	7 39·6	0·6	0·3	6·6	3·6	12·6	6·8
07	8 01·8	8 03·1	7 39·8	0·7	0·4	6·7	3·6	12·7	6·9
08	8 02·0	8 03·3	7 40·0	0·8	0·4	6·8	3·7	12·8	6·9
09	8 02·3	8 03·6	7 40·3	0·9	0·5	6·9	3·7	12·9	7·0
10	8 02·5	8 03·8	7 40·5	1·0	0·5	7·0	3·8	13·0	7·0
11	8 02·8	8 04·1	7 40·8	1·1	0·6	7·1	3·8	13·1	7·1
12	8 03·0	8 04·3	7 41·0	1·2	0·7	7·2	3·9	13·2	7·2
13	8 03·3	8 04·6	7 41·2	1·3	0·7	7·3	4·0	13·3	7·2
14	8 03·5	8 04·8	7 41·5	1·4	0·8	7·4	4·0	13·4	7·3
15	8 03·8	8 05·1	7 41·7	1·5	0·8	7·5	4·1	13·5	7·3
16	8 04·0	8 05·3	7 42·0	1·6	0·9	7·6	4·1	13·6	7·4
17	8 04·3	8 05·6	7 42·2	1·7	0·9	7·7	4·2	13·7	7·4
18	8 04·5	8 05·8	7 42·4	1·8	1·0	7·8	4·2	13·8	7·5
19	8 04·8	8 06·1	7 42·7	1·9	1·0	7·9	4·3	13·9	7·5
20	8 05·0	8 06·3	7 42·9	2·0	1·1	8·0	4·3	14·0	7·6
21	8 05·3	8 06·6	7 43·1	2·1	1·1	8·1	4·4	14·1	7·6
22	8 05·5	8 06·8	7 43·4	2·2	1·2	8·2	4·4	14·2	7·7
23	8 05·8	8 07·1	7 43·6	2·3	1·2	8·3	4·5	14·3	7·7
24	8 06·0	8 07·3	7 43·9	2·4	1·3	8·4	4·6	14·4	7·8
25	8 06·3	8 07·6	7 44·1	2·5	1·4	8·5	4·6	14·5	7·9
26	8 06·5	8 07·8	7 44·3	2·6	1·4	8·6	4·7	14·6	7·9
27	8 06·8	8 08·1	7 44·6	2·7	1·5	8·7	4·7	14·7	8·0
28	8 07·0	8 08·3	7 44·8	2·8	1·5	8·8	4·8	14·8	8·0
29	8 07·3	8 08·6	7 45·1	2·9	1·6	8·9	4·8	14·9	8·1
30	8 07·5	8 08·8	7 45·3	3·0	1·6	9·0	4·9	15·0	8·1
31	8 07·8	8 09·1	7 45·5	3·1	1·7	9·1	4·9	15·1	8·2
32	8 08·0	8 09·3	7 45·8	3·2	1·7	9·2	5·0	15·2	8·2
33	8 08·3	8 09·6	7 46·0	3·3	1·8	9·3	5·0	15·3	8·3
34	8 08·5	8 09·8	7 46·2	3·4	1·8	9·4	5·1	15·4	8·3
35	8 08·8	8 10·1	7 46·5	3·5	1·9	9·5	5·1	15·5	8·4
36	8 09·0	8 10·3	7 46·7	3·6	2·0	9·6	5·2	15·6	8·5
37	8 09·3	8 10·6	7 47·0	3·7	2·0	9·7	5·3	15·7	8·5
38	8 09·5	8 10·8	7 47·2	3·8	2·1	9·8	5·3	15·8	8·6
39	8 09·8	8 11·1	7 47·4	3·9	2·1	9·9	5·4	15·9	8·6
40	8 10·0	8 11·3	7 47·7	4·0	2·2	10·0	5·4	16·0	8·7
41	8 10·3	8 11·6	7 47·9	4·1	2·2	10·1	5·5	16·1	8·7
42	8 10·5	8 11·8	7 48·2	4·2	2·3	10·2	5·5	16·2	8·8
43	8 10·8	8 12·1	7 48·4	4·3	2·3	10·3	5·6	16·3	8·8
44	8 11·0	8 12·3	7 48·6	4·4	2·4	10·4	5·6	16·4	8·9
45	8 11·3	8 12·6	7 48·9	4·5	2·4	10·5	5·7	16·5	8·9
46	8 11·5	8 12·8	7 49·1	4·6	2·5	10·6	5·7	16·6	9·0
47	8 11·8	8 13·1	7 49·3	4·7	2·5	10·7	5·8	16·7	9·0
48	8 12·0	8 13·3	7 49·6	4·8	2·6	10·8	5·9	16·8	9·1
49	8 12·3	8 13·6	7 49·8	4·9	2·7	10·9	5·9	16·9	9·2
50	8 12·5	8 13·8	7 50·1	5·0	2·7	11·0	6·0	17·0	9·2
51	8 12·8	8 14·1	7 50·3	5·1	2·8	11·1	6·0	17·1	9·3
52	8 13·0	8 14·3	7 50·5	5·2	2·8	11·2	6·1	17·2	9·3
53	8 13·3	8 14·6	7 50·8	5·3	2·9	11·3	6·1	17·3	9·4
54	8 13·5	8 14·9	7 51·0	5·4	2·9	11·4	6·2	17·4	9·4
55	8 13·8	8 15·1	7 51·3	5·5	3·0	11·5	6·2	17·5	9·5
56	8 14·0	8 15·4	7 51·5	5·6	3·0	11·6	6·3	17·6	9·5
57	8 14·3	8 15·6	7 51·7	5·7	3·1	11·7	6·3	17·7	9·6
58	8 14·5	8 15·9	7 52·0	5·8	3·1	11·8	6·4	17·8	9·6
59	8 14·8	8 16·1	7 52·2	5·9	3·2	11·9	6·4	17·9	9·7
60	8 15·0	8 16·4	7 52·5	6·0	3·3	12·0	6·5	18·0	9·8

33ᵐ s	SUN PLANETS ° ′	ARIES ° ′	MOON ° ′	v or d ′	Corrⁿ ′	v or d ′	Corrⁿ ′	v or d ′	Corrⁿ ′
00	8 15·0	8 16·4	7 52·5	0·0	0·0	6·0	3·4	12·0	6·7
01	8 15·3	8 16·6	7 52·7	0·1	0·1	6·1	3·4	12·1	6·8
02	8 15·5	8 16·9	7 52·9	0·2	0·1	6·2	3·5	12·2	6·8
03	8 15·8	8 17·1	7 53·2	0·3	0·2	6·3	3·5	12·3	6·9
04	8 16·0	8 17·4	7 53·4	0·4	0·2	6·4	3·6	12·4	6·9
05	8 16·3	8 17·6	7 53·6	0·5	0·3	6·5	3·6	12·5	7·0
06	8 16·5	8 17·9	7 53·9	0·6	0·3	6·6	3·7	12·6	7·0
07	8 16·8	8 18·1	7 54·1	0·7	0·4	6·7	3·7	12·7	7·1
08	8 17·0	8 18·4	7 54·4	0·8	0·4	6·8	3·8	12·8	7·1
09	8 17·3	8 18·6	7 54·6	0·9	0·5	6·9	3·9	12·9	7·2
10	8 17·5	8 18·9	7 54·8	1·0	0·6	7·0	3·9	13·0	7·3
11	8 17·8	8 19·1	7 55·1	1·1	0·6	7·1	4·0	13·1	7·3
12	8 18·0	8 19·4	7 55·3	1·2	0·7	7·2	4·0	13·2	7·4
13	8 18·3	8 19·6	7 55·6	1·3	0·7	7·3	4·1	13·3	7·4
14	8 18·5	8 19·9	7 55·8	1·4	0·8	7·4	4·1	13·4	7·5
15	8 18·8	8 20·1	7 56·0	1·5	0·8	7·5	4·2	13·5	7·5
16	8 19·0	8 20·4	7 56·3	1·6	0·9	7·6	4·2	13·6	7·6
17	8 19·3	8 20·6	7 56·5	1·7	0·9	7·7	4·3	13·7	7·6
18	8 19·5	8 20·9	7 56·7	1·8	1·0	7·8	4·4	13·8	7·7
19	8 19·8	8 21·1	7 57·0	1·9	1·1	7·9	4·4	13·9	7·8
20	8 20·0	8 21·4	7 57·2	2·0	1·1	8·0	4·5	14·0	7·8
21	8 20·3	8 21·6	7 57·5	2·1	1·2	8·1	4·5	14·1	7·9
22	8 20·5	8 21·9	7 57·7	2·2	1·2	8·2	4·6	14·2	7·9
23	8 20·8	8 22·1	7 57·9	2·3	1·3	8·3	4·6	14·3	8·0
24	8 21·0	8 22·4	7 58·2	2·4	1·3	8·4	4·7	14·4	8·0
25	8 21·3	8 22·6	7 58·4	2·5	1·4	8·5	4·7	14·5	8·1
26	8 21·5	8 22·9	7 58·7	2·6	1·5	8·6	4·8	14·6	8·2
27	8 21·8	8 23·1	7 58·9	2·7	1·5	8·7	4·9	14·7	8·2
28	8 22·0	8 23·4	7 59·1	2·8	1·6	8·8	4·9	14·8	8·3
29	8 22·3	8 23·6	7 59·4	2·9	1·6	8·9	5·0	14·9	8·3
30	8 22·5	8 23·9	7 59·6	3·0	1·7	9·0	5·0	15·0	8·4
31	8 22·8	8 24·1	7 59·8	3·1	1·7	9·1	5·1	15·1	8·4
32	8 23·0	8 24·4	8 00·1	3·2	1·8	9·2	5·1	15·2	8·5
33	8 23·3	8 24·6	8 00·3	3·3	1·8	9·3	5·2	15·3	8·5
34	8 23·5	8 24·9	8 00·6	3·4	1·9	9·4	5·2	15·4	8·6
35	8 23·8	8 25·1	8 00·8	3·5	2·0	9·5	5·3	15·5	8·7
36	8 24·0	8 25·4	8 01·0	3·6	2·0	9·6	5·4	15·6	8·7
37	8 24·3	8 25·6	8 01·3	3·7	2·1	9·7	5·4	15·7	8·8
38	8 24·5	8 25·9	8 01·5	3·8	2·1	9·8	5·5	15·8	8·8
39	8 24·8	8 26·1	8 01·8	3·9	2·2	9·9	5·5	15·9	8·9
40	8 25·0	8 26·4	8 02·0	4·0	2·2	10·0	5·6	16·0	8·9
41	8 25·3	8 26·6	8 02·2	4·1	2·3	10·1	5·6	16·1	9·0
42	8 25·5	8 26·9	8 02·5	4·2	2·3	10·2	5·7	16·2	9·0
43	6 25·8	8 27·1	8 02·7	4·3	2·4	10·3	5·8	16·3	9·1
44	8 26·0	8 27·4	8 02·9	4·4	2·5	10·4	5·8	16·4	9·2
45	8 26·3	8 27·6	8 03·2	4·5	2·5	10·5	5·9	16·5	9·2
46	8 26·5	8 27·9	8 03·4	4·6	2·6	10·6	5·9	16·6	9·3
47	8 26·8	8 28·1	8 03·7	4·7	2·6	10·7	6·0	16·7	9·3
48	8 27·0	8 28·4	8 03·9	4·8	2·7	10·8	6·0	16·8	9·4
49	8 27·3	8 28·6	8 04·1	4·9	2·7	10·9	6·1	16·9	9·4
50	8 27·5	8 28·9	8 04·4	5·0	2·8	11·0	6·1	17·0	9·5
51	8 27·8	8 29·1	8 04·6	5·1	2·8	11·1	6·2	17·1	9·5
52	8 28·0	8 29·4	8 04·9	5·2	2·9	11·2	6·3	17·2	9·6
53	8 28·3	8 29·6	8 05·1	5·3	3·0	11·3	6·3	17·3	9·7
54	8 28·5	8 29·9	8 05·3	5·4	3·0	11·4	6·4	17·4	9·7
55	8 28·8	8 30·1	8 05·6	5·5	3·1	11·5	6·4	17·5	9·8
56	8 29·0	8 30·4	8 05·8	5·6	3·1	11·6	6·5	17·6	9·8
57	8 29·3	8 30·6	8 06·1	5·7	3·2	11·7	6·5	17·7	9·9
58	8 29·5	8 30·9	8 06·3	5·8	3·2	11·8	6·6	17·8	9·9
59	8 29·8	8 31·1	8 06·5	5·9	3·3	11·9	6·6	17·9	10·0
60	8 30·0	8 31·4	8 06·8	6·0	3·4	12·0	6·7	18·0	10·1

34m INCREMENTS AND CORRECTIONS 35m

34m s	SUN PLANETS ° ′	ARIES ° ′	MOON ° ′	v or d ′	Corrn ′	v or d ′	Corrn ′	v or d ′	Corrn ′
00	8 30·0	8 31·4	8 06·8	0·0	0·0	6·0	3·5	12·0	6·9
01	8 30·3	8 31·6	8 07·0	0·1	0·1	6·1	3·5	12·1	7·0
02	8 30·5	8 31·9	8 07·2	0·2	0·1	6·2	3·6	12·2	7·0
03	8 30·8	8 32·1	8 07·5	0·3	0·2	6·3	3·6	12·3	7·1
04	8 31·0	8 32·4	8 07·7	0·4	0·2	6·4	3·7	12·4	7·1
05	8 31·3	8 32·6	8 08·0	0·5	0·3	6·5	3·7	12·5	7·2
06	8 31·5	8 32·9	8 08·2	0·6	0·3	6·6	3·8	12·6	7·2
07	8 31·8	8 33·2	8 08·4	0·7	0·4	6·7	3·9	12·7	7·3
08	8 32·0	8 33·4	8 08·7	0·8	0·5	6·8	3·9	12·8	7·4
09	8 32·3	8 33·7	8 08·9	0·9	0·5	6·9	4·0	12·9	7·4
10	8 32·5	8 33·9	8 09·2	1·0	0·6	7·0	4·0	13·0	7·5
11	8 32·8	8 34·2	8 09·4	1·1	0·6	7·1	4·1	13·1	7·5
12	8 33·0	8 34·4	8 09·6	1·2	0·7	7·2	4·1	13·2	7·6
13	8 33·3	8 34·7	8 09·9	1·3	0·7	7·3	4·2	13·3	7·6
14	8 33·5	8 34·9	8 10·1	1·4	0·8	7·4	4·3	13·4	7·7
15	8 33·8	8 35·2	8 10·3	1·5	0·9	7·5	4·3	13·5	7·8
16	8 34·0	8 35·4	8 10·6	1·6	0·9	7·6	4·4	13·6	7·8
17	8 34·3	8 35·7	8 10·8	1·7	1·0	7·7	4·4	13·7	7·9
18	8 34·5	8 35·9	8 11·1	1·8	1·0	7·8	4·5	13·8	7·9
19	8 34·8	8 36·2	8 11·3	1·9	1·1	7·9	4·5	13·9	8·0
20	8 35·0	8 36·4	8 11·5	2·0	1·2	8·0	4·6	14·0	8·1
21	8 35·3	8 36·7	8 11·8	2·1	1·2	8·1	4·7	14·1	8·1
22	8 35·5	8 36·9	8 12·0	2·2	1·3	8·2	4·7	14·2	8·2
23	8 35·8	8 37·2	8 12·3	2·3	1·3	8·3	4·8	14·3	8·2
24	8 36·0	8 37·4	8 12·5	2·4	1·4	8·4	4·8	14·4	8·3
25	8 36·3	8 37·7	8 12·7	2·5	1·4	8·5	4·9	14·5	8·3
26	8 36·5	8 37·9	8 13·0	2·6	1·5	8·6	4·9	14·6	8·4
27	8 36·8	8 38·2	8 13·2	2·7	1·6	8·7	5·0	14·7	8·5
28	8 37·0	8 38·4	8 13·4	2·8	1·6	8·8	5·1	14·8	8·5
29	8 37·3	8 38·7	8 13·7	2·9	1·7	8·9	5·1	14·9	8·6
30	8 37·5	8 38·9	8 13·9	3·0	1·7	9·0	5·2	15·0	8·6
31	8 37·8	8 39·2	8 14·2	3·1	1·8	9·1	5·2	15·1	8·7
32	8 38·0	8 39·4	8 14·4	3·2	1·8	9·2	5·3	15·2	8·7
33	8 38·3	8 39·7	8 14·6	3·3	1·9	9·3	5·3	15·3	8·8
34	8 38·5	8 39·9	8 14·9	3·4	2·0	9·4	5·4	15·4	8·9
35	8 38·8	8 40·2	8 15·1	3·5	2·0	9·5	5·5	15·5	8·9
36	8 39·0	8 40·4	8 15·4	3·6	2·1	9·6	5·5	15·6	9·0
37	8 39·3	8 40·7	8 15·6	3·7	2·1	9·7	5·6	15·7	9·0
38	8 39·5	8 40·9	8 15·8	3·8	2·2	9·8	5·6	15·8	9·1
39	8 39·8	8 41·2	8 16·1	3·9	2·2	9·9	5·7	15·9	9·1
40	8 40·0	8 41·4	8 16·3	4·0	2·3	10·0	5·8	16·0	9·2
41	8 40·3	8 41·7	8 16·5	4·1	2·4	10·1	5·8	16·1	9·3
42	8 40·5	8 41·9	8 16·8	4·2	2·4	10·2	5·9	16·2	9·3
43	8 40·8	8 42·2	8 17·0	4·3	2·5	10·3	5·9	16·3	9·4
44	8 41·0	8 42·4	8 17·3	4·4	2·5	10·4	6·0	16·4	9·4
45	8 41·3	8 42·7	8 17·5	4·5	2·6	10·5	6·0	16·5	9·5
46	8 41·5	8 42·9	8 17·7	4·6	2·6	10·6	6·1	16·6	9·5
47	8 41·8	8 43·2	8 18·0	4·7	2·7	10·7	6·2	16·7	9·6
48	8 42·0	8 43·4	8 18·2	4·8	2·8	10·8	6·2	16·8	9·7
49	8 42·3	8 43·7	8 18·5	4·9	2·8	10·9	6·3	16·9	9·7
50	8 42·5	8 43·9	8 18·7	5·0	2·9	11·0	6·3	17·0	9·8
51	8 42·8	8 44·2	8 18·9	5·1	2·9	11·1	6·4	17·1	9·8
52	8 43·0	8 44·4	8 19·2	5·2	3·0	11·2	6·4	17·2	9·9
53	8 43·3	8 44·7	8 19·4	5·3	3·0	11·3	6·5	17·3	9·9
54	8 43·5	8 44·9	8 19·7	5·4	3·1	11·4	6·6	17·4	10·0
55	8 43·8	8 45·2	8 19·9	5·5	3·2	11·5	6·6	17·5	10·1
56	8 44·0	8 45·4	8 20·1	5·6	3·2	11·6	6·7	17·6	10·1
57	8 44·3	8 45·7	8 20·4	5·7	3·3	11·7	6·7	17·7	10·2
58	8 44·5	8 45·9	8 20·6	5·8	3·3	11·8	6·8	17·8	10·2
59	8 44·8	8 46·2	8 20·8	5·9	3·4	11·9	6·8	17·9	10·3
60	8 45·0	8 46·4	8 21·1	6·0	3·5	12·0	6·9	18·0	10·4

35m s	SUN PLANETS ° ′	ARIES ° ′	MOON ° ′	v or d ′	Corrn ′	v or d ′	Corrn ′	v or d ′	Corrn ′
00	8 45·0	8 46·4	8 21·1	0·0	0·0	6·0	3·6	12·0	7·1
01	8 45·3	8 46·7	8 21·3	0·1	0·1	6·1	3·6	12·1	7·2
02	8 45·5	8 46·9	8 21·6	0·2	0·1	6·2	3·7	12·2	7·2
03	8 45·8	8 47·2	8 21·8	0·3	0·2	6·3	3·7	12·3	7·3
04	8 46·0	8 47·4	8 22·0	0·4	0·2	6·4	3·8	12·4	7·3
05	8 46·3	8 47·7	8 22·3	0·5	0·3	6·5	3·8	12·5	7·4
06	8 46·5	8 47·9	8 22·5	0·6	0·4	6·6	3·9	12·6	7·5
07	8 46·8	8 48·2	8 22·8	0·7	0·4	6·7	4·0	12·7	7·5
08	8 47·0	8 48·4	8 23·0	0·8	0·5	6·8	4·0	12·8	7·6
09	8 47·3	8 48·7	8 23·2	0·9	0·5	6·9	4·1	12·9	7·6
10	8 47·5	8 48·9	8 23·5	1·0	0·6	7·0	4·1	13·0	7·7
11	8 47·8	8 49·2	8 23·7	1·1	0·7	7·1	4·2	13·1	7·8
12	8 48·0	8 49·4	8 23·9	1·2	0·7	7·2	4·3	13·2	7·8
13	8 48·3	8 49·7	8 24·2	1·3	0·8	7·3	4·3	13·3	7·9
14	8 48·5	8 49·9	8 24·4	1·4	0·8	7·4	4·4	13·4	7·9
15	8 48·8	8 50·2	8 24·7	1·5	0·9	7·5	4·4	13·5	8·0
16	8 49·0	8 50·4	8 24·9	1·6	0·9	7·6	4·5	13·6	8·0
17	8 49·3	8 50·7	8 25·1	1·7	1·0	7·7	4·6	13·7	8·1
18	8 49·5	8 50·9	8 25·4	1·8	1·1	7·8	4·6	13·8	8·2
19	8 49·8	8 51·2	8 25·6	1·9	1·1	7·9	4·7	13·9	8·2
20	8 50·0	8 51·5	8 25·9	2·0	1·2	8·0	4·7	14·0	8·3
21	8 50·3	8 51·7	8 26·1	2·1	1·2	8·1	4·8	14·1	8·3
22	8 50·5	8 52·0	8 26·3	2·2	1·3	8·2	4·9	14·2	8·4
23	8 50·8	8 52·2	8 26·6	2·3	1·4	8·3	4·9	14·3	8·5
24	8 51·0	8 52·5	8 26·8	2·4	1·4	8·4	5·0	14·4	8·5
25	8 51·3	8 52·7	8 27·0	2·5	1·5	8·5	5·0	14·5	8·6
26	8 51·5	8 53·0	8 27·3	2·6	1·5	8·6	5·1	14·6	8·6
27	8 51·8	8 53·2	8 27·5	2·7	1·6	8·7	5·1	14·7	8·7
28	8 52·0	8 53·5	8 27·8	2·8	1·7	8·8	5·2	14·8	8·8
29	8 52·3	8 53·7	8 28·0	2·9	1·7	8·9	5·3	14·9	8·8
30	8 52·5	8 54·0	8 28·2	3·0	1·8	9·0	5·3	15·0	8·9
31	8 52·8	8 54·2	8 28·5	3·1	1·8	9·1	5·4	15·1	8·9
32	8 53·0	8 54·5	8 28·7	3·2	1·9	9·2	5·4	15·2	9·0
33	8 53·3	8 54·7	8 29·0	3·3	2·0	9·3	5·5	15·3	9·1
34	8 53·5	8 55·0	8 29·2	3·4	2·0	9·4	5·6	15·4	9·1
35	8 53·8	8 55·2	8 29·4	3·5	2·1	9·5	5·6	15·5	9·2
36	8 54·0	8 55·5	8 29·7	3·6	2·1	9·6	5·7	15·6	9·2
37	8 54·3	8 55·7	8 29·9	3·7	2·2	9·7	5·7	15·7	9·3
38	8 54·5	8 56·0	8 30·2	3·8	2·2	9·8	5·8	15·8	9·3
39	8 54·8	8 56·2	8 30·4	3·9	2·3	9·9	5·9	15·9	9·4
40	8 55·0	8 56·5	8 30·6	4·0	2·4	10·0	5·9	16·0	9·5
41	8 55·3	8 56·7	8 30·9	4·1	2·4	10·1	6·0	16·1	9·5
42	8 55·5	8 57·0	8 31·1	4·2	2·5	10·2	6·0	16·2	9·6
43	8 55·8	8 57·2	8 31·3	4·3	2·5	10·3	6·1	16·3	9·6
44	8 56·0	8 57·5	8 31·6	4·4	2·6	10·4	6·2	16·4	9·7
45	8 56·3	8 57·7	8 31·8	4·5	2·7	10·5	6·2	16·5	9·8
46	8 56·5	8 58·0	8 32·1	4·6	2·7	10·6	6·3	16·6	9·8
47	8 56·8	8 58·2	8 32·3	4·7	2·8	10·7	6·3	16·7	9·9
48	8 57·0	8 58·5	8 32·5	4·8	2·8	10·8	6·4	16·8	9·9
49	8 57·3	8 58·7	8 32·8	4·9	2·9	10·9	6·4	16·9	10·0
50	8 57·5	8 59·0	8 33·0	5·0	3·0	11·0	6·5	17·0	10·1
51	8 57·8	8 59·2	8 33·3	5·1	3·0	11·1	6·6	17·1	10·1
52	8 58·0	8 59·5	8 33·5	5·2	3·1	11·2	6·6	17·2	10·2
53	8 58·3	8 59·7	8 33·7	5·3	3·1	11·3	6·7	17·3	10·2
54	8 58·5	9 00·0	8 34·0	5·4	3·2	11·4	6·7	17·4	10·3
55	8 58·8	9 00·2	8 34·2	5·5	3·3	11·5	6·8	17·5	10·4
56	8 59·0	9 00·5	8 34·4	5·6	3·3	11·6	6·9	17·6	10·4
57	8 59·3	9 00·7	8 34·7	5·7	3·4	11·7	6·9	17·7	10·5
58	8 59·5	9 01·0	8 34·9	5·8	3·4	11·8	7·0	17·8	10·5
59	8 59·8	9 01·2	8 35·2	5·9	3·5	11·9	7·0	17·9	10·6
60	9 00·0	9 01·5	8 35·4	6·0	3·6	12·0	7·1	18·0	10·7

APPENDIX 7

ALTITUDE CORRECTION TABLES 0°–35°—MOON

App. Alt.	0°–4° Corrⁿ	5°–9° Corrⁿ	10°–14° Corrⁿ	15°–19° Corrⁿ	20°–24° Corrⁿ	25°–29° Corrⁿ	30°–34° Corrⁿ	App. Alt.
′	° ′	° ′	° ′	° ′	° ′	° ′	° ′	′
00	0 33·8	5 58·2	10 62·1	15 62·8	20 62·2	25 60·8	30 58·9	00
10	35·9	58·5	62·2	62·8	62·1	60·8	58·8	10
20	37·8	58·7	62·2	62·8	62·1	60·7	58·8	20
30	39·6	58·9	62·3	62·8	62·1	60·7	58·7	30
40	41·2	59·1	62·3	62·8	62·0	60·6	58·6	40
50	42·6	59·3	62·4	62·7	62·0	60·6	58·5	50
00	1 44·0	6 59·5	11 62·4	16 62·7	21 62·0	26 60·5	31 58·5	00
10	45·2	59·7	62·4	62·7	61·9	60·4	58·4	10
20	46·3	59·9	62·5	62·7	61·9	60·4	58·3	20
30	47·3	60·0	62·5	62·7	61·9	60·3	58·2	30
40	48·3	60·2	62·5	62·7	61·8	60·3	58·2	40
50	49·2	60·3	62·6	62·7	61·8	60·2	58·1	50
00	2 50·0	7 60·5	12 62·6	17 62·7	22 61·7	27 60·1	32 58·0	00
10	50·8	60·6	62·6	62·6	61·7	60·1	57·9	10
20	51·4	60·7	62·6	62·6	61·6	60·0	57·8	20
30	52·1	60·9	62·7	62·6	61·6	59·9	57·8	30
40	52·7	61·0	62·7	62·6	61·5	59·9	57·7	40
50	53·3	61·1	62·7	62·6	61·5	59·8	57·6	50
00	3 53·8	8 61·2	13 62·7	18 62·5	23 61·5	28 59·7	33 57·5	00
10	54·3	61·3	62·7	62·5	61·4	59·7	57·4	10
20	54·8	61·4	62·7	62·5	61·4	59·6	57·4	20
30	55·2	61·5	62·8	62·5	61·3	59·6	57·3	30
40	55·6	61·6	62·8	62·4	61·3	59·5	57·2	40
50	56·0	61·6	62·8	62·4	61·2	59·4	57·1	50
00	4 56·4	9 61·7	14 62·8	19 62·4	24 61·2	29 59·3	34 57·0	00
10	56·7	61·8	62·8	62·3	61·1	59·3	56·9	10
20	57·1	61·9	62·8	62·3	61·1	59·2	56·9	20
30	57·4	61·9	62·8	62·3	61·0	59·1	56·8	30
40	57·7	62·0	62·8	62·2	60·9	59·1	56·7	40
50	57·9	62·1	62·8	62·2	60·9	59·0	56·6	50

H.P.	L	U	L	U	L	U	L	U	L	U	L	U	L	U	H.P.
′	′	′	′	′	′	′	′	′	′	′	′	′	′	′	′
54·0	0·3	0·9	0·3	0·9	0·4	1·0	0·5	1·1	0·6	1·2	0·7	1·3	0·9	1·5	54·0
54·3	0·7	1·1	0·7	1·2	0·7	1·2	0·8	1·3	0·9	1·4	1·1	1·5	1·2	1·7	54·3
54·6	1·1	1·4	1·1	1·4	1·1	1·4	1·2	1·5	1·3	1·6	1·4	1·7	1·5	1·8	54·6
54·9	1·4	1·6	1·5	1·6	1·5	1·6	1·6	1·7	1·6	1·8	1·8	1·9	1·9	2·0	54·9
55·2	1·8	1·8	1·8	1·8	1·9	1·9	1·9	1·9	2·0	2·0	2·1	2·1	2·2	2·2	55·2
55·5	2·2	2·0	2·2	2·0	2·3	2·1	2·3	2·1	2·4	2·2	2·4	2·3	2·5	2·4	55·5
55·8	2·6	2·2	2·6	2·2	2·6	2·3	2·7	2·3	2·7	2·4	2·8	2·4	2·9	2·5	55·8
56·1	3·0	2·4	3·0	2·5	3·0	2·5	3·0	2·5	3·1	2·6	3·1	2·6	3·2	2·7	56·1
56·4	3·4	2·7	3·4	2·7	3·4	2·7	3·4	2·7	3·4	2·8	3·5	2·8	3·5	2·9	56·4
56·7	3·7	2·9	3·7	2·9	3·8	2·9	3·8	2·9	3·8	3·0	3·8	3·0	3·9	3·0	56·7
57·0	4·1	3·1	4·1	3·1	4·1	3·1	4·1	3·1	4·2	3·1	4·2	3·2	4·2	3·2	57·0
57·3	4·5	3·3	4·5	3·3	4·5	3·3	4·5	3·3	4·5	3·3	4·5	3·4	4·6	3·4	57·3
57·6	4·9	3·5	4·9	3·5	4·9	3·5	4·9	3·5	4·9	3·5	4·9	3·5	4·9	3·6	57·6
57·9	5·3	3·8	5·3	3·8	5·2	3·8	5·2	3·7	5·2	3·7	5·2	3·7	5·2	3·7	57·9
58·2	5·6	4·0	5·6	4·0	5·6	4·0	5·6	4·0	5·6	3·9	5·6	3·9	5·6	3·9	58·2
58·5	6·0	4·2	6·0	4·2	6·0	4·2	6·0	4·2	6·0	4·1	5·9	4·1	5·9	4·1	58·5
58·8	6·4	4·4	6·4	4·4	6·4	4·4	6·3	4·4	6·3	4·3	6·3	4·3	6·2	4·2	58·8
59·1	6·8	4·6	6·8	4·6	6·7	4·6	6·7	4·6	6·7	4·5	6·6	4·5	6·6	4·4	59·1
59·4	7·2	4·8	7·1	4·8	7·1	4·8	7·1	4·8	7·0	4·7	7·0	4·7	6·9	4·6	59·4
59·7	7·5	5·1	7·5	5·0	7·5	5·0	7·5	5·0	7·4	4·9	7·3	4·8	7·2	4·7	59·7
60·0	7·9	5·3	7·9	5·3	7·9	5·2	7·8	5·2	7·8	5·1	7·7	5·0	7·6	4·9	60·0
60·3	8·3	5·5	8·3	5·5	8·2	5·4	8·2	5·4	8·1	5·3	8·0	5·2	7·9	5·1	60·3
60·6	8·7	5·7	8·7	5·7	8·6	5·7	8·6	5·6	8·5	5·5	8·4	5·4	8·2	5·3	60·6
60·9	9·1	5·9	9·0	5·9	9·0	5·9	8·9	5·8	8·8	5·7	8·7	5·6	8·6	5·4	60·9
61·2	9·5	6·2	9·4	6·1	9·4	6·1	9·3	6·0	9·2	5·9	9·1	5·8	8·9	5·6	61·2
61·5	9·8	6·4	9·8	6·3	9·7	6·3	9·7	6·2	9·5	6·1	9·4	5·9	9·2	5·8	61·5

DIP

Ht. of Eye	Corrⁿ	Ht. of Eye	Ht. of Eye	Corrⁿ	Ht. of Eye
m		ft.	m		ft.
2·4		8·0	9·5		31·5
	−2·8			−5·5	
2·6		8·6	9·9		32·7
	−2·9			−5·6	
2·8		9·2	10·3		33·9
	−3·0			−5·7	
3·0		9·8	10·6		35·1
	−3·1			−5·8	
3·2		10·5	11·0		36·3
	−3·2			−5·9	
3·4		11·2	11·4		37·6
	−3·3			−6·0	
3·6		11·9	11·8		38·9
	−3·4			−6·1	
3·8		12·6	12·2		40·1
	−3·5			−6·2	
4·0		13·3	12·6		41·5
	−3·6			−6·3	
4·3		14·1	13·0		42·8
	−3·7			−6·4	
4·5		14·9	13·4		44·2
	−3·8			−6·5	
4·7		15·7	13·8		45·5
	−3·9			−6·6	
5·0		16·5	14·2		46·9
	−4·0			−6·7	
5·2		17·4	14·7		48·4
	−4·1			−6·8	
5·5		18·3	15·1		49·8
	−4·2			−6·9	
5·8		19·1	15·5		51·3
	−4·3			−7·0	
6·1		20·1	16·0		52·8
	−4·4			−7·1	
6·3		21·0	16·5		54·3
	−4·5			−7·2	
6·6		22·0	16·9		55·8
	−4·6			−7·3	
6·9		22·9	17·4		57·4
	−4·7			−7·4	
7·2		23·9	17·9		58·9
	−4·8			−7·5	
7·5		24·9	18·4		60·5
	−4·9			−7·6	
7·9		26·0	18·8		62·1
	−5·0			−7·7	
8·2		27·1	19·3		63·8
	−5·1			−7·8	
8·5		28·1	19·8		65·4
	−5·2			−7·9	
8·8		29·2	20·4		67·1
	−5·3			−8·0	
9·2		30·4	20·9		68·8
	−5·4			−8·1	
9·5		31·5	21·4		70·5

MOON CORRECTION TABLE

The correction is in two parts; the first correction is taken from the upper part of the table with argument apparent altitude, and the second from the lower part, with argument H.P., in the same column as that from which the first correction was taken. Separate corrections are given in the lower part for lower (L) and upper (U) limbs. All corrections are to be **added** to apparent altitude, *but 30′ is to be subtracted from the altitude of the upper limb.*

For corrections for pressure and temperature see page A4.

For bubble sextant observations ignore dip, take the mean of upper and lower limb corrections and subtract 15′ from the altitude.

App. Alt. = Apparent altitude = Sextant altitude corrected for index error and dip.

SUN'S TRUE BEARING AT SUNRISE AND SUNSET

LATITUDES 0° to 66° DECLINATIONS 0° to 11°

LAT.	DECLINATION 0°	1°	2°	3°	4°	5°	6°	7°	8°	9°	10°	11°
	°	°	°	°	°	°	°	°	°	°	°	°
0° to 5°	90	89	88	87	86	85	84	83	82	81	80	79
6°	90	89	88	87	86	85	84	83	82	81	79.9	78.9
7°	90	89	88	87	86	85	84	83	81.9	80.9	79.9	78.9
8°	90	89	88	87	86	85	84	82.9	81.9	80.9	79.9	78.9
9°	90	89	88	87	86	85	83.9	82.9	81.9	80.9	79.8	78.9
10°	90	89	88	87	86	84.9	83.9	82.9	81.9	80.9	79.8	78.8
11°	90	89	88	87	86	84.9	83.9	82.9	81.9	80.8	79.8	78.8
12°	90	89	88	87	85.9	84.9	83.9	82.9	81.8	80.8	79.8	78.8
13°	90	89	88	86.9	85.9	84.9	83.8	82.8	81.8	80.8	79.7	78.7
14°	90	98	88	86.9	85.9	84.9	83.8	82.8	81.8	80.7	79.7	78.7
15°	90	89	88	86.9	85.9	84.8	83.8	82.8	81.7	80.7	79.6	78.6
16°	90	89	87.9	86.9	85.8	84.8	83.8	82.7	81.7	80.6	79.6	78.6
17°	90	89	87.9	86.9	85.8	84.8	83.7	82.7	81.6	80.6	79.5	78.5
18°	90	89	87.9	86.9	85.8	84.8	83.7	82.6	81.6	80.5	79.5	78.4
19°	90	89	87.9	86.8	85.8	84.7	83.7	82.6	81.5	80.5	79.4	78.4
20°	90	88.9	87.9	86.8	85.8	84.7	83.6	82.6	81.5	80.4	79.4	78.3
21°	90	88.9	87.9	86.8	85.7	84.7	83.6	82.5	81.4	80.4	79.3	78.2
22°	90	88.9	87.9	86.8	85.7	84.6	83.5	82.5	81.4	80.3	79.2	78.1
23°	90	88.9	87.9	86.7	85.7	84.6	83.5	82.4	81.3	80.2	79.1	78.0
24°	90	88.9	87.8	86.7	85.6	84.5	83.4	82.3	81.2	80.1	79.0	78.0
25°	90	88.9	87.8	86.7	85.6	84.5	83.4	82.3	81.2	80.1	79.0	77.9
26°	90	88.9	87.8	86.7	85.6	84.4	83.3	82.2	81.1	80.0	78.9	77.8
27°	90	88.9	87.8	86.6	85.5	84.4	83.3	82.1	81.0	79.9	78.8	77.6
28°	90	88.9	87.8	86.6	85.5	84.4	83.2	82.1	80.9	79.8	78.7	77.5
29°	90	88.9	87.8	86.6	85.5	84.3	83.1	82.0	80.9	79.7	78.6	77.4
30°	90	88.9	87.7	86.5	85.4	84.2	83.1	81.9	80.8	79.6	78.5	77.3
31°	90	88.9	87.7	86.5	85.4	84.2	83.0	81.8	80.7	79.5	78.3	77.1
32°	90	88.9	87.7	86.5	85.3	84.1	82.9	81.7	80.6	79.4	78.2	77.0
33°	90	88.8	87.7	86.4	85.3	84.0	82.8	81.7	80.5	79.3	78.0	76.9
34°	90	88.8	87.6	86.4	85.2	84.0	82.7	81.5	80.3	79.1	77.9	76.7
35°	90	88.8	87.5	86.3	85.1	83.9	82.7	81.4	80.2	79.0	77.8	76.5
36°	90	88.8	87.5	86.3	85.0	83.8	82.6	81.3	80.1	78.8	77.6	76.3
37°	90	88.7	87.5	86.2	85.0	83.7	82.5	81.2	80.0	78.7	77.4	76.2
38°	90	88.7	87.5	86.2	84.9	83.6	82.4	81.1	79.8	78.5	77.3	76.0
39°	90	88.7	87.4	86.1	84.8	83.6	82.3	81.0	79.7	78.4	77.1	75.8
40°	90	88.7	87.4	86.1	84.8	83.5	82.1	80.8	79.5	78.2	76.9	75.6
41°	90	88.7	87.3	86.0	84.7	83.4	82.0	80.7	79.4	78.0	76.7	75.3
42°	90	88.6	87.3	86.0	84.6	83.3	81.9	80.6	79.2	77.8	76.5	75.1
43°	90	88.6	87.3	85.9	84.5	83.1	81.8	80.4	79.0	77.6	76.3	74.9
44°	90	88.6	87.2	85.8	84.4	83.0	81.6	80.2	78.8	77.4	76.0	74.6
45°	90	88.6	87.2	85.7	84.3	82.9	81.5	80.1	78.6	77.2	75.8	74.3
46°	90	88.6	87.1	85.7	84.2	82.8	81.3	79.9	78.4	77.0	75.5	74.0
47°	90	88.5	87.1	85.6	84.1	82.6	81.2	79.7	78.2	76.7	75.2	73.7
48°	90	88.5	87.0	85.5	84.0	82.5	81.0	79.5	78.0	76.5	75.0	73.4
49°	90	88.5	86.9	85.4	83.9	82.4	80.8	79.3	77.7	76.2	74.6	73.1
50°	90	88.4	86.9	85.3	83.8	82.2	80.6	79.1	77.5	75.9	74.3	72.7
51°	90	88.4	86.8	85.2	83.6	82.0	80.4	78.8	77.2	75.6	74.0	72.3
52°	90	88.4	86.7	85.1	83.5	81.9	80.2	78.6	76.9	75.3	73.6	71.9
53°	90	88.3	86.7	85.0	83.3	81.7	80.0	78.3	76.6	74.9	73.2	71.5
54°	90	88.3	86.6	84.9	83.2	81.5	79.7	78.0	76.3	74.6	72.8	71.0
55°	90	88.2	86.5	84.8	83.0	81.3	79.5	77.7	75.9	74.2	72.4	70.6
56°	90	88.2	86.4	84.6	82.8	81.0	79.2	77.4	75.6	73.7	71.9	70.0
57°	90	88.2	86.3	84.5	82.6	80.8	78.9	77.1	75.2	73.3	71.4	69.5
58°	90	88.1	86.2	84.3	82.4	80.5	78.6	76.7	74.8	72.8	70.9	68.9
59°	90	88.0	86.1	84.2	82.2	80.2	78.3	76.3	74.3	72.3	70.3	68.2
60°	90	88.0	86.0	84.0	82.0	80.0	77.9	75.9	73.8	71.8	69.7	67.6
61°	90	87.9	85.9	83.8	81.7	79.6	77.5	75.4	73.3	71.2	69.0	66.8
62°	90	87.9	85.7	83.6	81.4	79.3	77.1	74.9	72.7	70.5	68.3	66.0
63°	90	87.8	85.6	83.4	81.2	78.9	76.7	74.4	72.1	69.8	67.5	65.1
64°	90	87.7	85.4	83.1	80.8	78.5	76.2	73.9	71.5	69.1	66.7	64.2
65°	90	87.6	85.3	82.9	80.5	78.1	75.7	73.2	70.8	68.3	65.7	63.2
66°	90	87.5	85.1	82.6	80.1	77.6	75.1	72.6	70.0	67.4	64.7	62.0

Name the Bearing the same as the Declination NORTH or SOUTH and EAST if rising, WEST if setting.

LAT 50°N

LHA ♈	Hc	Zn	Hc	Zn	Hc	Zn	Hc	Zn	Hc	Zn	Hc	Zn	Hc	Zn
	•CAPELLA		ALDEBARAN		Hamal		•Alpheratz		ALTAIR		•VEGA		Kochab	
0	39 37	062	26 11	095	53 48	126	68 56	176	24 13	254	33 58	292	37 31	347
1	40 11	063	26 49	096	54 19	127	68 58	178	23 36	255	33 22	292	37 22	347
2	40 45	063	27 27	097	54 49	128	68 59	180	22 59	256	32 46	293	37 13	347
3	41 20	064	28 06	098	55 19	130	68 58	183	22 21	257	32 11	294	37 05	347
4	41 55	064	28 44	099	55 49	131	68 55	185	21 44	257	31 36	294	36 56	348
5	42 29	065	29 22	099	56 17	132	68 51	188	21 06	258	31 01	295	36 48	348
6	43 04	065	30 00	100	56 46	134	68 45	190	20 28	259	30 26	295	36 40	348
7	43 39	066	30 38	101	57 13	135	68 37	192	19 50	260	29 51	296	36 33	349
8	44 15	066	31 16	102	57 40	137	68 28	195	19 12	261	29 16	297	36 25	349
9	44 50	067	31 53	103	58 06	138	68 17	197	18 34	261	28 42	297	36 18	349
10	45 26	067	32 31	104	58 31	140	68 05	199	17 56	262	28 08	298	36 11	350
11	46 01	068	33 08	105	58 56	141	67 52	202	17 18	263	27 34	298	36 04	350
12	46 37	068	33 45	105	59 19	143	67 37	204	16 39	264	27 00	299	35 57	350
13	47 13	069	34 23	106	59 42	145	67 20	206	16 01	265	26 26	300	35 50	350
14	47 49	069	34 59	107	60 04	146	67 03	208	15 23	265	25 53	300	35 44	351
	•CAPELLA		ALDEBARAN		Hamal		•Diphda		Alpheratz		•DENEB		Kochab	
15	48 25	070	35 36	108	60 25	148	21 48	184	66 44	210	47 25	290	35 38	351
16	49 02	070	36 13	109	60 44	150	21 44	185	66 24	212	46 49	290	35 32	351
17	49 38	071	36 49	110	61 03	152	21 40	186	66 03	214	46 13	291	35 27	352
18	50 15	072	37 25	111	61 21	153	21 36	188	65 41	216	45 37	291	35 21	352
19	50 51	072	38 01	112	61 38	155	21 30	189	65 17	218	45 01	292	35 16	352
20	51 28	073	38 37	113	61 53	157	21 24	190	64 53	220	44 25	292	35 11	353
21	52 05	073	39 12	114	62 08	159	21 17	191	64 28	222	43 50	293	35 06	353
22	52 42	074	39 47	115	62 21	161	21 10	192	64 02	224	43 14	293	35 01	353
23	53 19	074	40 22	116	62 33	163	21 02	193	63 35	225	42 39	294	34 57	354
24	53 56	075	40 57	117	62 44	165	20 53	194	63 07	227	42 04	294	34 53	354
25	54 33	075	41 31	118	62 53	167	20 44	195	62 38	228	41 28	295	34 49	354
26	55 11	076	42 05	119	63 01	169	20 34	196	62 09	230	40 54	295	34 45	355
27	55 48	076	42 39	120	63 08	171	20 23	197	61 39	232	40 19	296	34 41	355
28	56 25	077	43 12	121	63 14	173	20 12	198	61 09	233	39 44	296	34 38	355
29	57 03	077	43 45	122	63 18	175	20 00	199	60 38	235	39 10	297	34 35	356
	CAPELLA		•BETELGEUSE		RIGEL		Hamal		•Alpheratz		DENEB		•Kochab	
30	57 41	078	25 34	110	18 14	129	63 21	177	60 06	236	38 35	297	34 32	356
31	58 19	079	26 10	111	18 44	130	63 22	179	59 34	237	38 01	298	34 29	356
32	58 56	079	26 46	112	19 13	131	63 22	181	59 01	239	37 27	299	34 27	356
33	59 34	080	27 22	113	19 42	132	63 21	183	58 28	240	36 53	299	34 25	357
34	60 12	080	27 57	114	20 11	132	63 18	185	57 54	241	36 20	300	34 23	357
35	60 50	081	28 32	115	20 39	133	63 14	187	57 20	242	35 46	300	34 21	357
36	61 28	081	29 07	116	21 07	134	63 08	189	56 46	244	35 13	301	34 19	358
37	62 07	082	29 42	117	21 34	135	63 01	191	56 11	245	34 40	301	34 18	358
38	62 45	083	30 16	118	22 01	136	62 53	193	55 36	246	34 07	302	34 17	358
39	63 23	083	30 50	119	22 28	137	62 44	195	55 01	247	33 34	302	34 16	359
40	64 01	084	31 24	119	22 54	138	62 33	197	54 25	248	33 02	303	34 15	359
41	64 40	084	31 57	120	23 19	139	62 21	199	53 49	249	32 30	303	34 15	359
42	65 18	085	32 30	121	23 44	140	62 08	201	53 13	250	31 58	304	34 14	000
43	65 57	086	33 03	122	24 09	141	61 54	203	52 36	251	31 26	304	34 14	000
44	66 35	086	33 35	123	24 33	142	61 38	205	52 00	252	30 54	305	34 14	000

LAT 50°N

LHA ♈	Hc	Zn	Hc	Zn	Hc	Zn	Hc	Zn	Hc	Zn	Hc	Zn	Hc	Zn
	•Dubhe		REGULUS		PROCYON		•SIRIUS		RIGEL		ALDEBARAN		•Mirfak	
90	48 39	044	27 11	104	40 44	147	22 36	169	30 54	193	52 19	215	64 59	285
91	49 06	044	27 49	105	41 05	148	22 43	170	30 45	195	51 57	216	64 22	285
92	49 33	044	28 26	106	41 25	149	22 50	171	30 35	196	51 34	218	63 45	286
93	50 00	044	29 03	107	41 44	151	22 56	172	30 24	197	51 10	219	63 08	286
94	50 27	045	29 40	108	42 03	152	23 01	173	30 13	198	50 45	220	62 31	286
95	50 54	045	30 16	109	42 21	153	23 06	174	30 00	199	50 20	222	61 54	287
96	51 21	045	30 53	109	42 38	154	23 10	175	29 47	200	49 54	223	61 17	287
97	51 49	045	31 29	110	42 54	156	23 13	176	29 34	201	49 27	224	60 40	288
98	52 16	045	32 05	111	43 09	157	23 15	177	29 19	202	49 00	226	60 04	288
99	52 44	046	32 41	112	43 24	158	23 17	178	29 04	203	48 32	227	59 27	289
100	53 11	046	33 16	113	43 38	160	23 18	179	28 49	205	48 04	228	58 51	289
101	53 39	046	33 52	114	43 50	161	23 19	180	28 32	206	47 35	229	58 14	289
102	54 07	046	34 27	115	44 03	162	23 18	181	28 15	207	47 05	231	57 38	290
103	54 35	046	35 02	116	44 14	164	23 17	182	27 58	208	46 35	232	57 02	290
104	55 02	046	35 36	117	44 24	165	23 16	183	27 39	209	46 04	233	56 25	291
	•Dubhe		Denebola		REGULUS		•SIRIUS		RIGEL		ALDEBARAN		•Mirfak	
105	55 30	047	22 43	094	36 10	118	23 13	184	27 20	210	45 33	234	55 49	291
106	55 58	047	23 22	095	36 44	119	23 10	185	27 01	211	45 02	235	55 13	292
107	56 27	047	24 00	096	37 18	120	23 06	186	26 41	212	44 30	236	54 38	292
108	56 55	047	24 38	096	37 51	121	23 02	187	26 20	213	43 58	238	54 02	292
109	57 23	047	25 17	097	38 24	122	22 57	188	25 58	214	43 25	239	53 26	293
110	57 51	047	25 55	098	38 56	123	22 51	189	25 37	215	42 52	240	52 51	293
111	58 19	047	26 33	099	39 29	124	22 44	190	25 14	216	42 18	241	52 15	294
112	58 47	047	27 11	100	40 00	125	22 37	191	24 51	217	41 44	242	51 40	294
113	59 16	047	27 49	101	40 32	126	22 29	192	24 28	218	41 10	243	51 05	295
114	59 44	047	28 27	101	41 03	127	22 20	193	24 03	219	40 36	244	50 30	295
115	60 12	047	29 05	102	41 33	128	22 11	194	23 39	220	40 01	245	49 55	295
116	60 41	047	29 42	103	42 03	130	22 01	195	23 14	221	39 26	246	49 20	296
117	61 09	047	30 20	104	42 32	131	21 51	196	22 48	222	38 51	247	48 46	296
118	61 37	047	30 57	105	43 01	132	21 39	197	22 22	223	38 15	248	48 11	297
119	62 05	047	31 34	106	43 30	133	21 28	198	21 56	224	37 39	249	47 37	297
	•Kochab		Denebola		•REGULUS		SIRIUS		RIGEL		•ALDEBARAN		CAPELLA	
120	44 20	022	32 11	107	43 58	134	21 15	199	21 29	225	37 03	250	62 30	278
121	44 35	022	32 48	107	44 25	135	21 02	200	21 01	226	36 27	251	61 51	278
122	44 49	022	33 25	108	44 52	137	20 48	201	20 33	227	35 50	252	61 13	279
123	45 04	022	34 02	109	45 18	138	20 34	202	20 05	228	35 14	252	60 35	279
124	45 18	022	34 38	110	45 44	139	20 19	203	19 36	229	34 37	253	59 57	280
125	45 33	023	35 14	111	46 09	140	20 03	204	19 07	230	34 00	254	59 19	281
126	45 48	023	35 50	112	46 33	142	19 47	205	18 37	230	33 23	255	58 41	281
127	46 03	023	36 26	113	46 56	143	19 30	206	18 07	231	32 45	256	58 04	282
128	46 18	023	37 01	114	47 19	144	19 12	207	17 37	232	32 08	257	57 26	282
129	46 33	023	37 36	115	47 41	146	18 54	208	17 06	233	31 30	258	56 48	283
130	46 48	023	38 11	116	48 03	147	18 36	209	16 35	234	30 52	259	56 11	283
131	47 04	023	38 46	117	48 23	148	18 17	210	16 04	235	30 15	259	55 33	284
132	47 19	024	39 20	118	48 43	150	17 57	211	15 32	236	29 37	260	54 56	284
133	47 35	024	39 54	119	49 02	151	17 37	212	15 00	237	28 58	261	54 18	285
134	47 50	024	40 27	120	49 20	153	17 16	213	14 28	238	28 20	262	53 41	286

LHA	♦Dubhe	POLLUX	BETELGEUSE	♦RIGEL	Hamal	♦Alpheratz	DENEB
45	31 24 028	33 01 084	34 07 124	24 56 143	61 21 207	51 23 253	30 22 306
46	31 43 029	33 40 085	34 39 125	25 19 144	61 04 208	50 46 254	29 51 306
47	32 01 029	34 18 086	35 10 126	25 41 145	60 45 210	50 09 255	29 20 307
48	32 20 030	34 57 087	35 41 128	26 03 146	60 25 212	49 31 256	28 49 307
49	32 39 030	35 35 087	36 11 129	26 24 147	60 04 214	48 54 257	28 19 308
50	32 59 030	36 14 088	36 41 130	26 45 148	59 42 215	48 16 258	27 48 308
51	33 19 031	36 52 089	37 11 131	27 05 149	59 20 217	47 38 259	27 18 309
52	33 38 031	37 31 090	37 40 132	27 24 150	58 56 219	47 00 260	26 48 309
53	33 59 032	38 09 090	38 08 133	27 43 151	58 32 220	46 22 261	26 19 310
54	34 19 032	38 48 091	38 36 134	28 01 152	58 06 222	45 44 262	25 49 311
55	34 40 032	39 26 092	39 04 135	28 19 153	57 40 223	45 06 263	25 20 311
56	35 00 033	40 05 093	39 31 136	28 36 155	57 14 225	44 27 263	24 51 312
57	35 21 033	40 44 093	39 57 137	28 52 156	56 46 226	43 49 264	24 22 312
58	35 43 034	41 22 094	40 23 139	29 08 157	56 18 228	43 11 265	23 54 313
59	36 04 034	42 00 095	40 48 140	29 22 158	55 49 229	42 32 266	23 26 313
	♦Dubhe	POLLUX	SIRIUS	♦RIGEL	Hamal	♦Alpheratz	DENEB
60	36 26 034	42 39 096	14 08 140	29 37 159	55 20 230	41 54 267	22 58 314
61	36 48 035	43 17 097	14 33 140	29 50 160	54 50 232	41 15 268	22 30 315
62	37 10 035	43 55 098	14 57 141	30 03 161	54 19 233	40 37 268	22 03 315
63	37 32 035	44 34 098	15 21 142	30 15 162	53 48 234	39 58 269	21 36 316
64	37 54 036	45 12 099	15 45 143	30 26 163	53 17 236	39 20 270	21 09 316
65	38 17 036	45 50 100	16 07 144	30 37 165	52 45 237	38 41 271	20 42 317
66	38 40 037	46 28 101	16 30 145	30 47 166	52 12 238	38 02 271	20 16 317
67	39 03 037	47 05 102	16 52 146	30 56 167	51 39 239	37 24 272	19 50 318
68	39 26 037	47 43 103	17 13 147	31 05 168	51 06 240	36 45 273	19 25 319
69	39 50 038	48 21 104	17 34 148	31 12 169	50 32 242	36 07 274	18 59 319
70	40 13 038	48 58 105	17 54 149	31 19 170	49 58 243	35 28 274	18 34 320
71	40 37 038	49 35 106	18 14 150	31 25 171	49 24 244	34 50 275	18 10 320
72	41 01 039	50 12 107	18 33 151	31 31 173	48 49 245	34 12 276	17 45 321
73	41 25 039	50 49 108	18 52 152	31 35 174	48 14 246	33 33 277	17 21 322
74	41 50 039	51 26 109	19 10 153	31 39 175	47 39 247	32 55 277	16 57 322
	♦Dubhe	REGULUS	PROCYON	♦SIRIUS	RIGEL	♦Hamal	DENEB
75	42 14 040	17 40 092	34 20 130	19 27 153	31 42 176	47 03 248	16 34 323
76	42 39 040	18 18 093	34 49 131	19 44 154	31 44 177	46 27 249	16 11 323
77	43 04 040	18 57 094	35 18 132	20 01 155	31 46 178	45 51 250	15 48 324
78	43 29 040	19 35 095	35 46 133	20 16 156	31 47 180	45 15 251	15 26 325
79	43 54 041	20 14 095	36 14 134	20 32 157	31 46 181	44 38 252	15 03 325
80	44 19 041	20 52 096	36 42 135	20 46 158	31 46 182	44 01 253	14 42 326
81	44 44 041	21 30 097	37 09 136	21 00 159	31 44 183	43 24 254	14 20 327
82	45 10 042	22 09 098	37 35 137	21 13 160	31 41 184	42 47 255	13 59 327
83	45 36 042	22 47 098	38 01 139	21 26 161	31 38 185	42 10 256	13 39 328
84	46 01 042	23 25 099	38 26 140	21 38 162	31 34 187	41 32 257	13 18 329
85	46 27 042	24 03 100	38 51 141	21 49 163	31 30 188	40 55 258	12 58 329
86	46 54 043	24 41 101	39 15 142	22 00 164	31 24 189	40 17 258	12 39 330
87	47 20 043	25 19 102	39 38 143	22 10 165	31 18 190	39 39 259	12 19 330
88	47 46 043	25 56 103	40 01 144	22 19 166	31 11 191	39 01 260	12 01 331
89	48 13 044	26 34 103	40 23 146	22 28 167	31 03 192	38 23 261	11 42 332

LHA	♦Kochab	ARCTURUS	Denebola	♦REGULUS	SIRIUS	BETELGEUSE	♦CAPELLA
135	48 06 024	21 50 086	41 01 121	49 37 154	16 55 214	32 32 239	53 04 286
136	48 22 024	22 29 086	41 34 122	49 54 156	16 33 215	31 58 239	52 27 287
137	48 37 024	23 07 087	42 06 123	50 09 157	16 10 216	31 25 240	51 50 287
138	48 53 024	23 46 088	42 38 124	50 24 158	15 48 217	30 51 241	51 13 288
139	49 09 024	24 25 089	43 10 125	50 38 160	15 24 218	30 17 242	50 37 288
140	49 25 024	25 03 089	43 41 126	50 50 161	15 01 219	29 43 243	50 00 289
141	49 41 025	25 42 090	44 12 128	51 02 163	14 36 219	29 08 244	49 24 289
142	49 57 025	26 20 091	44 42 129	51 13 165	14 12 220	28 34 245	48 47 290
143	50 13 025	26 59 092	45 12 130	51 23 166	13 46 221	27 58 246	48 11 290
144	50 29 025	27 37 093	45 42 131	51 31 168	13 21 222	27 23 247	47 35 291
145	50 45 025	28 16 093	46 10 132	51 39 169	12 55 223	26 47 248	46 59 291
146	51 02 025	28 54 094	46 39 133	51 46 171	12 28 224	26 12 249	46 23 292
147	51 18 025	29 33 095	47 06 135	51 51 172	12 01 225	25 36 250	45 47 292
148	51 34 025	30 11 096	47 33 136	51 56 174	11 34 226	24 59 250	45 12 293
149	51 50 025	30 50 096	48 00 137	52 00 176	11 06 226	24 23 251	44 36 293
	♦Kochab	ARCTURUS	♦SPICA	REGULUS	PROCYON	♦BETELGEUSE	CAPELLA
150	52 07 025	31 28 097	14 28 128	52 02 177	36 18 226	23 46 252	44 01 294
151	52 23 025	32 06 098	14 58 129	52 04 179	35 50 227	23 09 253	43 26 294
152	52 39 025	32 44 099	15 28 130	52 04 180	35 21 228	22 33 254	42 51 295
153	52 56 025	33 22 100	15 57 131	52 03 182	34 53 229	21 55 255	42 16 295
154	53 12 025	34 00 101	16 27 132	52 01 183	34 23 230	21 18 256	41 41 296
155	53 28 025	34 38 101	16 55 132	51 59 185	33 54 231	20 41 256	41 06 296
156	53 44 025	35 16 102	17 23 133	51 55 187	33 23 232	20 03 257	40 32 297
157	54 01 025	35 53 103	17 51 134	51 50 188	32 53 233	19 25 258	39 57 297
158	54 17 025	36 31 104	18 19 135	51 44 190	32 22 234	18 48 259	39 23 298
159	54 33 025	37 08 105	18 46 136	51 37 191	31 50 235	18 10 260	38 49 298
160	54 49 025	37 45 106	19 12 137	51 28 193	31 18 236	17 32 260	38 15 299
161	55 05 025	38 22 107	19 38 138	51 19 194	30 46 237	16 54 261	37 42 300
162	55 22 025	38 59 108	20 04 139	51 09 196	30 14 238	16 16 262	37 08 300
163	55 38 025	39 36 109	20 29 140	50 58 198	29 41 239	15 37 263	36 35 301
164	55 54 024	40 12 110	20 54 141	50 46 199	29 07 240	14 59 264	36 02 301
	♦VEGA	ARCTURUS	♦SPICA	REGULUS	PROCYON	♦POLLUX	CAPELLA
165	15 59 048	40 49 110	21 18 142	50 33 201	28 34 241	47 07 258	35 29 302
166	16 27 048	41 25 111	21 42 143	50 19 202	28 00 242	46 29 259	34 56 302
167	16 56 049	42 00 112	22 05 144	50 04 204	27 26 243	45 52 260	34 24 303
168	17 26 050	42 36 113	22 27 145	49 48 205	26 51 244	45 14 261	33 51 303
169	17 55 050	43 11 114	22 49 146	49 31 206	26 17 245	44 35 262	33 19 304
170	18 25 051	43 46 115	23 11 147	49 14 208	25 42 246	43 57 262	32 47 304
171	18 55 052	44 21 117	23 32 148	48 55 209	25 06 246	43 19 263	32 15 305
172	19 25 052	44 55 118	23 52 149	48 36 211	24 31 247	42 41 264	31 44 305
173	19 56 053	45 29 119	24 12 150	48 16 212	23 55 248	42 02 265	31 13 306
174	20 27 053	46 03 120	24 31 151	47 55 213	23 19 249	41 24 266	30 41 306
175	20 58 054	46 36 121	24 50 152	47 34 215	22 43 250	40 45 267	30 10 307
176	21 29 055	47 09 122	25 08 153	47 11 216	22 07 251	40 07 267	29 40 307
177	22 01 055	47 42 123	25 25 154	46 48 217	21 30 252	39 28 268	29 09 308
178	22 33 056	48 14 124	25 42 155	46 24 219	20 54 252	38 50 269	28 39 309
179	23 05 057	48 45 125	25 58 156	46 00 220	20 17 253	38 11 270	28 09 309

LAT 50°N

LHA ♈	Hc	Zn	Hc	Zn	Hc	Zn	Hc	Zn	Hc	Zn	Hc	Zn	Hc	Zn
	♦DENEB		VEGA		ARCTURUS		♦SPICA		REGULUS		♦POLLUX		CAPELLA	
180	14 34	034	23 37	057	49 16	127	26 14	157	45 35	221	37 33	270	27 39	310
181	14 55	034	24 10	058	49 47	128	26 28	158	45 09	223	36 54	271	27 10	310
182	15 17	035	24 42	058	50 17	129	26 42	159	44 43	224	36 15	272	26 40	311
183	15 40	036	25 15	059	50 47	130	26 56	160	44 16	225	35 37	273	26 11	311
184	16 02	036	25 49	060	51 16	132	27 09	161	43 48	226	34 58	273	25 42	312
185	16 25	037	26 22	060	51 45	133	27 21	162	43 20	227	34 20	274	25 14	312
186	16 49	038	26 56	061	52 13	134	27 32	163	42 51	229	33 41	275	24 45	313
187	17 12	038	27 29	061	52 40	136	27 43	164	42 22	230	33 03	276	24 17	314
188	17 36	039	28 03	062	53 06	137	27 53	165	41 53	231	32 25	276	23 50	314
189	18 00	039	28 37	063	53 32	138	28 02	167	41 23	232	31 46	277	23 22	315
190	18 25	040	29 12	063	53 58	140	28 11	168	40 52	233	31 08	278	22 55	315
191	18 50	041	29 46	064	54 22	141	28 19	169	40 21	234	30 30	278	22 28	316
192	19 15	041	30 21	064	54 46	143	28 26	170	39 49	235	29 52	279	22 01	316
193	19 41	042	30 56	065	55 09	144	28 32	171	39 18	236	29 14	280	21 35	317
194	20 06	042	31 31	066	55 31	146	28 38	172	38 45	237	28 36	281	21 09	318
	♦DENEB		VEGA		Rasalhague		♦ARCTURUS		REGULUS		♦POLLUX		CAPELLA	
195	20 33	043	32 06	066	23 22	098	55 52	147	38 13	238	27 58	281	20 43	318
196	20 59	043	32 42	067	24 00	099	56 12	149	37 40	239	27 20	282	20 17	319
197	21 26	044	33 17	067	24 38	100	56 32	151	37 06	240	26 43	283	19 52	319
198	21 53	045	33 53	068	25 16	101	56 50	152	36 33	241	26 05	283	19 27	320
199	22 20	045	34 29	069	25 54	102	57 08	154	35 58	242	25 28	284	19 02	321
200	22 47	046	35 05	069	26 32	103	57 24	156	35 24	243	24 50	285	18 38	321
201	23 15	046	35 41	070	27 09	103	57 40	157	34 50	244	24 13	285	18 14	322
202	23 43	047	36 17	071	27 47	104	57 54	159	34 15	245	23 36	286	17 50	322
203	24 12	048	36 54	071	28 24	105	58 08	161	33 39	246	22 59	287	17 27	323
204	24 40	048	37 30	072	29 01	106	58 20	162	33 04	247	22 22	288	17 04	324
205	25 09	049	38 07	072	29 38	107	58 31	164	32 28	248	21 45	288	16 41	324
206	25 38	049	38 44	073	30 15	108	58 41	166	31 52	249	21 09	289	16 18	325
207	26 07	050	39 21	074	30 52	109	58 50	168	31 16	250	20 32	290	15 56	325
208	26 37	050	39 58	074	31 28	109	58 57	170	30 40	251	19 56	290	15 35	326
209	27 07	051	40 35	075	32 05	110	59 04	171	30 04	252	19 20	291	15 13	327
	♦DENEB		VEGA		Rasalhague		♦ARCTURUS		REGULUS		♦POLLUX		CAPELLA	
210	27 37	051	41 12	075	32 41	111	59 09	173	29 27	253	18 44	292	14 52	327
211	28 07	052	41 50	076	33 17	112	59 13	175	28 50	253	18 08	292	14 32	328
212	28 38	053	42 27	077	33 52	113	59 15	177	28 13	254	17 33	293	14 11	328
213	29 09	053	43 05	077	34 28	114	59 17	179	27 36	255	16 57	294	13 51	329
214	29 40	054	43 42	078	35 03	115	59 17	181	26 58	256	16 22	294	13 32	330
215	30 11	054	44 20	079	35 37	116	59 16	182	26 21	257	15 47	295	13 12	330
216	30 42	055	44 58	079	36 12	117	59 14	184	25 43	258	15 12	296	12 54	331
217	31 14	055	45 36	080	36 46	118	59 10	186	25 05	259	14 38	296	12 35	332
218	31 46	056	46 14	081	37 20	119	59 06	188	24 28	259	14 03	297	12 17	332
219	32 18	056	46 52	081	37 54	120	59 00	190	23 50	260	13 29	298	11 59	333
220	32 50	057	47 30	082	38 27	121	58 53	192	23 12	261	12 55	299	11 42	334
221	33 22	058	48 08	083	39 00	122	58 44	193	22 33	262	12 21	299	11 25	334
222	33 55	058	48 47	083	39 32	123	58 35	195	21 55	263	11 48	300	11 08	335
223	34 28	059	49 25	084	40 05	124	58 24	197	21 17	263	11 14	301	10 52	336
224	35 01	059	50 03	085	40 36	125	58 12	199	20 39	264	10 41	301	10 36	336

LAT 50°N

LHA ♈	Hc	Zn	Hc	Zn	Hc	Zn	Hc	Zn	Hc	Zn	Hc	Zn	Hc	Zn
	♦Mirfak		Alpheratz		♦ALTAIR		Rasalhague		♦ARCTURUS		Alkaid		Kochab	
270	15 18	025	20 41	069	42 56	142	52 12	190	36 07	256	50 19	294	58 50	337
271	15 34	026	21 17	070	43 19	143	52 04	192	35 30	257	49 44	295	58 35	337
272	15 51	026	21 53	071	43 42	144	51 56	194	34 52	258	49 09	295	58 20	337
273	16 08	027	22 30	071	44 05	145	51 46	195	34 14	259	48 34	296	58 05	337
274	16 26	027	23 06	072	44 26	147	51 36	197	33 36	260	48 00	296	57 49	337
275	16 44	028	23 43	073	44 47	148	51 24	198	32 58	261	47 25	297	57 34	336
276	17 02	029	24 20	073	45 07	149	51 12	200	32 20	262	46 51	297	57 18	336
277	17 21	029	24 57	074	45 27	151	50 58	201	31 42	262	46 16	298	57 03	336
278	17 40	030	25 34	075	45 45	152	50 44	203	31 04	263	45 42	298	56 47	336
279	17 59	030	26 11	075	46 03	153	50 28	204	30 26	264	45 08	299	56 31	336
280	18 19	031	26 48	076	46 20	155	50 12	206	29 47	265	44 34	299	56 15	336
281	18 39	032	27 26	077	46 36	156	49 55	207	29 09	266	44 01	299	56 00	336
282	19 00	032	28 03	077	46 51	157	49 37	209	28 30	266	43 27	300	55 44	335
283	19 20	033	28 41	078	47 06	159	49 18	210	27 52	267	42 54	300	55 28	335
284	19 41	033	29 19	079	47 19	160	48 58	211	27 13	268	42 21	301	55 11	335
	♦Mirfak		Alpheratz		♦ALTAIR		Rasalhague		♦ARCTURUS		Alkaid		Kochab	
285	20 03	034	29 57	079	47 32	162	48 38	213	26 35	269	41 48	301	54 55	335
286	20 24	034	30 35	080	47 44	163	48 17	214	25 56	270	41 15	302	54 39	335
287	20 46	035	31 13	081	47 54	164	47 55	215	25 17	270	40 42	302	54 23	335
288	21 09	036	31 51	082	48 04	166	47 32	217	24 39	271	40 10	303	54 07	335
289	21 31	036	32 29	082	48 13	167	47 08	218	24 00	272	39 37	303	53 50	335
290	21 54	037	33 07	083	48 21	169	46 44	219	23 22	273	39 05	304	53 34	335
291	22 17	037	33 46	084	48 28	170	46 19	221	22 43	273	38 33	304	53 18	335
292	22 41	038	34 24	084	48 34	172	45 54	222	22 05	274	38 01	305	53 02	335
293	23 05	038	35 02	085	48 39	173	45 28	223	21 26	275	37 30	305	52 45	335
294	23 29	039	35 41	086	48 43	175	45 01	224	20 48	276	36 58	306	52 29	335
295	23 53	040	36 19	087	48 46	176	44 34	226	20 10	276	36 27	306	52 13	335
296	24 18	040	36 58	087	48 48	178	44 06	227	19 31	277	35 56	307	51 56	335
297	24 43	041	37 36	088	48 49	179	43 37	228	18 53	278	35 25	307	51 40	335
298	25 08	041	38 15	089	48 49	181	43 08	229	18 15	279	34 54	308	51 24	335
299	25 34	042	38 54	090	48 48	182	42 39	230	17 37	279	34 24	308	51 08	335
	CAPELLA		♦Alpheratz		Enif		ALTAIR		♦Rasalhague		Alphecca		♦Kochab	
300	12 24	028	39 32	090	44 28	143	48 46	184	42 09	232	35 00	271	50 51	335
301	12 42	029	40 11	091	44 51	144	48 43	185	41 39	233	34 22	272	50 35	335
302	13 01	029	40 49	092	45 13	146	48 38	187	41 08	234	33 43	273	50 19	335
303	13 20	030	41 28	093	45 34	147	48 33	188	40 36	235	33 05	273	50 03	335
304	13 39	030	42 06	093	45 55	148	48 27	190	40 05	236	32 26	274	49 47	335
305	13 59	031	42 45	094	46 15	150	48 20	191	39 33	237	31 48	275	49 31	336
306	14 19	032	43 23	095	46 34	151	48 12	193	39 00	238	31 09	276	49 15	336
307	14 40	032	44 02	096	46 52	152	48 03	194	38 27	239	30 31	276	48 59	336
308	15 01	033	44 40	097	47 10	154	47 53	196	37 54	240	29 53	277	48 43	336
309	15 22	034	45 18	098	47 26	155	47 42	197	37 20	241	29 14	278	48 27	336
310	15 43	034	45 56	098	47 42	157	47 31	199	36 46	242	28 36	279	48 12	336
311	16 05	035	46 34	099	47 57	158	47 18	200	36 12	243	27 58	279	47 56	336
312	16 27	035	47 12	100	48 11	159	47 04	201	35 38	244	27 20	280	47 40	336
313	16 50	036	47 50	101	48 24	161	46 50	203	35 03	245	26 42	281	47 25	336
314	17 13	037	48 28	102	48 37	162	46 34	204	34 28	246	26 04	281	47 10	336

LHA	DENEB	♦VEGA	Rasalhague	ANTARES	♦ARCTURUS	Denebola	♦Dubhe
225	35 34 060	50 42 085	41 08 126	11 09 160	57 59 200	37 37 245	56 06 313
226	36 07 060	51 20 086	41 39 127	11 21 161	57 45 202	37 02 246	55 37 313
227	36 41 061	51 59 087	42 09 128	11 34 162	57 30 204	36 26 247	55 10 314
228	37 15 061	52 37 087	42 39 130	11 46 163	57 14 206	35 51 248	54 42 314
229	37 49 062	53 16 088	43 08 131	11 57 164	56 57 207	35 15 249	54 14 314
230	38 23 062	53 54 089	43 37 132	12 07 164	56 39 209	34 39 250	53 46 314
231	38 57 063	54 33 090	44 06 133	12 18 165	56 20 210	34 02 251	53 18 314
232	39 31 063	55 11 090	44 34 134	12 27 166	56 00 212	33 26 252	52 51 314
233	40 06 064	55 50 091	45 01 136	12 36 167	55 39 214	32 49 253	52 23 314
234	40 40 064	56 28 092	45 28 137	12 44 168	55 17 215	32 12 253	51 56 315
235	41 15 065	57 07 093	45 54 138	12 52 169	54 54 217	31 35 254	51 28 315
236	41 50 065	57 45 094	46 19 139	12 59 170	54 31 218	30 58 255	51 01 315
237	42 26 066	58 24 094	46 44 141	13 05 171	54 07 220	30 21 256	50 34 315
238	43 01 067	59 02 095	47 08 142	13 11 172	53 42 221	29 43 257	50 07 315
239	43 36 067	59 41 096	47 32 143	13 17 173	53 16 222	29 05 258	49 40 316
	♦DENEB	ALTAIR	Rasalhague	♦ANTARES	ARCTURUS	Denebola	♦Dubhe
240	44 12 068	27 20 110	47 55 145	13 21 174	52 50 224	28 28 259	49 13 316
241	44 48 068	27 56 111	48 17 146	13 25 174	52 23 225	27 50 259	48 46 316
242	45 23 069	28 32 112	48 38 147	13 29 175	51 55 227	27 12 260	48 19 316
243	45 59 069	29 07 113	48 58 149	13 32 176	51 27 228	26 34 261	47 53 317
244	46 36 070	29 43 114	49 18 150	13 34 177	50 58 229	25 56 262	47 26 317
245	47 12 070	30 18 115	49 37 151	13 35 178	50 29 230	25 17 263	47 00 317
246	47 48 071	30 53 116	49 55 153	13 36 179	49 59 232	24 39 264	46 34 317
247	48 25 071	31 27 117	50 12 154	13 37 180	49 28 233	24 01 264	46 08 318
248	49 01 072	32 02 118	50 28 156	13 36 181	48 57 234	23 22 265	45 42 318
249	49 38 072	32 36 119	50 44 157	13 35 182	48 26 235	22 44 266	45 16 318
250	50 15 073	33 09 120	50 58 159	13 34 183	47 54 236	22 05 267	44 51 319
251	50 52 073	33 43 121	51 12 160	13 32 184	47 21 238	21 27 267	44 25 319
252	51 29 074	34 16 122	51 24 162	13 29 185	46 48 239	20 48 268	44 00 319
253	52 06 075	34 48 123	51 36 163	13 26 185	46 15 240	20 10 269	43 35 319
254	52 43 075	35 21 124	51 46 165	13 22 186	45 42 241	19 31 270	43 10 320
	♦Schedar	DENEB	ALTAIR	♦Rasalhague	ARCTURUS	♦Alkaid	Kochab
255	29 16 035	53 20 076	35 53 125	51 56 166	45 08 242	59 18 288	62 14 342
256	29 39 036	53 58 076	36 24 126	52 04 168	44 34 243	58 42 288	62 02 341
257	30 01 036	54 35 077	36 55 127	52 12 170	43 59 244	58 05 289	61 49 341
258	30 24 037	55 13 077	37 26 128	52 18 171	43 24 245	57 28 289	61 37 341
259	30 47 037	55 50 078	37 56 129	52 23 173	42 49 246	56 52 290	61 24 340
260	31 10 037	56 28 078	38 26 130	52 28 174	42 14 247	56 16 290	61 11 340
261	31 34 038	57 06 079	38 56 131	52 31 176	41 38 248	55 40 290	60 57 340
262	31 58 038	57 44 080	39 24 132	52 33 178	41 02 249	55 04 291	60 44 339
263	32 22 039	58 22 080	39 53 133	52 34 179	40 26 250	54 28 291	60 30 339
264	32 46 039	59 00 081	40 21 134	52 34 181	39 50 251	53 52 292	60 16 339
265	33 11 040	59 38 081	40 48 136	52 33 182	39 13 252	53 16 292	60 02 339
266	33 35 040	60 16 082	41 15 137	52 31 184	38 36 253	52 40 293	59 48 338
267	34 00 041	60 54 083	41 41 138	52 28 186	37 59 254	52 05 293	59 34 338
268	34 25 041	61 33 083	42 06 139	52 24 187	37 22 255	51 29 294	59 19 338
269	34 51 041	62 11 084	42 31 140	52 18 189	36 45 256	50 54 294	59 05 338

LHA	CAPELLA	♦Hamal	Alpheratz	Enif	♦ALTAIR	VEGA	♦Kochab
315	17 36 037	26 12 084	49 06 103	48 48 164	46 18 206	62 18 260	46 54 337
316	17 59 038	26 50 085	49 43 104	48 58 165	46 01 207	61 40 261	46 39 337
317	18 23 038	27 29 086	50 21 105	49 08 167	45 43 208	61 02 262	46 24 337
318	18 47 039	28 07 086	50 58 106	49 16 168	45 25 210	60 24 263	46 09 337
319	19 12 040	28 46 087	51 35 107	49 23 170	45 05 211	59 46 264	45 54 337
320	19 37 040	29 24 088	52 12 108	49 30 171	44 45 212	59 07 265	45 39 337
321	20 02 041	30 03 089	52 48 109	49 35 173	44 24 214	58 29 265	45 24 337
322	20 27 041	30 41 089	53 25 110	49 40 174	44 02 215	57 50 266	45 09 338
323	20 53 042	31 20 090	54 01 111	49 43 176	43 40 216	57 12 267	44 55 338
324	21 19 043	31 59 091	54 37 112	49 45 177	43 17 217	56 33 268	44 40 338
325	21 45 043	32 37 092	55 12 113	49 47 179	42 53 219	55 55 269	44 26 338
326	22 12 044	33 16 093	55 48 114	49 47 180	42 29 220	55 16 269	44 11 338
327	22 38 044	33 54 093	56 22 116	49 46 182	42 04 221	54 38 270	43 57 339
328	23 06 045	34 33 094	56 57 117	49 44 183	41 38 222	53 59 271	43 43 339
329	23 33 045	35 11 095	57 31 118	49 42 185	41 12 223	53 21 272	43 29 339
	CAPELLA	♦Hamal	Diphda	Enif	♦ALTAIR	VEGA	♦Kochab
330	24 01 046	35 49 096	13 02 141	49 38 186	40 45 225	52 42 272	43 15 339
331	24 28 047	36 28 097	13 27 141	49 33 188	40 18 226	52 04 273	43 02 339
332	24 57 047	37 06 097	13 51 142	49 27 189	39 50 227	51 25 274	42 48 340
333	25 25 048	37 44 098	14 14 143	49 20 191	39 22 228	50 47 275	42 35 340
334	25 54 048	38 22 099	14 37 144	49 13 192	38 53 229	50 08 275	42 22 340
335	26 23 049	39 00 100	14 59 145	49 04 194	38 23 230	49 30 276	42 08 340
336	26 52 049	39 38 101	15 21 146	48 54 195	37 53 231	48 51 277	41 55 340
337	27 21 050	40 16 102	15 42 147	48 43 197	37 23 232	48 13 277	41 43 341
338	27 51 051	40 54 102	16 03 148	48 32 198	36 52 233	47 35 278	41 30 341
339	28 21 051	41 32 103	16 23 149	48 19 200	36 21 234	46 57 279	41 17 341
340	28 51 052	42 09 104	16 43 150	48 06 201	35 50 236	46 19 279	41 05 341
341	29 21 052	42 46 105	17 02 151	47 51 203	35 18 237	45 41 280	40 53 342
342	29 52 053	43 23 106	17 21 151	47 36 204	34 45 238	45 03 281	40 40 342
343	30 23 053	44 00 107	17 39 152	47 20 205	34 13 239	44 25 281	40 28 342
344	30 54 054	44 37 108	17 57 153	47 03 207	33 39 240	43 47 282	40 17 342
	♦CAPELLA	ALDEBARAN	♦Diphda	Enif	ALTAIR	♦VEGA	Kochab
345	31 25 054	16 33 084	18 14 154	46 45 208	33 06 241	43 09 283	40 05 343
346	31 56 055	17 12 085	18 30 155	46 26 210	32 32 241	42 32 283	39 53 343
347	32 28 055	17 50 085	18 46 156	46 07 211	31 58 242	41 54 284	39 42 343
348	33 00 056	18 28 086	19 01 157	45 47 212	31 24 243	41 17 284	39 31 343
349	33 32 056	19 07 087	19 16 158	45 26 214	30 49 244	40 40 285	39 20 344
350	34 04 057	19 45 088	19 30 159	45 04 215	30 14 245	40 03 286	39 09 344
351	34 37 058	20 24 088	19 43 160	44 42 216	29 39 246	39 25 286	38 59 344
352	35 09 058	21 03 089	19 56 161	44 19 217	29 04 247	38 48 287	38 48 344
353	35 42 059	21 41 090	20 08 162	43 55 219	28 28 248	38 12 288	38 38 345
354	36 15 059	22 20 091	20 20 163	43 30 220	27 52 249	37 35 288	38 28 345
355	36 48 060	22 58 091	20 31 164	43 05 221	27 16 250	36 58 289	38 18 345
356	37 22 060	23 37 092	20 41 165	42 40 222	26 40 251	36 22 289	38 08 345
357	37 55 061	24 15 093	20 51 166	42 13 224	26 04 251	35 46 290	37 58 346
358	38 29 061	24 54 094	20 59 167	41 46 225	25 27 252	35 09 291	37 49 346
359	39 03 062	25 32 095	21 08 168	41 19 226	24 50 253	34 33 291	37 40 346

N. Lat. {LHA greater than 180°....... Zn=Z
{LHA less than 180°........... Zn=360−Z

DECLINATION (0°-14°) SAME

LHA	0° Hc	d	Z	1° Hc	d	Z	2° Hc	d	Z	3° Hc	d	Z
	° ′	′	°	° ′	′	°	° ′	′	°	° ′	′	°
0	40 00	+60	180	41 00	+60	180	42 00	+60	180	43 00	+60	180
1	40 00	60	179	41 00	60	179	42 00	60	179	43 00	60	179
2	39 58	60	177	40 58	60	177	41 58	60	177	42 58	60	177
3	39 56	60	176	40 56	60	176	41 56	60	176	42 56	60	176
4	39 53	60	175	40 53	60	175	41 53	60	175	42 53	60	175
5	39 49	+60	174	40 49	+60	173	41 49	+60	173	42 49	+59	173
6	39 44	60	172	40 44	60	172	41 44	60	172	42 44	59	172
7	39 39	59	171	40 38	60	171	41 38	60	171	42 38	59	171
8	39 32	60	170	40 32	59	170	41 31	60	169	42 31	59	169
9	39 25	59	168	40 24	60	168	41 24	59	168	42 23	60	168
10	39 16	+60	167	40 16	+59	167	41 15	+59	167	42 14	+60	167
11	39 07	60	166	40 07	59	166	41 06	59	165	42 05	59	165
12	38 57	60	165	39 57	59	164	40 56	59	164	41 55	59	164
13	38 47	59	163	39 46	59	163	40 45	59	163	41 44	58	163
14	38 35	59	162	39 34	59	162	40 33	58	161	41 31	59	161
15	38 23	+59	161	39 22	+58	160	40 20	+59	160	41 19	+58	160
16	38 10	58	160	39 08	59	159	40 07	58	159	41 05	58	159
17	37 56	58	158	38 54	58	158	39 52	58	158	40 50	59	157
18	37 41	58	157	38 39	58	157	39 37	58	156	40 35	58	156
19	37 26	58	156	38 24	57	156	39 21	58	155	40 19	58	155
20	37 10	+57	155	38 07	+58	154	39 05	+57	154	40 02	+58	154
21	36 53	57	153	37 50	57	153	38 47	58	153	39 45	57	152
22	36 35	57	152	37 32	57	152	38 29	57	151	39 26	57	151
23	36 17	57	151	37 14	57	151	38 11	56	150	39 07	57	150
24	35 58	56	150	36 54	57	149	37 51	57	149	38 48	56	149
25	35 38	+56	149	36 34	+57	148	37 31	+56	148	38 27	+56	147
26	35 18	56	148	36 14	56	147	37 10	56	147	38 06	56	146
27	34 56	57	146	35 53	55	146	36 48	56	146	37 44	56	145
28	34 35	56	145	35 31	55	145	36 26	56	144	37 22	55	144
29	34 13	55	144	35 08	55	144	36 03	56	143	36 59	55	143
30	33 50	+55	143	34 45	+55	143	35 40	+55	142	36 35	+55	142
31	33 26	55	142	34 21	55	141	35 16	55	141	36 11	54	140
32	33 02	55	141	33 57	54	140	34 51	55	140	35 46	54	139
33	32 37	55	140	33 32	54	139	34 26	55	139	35 21	54	138
34	32 12	54	139	33 06	55	138	34 01	54	138	34 55	53	137
35	31 46	+54	138	32 40	+54	137	33 34	+54	137	34 28	+54	136
36	31 20	54	137	32 14	53	136	33 07	54	136	34 01	53	135
37	30 53	54	136	31 47	53	135	32 40	53	134	33 33	53	134
38	30 26	53	134	31 19	53	134	32 12	53	133	33 05	53	133
39	29 58	53	133	30 51	53	133	31 44	53	132	32 37	52	132
40	29 30	+53	132	30 23	+52	132	31 15	+53	131	32 08	+52	131
41	29 01	53	131	29 54	52	131	30 46	52	130	31 38	52	130
42	28 32	52	130	29 24	52	130	30 16	52	129	31 08	52	129
43	28 03	52	129	28 55	51	129	29 46	52	128	30 38	52	128
44	27 33	51	128	28 24	52	128	29 16	51	127	30 07	52	127
45	27 02	+52	128	27 54	+51	127	28 45	+51	126	29 36	+51	126
46	26 31	52	127	27 23	51	126	28 14	51	125	29 05	51	125
47	26 00	51	126	26 51	51	125	27 42	51	124	28 33	50	124
48	25 29	50	125	26 19	51	124	27 10	51	123	28 01	50	123
49	24 57	50	124	25 47	51	123	26 38	50	123	27 28	50	122
50	24 24	+51	123	25 15	+50	122	26 05	+50	122	26 55	+50	121
51	23 52	50	122	24 42	50	121	25 32	50	121	26 22	50	120
52	23 19	50	121	24 09	50	120	24 59	49	120	25 48	50	119
53	22 46	49	120	23 35	50	119	24 25	49	119	25 14	50	118
54	22 12	50	119	23 02	49	119	23 51	49	118	24 40	49	117
55	21 38	+50	118	22 28	+49	118	23 17	+49	117	24 06	+49	116
56	21 04	49	117	21 53	49	117	22 42	49	116	23 31	49	116
57	20 30	49	116	21 19	48	116	22 07	49	115	22 56	49	115
58	19 55	49	116	20 44	48	115	21 32	49	114	22 21	48	114
59	19 20	49	115	20 09	48	114	20 57	49	114	21 46	48	113
60	18 45	+48	114	19 33	+49	113	20 22	+48	113	21 10	+48	112
61	18 09	49	113	18 58	48	112	19 46	48	112	20 34	48	111
62	17 34	48	112	18 22	48	112	19 10	48	111	19 58	48	110
63	16 58	48	111	17 46	48	111	18 34	48	110	19 22	47	109
64	16 22	48	111	17 10	48	110	17 58	47	109	18 45	48	109
65	15 46	+48	110	16 34	+47	109	17 21	+48	108	18 09	+47	108
66	15 09	48	109	15 57	47	108	16 44	48	108	17 32	47	107
67	14 33	47	108	15 20	48	107	16 08	47	107	16 55	47	106
68	13 56	47	107	14 43	48	107	15 31	47	106	16 18	47	105
69	13 19	47	106	14 06	47	106	14 53	47	105	15 40	47	105

LHA	4° Hc	d	Z	5° Hc	d	Z	6° Hc	d	Z	7° Hc	d	Z
	° ′	′	°	° ′	′	°	° ′	′	°	° ′	′	°
0	44 00	+60	180	45 00	+60	180	46 00	+60	180	47 00	+60	180
1	44 00	60	179	45 00	60	179	46 00	60	179	47 00	60	179
2	43 58	60	177	44 58	60	177	45 58	60	177	46 58	60	177
3	43 56	60	176	44 56	60	176	45 56	60	176	46 56	60	176
4	43 53	59	175	44 52	60	174	45 52	60	174	46 52	60	174
5	43 48	+60	173	44 48	+60	173	45 48	+60	173	46 48	+60	173
6	43 43	60	172	44 43	60	172	45 43	59	171	46 42	60	171
7	43 37	60	170	44 37	60	170	45 37	59	170	46 36	60	170
8	43 30	60	169	44 30	59	169	45 29	60	169	46 29	59	168
9	43 23	59	168	44 22	59	167	45 21	60	167	46 21	59	167
10	43 14	+59	166	44 13	+59	166	45 12	+60	166	46 12	+59	166
11	43 04	59	165	44 03	59	165	45 02	59	164	46 01	60	164
12	42 54	59	164	43 53	59	163	44 52	59	163	45 51	58	163
13	42 42	59	162	43 41	59	162	44 40	59	162	45 39	58	161
14	42 30	59	161	43 29	58	161	44 27	59	160	45 26	58	160
15	42 17	+59	160	43 16	+58	159	44 14	+58	159	45 12	+59	159
16	42 03	58	158	43 01	59	158	44 00	58	158	44 58	58	157
17	41 49	58	157	42 47	58	157	43 45	57	156	44 42	58	156
18	41 33	58	156	42 31	58	155	43 29	57	155	44 26	58	155
19	41 17	57	154	42 14	58	154	43 12	57	154	44 09	58	153
20	41 00	+57	153	41 57	+57	153	42 54	+58	152	43 52	+57	152
21	40 42	57	152	41 39	57	152	42 36	57	151	43 33	57	151
22	40 23	57	151	41 20	57	150	42 17	57	150	43 14	56	149
23	40 04	57	149	41 01	56	149	41 57	57	149	42 54	56	148
24	39 44	56	148	40 40	57	148	41 37	56	147	42 33	56	147
25	39 23	+57	147	40 20	+56	147	41 16	+55	146	42 11	+56	146
26	39 02	56	146	39 58	56	145	40 54	55	145	41 49	56	144
27	38 40	56	145	39 36	55	144	40 31	55	144	41 26	56	143
28	38 17	56	143	39 13	55	143	40 08	55	142	41 03	55	142
29	37 54	55	142	38 49	55	142	39 44	55	141	40 39	54	141
30	37 30	+55	141	38 25	+54	141	39 19	+55	140	40 14	+54	140
31	37 05	55	140	38 00	54	139	38 54	55	139	39 49	54	138
32	36 40	55	139	37 35	54	138	38 29	54	138	39 23	53	137
33	36 15	54	138	37 09	53	137	38 02	54	137	38 56	54	136
34	35 48	54	137	36 42	54	136	37 36	53	135	38 29	53	135
35	35 22	+53	135	36 15	+53	135	37 08	+53	134	38 01	+53	134
36	34 54	53	134	35 47	53	134	36 40	53	133	37 33	53	133
37	34 26	53	133	35 19	53	133	36 12	53	132	37 05	52	132
38	33 58	53	132	34 51	52	132	35 43	53	131	36 36	52	130
39	33 29	53	131	34 22	52	131	35 14	52	130	36 06	52	129
40	33 00	+52	130	33 52	+52	130	34 44	+52	129	35 36	+51	128
41	32 30	52	129	33 22	52	129	34 14	51	128	35 05	52	127
42	32 00	52	128	32 52	51	128	33 43	52	127	34 35	51	126
43	31 30	51	127	32 21	51	127	33 12	51	126	34 03	51	125
44	30 59	51	126	31 50	51	126	32 41	51	125	33 32	50	124
45	30 27	+51	125	31 18	+51	125	32 09	+50	124	32 59	+51	123
46	29 56	50	124	30 46	51	124	31 37	50	123	32 27	50	122
47	29 23	51	123	30 14	50	123	31 04	50	122	31 54	50	121
48	28 51	50	122	29 41	50	122	30 31	50	121	31 21	50	120
49	28 18	50	121	29 08	50	121	29 58	50	120	30 48	49	119
50	27 45	+50	120	28 35	+49	120	29 24	+50	119	30 14	+49	118
51	27 12	49	119	28 01	49	119	28 50	50	118	29 40	49	117
52	26 38	49	118	27 27	49	118	28 16	49	117	29 05	49	117
53	26 04	49	118	26 53	49	117	27 42	49	116	28 31	48	116
54	25 29	49	117	26 18	49	116	27 07	49	115	27 56	48	115
55	24 55	+49	116	25 44	+48	115	26 32	+49	114	27 21	+48	114
56	24 20	48	115	25 08	49	114	25 57	48	114	26 45	48	113
57	23 45	48	114	24 33	48	113	25 21	48	113	26 09	48	112
58	23 09	49	113	23 58	48	112	24 46	48	112	25 34	47	111
59	22 34	48	112	23 22	48	112	24 10	48	111	24 58	47	110
60	21 58	+48	111	22 46	+48	111	23 34	+47	110	24 21	+48	109
61	21 22	48	111	22 10	47	110	22 57	48	109	23 45	47	109
62	20 46	47	110	21 33	48	109	22 21	47	108	23 08	47	108
63	20 09	48	109	20 57	47	108	21 44	47	108	22 31	47	107
64	19 33	47	108	20 20	47	107	21 07	47	107	21 54	47	106
65	18 56	+47	107	19 43	+47	106	20 30	+47	106	21 17	+47	105
66	18 19	47	106	19 06	47	106	19 53	47	105	20 40	46	104
67	17 42	47	105	18 29	47	105	19 16	46	104	20 02	47	104
68	17 05	46	105	17 51	47	104	18 38	47	103	19 25	46	103
69	16 27	47	104	17 14	47	103	18 01	46	103	18 47	46	102

S. Lat. {LHA greater than 180°....... Zn=180−Z
{LHA less than 180°........... Zn=180+Z

DECLINATION (0°-14°) SAME

8°			9°			10°			11°			12°			13°			14°			
Hc	d	Z	Hc	d	Z	Hc	d	Z	Hc	d	Z	Hc	d	Z	Hc	d	Z	Hc	d	Z	LHA
° ′	′	°	° ′	′	°	° ′	′	°	° ′	′	°	° ′	′	°	° ′	′	°	° ′	′	°	
48 00	+60	180	49 00	+60	180	50 00	+60	180	51 00	+60	180	52 00	+60	180	53 00	+60	180	54 00	+60	180	360
48 00	60	179	49 00	60	179	50 00	60	179	51 00	60	178	52 00	60	178	53 00	59	178	53 59	60	178	359
47 58	60	177	48 58	60	177	49 58	60	177	50 58	60	177	51 58	60	177	52 58	60	177	53 58	60	177	358
47 56	59	176	48 55	60	176	49 55	60	175	50 55	60	175	51 55	60	175	52 55	60	175	53 55	60	175	357
47 52	60	174	48 52	60	174	49 52	60	174	50 52	60	174	51 52	59	174	52 51	60	174	53 51	60	173	356
47 48	+59	173	48 47	+60	173	49 47	+60	172	50 47	+60	172	51 47	+59	172	52 46	+60	172	53 46	+60	172	355
47 42	60	171	48 42	60	171	49 42	59	171	50 41	60	171	51 41	60	171	52 41	59	170	53 40	60	170	354
47 36	59	170	48 35	60	170	49 35	59	169	50 34	60	169	51 34	60	169	52 34	59	169	53 33	59	169	353
47 28	60	168	48 28	59	168	49 27	60	168	50 27	59	168	51 26	59	167	52 25	60	167	53 25	59	167	352
47 20	59	167	48 19	60	167	49 19	59	166	50 18	59	166	51 17	59	166	52 16	60	166	53 16	59	165	351
47 11	+59	165	48 10	+59	165	49 09	+59	165	50 08	+59	165	51 07	+59	164	52 06	+59	164	53 05	+59	164	350
47 01	59	164	48 00	59	164	48 59	58	163	49 57	59	163	50 56	59	163	51 55	59	163	52 54	59	162	349
46 49	59	163	47 48	59	162	48 47	59	162	49 46	58	162	50 44	59	161	51 43	59	161	52 42	58	161	348
46 37	59	161	47 36	59	161	48 35	58	160	49 33	59	160	50 32	58	160	51 30	58	159	52 28	58	159	347
46 24	59	160	47 23	58	159	48 21	53	159	49 19	59	159	50 18	58	158	51 16	58	158	52 14	58	158	346
46 11	+58	158	47 09	+58	158	48 07	+58	158	49 05	+58	157	50 03	+58	157	51 01	+58	156	51 59	+57	156	345
45 56	58	157	46 54	58	157	47 52	58	156	48 50	57	156	49 47	58	155	50 45	57	155	51 42	58	154	344
45 40	58	156	46 38	58	155	47 36	57	155	48 33	58	154	49 31	57	154	50 28	57	153	51 25	58	153	343
45 24	57	154	46 21	58	154	47 19	57	153	48 16	57	153	49 13	57	152	50 10	57	152	51 07	57	152	342
45 07	57	153	46 04	57	152	47 01	57	152	47 58	57	152	48 55	57	151	49 52	57	151	50 49	56	150	341
44 49	+57	152	45 46	+57	151	46 43	+56	151	47 39	+57	150	48 36	+56	150	49 32	+57	149	50 29	+56	149	340
44 30	57	150	45 27	56	150	46 23	57	149	47 20	56	149	48 16	56	148	49 12	56	148	50 08	56	147	339
44 10	57	149	45 07	56	148	46 03	56	148	46 59	56	147	47 55	56	147	48 51	56	146	49 47	56	146	338
43 50	56	148	44 46	56	147	45 42	56	147	46 38	56	146	47 34	55	146	48 29	56	145	49 25	55	144	337
43 29	56	146	44 25	56	146	45 21	55	145	46 16	56	145	47 12	55	144	48 07	55	144	49 02	55	143	336
43 07	+56	145	44 03	+55	145	44 58	+56	144	45 54	+55	143	46 49	+55	143	47 44	+54	142	48 38	+55	142	335
42 45	55	144	43 40	55	143	44 35	55	143	45 30	55	142	46 25	55	142	47 20	54	141	48 14	54	140	334
42 22	55	143	43 17	54	142	44 11	55	141	45 06	55	141	46 01	54	140	46 55	54	140	47 49	54	139	333
41 58	55	141	42 53	54	141	43 47	55	140	44 42	54	140	45 36	54	139	46 30	54	138	47 24	53	138	332
41 33	55	140	42 28	54	140	43 22	54	139	44 16	54	138	45 10	54	138	46 04	53	137	46 57	54	136	331
41 08	+54	139	42 02	+54	138	42 56	+54	138	43 50	+54	137	44 44	+53	137	45 37	+53	136	46 30	+53	135	330
40 43	54	138	41 37	53	137	42 30	54	137	43 24	53	136	44 17	53	135	45 10	53	135	46 03	53	134	329
40 16	54	137	41 10	53	136	42 03	54	135	42 57	53	135	43 50	52	134	44 42	53	133	45 35	52	133	328
39 50	53	135	40 43	53	135	41 36	53	134	42 29	53	134	43 22	52	133	44 14	52	132	45 06	52	132	327
39 22	53	134	40 15	53	134	41 08	53	133	42 01	52	132	42 53	52	132	43 45	52	131	44 37	52	130	326
38 54	+53	133	39 47	+53	133	40 40	+52	132	41 32	+52	131	42 24	+52	131	43 16	+52	130	44 08	+51	129	325
38 26	52	132	39 18	53	131	40 11	52	131	41 03	52	130	41 55	51	129	42 46	51	129	43 37	51	128	324
37 57	52	131	38 49	52	130	39 41	52	130	40 33	51	129	41 24	52	128	42 16	51	128	43 07	51	127	323
37 28	52	130	38 20	51	129	39 11	52	129	40 03	51	128	40 54	51	127	41 45	51	127	42 36	50	126	322
36 58	51	129	37 49	52	128	38 41	51	127	39 32	51	127	40 23	51	126	41 14	50	125	42 04	50	125	321
36 27	+52	128	37 19	+51	127	38 10	+51	126	39 01	+51	126	39 52	+50	125	40 42	+50	124	41 32	+50	124	320
35 57	51	127	36 48	51	126	37 39	50	125	38 29	51	125	39 20	50	124	40 10	50	123	41 00	50	123	319
35 26	50	126	36 16	51	125	37 07	50	124	37 57	51	124	38 48	50	123	39 38	49	122	40 27	50	121	318
34 54	51	125	35 45	50	124	36 35	50	123	37 25	50	123	38 15	50	122	39 05	49	121	39 54	49	120	317
34 22	50	124	35 12	51	123	36 03	49	122	36 52	50	122	37 42	50	121	38 32	49	120	39 21	49	119	316
33 50	+50	123	34 40	+50	122	35 30	+49	121	36 19	+50	121	37 09	+49	120	37 58	+49	119	38 47	+48	118	315
33 17	50	122	34 07	50	121	34 57	49	120	35 46	49	120	36 35	49	119	37 24	49	118	38 13	48	117	314
32 44	50	121	33 34	49	120	34 23	49	119	35 12	49	119	36 01	49	118	36 50	48	117	37 38	49	116	313
32 11	49	120	33 00	49	119	33 49	49	118	34 38	49	118	35 27	48	117	36 15	49	116	37 04	48	115	312
31 37	49	119	32 26	49	118	33 15	49	117	34 04	48	117	34 52	49	116	35 41	48	115	36 29	47	114	311
31 03	+49	118	31 52	+49	117	32 41	+48	116	33 29	+49	116	34 18	+48	115	35 06	+47	114	35 53	+48	113	310
30 29	48	117	31 17	49	116	32 06	48	115	32 54	48	115	33 42	48	114	34 30	48	113	35 18	47	113	309
29 54	49	116	30 43	48	115	31 31	48	115	32 19	48	114	33 07	48	113	33 55	47	112	34 42	47	112	308
29 19	49	115	30 08	48	114	30 56	48	114	31 44	48	113	32 32	47	112	33 19	47	111	34 06	47	111	307
28 44	48	114	29 32	48	113	30 20	48	113	31 08	48	112	31 56	47	111	32 43	47	111	33 30	47	110	306
28 09	+48	113	28 57	+48	112	29 45	+47	112	30 32	+48	111	31 20	+47	110	32 07	+47	110	32 54	+46	109	305
27 33	48	112	28 21	48	112	29 09	47	111	29 56	47	110	30 43	47	109	31 30	47	109	32 17	46	108	304
26 57	48	111	27 45	48	111	28 33	47	110	29 20	47	109	30 07	47	109	30 54	46	108	31 40	46	107	303
26 21	48	110	27 09	47	110	27 56	47	109	28 43	47	108	29 30	47	108	30 17	46	107	31 03	46	106	302
25 45	47	110	26 32	48	109	27 20	47	108	28 07	46	108	28 53	47	107	29 40	46	106	30 26	46	105	301
25 09	+47	109	25 56	+47	108	26 43	+47	107	27 30	+46	107	28 16	+47	106	29 03	+46	105	29 49	+46	104	300
24 32	47	108	25 19	47	107	26 06	47	106	26 53	46	106	27 39	46	105	28 25	46	104	29 11	46	104	299
23 55	47	107	24 42	47	106	25 29	46	106	26 15	47	105	27 02	46	104	27 48	46	104	28 34	46	103	298
23 18	47	106	24 05	47	105	24 52	46	105	25 38	46	104	26 24	46	103	27 10	46	103	27 56	46	102	297
22 41	47	105	23 28	46	105	24 14	47	104	25 01	46	103	25 47	46	103	26 33	45	102	27 18	46	101	296
22 04	+46	104	22 50	+47	104	23 37	+46	103	24 23	+46	102	25 09	+46	102	25 55	+45	101	26 40	+46	100	295
21 26	47	104	22 13	46	103	22 59	46	102	23 45	46	102	24 31	46	101	25 17	45	100	26 02	46	99	294
20 49	46	103	21 35	46	102	22 21	46	101	23 07	46	101	23 53	46	100	24 39	45	99	25 24	46	99	293
20 11	46	102	20 57	47	101	21 44	46	101	22 30	45	100	23 15	46	99	24 01	45	99	24 46	45	98	292
19 33	47	101	20 20	46	101	21 06	45	100	21 51	46	99	22 37	46	98	23 23	45	98	24 08	45	97	291
8°			9°			10°			11°			12°			13°			14°			

N. Lat. {LHA greater than 180°....... Zn=Z
{LHA less than 180°........... Zn=360−Z

DECLINATION (0°-14°) **SAME**

LHA	0° Hc	d	Z	1° Hc	d	Z	2° Hc	d	Z	3° Hc	d	Z	4° Hc	d	Z	5° Hc	d	Z	6° Hc	d	Z	7° Hc	d	Z
	° ′	′	°	° ′	′	°	° ′	′	°	° ′	′	°	° ′	′	°	° ′	′	°	° ′	′	°	° ′	′	°
70	12 42	+47	106	13 29	+47	105	14 16	+47	104	15 03	+47	104	15 50	+46	103	16 36	+47	102	17 23	+46	102	18 09	+47	101
71	12 05	47	105	12 52	47	104	13 39	46	104	14 25	47	103	15 12	47	102	15 59	46	102	16 45	46	101	17 31	47	100
72	11 27	47	104	12 14	47	103	13 01	47	103	13 48	46	102	14 34	47	101	15 21	46	101	16 07	46	100	16 53	46	99
73	10 50	47	103	11 37	46	103	12 23	47	102	13 10	46	101	13 56	47	101	14 43	46	100	15 29	46	99	16 15	46	99
74	10 12	47	102	10 59	47	102	11 46	46	101	12 32	47	101	13 19	46	100	14 05	46	99	14 51	46	99	15 37	46	98
75	09 35	+46	102	10 21	+47	101	11 08	+46	100	11 54	+46	100	12 40	+47	99	13 27	+46	98	14 13	+46	98	14 59	+46	97
76	08 57	46	101	09 43	47	100	10 30	46	100	11 16	46	99	12 02	47	98	12 49	46	98	13 35	46	97	14 21	45	96
77	08 19	46	100	09 05	47	99	09 52	46	99	10 38	46	98	11 24	46	97	12 10	46	97	12 56	46	96	13 42	46	96
78	07 41	46	99	08 27	46	99	09 13	47	98	10 00	46	97	10 46	46	97	11 32	46	96	12 18	46	95	13 04	46	95
79	07 03	46	99	07 49	46	98	08 35	46	97	09 21	47	97	10 08	46	96	10 54	45	95	11 39	46	95	12 25	46	94
80	06 25	+46	98	07 11	+46	97	07 57	+46	96	08 43	+46	96	09 29	+46	95	10 15	+46	95	11 01	+46	94	11 47	+46	93
81	05 46	46	97	06 32	47	96	07 19	46	96	08 05	46	95	08 51	46	94	09 37	46	94	10 23	45	93	11 08	46	92
82	05 08	46	96	05 54	46	96	06 40	46	95	07 26	46	94	08 12	46	94	08 58	46	93	09 44	46	92	10 30	45	92
83	04 30	46	95	05 16	46	95	06 02	46	94	06 48	46	93	07 34	46	93	08 20	45	92	09 05	46	92	09 51	46	91
84	03 51	46	95	04 37	46	94	05 23	46	93	06 09	46	93	06 55	46	92	07 41	46	91	08 27	46	91	09 13	45	90
85	03 13	+46	94	03 59	+46	93	04 45	+46	93	05 31	+46	92	06 17	+45	91	07 02	+46	91	07 48	+46	90	08 34	+46	89
86	02 34	46	93	03 20	46	92	04 06	46	92	04 52	46	91	05 38	46	91	06 24	46	90	07 10	45	89	07 55	46	89
87	01 56	46	92	02 42	46	92	03 28	46	91	04 14	45	90	04 59	46	90	05 45	46	89	06 31	46	88	07 17	46	88
88	01 17	46	92	02 03	46	91	02 49	46	90	03 35	46	90	04 21	46	89	05 07	46	88	05 53	45	88	06 38	46	87
89	00 39	46	91	01 25	45	90	02 10	46	89	02 56	46	89	03 42	46	88	04 28	46	88	05 14	46	87	06 00	46	86
90	00 00	+46	90	00 46	+46	89	01 32	+46	89	02 18	+46	88	03 04	+46	87	03 50	+46	87	04 36	+45	86	05 21	+46	86
91	−0 39	46	89	00 07	46	89	00 53	46	88	01 39	46	87	02 25	46	87	03 11	46	86	03 57	46	85	04 43	46	85
92	−1 17	46	88	−0 31	46	88	00 15	46	87	01 01	46	87	01 47	46	86	02 33	46	85	03 19	46	85	04 05	45	84
93	−1 56	46	88	−1 10	46	87	−0 24	46	86	00 22	46	86	01 08	46	85	01 54	46	84	02 40	46	84	03 26	46	83
94	−2 34	46	87	−1 48	46	86	−1 02	46	86	−0 16	46	85	00 30	46	84	01 16	46	84	02 02	46	83	02 48	46	82
95	−3 13	+46	86	−2 27	+46	86	−1 41	+46	85	−0 55	+47	84	−0 08	+46	84	00 38	+46	83	01 24	+46	82	02 10	+47	82
96	−3 51	46	85	−3 05	46	85	−2 19	46	84	−1 33	46	83	−0 47	46	83	−0 01	47	82	00 46	46	82	01 32	46	81
97	−4 30	47	85	−3 43	46	84	−2 57	46	83	−2 11	46	83	−1 25	46	82	−0 39	46	81	00 07	47	81	00 54	46	80
98	−5 08	46	84	−4 22	46	83	−3 36	47	83	−2 49	46	82	−2 03	46	81	−1 17	46	81	−0 31	47	80	00 16	46	79
99	−5 46	46	83	−5 00	46	82	−4 14	46	82	−3 28	47	81	−2 41	46	81	−1 55	46	80	−1 09	47	79	−0 22	46	79
100				−5 38	+46	82	−4 52	+46	81	−4 06	+47	80	−3 19	+46	80	−2 33	+47	79	−1 46	+46	78	−1 00	+47	78
101							−5 30	46	80	−4 44	47	80	−3 57	46	79	−3 11	47	78	−2 24	46	78	−1 38	47	77
102							−6 08	47	79	−5 21	46	79	−4 35	47	78	−3 48	46	78	−3 02	47	77	−2 15	47	76
103										−5 59	46	78	−5 13	47	77	−4 26	47	77	−3 39	46	76	−2 53	47	76
104													−5 50	47	77	−5 03	46	76	−4 17	47	75	−3 30	47	75
105																−5 41	+47	75	−4 54	+47	75	−4 07	+47	74
106																			−5 31	47	74	−4 44	47	73
107																			−6 08	47	73	−5 21	47	72
108																						−5 58	48	72
109																								

0°	1°	2°	3°	4°	5°	6°	7°

S. Lat. {LHA greater than 180°....... Zn=180−Z
{LHA less than 180°........... Zn=180+Z

DECLINATION (0°-14°) **SAME**

NAME AS LATITUDE

8°			9°			10°			11°			12°			13°			14°			
Hc	d	Z	Hc	d	Z	Hc	d	Z	Hc	d	Z	Hc	d	Z	Hc	d	Z	Hc	d	Z	LHA
° ′	′	°	° ′	′	°	° ′	′	°	° ′	′	°	° ′	′	°	° ′	′	°	° ′	′	°	
18 56	+46	100	19 42	+46	100	20 28	+45	99	21 13	+46	98	21 59	+45	98	22 44	+46	97	23 30	+45	96	290
18 18	46	100	19 04	45	99	19 49	46	98	20 35	46	98	21 21	45	97	22 06	45	96	22 51	45	95	289
17 39	46	99	18 25	46	98	19 11	46	97	19 57	45	97	20 42	46	96	21 28	45	95	22 13	45	95	288
17 01	46	98	17 47	46	97	18 33	46	97	19 19	45	96	20 04	45	95	20 49	45	95	21 34	45	94	287
16 23	46	97	17 09	46	97	17 55	45	96	18 40	46	95	19 26	45	94	20 11	45	94	20 56	45	93	286
15 45	+46	96	16 31	+45	96	17 16	+46	95	18 02	+45	94	18 47	+45	94	19 32	+45	93	20 17	+45	92	285
15 06	46	96	15 52	46	95	16 38	45	94	17 23	46	94	18 09	45	93	18 54	45	92	19 39	45	92	284
14 28	46	95	15 14	45	94	15 59	46	94	16 45	45	93	17 30	45	92	18 15	45	91	19 00	45	91	283
13 50	45	94	14 35	46	93	15 21	45	93	16 06	45	92	16 51	46	91	17 37	45	91	18 22	45	90	282
13 11	46	93	13 57	45	93	14 42	46	92	15 28	45	91	16 13	45	91	16 58	45	90	17 43	45	89	281
12 33	+45	93	13 18	+46	92	14 04	+45	91	14 49	+45	91	15 34	+46	90	16 20	+45	89	17 05	+44	88	280
11 54	46	92	12 40	45	91	13 25	46	90	14 11	45	90	14 56	45	89	15 41	45	88	16 26	45	88	279
11 15	46	91	12 01	46	90	12 47	45	90	13 32	45	89	14 17	45	88	15 02	45	88	15 47	45	87	278
10 37	45	90	11 22	46	90	12 08	45	89	12 53	46	88	13 39	45	88	14 24	45	87	15 09	45	86	277
09 58	46	89	10 44	45	89	11 29	46	88	12 15	45	87	13 00	45	87	13 45	46	86	14 31	45	85	276
09 20	+45	89	10 05	+46	88	10 51	+45	87	11 36	+46	87	12 22	+45	86	13 07	+45	85	13 52	+45	85	275
08 41	46	88	09 27	45	87	10 12	46	87	10 58	45	86	11 43	46	85	12 29	45	85	13 14	45	84	274
08 03	45	87	08 48	46	87	09 34	45	86	10 19	46	85	11 05	45	85	11 50	45	84	12 35	46	83	273
07 24	46	86	08 10	45	86	08 55	46	85	09 41	45	84	10 26	46	84	11 12	45	83	11 57	45	82	272
06 46	45	86	07 31	46	85	08 17	46	84	09 03	45	84	09 48	46	83	10 34	45	82	11 19	45	82	271
06 07	+46	85	06 53	+46	84	07 39	+45	84	08 24	+46	83	09 10	+45	82	09 55	+46	82	10 41	+45	81	270
05 29	46	84	06 15	45	83	07 00	46	83	07 46	46	82	08 32	45	82	09 17	46	81	10 03	45	80	269
04 50	46	83	05 36	46	83	06 22	46	82	07 08	46	81	07 54	45	81	08 39	46	80	09 25	45	79	268
04 12	46	83	04 58	46	82	05 44	46	81	06 30	46	81	07 16	45	80	08 01	46	79	08 47	46	79	267
03 34	46	82	04 20	46	81	05 06	46	81	05 52	46	80	06 38	45	79	07 23	46	79	08 09	46	78	266
02 57	+45	81	03 42	+46	80	04 28	+46	80	05 14	+46	79	06 00	+46	79	06 46	+46	78	07 32	+45	77	265
02 18	46	80	03 04	46	80	03 50	46	79	04 36	46	78	05 22	46	78	06 08	46	77	06 54	46	76	264
01 40	46	80	02 26	46	79	03 12	46	78	03 58	46	78	04 44	47	77	05 31	46	76	06 17	46	76	263
01 02	46	79	01 48	46	78	02 34	47	77	03 21	46	77	04 07	46	76	04 53	46	76	05 39	46	75	262
00 24	47	78	01 11	46	77	01 57	46	77	02 43	47	76	03 30	46	76	04 16	46	75	05 02	46	74	261
−0 13	+46	77	00 33	+46	77	01 19	+47	76	02 06	+46	75	02 52	+47	75	03 39	+46	74	04 25	+46	73	260
−0 51	47	76	−0 04	46	76	00 42	47	75	01 29	46	75	02 15	47	74	03 02	46	73	03 48	47	73	259
−1 28	46	76	−0 42	47	75	00 05	47	74	00 52	46	74	01 38	47	73	02 25	46	73	03 11	47	72	258
−2 06	47	75	−1 19	47	74	−0 32	47	74	00 15	46	73	01 01	47	72	01 48	47	72	02 35	47	71	257
−2 43	47	74	−1 56	47	74	−1 09	47	73	−0 22	47	72	00 25	47	72	01 12	46	71	01 58	47	70	256
−3 20	+47	73	−2 33	+47	73	−1 46	+47	72	−0 59	+47	71	−0 12	+47	71	00 35	+47	70	01 22	+47	70	255
−3 57	47	73	−3 10	47	72	−2 23	48	71	−1 35	47	71	−0 48	47	70	−0 01	47	69	00 46	47	69	254
−4 34	48	72	−3 46	47	71	−2 59	47	71	−2 12	48	70	−1 24	47	69	−0 37	47	69	00 10	48	68	253
−5 10	47	71	−4 23	48	70	−3 35	47	70	−2 48	48	69	−2 00	47	69	−1 13	48	68	−0 25	47	67	252
−5 47	48	70	−4 59	48	70	−4 11	47	69	−3 24	48	68	−2 36	47	68	−1 49	48	67	−1 01	48	67	251
		110	−5 35	+48	69	−4 47	+47	68	−4 00	+48	68	−3 12	+48	67	−2 24	+48	66	−1 36	+48	66	250
		111	−6 11	48	68	−5 23	48	67	−4 35	48	67	−3 47	48	66	−2 59	48	66	−2 11	48	65	249
					112	−5 59	48	67	−5 11	49	66	−4 22	48	65	−3 34	48	65	−2 46	48	64	248
								113	−5 46	49	65	−4 57	48	65	−4 09	48	64	−3 21	49	63	247
											114	−5 32	48	64	−4 44	49	63	−3 55	48	63	246
											115	−6 07	+49	63	−5 18	+49	62	−4 29	+48	62	245
														116	−5 52	49	62	−5 03	49	61	244
																	117	−5 37	49	60	243

LAT 50°

8°	9°	10°	11°	12°	13°	14°

NAME AS LATITUDE

LAT 50°

N. Lat. {LHA greater than 180°....... Zn=Z
{LHA less than 180°........... Zn=360−Z

DECLINATION (0°-14°) CONTRARY

LHA	0° Hc	d	Z	1° Hc	d	Z	2° Hc	d	Z	3° Hc	d	Z	4° Hc	d	Z	5° Hc	d	Z	6° Hc	d	Z	7° Hc	d	Z
	° ′	′	°	° ′	′	°	° ′	′	°	° ′	′	°	° ′	′	°	° ′	′	°	° ′	′	°	° ′	′	°
99	-5 46	46	83	261																				
98	-5 08	46	84	-5 54	46	84	262																	
97	-4 30	46	85	-5 16	46	85	-6 02	46	86	263														
96	-3 51	46	85	-4 37	46	86	-5 23	46	87	-6 09	46	87	264											
95	-3 13	-46	86	-3 59	-46	87	-4 45	-46	87	-5 31	-46	88	-6 17	-45	89	265								
94	-2 34	46	87	-3 20	46	88	-4 06	46	88	-4 52	46	89	-5 38	46	89	266								
93	-1 56	46	88	-2 42	46	88	-3 28	46	89	-4 14	45	90	-4 59	46	90	-5 45	46	91	267					
92	-1 17	46	88	-2 03	46	89	-2 49	46	90	-3 35	46	90	-4 21	46	91	-5 07	46	92	-5 53	45	92	268		
91	-0 39	46	89	-1 25	45	90	-2 10	46	91	-2 56	46	91	-3 42	46	92	-4 28	46	92	-5 14	46	93	-6 00	46	94
90	00 00	-46	90	-0 46	-46	91	-1 32	-46	91	-2 18	-46	92	-3 04	-46	93	-3 50	-46	93	-4 36	-45	94	-5 21	-46	94
89	00 39	46	91	-0 07	46	91	-0 53	46	92	-1 39	46	93	-2 25	46	93	-3 11	46	94	-3 57	46	95	-4 43	46	95
88	01 17	46	92	00 31	46	92	-0 15	46	93	-1 01	46	93	-1 47	46	94	-2 33	46	95	-3 19	46	95	-4 05	45	96
87	01 56	46	92	01 10	46	93	00 24	46	94	-0 22	46	94	-1 08	46	95	-1 54	46	96	-2 40	46	96	-3 26	46	97
86	02 34	46	93	01 48	46	94	01 02	46	94	00 16	46	95	-0 30	46	96	-1 16	46	96	-2 02	46	97	-2 48	46	98
85	03 13	-46	94	02 27	-46	94	01 41	-46	95	00 55	-47	96	00 08	-46	96	-0 38	-46	97	-1 24	-46	98	-2 10	-47	98
84	03 51	46	95	03 05	46	95	02 19	46	96	01 33	46	97	00 47	46	97	00 01	47	98	-0 46	46	98	-1 32	46	99
83	04 30	47	95	03 43	46	96	02 57	46	97	02 11	46	97	01 25	46	98	00 39	46	99	-0 07	47	99	-0 54	46	100
82	05 08	46	96	04 22	46	97	03 36	47	97	02 49	46	98	02 03	46	99	01 17	46	99	00 31	47	100	-0 16	46	101
81	05 46	46	97	05 00	46	98	04 14	46	98	03 28	47	99	02 41	46	99	01 55	46	100	01 09	47	101	00 22	46	101
80	06 25	-47	98	05 38	-46	98	04 52	-46	99	04 06	-47	100	03 19	-46	100	02 33	-47	101	01 46	-46	102	01 00	-47	102
79	07 03	47	99	06 16	46	99	05 30	46	100	04 44	47	100	03 57	46	101	03 11	47	102	02 24	46	102	01 38	47	103
78	07 41	47	99	06 54	46	100	06 08	47	101	05 21	46	101	04 35	47	102	03 48	46	102	03 02	47	103	02 15	47	104
77	08 19	47	100	07 32	46	101	06 46	47	101	05 59	46	102	05 13	47	103	04 26	47	103	03 39	46	104	02 53	47	104
76	08 57	47	101	08 10	46	102	07 24	47	102	06 37	47	103	05 50	47	103	05 03	46	104	04 17	47	105	03 30	47	105
75	09 35	-47	102	08 48	-47	102	08 01	-46	103	07 15	-47	104	06 28	-47	104	05 41	-47	105	04 54	-47	105	04 07	-47	106
74	10 12	46	102	09 26	47	103	08 39	47	104	07 52	47	104	07 05	47	105	06 18	47	106	05 31	47	106	04 44	47	107
73	10 50	47	103	10 03	47	104	09 16	47	104	08 29	47	105	07 42	47	106	06 55	47	106	06 08	47	107	05 21	47	108
72	11 27	46	104	10 41	47	105	09 54	48	105	09 06	47	106	08 19	47	107	07 32	47	107	06 45	47	108	05 58	48	108
71	12 05	47	105	11 18	47	105	10 31	48	106	09 43	47	107	08 56	47	107	08 09	48	108	07 21	47	109	06 34	47	109
70	12 42	-47	106	11 55	-47	106	11 08	-48	107	10 20	-47	108	09 33	-48	108	08 45	-47	109	07 58	-48	109	07 10	-47	110
	0°			1°			2°			3°			4°			5°			6°			7°		

S. Lat. {LHA greater than 180°....... Zn=180−Z
{LHA less than 180°........... Zn=180+Z

DECLINATION (0°-14°) CONTRARY

NAME TO LATITUDE

LAT 50°

8°			9°			10°			11°			12°			13°			14°			
Hc	d	Z	Hc	d	Z	Hc	d	Z	Hc	d	Z	Hc	d	Z	Hc	d	Z	Hc	d	Z	LHA
° ′	′	°	° ′	′	°	° ′	′	°	° ′	′	°	° ′	′	°	° ′	′	°	° ′	′	°	
269																					
-6 07	-46	95	270																		
-5 29	46	96	-6 15	45	97	271															
-4 50	46	97	-5 36	46	97	272															
-4 12	46	97	-4 58	46	98	-5 44	46	99	273												
-3 34	46	98	-4 20	46	99	-5 06	46	99	-5 52	46	100	274									
-2 57	-45	99	-3 42	-46	100	-4 28	-46	100	-5 14	-46	101	-6 00	-46	101	275						
-2 18	46	100	-3 04	46	100	-3 50	46	101	-4 36	46	102	-5 22	46	102	-6 08	46	103	276			
-1 40	46	100	-2 26	46	101	-3 12	46	102	-3 58	46	102	-4 44	47	103	-5 31	46	104	277			
-1 02	46	101	-1 48	46	102	-2 34	47	103	-3 21	46	103	-4 07	46	104	-4 53	46	104	-5 39	46	105	278
-0 24	47	102	-1 11	46	103	-1 57	46	103	-2 43	47	104	-3 30	46	104	-4 16	46	105	-5 02	46	106	279
00 13	-46	103	-0 33	-46	103	-1 19	-47	104	-2 06	-46	105	-2 52	-47	105	-3 39	-46	106	-4 25	-46	107	280
00 51	47	104	00 04	46	104	-0 42	47	105	-1 29	46	105	-2 15	47	106	-3 02	46	107	-3 48	47	107	281
01 28	46	104	00 42	47	105	-0 05	47	106	-0 52	46	106	-1 38	47	107	-2 25	46	107	-3 11	47	108	282
02 06	47	105	01 19	47	106	00 32	47	106	-0 15	46	107	-1 01	47	108	-1 48	47	108	-2 35	47	109	283
02 43	47	106	01 56	47	106	01 09	47	107	00 22	47	108	-0 25	47	108	-1 12	46	109	-1 58	47	110	284
03 20	-47	107	02 33	-47	107	01 46	-47	108	00 59	-47	109	00 12	-47	109	-0 35	-47	110	-1 22	-47	110	285
03 57	47	107	03 10	47	108	02 23	48	109	01 35	47	109	00 48	47	110	00 01	47	111	-0 46	47	111	286
04 34	48	108	03 46	47	109	02 59	47	109	02 12	48	110	01 24	47	111	00 37	47	111	-0 10	48	112	287
05 10	47	109	04 23	48	110	03 35	47	110	02 48	48	111	02 00	47	111	01 13	48	112	00 25	47	113	288
05 47	48	110	04 59	48	110	04 11	47	111	03 24	48	112	02 36	47	112	01 49	48	113	01 01	48	113	289
06 23	-48	111	05 35	-48	111	04 47	-47	112	04 00	-48	112	03 12	-48	113	02 24	-48	114	01 36	-48	114	290
8°			9°			10°			11°			12°			13°			14°			

NAME TO LATITUDE

N. Lat. {LHA greater than 180°....... Zn=Z
{LHA less than 180°........... Zn=360−Z

DECLINATION (0°-14°) CONTRARY

LHA	0° Hc	d	Z	1° Hc	d	Z	2° Hc	d	Z	3° Hc	d	Z	4° Hc	d	Z	5° Hc	d	Z	6° Hc	d	Z	7° Hc	d	Z
	° ′	′	°	° ′	′	°	° ′	′	°	° ′	′	°	° ′	′	°	° ′	′	°	° ′	′	°	° ′	′	°
69	13 19	47	106	12 32	48	107	11 44	47	108	10 57	47	108	10 10	48	109	09 22	48	110	08 34	47	110	07 47	48	111
68	13 56	47	107	13 09	48	108	12 21	47	109	11 34	48	109	10 46	48	110	09 58	48	110	09 10	47	111	08 23	48	112
67	14 33	48	108	13 45	47	109	12 58	48	109	12 10	48	110	11 22	48	111	10 34	48	111	09 46	48	112	08 58	48	112
66	15 09	47	109	14 22	48	110	13 34	48	110	12 46	48	111	11 58	48	111	11 10	48	112	10 22	48	113	09 34	48	113
65	15 46	−48	110	14 58	−48	110	14 10	−48	111	13 22	−48	112	12 34	−48	112	11 46	−48	113	10 58	−49	113	10 09	−48	114
64	16 22	48	111	15 34	48	111	14 46	48	112	13 58	48	112	13 10	49	113	12 21	48	114	11 33	49	114	10 44	48	115
63	16 58	48	111	16 10	48	112	15 22	49	113	14 33	48	113	13 45	49	114	12 56	48	114	12 08	49	115	11 19	48	116
62	17 34	48	112	16 46	49	113	15 57	48	113	15 09	49	114	14 20	48	115	13 32	49	115	12 43	49	116	11 54	49	116
61	18 09	48	113	17 21	48	114	16 33	49	114	15 44	49	115	14 55	49	116	14 06	49	116	13 17	49	117	12 28	49	117
60	18 45	−49	114	17 56	−48	115	17 08	−49	115	16 19	−49	116	15 30	−49	116	14 41	−49	117	13 52	−50	118	13 02	−49	118
59	19 20	49	115	18 31	49	115	17 42	49	116	16 53	49	117	16 04	49	117	15 15	49	118	14 26	50	118	13 36	49	119
58	19 55	49	116	19 06	49	116	18 17	49	117	17 28	50	117	16 38	49	118	15 49	49	119	15 00	50	119	14 10	50	120
57	20 30	50	116	19 40	49	117	18 51	49	118	18 02	50	118	17 12	49	119	16 23	50	119	15 33	50	120	14 43	50	121
56	21 04	49	117	20 15	50	118	19 25	49	119	18 36	50	119	17 46	50	120	16 56	50	120	16 06	50	121	15 16	50	122
55	21 38	−49	118	20 49	−50	119	19 59	−50	119	19 09	−50	120	18 19	−50	121	17 29	−50	121	16 39	−50	122	15 49	−50	122
54	22 12	50	119	21 22	50	120	20 32	50	120	19 42	50	121	18 52	50	122	18 02	50	122	17 12	50	123	16 22	51	123
53	22 46	50	120	21 56	50	121	21 06	51	121	20 15	50	122	19 25	50	122	18 35	51	123	17 44	50	124	16 54	51	124
52	23 19	50	121	22 29	51	122	21 38	50	122	20 48	50	123	19 58	51	123	19 07	51	124	18 16	51	124	17 25	50	125
51	23 52	51	122	23 01	50	122	22 11	51	123	21 20	50	124	20 30	51	124	19 39	51	125	18 48	51	125	17 57	51	126
50	24 24	−50	123	23 34	−51	123	22 43	−51	124	21 52	−51	125	21 01	−51	125	20 10	−51	126	19 19	−51	126	18 28	−51	127
49	24 57	51	124	24 06	51	124	23 15	51	125	22 24	51	125	21 33	51	126	20 42	52	127	19 50	51	127	18 59	52	128
48	25 29	51	125	24 38	52	125	23 46	51	126	22 55	51	126	22 04	52	127	21 12	51	127	20 21	52	128	19 29	52	129
47	26 00	51	126	25 09	51	126	24 18	52	127	23 26	52	127	22 34	51	128	21 43	52	128	20 51	52	129	19 59	52	129
46	26 31	51	127	25 40	52	127	24 48	51	128	23 57	52	128	23 05	52	129	22 13	52	129	21 21	52	130	20 29	53	130
45	27 02	−52	128	26 10	−51	128	25 19	−52	129	24 27	−52	129	23 35	−53	130	22 42	−52	130	21 50	−52	131	20 58	−53	131
44	27 33	52	128	26 41	52	129	25 49	53	130	24 56	52	130	24 04	52	131	23 12	53	131	22 19	52	132	21 27	53	132
43	28 03	53	129	27 10	52	130	26 18	52	131	25 26	53	131	24 33	52	132	23 41	53	132	22 48	53	133	21 55	53	133
42	28 32	52	130	27 40	53	131	26 47	52	132	25 55	53	132	25 02	53	133	24 09	53	133	23 16	53	134	22 23	53	134
41	29 01	52	131	28 09	53	132	27 16	53	133	26 23	53	133	25 30	53	134	24 37	53	134	23 44	54	135	22 50	53	135
40	29 30	−53	132	28 37	−53	133	27 44	−53	134	26 51	−53	134	25 58	−54	135	25 04	−53	135	24 11	−54	136	23 17	−53	136
39	29 58	53	133	29 05	53	134	28 12	54	135	27 18	53	135	26 25	54	136	25 31	53	136	24 38	54	137	23 44	54	137
38	30 26	53	134	29 33	54	135	28 39	53	136	27 46	54	136	26 52	54	137	25 58	54	137	25 04	54	138	24 10	54	138
37	30 53	53	136	30 00	54	136	29 06	54	137	28 12	54	137	27 18	54	138	26 24	54	138	25 30	54	139	24 36	55	139
36	31 20	54	137	30 26	54	137	29 32	54	138	28 38	54	138	27 44	54	139	26 50	55	139	25 55	54	140	25 01	55	140
35	31 46	−54	138	30 52	−54	138	29 58	−54	139	29 04	−55	139	28 09	−54	140	27 15	−55	140	26 20	−55	141	25 25	−55	141
34	32 12	54	139	31 18	55	139	30 23	54	140	29 29	55	140	28 34	55	141	27 39	55	141	26 44	55	142	25 49	55	142
33	32 37	54	140	31 43	55	140	30 48	55	141	29 53	55	141	28 58	55	142	28 03	55	142	27 08	55	143	26 13	55	143
32	33 02	55	141	32 07	55	141	31 12	55	142	30 17	55	142	29 22	55	143	28 27	56	143	27 31	55	144	26 36	56	144
31	33 26	55	142	32 31	55	142	31 36	56	143	30 40	55	143	29 45	56	144	28 49	55	144	27 54	56	145	26 58	56	145
30	33 50	−56	143	32 54	−55	144	31 59	−56	144	31 03	−55	144	30 08	−56	145	29 12	−56	145	28 16	−56	146	27 20	−56	146
29	34 13	56	144	33 17	56	145	32 21	56	145	31 25	56	145	30 29	56	146	29 33	56	146	28 37	56	147	27 41	56	147
28	34 35	56	145	33 39	56	146	32 43	56	146	31 47	56	147	30 51	56	147	29 55	57	147	28 58	56	148	28 02	56	148
27	34 56	56	146	34 00	56	147	33 04	56	147	32 08	56	148	31 12	57	148	30 15	56	148	29 19	57	149	28 22	57	149
26	35 18	57	148	34 21	56	148	33 25	57	148	32 28	56	149	31 32	57	149	30 35	57	150	29 38	57	150	28 41	56	150
25	35 38	−57	149	34 41	−56	149	33 45	−57	150	32 48	−57	150	31 51	−57	150	30 54	−57	151	29 57	−57	151	29 00	−57	151
24	35 58	57	150	35 01	57	150	34 04	57	151	33 07	57	151	32 10	57	151	31 13	57	152	30 16	58	152	29 18	57	152
23	36 17	57	151	35 20	58	151	34 22	57	152	33 25	57	152	32 28	57	153	31 31	58	153	30 33	57	153	29 36	57	154
22	36 35	57	152	35 38	58	153	34 40	57	153	33 43	57	153	32 46	58	154	31 48	58	154	30 50	57	154	29 53	58	155
21	36 53	58	153	35 55	57	154	34 58	58	154	34 00	58	154	33 02	57	155	32 05	58	155	31 07	58	155	30 09	58	156
20	37 10	−58	155	36 12	−58	155	35 14	−58	155	34 16	−58	156	33 18	−57	156	32 21	−58	156	31 23	−58	157	30 25	−58	157
19	37 26	58	156	36 28	58	156	35 30	58	156	34 32	58	157	33 34	58	157	32 36	58	157	31 38	59	158	30 39	58	158
18	37 41	58	157	36 43	58	157	35 45	58	158	34 47	59	158	33 48	58	158	32 50	58	159	31 52	58	159	30 54	59	159
17	37 56	58	158	36 58	59	159	35 59	58	159	35 01	59	159	34 02	58	159	33 04	59	160	32 05	58	160	31 07	59	160
16	38 10	59	160	37 11	58	160	36 13	59	160	35 14	58	160	34 16	59	161	33 17	59	161	32 18	58	161	31 20	59	161
15	38 23	−59	161	37 24	−58	161	36 26	−59	161	35 27	−59	162	34 28	−59	162	33 29	−58	162	32 31	−59	162	31 32	−59	163
14	38 35	59	162	37 36	58	162	36 38	59	163	35 39	59	163	34 40	59	163	33 41	59	163	32 42	59	163	31 43	59	164
13	38 47	59	163	37 48	59	164	36 49	59	164	35 50	59	164	34 51	59	164	33 52	59	164	32 53	60	165	31 53	59	165
12	38 57	59	165	37 58	59	165	36 59	59	165	36 00	59	165	35 01	59	165	34 02	60	166	33 02	59	166	32 03	59	166
11	39 07	59	166	38 08	59	166	37 09	59	166	36 10	60	166	35 10	59	167	34 11	59	167	33 12	60	167	32 12	59	167
10	39 16	−59	167	38 17	−59	167	37 18	−60	167	36 18	−59	168	35 19	−60	168	34 19	−59	168	33 20	−60	168	32 20	−59	168
9	39 25	60	168	38 25	59	169	37 26	60	169	36 26	59	169	35 27	60	169	34 27	59	169	33 28	60	169	32 28	60	169
8	39 32	60	170	38 32	59	170	37 33	60	170	36 33	59	170	35 34	60	170	34 34	60	170	33 34	59	170	32 35	60	171
7	39 39	60	171	38 39	60	171	37 39	59	171	36 40	60	171	35 40	60	171	34 40	60	172	33 40	59	172	32 41	60	172
6	39 44	59	172	38 45	60	172	37 45	60	172	36 45	60	173	35 45	60	173	34 45	59	173	33 46	60	173	32 46	60	173
5	39 49	−60	174	38 49	−60	174	37 49	−59	174	36 50	−60	174	35 50	−60	174	34 50	−60	174	33 50	−60	174	32 50	−60	174
4	39 53	60	175	38 53	60	175	37 53	60	175	36 53	60	175	35 53	59	175	34 54	60	175	33 54	60	175	32 54	60	175
3	39 56	60	176	38 56	60	176	37 56	60	176	36 56	60	176	35 56	60	176	34 56	60	176	33 56	60	176	32 56	59	177
2	39 58	60	177	38 58	60	177	37 58	60	178	36 58	60	178	35 58	60	178	34 58	60	178	33 58	60	178	32 58	60	178
1	40 00	60	179	39 00	60	179	38 00	60	179	37 00	60	179	36 00	60	179	35 00	60	179	34 00	60	179	33 00	60	179
0	40 00	−60	180	39 00	−60	180	38 00	−60	180	37 00	−60	180	36 00	−60	180	35 00	−60	180	34 00	−60	180	33 00	−60	180
	0°			1°			2°			3°			4°			5°			6°			7°		

S. Lat. {LHA greater than 180°....... Zn=180−Z
{LHA less than 180°........... Zn=180+Z

DECLINATION (0°-14°) CONTRARY

8°			9°			10°			11°			12°			13°			14°			
Hc	d	Z	Hc	d	Z	Hc	d	Z	Hc	d	Z	Hc	d	Z	Hc	d	Z	Hc	d	Z	LHA
° ′	′	°	° ′	′	°	° ′	′	°	° ′	′	°	° ′	′	°	° ′	′	°	° ′	′	°	
06 59	48	111	06 11	48	112	05 23	48	113	04 35	48	113	03 47	48	114	02 59	48	114	02 11	48	115	291
07 35	48	112	06 47	48	113	05 59	48	113	05 11	49	114	04 22	48	115	03 34	48	115	02 46	48	116	292
08 10	48	113	07 22	48	114	06 34	48	114	05 46	49	115	04 57	48	115	04 09	48	116	03 21	49	117	293
08 46	49	114	07 57	48	114	07 09	48	115	06 21	49	116	05 32	48	116	04 44	49	117	03 55	48	117	294
09 21	-49	115	08 32	-48	115	07 44	-49	116	06 55	-48	116	06 07	-49	117	05 18	-49	118	04 29	-48	118	295
09 56	49	115	09 07	49	116	08 18	48	117	07 30	49	117	06 41	49	118	05 52	49	118	05 03	49	119	296
10 31	49	116	09 42	49	117	08 53	49	117	08 04	49	118	07 15	49	119	06 26	49	119	05 37	49	120	297
11 05	49	117	10 16	49	118	09 27	49	118	08 38	49	119	07 49	49	119	07 00	50	120	06 10	49	121	298
11 39	49	118	10 50	49	118	10 01	49	119	09 12	50	120	08 22	49	120	07 33	50	121	06 43	49	121	299
12 13	-49	119	11 24	-50	119	10 34	-49	120	09 45	-50	120	08 55	-49	121	08 06	-50	122	07 16	-50	122	300
12 47	50	120	11 57	49	120	11 08	50	121	10 18	50	121	09 28	49	122	08 39	50	122	07 49	50	123	301
13 20	49	120	12 31	50	121	11 41	50	122	10 51	50	122	10 01	50	123	09 11	50	123	08 21	50	124	302
13 53	49	121	13 04	50	122	12 14	51	122	11 23	50	123	10 33	50	123	09 43	50	124	08 53	50	125	303
14 26	50	122	13 36	50	123	12 46	50	123	11 56	51	124	11 05	50	124	10 15	51	125	09 24	50	125	304
14 59	-50	123	14 09	-51	124	13 18	-50	124	12 28	-51	125	11 37	-51	125	10 46	-50	126	09 56	-51	126	305
15 31	50	124	14 41	51	124	13 50	51	125	12 59	51	125	12 08	50	126	11 18	51	127	10 27	51	127	306
16 03	51	125	15 12	51	125	14 21	51	126	13 30	51	126	12 39	51	127	11 48	51	127	10 57	51	128	307
16 35	51	126	15 44	51	126	14 53	52	127	14 01	51	127	13 10	51	128	12 19	51	128	11 28	52	129	308
17 06	51	126	16 15	52	127	15 23	51	128	14 32	51	128	13 41	52	129	12 49	52	129	11 57	51	130	309
17 37	-52	127	16 45	-51	128	15 54	-52	128	15 02	-51	129	14 11	-52	129	13 19	-52	130	12 27	-52	130	310
18 07	51	128	17 16	52	129	16 24	52	129	15 32	52	130	14 40	52	130	13 48	52	131	12 56	52	131	311
18 37	52	129	17 45	51	130	16 54	53	130	16 01	52	131	15 09	52	131	14 17	52	132	13 25	52	132	312
19 07	52	130	18 15	52	131	17 23	52	131	16 31	53	132	15 38	52	132	14 46	53	133	13 53	52	133	313
19 36	52	131	18 44	52	131	17 52	53	132	16 59	52	132	16 07	53	133	15 14	53	133	14 21	52	134	314
20 05	-52	132	19 13	-53	132	18 20	-52	133	17 28	-53	133	16 35	-53	134	15 42	-53	134	14 49	-53	135	315
20 34	53	133	19 41	53	133	18 48	53	134	17 55	53	134	17 02	53	135	16 09	53	135	15 16	53	136	316
21 02	53	134	20 09	53	134	19 16	53	135	18 23	53	135	17 30	54	136	16 36	53	136	15 43	54	137	317
21 30	53	135	20 37	54	135	19 43	53	136	18 50	54	136	17 56	53	137	17 03	54	137	16 09	54	138	318
21 57	53	136	21 04	54	136	20 10	54	137	19 16	53	137	18 23	54	138	17 29	54	138	16 35	54	138	319
22 24	-54	137	21 30	-54	137	20 36	-54	137	19 42	-54	138	18 48	-54	138	17 54	-54	139	17 00	-54	139	320
22 50	54	138	21 56	54	138	21 02	54	138	20 08	54	139	19 14	54	139	18 20	55	140	17 25	54	140	321
23 16	54	138	22 22	55	139	21 27	54	139	20 33	54	140	19 39	55	140	18 44	54	141	17 50	55	141	322
23 41	54	139	22 47	55	140	21 52	54	140	20 58	55	141	20 03	55	141	19 08	54	142	18 14	55	142	323
24 06	55	140	23 11	54	141	22 17	55	141	21 22	55	142	20 27	55	142	19 32	55	143	18 37	55	143	324
24 30	-54	141	23 36	-55	142	22 41	-55	142	21 46	-56	143	20 50	-55	143	19 55	-55	144	19 00	-55	144	325
24 54	55	142	23 59	55	143	23 04	55	143	22 09	56	144	21 13	55	144	20 18	55	145	19 23	56	145	326
25 18	56	143	24 22	55	144	23 27	56	144	22 31	55	145	21 36	56	145	20 40	56	145	19 44	55	146	327
25 40	55	144	24 45	56	145	23 49	56	145	22 53	55	146	21 58	56	146	21 02	56	146	20 06	56	147	328
26 02	55	145	25 07	56	146	24 11	56	146	23 15	56	147	22 19	56	147	21 23	56	147	20 27	56	148	329
26 24	-56	146	25 28	-56	147	24 32	-56	147	23 36	-56	148	22 40	-57	148	21 43	-56	148	20 47	-56	149	330
26 45	56	148	25 49	56	148	24 53	57	148	23 56	56	149	23 00	57	149	22 03	56	149	21 07	57	150	331
27 06	57	149	26 09	56	149	25 13	57	149	24 16	57	150	23 19	56	150	22 23	57	150	21 26	57	151	332
27 25	56	150	26 29	57	150	25 32	57	150	24 35	57	151	23 38	57	151	22 41	57	151	21 44	57	152	333
27 45	57	151	26 48	57	151	25 51	57	151	24 54	57	152	23 57	57	152	23 00	58	152	22 02	57	153	334
28 03	-57	152	27 06	-57	152	26 09	-57	152	25 12	-58	153	24 14	-57	153	23 17	-57	153	22 20	-58	154	335
28 21	57	153	27 24	58	153	26 26	57	153	25 29	57	154	24 32	58	154	23 34	57	154	22 37	58	155	336
28 39	58	154	27 41	58	154	26 43	57	155	25 46	58	155	24 48	57	155	23 51	58	155	22 53	58	156	337
28 55	58	155	27 57	57	155	27 00	58	156	26 02	58	156	25 04	58	156	24 06	58	156	23 08	58	157	338
29 11	58	156	28 13	58	156	27 15	58	157	26 17	58	157	25 19	58	157	24 21	58	158	23 23	58	158	339
29 27	-59	157	28 28	-58	157	27 30	-58	158	26 32	-58	158	25 34	-58	158	24 36	-58	159	23 38	-59	159	340
29 41	58	158	28 43	58	159	27 45	59	159	26 46	58	159	25 48	58	159	24 50	59	160	23 51	58	160	341
29 55	58	159	28 57	59	160	27 58	58	160	27 00	59	160	26 01	58	160	25 03	59	161	24 04	58	161	342
30 08	58	160	29 10	59	161	28 11	58	161	27 13	59	161	26 14	59	161	25 15	58	162	24 17	59	162	343
30 21	59	162	29 22	59	162	28 23	58	162	27 25	59	162	26 26	59	163	25 27	59	163	24 28	59	163	344
30 33	-59	163	29 34	-59	163	28 35	-59	163	27 36	-59	163	26 37	-59	164	25 38	-59	164	24 39	-59	164	345
30 44	59	164	29 45	59	164	28 46	59	164	27 47	59	164	26 48	59	165	25 49	59	165	24 50	60	165	346
30 54	59	165	29 55	59	165	28 56	59	165	27 57	59	166	26 58	60	166	25 58	59	166	24 59	59	166	347
31 04	59	166	30 05	60	166	29 05	59	166	28 06	59	167	27 07	60	167	26 07	59	167	25 08	59	167	348
31 13	60	167	30 13	59	167	29 14	59	168	28 15	60	168	27 15	59	168	26 16	60	168	25 16	59	168	349
31 21	-60	168	30 21	-59	169	29 22	-60	169	28 22	-59	169	27 23	-60	169	26 23	-59	169	25 24	-60	169	350
31 28	59	170	30 29	60	170	29 29	59	170	28 30	60	170	27 30	60	170	26 30	59	170	25 31	60	170	351
31 35	60	171	30 35	59	171	29 36	60	171	28 36	60	171	27 36	59	171	26 37	60	171	25 37	60	171	352
31 41	60	172	30 41	60	172	29 41	59	172	28 42	60	172	27 42	60	172	26 42	60	172	25 42	59	173	353
31 46	60	173	30 46	60	173	29 46	60	173	28 46	59	173	27 47	60	173	26 47	60	173	25 47	60	174	354
31 50	-60	174	30 50	-60	174	29 50	-59	174	28 51	-60	174	27 51	-60	175	26 51	-60	175	25 51	-60	175	355
31 54	60	175	30 54	60	175	29 54	60	176	28 54	60	176	27 54	60	176	26 54	60	176	25 54	60	176	356
31 57	60	177	30 57	60	177	29 57	60	177	28 57	60	177	27 57	60	177	26 57	60	177	25 57	60	177	357
31 58	60	178	30 58	59	178	29 59	60	178	28 59	60	178	27 59	60	178	26 59	60	178	25 59	60	178	358
32 00	60	179	31 00	60	179	30 00	60	179	29 00	60	179	28 00	60	179	27 00	60	179	26 00	60	179	359
32 00	-60	180	31 00	-60	180	30 00	-60	180	29 00	-60	180	28 00	-60	180	27 00	-60	180	26 00	-60	180	360
8°			9°			10°			11°			12°			13°			14°			

LAT 50°

N. Lat. {LHA greater than 180°....... Zn=Z; LHA less than 180°........... Zn=360−Z}

DECLINATION (15°-29°) SAME

LHA	15° Hc	d	Z	16° Hc	d	Z	17° Hc	d	Z	18° Hc	d	Z	19° Hc	d	Z	20° Hc	d	Z	21° Hc	d	Z	22° Hc	d	Z
	° ′	′	°	° ′	′	°	° ′	′	°	° ′	′	°	° ′	′	°	° ′	′	°	° ′	′	°	° ′	′	°
0	55 00	+60	180	56 00	+60	180	57 00	+60	180	58 00	+60	180	59 00	+60	180	60 00	+60	180	61 00	+60	180	62 00	+60	180
1	54 59	60	178	55 59	60	178	56 59	60	178	57 59	60	178	58 59	60	178	59 59	60	178	60 59	60	178	61 59	60	178
2	54 58	60	177	55 58	60	177	56 58	60	177	57 58	60	176	58 58	60	176	59 58	59	176	60 57	60	176	61 57	60	176
3	54 55	60	175	55 55	60	175	56 55	60	175	57 55	59	175	58 54	60	175	59 54	60	174	60 54	60	174	61 54	60	174
4	54 51	60	173	55 51	60	173	56 51	59	173	57 50	60	173	58 50	60	173	59 50	60	173	60 50	59	172	61 49	60	172
5	54 46	+60	172	55 46	+59	171	56 45	+60	171	57 45	+60	171	58 45	+59	171	59 44	+60	171	60 44	+60	170	61 44	+59	170
6	54 40	59	170	55 39	60	170	56 39	59	170	57 38	60	169	58 38	59	169	59 37	60	169	60 37	59	169	61 36	60	168
7	54 32	60	168	55 32	59	168	56 31	60	168	57 31	59	168	58 30	59	167	59 29	60	167	60 29	59	167	61 28	59	166
8	54 24	59	167	55 23	60	166	56 23	59	166	57 22	59	166	58 21	59	166	59 20	59	165	60 19	59	165	61 18	59	164
9	54 15	59	165	55 14	59	165	56 13	59	164	57 12	59	164	58 11	59	164	59 10	58	163	60 08	59	163	61 07	59	163
10	54 04	+59	163	55 03	+59	163	56 02	+59	163	57 01	+58	162	57 59	+59	162	58 58	+58	162	59 56	+59	161	60 55	+58	161
11	53 53	58	162	54 51	59	161	55 50	58	161	56 48	59	161	57 47	58	160	58 45	58	160	59 43	59	159	60 42	58	159
12	53 40	58	160	54 38	59	160	55 37	58	159	56 35	58	159	57 33	58	159	58 31	58	158	59 29	58	158	60 27	58	157
13	53 26	59	159	54 25	58	158	55 23	58	158	56 21	58	157	57 19	57	157	58 16	58	156	59 14	57	156	60 11	58	155
14	53 12	58	157	54 10	58	157	55 08	57	156	56 05	58	156	57 03	57	155	58 00	58	155	58 58	57	154	59 55	57	153
15	52 56	+58	156	53 54	+58	155	54 52	+57	155	55 49	+57	154	56 46	+57	154	57 43	+57	153	58 40	+57	152	59 37	+56	152
16	52 40	57	154	53 37	57	154	54 34	58	153	55 32	56	152	56 28	57	152	57 25	57	151	58 22	56	151	59 18	56	150
17	52 23	57	152	53 20	56	152	54 16	57	151	55 13	57	151	56 10	56	150	57 06	56	150	58 02	56	149	58 58	56	148
18	52 04	57	151	53 01	57	150	53 58	56	150	54 54	56	149	55 50	56	149	56 46	56	148	57 42	56	147	58 38	55	147
19	51 45	56	150	52 41	57	149	53 38	56	148	54 34	56	148	55 30	55	147	56 25	56	146	57 21	55	146	58 16	55	145
20	51 25	+56	148	52 21	+56	147	53 17	+56	147	54 13	+55	146	55 08	+56	146	56 04	+55	145	56 59	+54	144	57 53	+55	143
21	51 04	56	147	52 00	56	146	52 56	55	145	53 51	55	145	54 46	55	144	55 41	55	143	56 36	54	143	57 30	54	142
22	50 43	55	145	51 38	55	145	52 33	55	144	53 28	55	143	54 23	54	143	55 17	55	142	56 12	54	141	57 06	53	140
23	50 20	55	144	51 15	55	143	52 10	55	143	53 05	54	142	53 59	54	141	54 53	54	140	55 47	54	140	56 41	53	139
24	49 57	55	142	50 52	54	142	51 46	54	141	52 40	54	140	53 34	54	140	54 28	54	139	55 22	53	138	56 15	53	137
25	49 33	+54	141	50 27	+55	140	51 22	+54	140	52 16	+53	139	53 09	+53	138	54 02	+54	137	54 56	+52	137	55 48	+53	136
26	49 08	55	140	50 03	53	139	50 56	54	138	51 50	53	138	52 43	53	137	53 36	53	136	54 29	52	135	55 21	52	134
27	48 43	54	138	49 37	53	138	50 30	53	137	51 23	53	136	52 16	53	136	53 09	52	135	54 01	52	134	54 53	52	133
28	48 17	54	137	49 11	53	136	50 04	52	136	50 56	53	135	51 49	52	134	52 41	52	133	53 33	52	133	54 25	51	132
29	47 51	53	136	48 44	52	135	49 36	53	134	50 29	52	134	51 21	52	133	52 13	51	132	53 04	51	131	53 55	51	130
30	47 23	+53	135	48 16	+52	134	49 08	+53	133	50 01	+51	132	50 52	+52	132	51 44	+51	131	52 35	+51	130	53 26	+50	129
31	46 56	52	133	47 48	52	133	48 40	52	132	49 32	51	131	50 23	51	130	51 14	51	129	52 05	50	129	52 55	50	128
32	46 27	52	132	47 19	52	131	48 11	51	131	49 02	51	130	49 53	51	129	50 44	51	128	51 35	50	127	52 25	49	126
33	45 58	52	131	46 50	51	130	47 41	51	129	48 32	51	129	49 23	51	128	50 14	50	127	51 04	49	126	51 53	49	125
34	45 29	51	130	46 20	51	129	47 11	51	128	48 02	50	127	48 52	51	127	49 43	49	126	50 32	49	125	51 21	49	124
35	44 59	+51	128	45 50	+51	128	46 41	+50	127	47 31	+50	126	48 21	+50	125	49 11	+49	125	50 00	+49	124	50 49	+49	123
36	44 28	51	127	45 19	51	127	46 10	50	126	47 00	50	125	47 50	49	124	48 39	49	123	49 28	49	122	50 17	48	122
37	43 58	50	126	44 48	50	125	45 38	50	125	46 28	49	124	47 17	49	123	48 06	49	122	48 55	48	121	49 43	48	120
38	43 26	50	125	44 16	50	124	45 06	50	124	45 56	49	123	46 45	49	122	47 34	48	121	48 22	48	120	49 10	48	119
39	42 54	50	124	43 44	50	123	44 34	49	122	45 23	49	122	46 12	48	121	47 00	48	120	47 48	48	119	48 36	47	118
40	42 22	+50	123	43 12	+49	122	44 01	+49	121	44 50	+49	121	45 39	+48	120	46 27	+48	119	47 15	+47	118	48 02	+47	117
41	41 50	49	122	42 39	49	121	43 28	49	120	44 17	48	119	45 05	48	119	45 53	47	118	46 40	47	117	47 27	47	116
42	41 17	49	121	42 06	48	120	42 54	49	119	43 43	48	118	44 31	47	118	45 18	48	117	46 06	47	116	46 53	46	115
43	40 43	49	120	41 32	48	119	42 20	49	118	43 09	47	117	43 56	48	116	44 44	47	116	45 31	46	115	46 17	47	114
44	40 10	48	119	40 58	48	118	41 46	48	117	42 34	48	116	43 22	47	115	44 09	47	115	44 56	46	114	45 42	46	113
45	39 35	+49	118	40 24	+48	117	41 12	+47	116	41 59	+48	115	42 47	+47	114	43 34	+46	114	44 20	+46	113	45 06	+46	112
46	39 01	48	117	39 49	48	116	40 37	47	115	41 24	47	114	42 11	47	113	42 58	46	113	43 44	46	112	44 30	46	111
47	38 27	47	116	39 14	48	115	40 02	47	114	40 49	47	113	41 36	46	112	42 22	46	112	43 08	46	111	43 54	45	110
48	37 52	47	115	38 39	48	114	39 27	46	113	40 13	47	112	41 00	46	111	41 46	46	111	42 32	46	110	43 18	45	109
49	37 16	48	114	38 04	47	113	38 51	47	112	39 38	46	111	40 24	46	110	41 10	46	110	41 56	45	109	42 41	45	108
50	36 41	+47	113	37 28	+47	112	38 15	+47	111	39 02	+46	110	39 48	+46	110	40 34	+45	109	41 19	+45	108	42 04	+45	107
51	36 05	47	112	36 52	47	111	37 39	46	110	38 25	46	109	39 11	46	109	39 57	45	108	40 42	45	107	41 27	45	106
52	35 29	47	111	36 16	47	110	37 03	46	109	37 49	46	108	38 35	45	108	39 20	45	107	40 05	45	106	40 50	45	105
53	34 53	47	110	35 40	46	109	36 26	46	108	37 12	46	108	37 58	45	107	38 43	45	106	39 28	45	105	40 13	44	104
54	34 17	46	109	35 03	46	108	35 49	46	107	36 35	46	107	37 21	45	106	38 06	45	105	38 51	44	104	39 35	44	103
55	33 40	+47	108	34 27	+46	107	35 13	+45	107	35 58	+46	106	36 44	+45	105	37 29	+44	104	38 13	+45	103	38 58	+44	102
56	33 03	47	107	33 50	45	106	34 35	46	106	35 21	45	105	36 06	45	104	36 51	45	103	37 36	44	102	38 20	44	102
57	32 26	47	106	33 13	45	106	33 58	46	105	34 44	45	104	35 29	45	103	36 14	44	102	36 58	44	102	37 42	44	101
58	31 49	46	105	32 35	46	105	33 21	45	104	34 06	45	103	34 51	45	102	35 36	44	102	36 20	44	101	37 04	44	100
59	31 12	46	105	31 58	45	104	32 43	46	103	33 29	44	102	34 13	45	101	34 58	44	101	35 42	44	100	36 26	44	99
60	30 35	+45	104	31 20	+46	103	32 06	+45	102	32 51	+45	101	33 36	+44	101	34 20	+44	100	35 04	+44	99	35 48	+44	98
61	29 57	46	103	30 43	45	102	31 28	45	101	32 13	45	101	32 58	44	100	33 42	44	99	34 26	44	98	35 10	43	97
62	29 20	45	102	30 05	45	101	30 50	45	101	31 35	45	100	32 20	44	99	33 04	44	98	33 48	44	97	34 32	43	97
63	28 42	45	101	29 27	45	100	30 12	45	100	30 57	44	99	31 41	45	98	32 26	44	97	33 10	43	97	33 53	43	96
64	28 04	45	100	28 49	45	100	29 34	45	99	30 19	44	98	31 03	44	97	31 47	44	97	32 31	44	96	33 15	43	95
65	27 26	+45	100	28 11	+45	99	28 56	+45	98	29 41	+44	97	30 25	+44	96	31 09	+44	96	31 53	+43	95	32 36	+44	94
66	26 48	45	99	27 33	45	98	28 18	44	97	29 02	45	96	29 47	44	96	30 31	43	95	31 14	44	94	31 58	43	93
67	26 10	45	98	26 55	44	97	27 39	45	96	28 24	44	96	29 08	44	95	29 52	44	94	30 36	43	93	31 19	43	93
68	25 31	45	97	26 16	45	96	27 01	44	96	27 45	45	95	28 30	44	94	29 14	43	93	29 57	44	93	30 41	43	92
69	24 53	45	96	25 38	45	96	26 23	44	95	27 07	44	94	27 51	44	93	28 35	44	93	29 19	43	92	30 02	43	91
	15°			16°			17°			18°			19°			20°			21°			22°		

S. Lat. {LHA greater than 180°....... Zn=180−Z; LHA less than 180°........... Zn=180+Z}

DECLINATION (15°-29°) SAME

23°			24°			25°			26°			27°			28°			29°			
Hc	d	Z	Hc	d	Z	Hc	d	Z	Hc	d	Z	Hc	d	Z	Hc	d	Z	Hc	d	Z	LHA
° ′	′	°	° ′	′	°	° ′	′	°	° ′	′	°	° ′	′	°	° ′	′	°	° ′	′	°	
63 00	+60	180	64 00	+60	180	65 00	+60	180	66 00	+60	180	67 00	+60	180	68 00	+60	180	69 00	+60	180	360
62 59	60	178	63 59	60	178	64 59	60	178	65 59	60	178	66 59	60	178	67 59	60	178	68 59	60	178	359
62 57	60	176	63 57	60	176	64 57	60	176	65 57	60	176	66 57	60	175	67 57	60	175	68 57	60	175	358
62 54	60	174	63 54	60	174	64 54	59	174	65 53	60	173	66 53	60	173	67 53	60	173	68 53	59	173	357
62 49	60	172	63 49	60	172	64 49	59	172	65 48	60	171	66 48	59	171	67 47	60	171	68 47	59	170	356
62 43	+60	170	63 43	+59	170	64 42	+60	169	65 42	+59	169	66 41	+59	169	67 40	+60	168	68 40	+59	168	355
62 36	59	168	63 35	59	168	64 34	60	167	65 34	59	167	66 33	59	167	67 32	59	166	68 31	59	166	354
62 27	59	166	63 26	59	166	64 25	59	165	65 24	59	165	66 23	59	164	67 22	58	164	68 20	59	163	353
62 17	59	164	63 16	59	164	64 15	58	163	65 13	59	163	66 12	58	162	67 10	59	162	68 09	58	161	352
62 06	58	162	63 04	59	162	64 03	58	161	65 01	58	161	65 59	58	160	66 57	58	159	67 55	58	159	351
61 53	+58	160	62 51	+59	160	63 50	+58	159	64 48	+57	159	65 45	+58	158	66 43	+58	157	67 41	+57	156	350
61 40	57	158	62 37	58	158	63 35	58	157	64 33	57	157	65 30	57	156	66 27	57	155	67 24	57	154	349
61 25	57	156	62 22	58	156	63 20	57	155	64 17	57	155	65 14	57	154	66 11	56	153	67 07	56	152	348
61 09	57	155	62 06	57	154	63 03	57	153	64 00	56	153	64 56	56	152	65 52	56	151	66 48	56	150	347
60 52	56	153	61 48	57	152	62 45	56	151	63 41	56	151	64 37	56	150	65 33	56	149	66 29	55	148	346
60 33	+57	151	61 30	+56	150	62 26	+56	150	63 22	+55	149	64 17	+56	148	65 13	+54	147	66 07	+55	146	345
60 14	56	149	61 10	56	149	62 06	55	148	63 01	55	147	63 56	55	146	64 51	54	145	65 45	54	144	344
59 54	56	148	60 50	55	147	61 45	55	146	62 40	54	145	63 34	54	144	64 28	54	143	65 22	54	142	343
59 33	55	146	60 28	55	145	61 23	54	144	62 17	54	143	63 11	54	142	64 05	53	141	64 58	53	140	342
59 11	54	144	60 05	55	143	61 00	54	143	61 54	53	142	62 47	53	141	63 40	53	140	64 33	52	139	341
58 48	+54	143	59 42	+54	142	60 36	+53	141	61 29	+53	140	62 22	+53	139	63 15	+52	138	64 07	+52	137	340
58 24	54	141	59 18	53	140	60 11	53	139	61 04	53	138	61 57	52	137	62 49	51	136	63 40	51	135	339
57 59	54	139	58 53	52	139	59 45	53	138	60 38	52	137	61 30	51	136	62 21	51	135	63 12	51	133	338
57 34	53	138	58 27	52	137	59 19	52	136	60 11	52	135	61 03	51	134	61 54	50	133	62 44	50	132	337
57 08	52	136	58 00	52	136	58 52	51	135	59 43	51	134	60 34	51	133	61 25	50	131	62 15	49	130	336
56 41	+52	135	57 33	+51	134	58 24	+51	133	59 15	+51	132	60 06	+50	131	60 56	+49	130	61 45	+49	129	335
56 13	51	134	57 04	52	133	57 56	50	132	58 46	50	131	59 36	50	130	60 26	49	128	61 15	48	127	334
55 45	51	132	56 36	50	131	57 26	51	130	58 17	49	129	59 06	49	128	59 55	49	127	60 44	48	126	333
55 16	50	131	56 06	51	130	56 57	49	129	57 46	49	128	58 35	49	127	59 24	48	126	60 12	47	124	332
54 46	50	129	55 36	50	128	56 26	49	127	57 15	49	126	58 04	48	125	58 52	48	124	59 40	47	123	331
54 16	+50	128	55 06	+49	127	55 55	+49	126	56 44	+48	125	57 32	+48	124	58 20	+47	123	59 07	+47	122	330
53 45	50	127	54 35	49	126	55 24	48	125	56 12	48	124	57 00	48	123	57 48	46	121	58 34	46	120	329
53 14	49	125	54 03	49	124	54 52	48	123	55 40	48	122	56 28	46	121	57 14	47	120	58 01	45	119	328
52 42	49	124	53 31	48	123	54 19	48	122	55 07	47	121	55 54	47	120	56 41	46	119	57 27	45	118	327
52 10	49	123	52 59	48	122	53 47	47	121	54 34	47	120	55 21	46	119	56 07	45	118	56 52	45	117	326
51 38	+48	122	52 26	+47	121	53 13	+47	120	54 00	+47	119	54 47	+46	118	55 33	+45	117	56 18	+44	115	325
51 05	47	121	51 52	48	120	52 40	46	119	53 26	46	118	54 12	46	116	54 58	45	115	55 43	44	114	324
50 31	48	119	51 19	47	118	52 06	46	117	52 52	46	116	53 38	45	115	54 23	44	114	55 07	44	113	323
49 58	47	118	50 45	46	117	51 31	46	116	52 17	46	115	53 03	45	114	53 48	44	113	54 32	43	112	322
49 23	47	117	50 10	46	116	50 56	46	115	51 42	45	114	52 27	45	113	53 12	44	112	53 56	43	111	321
48 49	+46	116	49 35	+46	115	50 21	+46	114	51 07	+45	113	51 52	+44	112	52 36	+44	111	53 20	+43	110	320
48 14	46	115	49 00	46	114	49 46	45	113	50 31	45	112	51 16	44	111	52 00	43	110	52 43	43	109	319
47 39	46	114	48 25	45	113	49 10	45	112	49 55	45	111	50 40	43	110	51 23	44	109	52 07	42	108	318
47 04	45	113	47 49	45	112	48 34	45	111	49 19	44	110	50 03	44	109	50 47	43	108	51 30	42	107	317
46 28	45	112	47 13	45	111	47 58	45	110	48 43	44	109	49 27	43	108	50 10	43	107	50 53	42	106	316
45 52	+45	111	46 37	+45	110	47 22	+44	109	48 06	+44	108	48 50	+43	107	49 33	+42	106	50 15	+42	105	315
45 16	45	110	46 01	44	109	46 45	44	108	47 29	44	107	48 13	43	106	48 56	42	105	49 38	42	104	314
44 39	45	109	45 24	45	108	46 09	43	107	46 52	44	106	47 36	42	105	48 18	43	104	49 01	41	103	313
44 03	44	108	44 47	45	107	45 32	43	106	46 15	43	105	46 58	43	104	47 41	42	103	48 23	41	102	312
43 26	44	107	44 10	44	106	44 54	44	105	45 38	43	104	46 21	42	103	47 03	42	102	47 45	41	101	311
42 49	+44	106	43 33	+44	105	44 17	+43	104	45 00	+43	103	45 43	+42	102	46 25	+42	101	47 07	+41	100	310
42 12	44	105	42 56	44	104	43 40	43	103	44 23	42	102	45 05	43	101	45 48	41	100	46 29	41	99	309
41 35	43	104	42 18	44	103	43 02	43	102	43 45	43	101	44 28	42	100	45 10	41	99	45 51	41	98	308
40 57	44	103	41 41	43	102	42 24	43	101	43 07	43	101	43 50	41	100	44 31	42	99	45 13	41	98	307
40 19	44	102	41 03	43	102	41 46	43	101	42 29	42	100	43 11	42	99	43 53	42	98	44 35	40	97	306
39 42	+43	102	40 25	+43	101	41 08	+43	100	41 51	+42	99	42 33	+42	98	43 15	+41	97	43 56	+41	96	305
39 04	43	101	39 47	43	100	40 30	43	99	41 13	42	98	41 55	42	97	42 37	41	96	43 18	40	95	304
38 26	43	100	39 09	43	99	39 52	43	98	40 35	42	97	41 17	41	96	41 58	41	95	42 39	41	94	303
37 48	43	99	38 31	43	98	39 14	42	97	39 56	42	96	40 38	42	95	41 20	41	94	42 01	40	93	302
37 10	43	98	37 53	43	97	38 36	42	96	39 18	42	95	40 00	41	95	40 41	41	94	41 22	41	93	301
36 32	+43	97	37 15	+42	96	37 57	+43	96	38 40	+41	95	39 21	+42	94	40 03	+41	93	40 44	+40	92	300
35 53	43	96	36 36	43	96	37 19	42	95	38 01	42	94	38 43	41	93	39 24	41	92	40 05	41	91	299
35 15	43	96	35 58	42	95	36 40	43	94	37 23	41	93	38 04	42	92	38 46	41	91	39 27	40	90	298
34 36	43	95	35 19	43	94	36 02	42	93	36 44	42	92	37 26	41	91	38 07	41	90	38 48	41	90	297
33 58	43	94	34 41	42	93	35 23	43	92	36 06	41	91	36 47	42	91	37 29	41	90	38 10	40	89	296
33 20	+42	93	34 02	+43	92	34 45	+42	92	35 27	+42	91	36 09	+41	90	36 50	+41	89	37 31	+40	88	295
32 41	43	92	33 24	42	92	34 06	42	91	34 48	42	90	35 30	42	89	36 12	40	88	36 52	41	87	294
32 02	43	92	32 45	43	91	33 28	42	90	34 10	42	89	34 52	41	88	35 33	41	87	36 14	41	87	293
31 24	43	91	32 07	42	90	32 49	42	89	33 31	42	88	34 13	41	88	34 54	41	87	35 35	41	86	292
30 45	43	90	31 28	43	89	32 11	42	89	32 53	42	88	33 35	41	87	34 16	41	86	34 57	41	85	291
23°			24°			25°			26°			27°			28°			29°			

LAT 50°

N. Lat. {LHA greater than 180°....... Zn=Z; LHA less than 180°.......... Zn=360−Z}

DECLINATION (15°-29°) SAME

LHA	15° Hc	d	Z	16° Hc	d	Z	17° Hc	d	Z	18° Hc	d	Z
	° ′	′	°	° ′	′	°	° ′	′	°	° ′	′	°
70	24 15	+45	96	25 00	+44	95	25 44	+45	94	26 29	+44	93
71	23 36	45	95	24 21	45	94	25 06	44	93	25 50	44	93
72	22 58	45	94	23 43	44	93	24 27	44	92	25 11	45	92
73	22 19	45	93	23 04	45	92	23 49	44	92	24 33	44	91
74	21 41	45	92	22 26	44	92	23 10	44	91	23 54	44	90
75	21 02	+45	92	21 47	+44	91	22 31	+45	90	23 16	+44	89
76	20 24	44	91	21 08	45	90	21 53	44	89	22 37	44	89
77	19 45	45	90	20 30	44	89	21 14	45	89	21 59	44	88
78	19 07	44	89	19 51	45	89	20 36	44	88	21 20	44	87
79	18 28	45	89	19 13	44	88	19 57	45	87	20 42	44	86
80	17 49	+45	88	18 34	+45	87	19 19	+44	86	20 03	+44	86
81	17 11	45	87	17 56	44	86	18 40	45	86	19 25	44	85
82	16 32	45	86	17 17	45	86	18 02	44	85	18 46	45	84
83	15 54	45	86	16 39	44	85	17 23	45	84	18 08	44	83
84	15 16	44	85	16 00	45	84	16 45	45	83	17 30	44	83
85	14 37	+45	84	15 22	+45	83	16 07	+45	83	16 52	+44	82
86	13 59	45	83	14 44	45	83	15 29	44	82	16 13	45	81
87	13 21	45	83	14 06	45	82	14 51	44	81	15 35	45	80
88	12 42	45	82	13 27	45	81	14 12	45	80	14 57	45	80
89	12 04	45	81	12 49	45	80	13 34	45	80	14 19	45	79
90	11 26	+45	80	12 11	+46	80	12 57	+45	79	13 42	+45	78
91	10 48	46	80	11 34	45	79	12 19	45	78	13 04	45	78
92	10 10	46	79	10 56	45	78	11 41	45	77	12 26	45	77
93	09 33	45	78	10 18	46	77	11 04	45	77	11 49	45	76
94	08 55	46	77	09 41	45	77	10 26	45	76	11 11	46	75
95	08 17	+46	77	09 03	+46	76	09 49	+45	75	10 34	+46	75
96	07 40	46	76	08 26	45	75	09 11	46	75	09 57	46	74
97	07 03	46	75	07 49	45	74	08 34	46	74	09 20	46	73
98	06 25	46	74	07 11	46	74	07 57	46	73	08 43	46	72
99	05 48	47	74	06 35	46	73	07 21	46	72	08 07	46	72
100	05 11	+47	73	05 58	+46	72	06 44	+46	72	07 30	+46	71
101	04 35	46	72	05 21	46	71	06 07	47	71	06 54	46	70
102	03 58	47	71	04 45	46	71	05 31	47	70	06 18	46	69
103	03 22	46	71	04 08	47	70	04 55	47	69	05 42	46	69
104	02 45	47	70	03 32	47	69	04 19	47	69	05 06	47	68
105	02 09	+47	69	02 56	+47	68	03 43	+47	68	04 30	+47	67
106	01 33	47	68	02 20	48	68	03 08	47	67	03 55	47	66
107	00 58	47	68	01 45	47	67	02 32	47	66	03 19	48	66
108	00 22	47	67	01 09	48	66	01 57	47	66	02 44	48	65
109	−0 13	47	66	00 34	48	65	01 22	48	65	02 10	47	64
110	−0 48	+47	65	−0 01	+48	65	00 47	+48	64	01 35	+48	63
111	−1 23	48	64	−0 35	48	64	00 13	48	63	01 01	48	63
112	−1 58	48	64	−1 10	48	63	−0 22	49	62	00 27	48	62
113	−2 32	48	63	−1 44	48	62	−0 56	49	62	−0 07	48	61
114	−3 07	49	62	−2 18	48	62	−1 30	49	61	−0 41	49	60
115	−3 41	+49	61	−2 52	+49	61	−2 03	+49	60	−1 14	+48	60
116	−4 14	49	61	−3 25	49	60	−2 36	48	59	−1 48	49	59
117	−4 48	49	60	−3 59	49	59	−3 10	50	59	−2 20	49	58
118	−5 21	49	59	−4 32	50	58	−3 42	49	58	−2 53	49	57
119	−5 54	50	58	−5 04	49	58	−4 15	50	57	−3 25	49	56
120				−5 37	+50	57	−4 47	+50	56	−3 57	+50	56
121							−5 19	50	55	−4 29	50	55
122							−5 51	51	55	−5 00	50	54
123										−5 31	50	53

LHA	19° Hc	d	Z	20° Hc	d	Z	21° Hc	d	Z	22° Hc	d	Z
	° ′	′	°	° ′	′	°	° ′	′	°	° ′	′	°
70	27 13	+44	93	27 57	+43	92	28 40	+44	91	29 24	+43	90
71	26 34	44	92	27 18	44	91	28 02	43	90	28 45	43	89
72	25 56	43	91	26 39	44	90	27 23	44	89	28 07	43	89
73	25 17	44	90	26 01	44	89	26 45	43	89	27 28	43	88
74	24 38	44	89	25 22	44	89	26 06	43	88	26 49	44	87
75	24 00	+44	89	24 44	+44	88	25 28	+43	87	26 11	+43	86
76	23 21	44	88	24 05	44	87	24 49	43	86	25 32	44	86
77	22 43	44	87	23 27	44	86	24 11	43	86	24 54	43	85
78	22 04	44	86	22 48	44	86	23 32	44	85	24 16	43	84
79	21 26	44	86	22 10	44	85	22 54	43	84	23 37	44	83
80	20 47	+44	85	21 31	+44	84	22 15	+44	83	22 59	+43	83
81	20 09	44	84	20 53	44	83	21 37	44	83	22 21	43	82
82	19 31	44	83	20 15	44	83	20 59	44	82	21 43	43	81
83	18 52	45	83	19 37	44	82	20 21	44	81	21 05	43	81
84	18 14	44	82	18 58	45	81	19 43	44	81	20 27	43	80
85	17 36	+44	81	18 20	+45	81	19 05	+44	80	19 49	+44	79
86	16 58	44	80	17 42	45	80	18 27	44	79	19 11	44	78
87	16 20	45	80	17 05	44	79	17 49	44	78	18 33	44	78
88	15 42	45	79	16 27	44	78	17 11	45	78	17 56	44	77
89	15 04	45	78	15 49	45	78	16 34	44	77	17 18	44	76
90	14 27	+44	78	15 11	+45	77	15 56	+45	76	16 41	+44	75
91	13 49	45	77	14 34	45	76	15 19	44	75	16 03	45	75
92	13 11	46	76	13 57	44	75	14 41	45	75	15 26	45	74
93	12 34	45	75	13 19	45	75	14 04	45	74	14 49	45	73
94	11 57	45	75	12 42	45	74	13 27	45	73	14 12	45	73
95	11 20	+45	74	12 05	+45	73	12 50	+46	73	13 36	+45	72
96	10 43	45	73	11 28	46	73	12 14	45	72	12 59	45	71
97	10 06	46	72	10 52	45	72	11 37	46	71	12 23	45	70
98	09 29	46	72	10 15	46	71	11 01	45	70	11 46	46	70
99	08 53	46	71	09 39	46	70	10 25	45	70	11 10	46	69
100	08 16	+46	70	09 02	+46	70	09 48	+46	69	10 34	+46	68
101	07 40	46	70	08 26	47	69	09 13	46	68	09 59	46	68
102	07 04	46	69	07 50	47	68	08 37	46	68	09 23	46	67
103	06 28	47	68	07 15	46	67	08 01	47	67	08 48	46	66
104	05 53	46	67	06 39	47	67	07 26	47	66	08 13	46	65
105	05 17	+47	67	06 04	+47	66	06 51	+47	65	07 38	+46	65
106	04 42	47	66	05 29	47	65	06 16	47	65	07 03	47	64
107	04 07	47	65	04 54	47	64	05 41	47	64	06 28	47	63
108	03 32	47	64	04 19	48	64	05 07	47	63	05 54	47	62
109	02 57	48	64	03 45	47	63	04 32	48	62	05 20	47	62
110	02 23	+48	63	03 11	+47	62	03 58	+48	62	04 46	+48	61
111	01 49	48	62	02 37	48	61	03 25	48	61	04 13	47	60
112	01 15	48	61	02 03	48	61	02 51	48	60	03 39	48	59
113	00 41	48	61	01 29	49	60	02 18	48	59	03 06	48	59
114	00 08	48	60	00 56	49	59	01 45	48	59	02 33	49	58
115	−0 26	+49	59	00 23	+49	58	01 12	+49	58	02 01	+48	57
116	−0 59	49	58	−0 10	49	58	00 39	49	57	01 28	49	56
117	−1 31	49	57	−0 42	49	57	00 07	49	56	00 56	50	56
118	−2 04	50	57	−1 14	49	56	−0 25	50	56	00 25	49	55
119	−2 36	50	56	−1 46	50	55	−0 56	49	55	−0 07	50	54
120	−3 07	+49	55	−2 18	+50	55	−1 28	+50	54	−0 38	+50	53
121	−3 39	50	54	−2 49	50	54	−1 59	50	53	−1 09	50	53
122	−4 10	50	54	−3 20	50	53	−2 30	51	52	−1 39	50	52
123	−4 41	51	53	−3 50	50	52	−3 00	51	52	−2 09	50	51
124	−5 11	50	52	−4 21	51	51	−3 30	51	51	−2 39	51	50
125	−5 42	+51	51	−4 51	+51	51	−4 00	+51	50	−3 09	+51	50
126				−5 20	51	50	−4 29	51	49	−3 38	51	49
127				−5 50	52	49	−4 58	51	48	−4 07	52	48
128							−5 27	52	48	−4 35	52	47
129							−5 55	52	47	−5 03	52	46
130										−5 31	+52	45
131												
132												

15°	16°	17°	18°	19°	20°	21°	22°

S. Lat. {LHA greater than 180°....... Zn=180−Z; LHA less than 180°.......... Zn=180+Z}

DECLINATION (15°-29°) SAME

	23°			24°			25°			26°			27°			28°			29°			
Hc	d	Z	Hc	d	Z	Hc	d	Z	Hc	d	Z	Hc	d	Z	Hc	d	Z	Hc	d	Z	LHA
° ′	′	°	° ′	′	°	° ′	′	°	° ′	′	°	° ′	′	°	° ′	′	°	° ′	′	°	
30 07	+43	89	30 50	+42	89	31 32	+42	88	32 14	+42	87	32 56	+42	86	33 38	+41	85	34 19	+40	84	290
29 28	43	89	30 11	43	88	30 54	42	87	31 36	42	86	32 18	41	85	32 59	41	84	33 40	41	84	289
28 50	42	88	29 32	43	87	30 15	42	86	30 57	42	85	31 39	42	85	32 21	41	84	33 02	41	83	288
28 11	43	87	28 54	43	86	29 37	42	86	30 19	42	85	31 01	41	84	31 42	42	83	32 24	41	82	287
27 33	43	86	28 16	42	86	28 58	42	85	29 40	42	84	30 22	42	83	31 04	42	82	31 46	41	81	286
26 54	+43	86	27 37	+43	85	28 20	+42	84	29 02	+42	83	29 44	+42	82	30 26	+41	82	31 07	+42	81	285
26 16	43	85	26 59	42	84	27 41	43	83	28 24	42	83	29 06	42	82	29 48	41	81	30 29	42	80	284
25 37	43	84	26 20	43	83	27 03	43	83	27 46	42	82	28 28	42	81	29 10	42	80	29 52	41	79	283
24 59	43	83	25 42	43	83	26 25	43	82	27 08	42	81	27 50	42	80	28 32	42	79	29 14	41	79	282
24 21	43	83	25 04	43	82	25 47	42	81	26 29	43	80	27 12	42	80	27 54	42	79	28 36	41	78	281
23 42	+44	82	24 26	+43	81	25 09	+42	80	25 51	+43	80	26 34	+42	79	27 16	+42	78	27 58	+42	77	280
23 04	44	81	23 48	43	80	24 31	43	80	25 14	42	79	25 56	43	78	26 39	42	77	27 21	42	77	279
22 26	44	81	23 10	43	80	23 53	43	79	24 36	43	78	25 19	42	77	26 01	42	77	26 43	42	76	278
21 48	44	80	22 32	43	79	23 15	43	78	23 58	43	78	24 41	43	77	25 24	42	76	26 06	42	75	277
21 10	44	79	21 54	43	78	22 37	44	78	23 21	42	77	24 03	43	76	24 46	43	75	25 29	42	75	276
20 33	+43	78	21 16	+44	78	22 00	+43	77	22 43	+43	76	23 26	+43	75	24 09	+43	75	24 52	+42	74	275
19 55	44	78	20 39	43	77	21 22	44	76	22 06	43	75	22 49	43	75	23 32	43	74	24 15	42	73	274
19 17	44	77	20 01	44	76	20 45	43	75	21 28	44	75	22 12	43	74	22 55	43	73	23 38	42	72	273
18 40	44	76	19 24	44	75	20 08	43	75	20 51	44	74	21 35	43	73	22 18	43	73	23 01	43	72	272
18 02	44	76	18 46	44	75	19 30	44	74	20 14	44	73	20 58	43	73	21 41	44	72	22 25	43	71	271
17 25	+44	75	18 09	+44	74	18 53	+44	73	19 37	+44	73	20 21	+44	72	21 05	+43	71	21 48	+43	70	270
16 48	44	74	17 32	45	73	18 17	44	73	19 01	44	72	19 45	43	71	20 28	44	70	21 12	43	70	269
16 11	44	73	16 55	45	73	17 40	44	72	18 24	44	71	19 08	44	71	19 52	44	70	20 36	43	69	268
15 34	45	73	16 19	44	72	17 03	45	71	17 48	44	71	18 22	44	70	19 16	44	69	20 00	44	68	267
14 57	45	72	15 42	45	71	16 27	44	71	17 11	45	70	17 56	44	69	18 40	44	68	19 24	44	68	266
14 21	+45	71	15 06	+45	71	15 51	+44	70	16 35	+45	69	17 20	+44	68	18 04	+44	68	18 48	+45	67	265
13 44	45	71	14 29	45	70	15 14	45	69	15 59	45	68	16 44	45	68	17 29	44	67	18 13	44	66	264
13 08	45	70	13 53	45	69	14 38	46	68	15 24	44	68	16 08	45	67	16 53	45	66	17 38	44	66	263
12 32	45	69	13 17	46	68	14 03	45	68	14 48	45	67	15 33	45	66	16 18	45	66	17 03	45	65	262
11 56	46	68	12 42	45	68	13 27	46	67	14 13	45	66	14 58	45	66	15 43	45	65	16 28	45	64	261
11 20	+46	68	12 06	+46	67	12 52	+45	66	13 37	+46	66	14 23	+45	65	15 08	+45	64	15 53	+45	64	260
10 45	46	67	11 31	45	66	12 16	46	66	13 02	46	65	13 48	45	64	14 33	46	64	15 19	45	63	259
10 09	46	66	10 55	46	66	11 41	46	65	12 27	46	64	13 13	46	64	13 59	46	63	14 45	45	62	258
09 34	46	65	10 20	47	65	11 07	46	64	11 53	46	64	12 39	46	63	13 25	46	62	14 11	45	62	257
08 59	47	65	09 46	46	64	10 32	46	63	11 18	47	63	12 05	46	62	12 51	46	62	13 37	46	61	256
08 24	+47	64	09 11	+47	63	09 58	+46	63	10 44	+47	62	11 31	+46	61	12 17	+46	61	13 03	+47	60	255
07 50	47	63	08 37	47	63	09 24	46	62	10 10	47	61	10 57	46	61	11 43	47	60	12 30	46	59	254
07 15	48	63	08 03	47	62	08 50	47	61	09 37	46	61	10 23	47	60	11 10	47	59	11 57	47	59	253
06 41	48	62	07 29	47	61	08 16	47	61	09 03	47	60	09 50	47	59	10 37	47	59	11 24	47	58	252
06 07	48	61	06 55	47	61	07 42	48	60	08 30	47	59	09 17	47	59	10 04	47	58	10 51	48	57	251
05 34	+48	60	06 22	+47	60	07 09	+48	59	07 57	+47	59	08 44	+48	58	09 32	+47	57	10 19	+47	57	250
05 00	48	60	05 48	48	59	06 36	48	58	07 24	48	58	08 12	47	57	08 59	48	57	09 47	48	56	249
04 27	48	59	05 15	48	58	06 03	48	58	06 51	48	57	07 39	48	57	08 27	48	56	09 15	48	55	248
03 54	49	58	04 43	48	58	05 31	48	57	06 19	48	56	07 07	49	56	07 56	48	55	08 44	48	55	247
03 22	48	57	04 10	49	57	04 59	48	56	05 47	49	56	06 36	48	55	07 24	48	54	08 12	49	54	246
02 49	+49	57	03 38	+49	56	04 27	+49	55	05 16	+48	55	06 04	+49	54	06 53	+48	54	07 41	+49	53	245
02 17	49	56	03 06	49	55	03 55	49	55	04 44	49	54	05 33	49	54	06 22	49	53	07 11	48	52	244
01 46	49	55	02 35	49	55	03 24	49	54	04 13	49	53	05 02	49	53	05 51	49	52	06 40	49	52	243
01 14	49	54	02 03	50	54	02 53	49	53	03 42	50	53	04 32	49	52	05 21	49	52	06 10	49	51	242
00 43	49	54	01 32	50	53	02 22	50	53	03 12	49	52	04 01	50	51	04 51	49	51	05 40	50	50	241
00 12	+50	53	01 02	+50	52	01 52	+49	52	02 41	+50	51	03 31	+50	51	04 21	+50	50	05 11	+50	50	240
−0 19	50	52	00 31	50	52	01 21	51	51	02 12	50	50	03 02	50	50	03 52	50	49	04 42	50	49	239
−0 49	50	51	00 01	51	51	00 52	50	50	01 42	50	50	02 32	51	49	03 23	50	49	04 13	50	48	238
−1 19	51	51	−0 28	50	50	00 22	51	49	01 13	50	49	02 03	51	48	02 54	50	48	03 44	51	47	237
−1 48	50	50	−0 58	51	49	−0 07	51	49	00 44	51	48	01 35	50	48	02 25	51	47	03 16	51	47	236
−2 18	+51	49	−1 27	+51	48	−0 36	+51	48	00 15	+51	47	01 06	+51	47	01 57	+51	46	02 48	+51	46	235
−2 47	52	48	−1 55	51	48	−1 04	51	47	−0 13	51	47	00 38	52	46	01 30	51	46	02 21	51	45	234
−3 15	51	47	−2 24	52	47	−1 32	51	46	−0 41	52	46	00 11	51	45	01 02	52	45	01 54	51	44	233
−3 43	51	47	−2 52	52	46	−2 00	52	46	−1 08	51	45	−0 17	52	45	00 35	52	44	01 27	52	44	232
−4 11	52	46	−3 19	52	45	−2 27	52	45	−1 35	52	44	−0 43	51	44	00 08	52	43	01 00	53	43	231
−4 39	+52	45	−3 47	+53	45	−2 54	+52	44	−2 02	+52	44	−1 10	+52	43	−0 18	+52	43	00 34	+53	42	230
−5 06	53	44	−4 13	52	44	−3 21	52	43	−2 29	53	43	−1 36	52	42	−0 44	53	42	00 09	52	41	229
−5 33	53	43	−4 40	53	43	−3 47	52	42	−2 55	53	42	−2 02	53	41	−1 09	53	41	−0 16	52	41	228
		133	−5 06	53	42	−4 13	53	42	−3 20	53	41	−2 27	53	41	−1 34	53	40	−0 41	52	40	227
		134	−5 32	53	41	−4 39	54	41	−3 45	53	40	−2 52	53	40	−1 59	53	39	−1 06	53	39	226
					135	−5 04	+54	40	−4 10	+53	40	−3 17	+54	39	−2 23	+53	39	−1 30	+53	38	225
					136	−5 28	53	39	−4 35	54	39	−3 41	54	38	−2 47	53	38	−1 54	54	37	224
								137	−4 58	53	38	−4 05	54	38	−3 11	54	37	−2 17	54	37	223
								138	−5 22	54	37	−4 28	54	37	−3 34	54	36	−2 40	54	36	222
								139	−5 45	54	36	−4 51	55	36	−3 56	54	35	−3 02	54	35	221
23°			24°			25°			26°			27°			28°			29°			

LAT 50°

N. Lat. {LHA greater than 180°....... Zn=Z
LHA less than 180°........... Zn=360−Z}

DECLINATION (15°-29°) SAME

LHA	15° Hc	d	Z	16° Hc	d	Z	17° Hc	d	Z	18° Hc	d	Z	19° Hc	d	Z	20° Hc	d	Z	21° Hc	d	Z	22° Hc	d	Z
	° ′	′	°	° ′	′	°	° ′	′	°	° ′	′	°	° ′	′	°	° ′	′	°	° ′	′	°	° ′	′	°
81	−5 48	47	106	279																				
80	−5 11	−47	107	−5 58	−46	108	280																	
79	−4 35	46	108	−5 21	46	109	−6 07	47	109	281														
78	−3 58	47	109	−4 45	46	109	−5 31	47	110	282														
77	−3 22	46	109	−4 08	47	110	−4 55	47	111	−5 42	46	111	283											
76	−2 45	47	110	−3 32	47	111	−4 19	47	111	−5 06	47	112	−5 53	46	113	284								
75	−2 09	−47	111	−2 56	−47	112	−3 43	−47	112	−4 30	−47	113	−5 17	−47	113	−6 04	−47	114	285					
74	−1 33	47	112	−2 20	48	112	−3 08	47	113	−3 55	47	114	−4 42	47	114	−5 29	47	115	286					
73	−0 58	47	112	−1 45	47	113	−2 32	47	114	−3 19	48	114	−4 07	47	115	−4 54	47	116	−5 41	47	116	287		
72	−0 22	47	113	−1 09	48	114	−1 57	47	114	−2 44	48	115	−3 32	47	116	−4 19	48	116	−5 07	47	117	−5 54	47	118
71	00 13	47	114	−0 34	48	115	−1 22	48	115	−2 10	47	116	−2 57	48	116	−3 45	47	117	−4 32	48	118	−5 20	47	118
70	00 48	−47	115	00 01	−48	115	−0 47	−48	116	−1 35	−48	117	−2 23	−48	117	−3 11	−47	118	−3 58	−48	118	−4 46	−48	119
	15°			16°			17°			18°			19°			20°			21°			22°		

S. Lat. {LHA greater than 180°....... Zn=180−Z
LHA less than 180°........... Zn=180+Z}

DECLINATION (15°-29°) CONTRARY

NAME AS LATITUDE

LAT 50°

23°			24°			25°			26°			27°			28°			29°			
Hc	d	Z	Hc	d	Z	Hc	d	Z	Hc	d	Z	Hc	d	Z	Hc	d	Z	Hc	d	Z	LHA
° ′	′	°	° ′	′	°	° ′	′	°	° ′	′	°	° ′	′	°	° ′	′	°	° ′	′	°	
											140	−5 13	+54	35	−4 19	+55	35	−3 24	+55	34	220
											141	−5 35	55	34	−4 40	55	34	−3 45	55	33	219
														142	−5 02	56	33	−4 06	55	33	218
														143	−5 22	55	32	−4 27	55	32	217
																	144	−4 47	55	31	216
																	145	−5 07	+56	30	215
																	146	−5 26	56	29	214

LAT 50°

Hc	d	Z																		
288																				
289																				
−5 34	−48	120	290																	
23°			24°			25°			26°			27°			28°			29°		

NAME TO LATITUDE

N. Lat. {LHA greater than 180°....... Zn=Z
LHA less than 180°........... Zn=360−Z}

DECLINATION (15°-29°) CONTRARY

LHA	15° Hc	d	Z	16° Hc	d	Z	17° Hc	d	Z	18° Hc	d	Z	19° Hc	d	Z	20° Hc	d	Z	21° Hc	d	Z	22° Hc	d	Z
	° ′	′	°	° ′	′	°	° ′	′	°	° ′	′	°	° ′	′	°	° ′	′	°	° ′	′	°	° ′	′	°
69	01 23	48	116	00 35	48	116	−0 13	48	117	−1 01	48	117	−1 49	48	118	−2 37	48	119	−3 25	48	119	−4 13	47	120
68	01 58	48	116	01 10	48	117	00 22	49	118	−0 27	48	118	−1 15	48	119	−2 03	48	119	−2 51	48	120	−3 39	48	121
67	02 32	48	117	01 44	48	118	00 56	49	118	00 07	48	119	−0 41	48	119	−1 29	49	120	−2 18	48	121	−3 06	48	121
66	03 07	49	118	02 18	48	118	01 30	49	119	00 41	49	120	−0 08	48	120	−0 56	49	121	−1 45	48	121	−2 33	49	122
65	03 41	−49	119	02 52	−49	119	02 03	−49	120	01 14	−48	120	00 26	−49	121	−0 23	−49	122	−1 12	−49	122	−2 01	−48	123
64	04 14	49	119	03 25	49	120	02 36	48	121	01 48	49	121	00 59	49	122	00 10	49	122	−0 39	49	123	−1 28	49	124
63	04 48	49	120	03 59	49	121	03 10	50	121	02 20	49	122	01 31	49	123	00 42	49	123	−0 07	49	124	−0 56	50	124
62	05 21	49	121	04 32	50	122	03 42	49	122	02 53	49	123	02 04	50	123	01 14	49	124	00 25	50	124	−0 25	49	125
61	05 54	50	122	05 04	49	122	04 15	50	123	03 25	49	124	02 36	50	124	01 46	50	125	00 56	49	125	00 07	50	126
60	06 26	−49	123	05 37	−50	123	04 47	−50	124	03 57	−50	124	03 07	−49	125	02 18	−50	125	01 28	−50	126	00 38	−50	127
59	06 59	50	124	06 09	50	124	05 19	50	125	04 29	50	125	03 39	50	126	02 49	50	126	01 59	50	127	01 09	50	127
58	07 31	50	124	06 41	50	125	05 51	51	125	05 00	50	126	04 10	50	126	03 20	50	127	02 30	51	128	01 39	50	128
57	08 03	51	125	07 12	50	126	06 22	51	126	05 31	50	127	04 41	51	127	03 50	50	128	03 00	51	128	02 09	50	129
56	08 34	51	126	07 43	50	127	06 53	51	127	06 02	51	128	05 11	50	128	04 21	51	129	03 30	51	129	02 39	51	130
55	09 05	−51	127	08 14	−51	127	07 23	−50	128	06 33	−51	128	05 42	−51	129	04 51	−51	129	04 00	−51	130	03 09	−51	130
54	09 36	51	128	08 45	51	128	07 54	51	129	07 03	52	129	06 11	51	130	05 20	51	130	04 29	51	131	03 38	51	131
53	10 06	51	128	09 15	51	129	08 24	52	130	07 32	51	130	06 41	51	131	05 50	52	131	04 58	51	132	04 07	52	132
52	10 36	51	129	09 45	52	130	08 53	51	130	08 02	52	131	07 10	51	131	06 19	52	132	05 27	52	132	04 35	52	133
51	11 06	52	130	10 14	52	131	09 22	51	131	08 31	52	132	07 39	52	132	06 47	52	133	05 55	52	133	05 03	52	134
50	11 35	−52	131	10 43	−52	132	09 51	−52	132	08 59	−52	133	08 07	−52	133	07 15	−52	134	06 23	−52	134	05 31	−52	135
49	12 04	52	132	11 12	52	132	10 20	52	133	09 28	53	133	08 35	52	134	07 43	52	134	06 51	53	135	05 58	52	135
48	12 33	53	133	11 40	52	133	10 48	53	134	09 55	52	134	09 03	53	135	08 10	52	135	07 18	53	136	06 25	52	136
47	13 01	53	134	12 08	52	134	11 16	53	135	10 23	53	135	09 30	53	136	08 37	52	136	07 45	53	136	06 52	53	137
46	13 29	53	134	12 36	53	135	11 43	53	135	10 50	53	136	09 57	53	136	09 04	53	137	08 11	53	137	07 18	53	138
45	13 56	−53	135	13 03	−53	136	12 10	−53	136	11 17	−54	137	10 23	−53	137	09 30	−53	138	08 37	−53	138	07 44	−54	139
44	14 23	53	136	13 30	54	137	12 36	53	137	11 43	54	138	10 49	53	138	09 56	53	139	09 03	54	139	08 09	54	139
43	14 49	53	137	13 56	54	138	13 02	53	138	12 09	54	138	11 15	54	139	10 21	53	139	09 28	54	140	08 34	54	140
42	15 15	53	138	14 22	54	138	13 28	54	139	12 34	54	139	11 40	54	140	10 46	54	140	09 52	54	141	08 58	54	141
41	15 41	54	139	14 47	54	139	13 53	54	140	12 59	54	140	12 05	54	141	11 11	54	141	10 17	55	142	09 22	54	142
40	16 06	−54	140	15 12	−54	140	14 18	−55	141	13 23	−54	141	12 29	−54	142	11 35	−55	142	10 40	−54	142	09 46	−55	143
39	16 31	55	141	15 36	54	141	14 42	55	142	13 47	54	142	12 53	55	142	11 58	54	143	11 04	55	143	10 09	55	144
38	16 55	55	142	16 00	54	142	15 06	55	142	14 11	55	143	13 16	55	143	12 21	55	144	11 26	54	144	10 32	55	145
37	17 19	55	143	16 24	55	143	15 29	55	143	14 34	55	144	13 39	55	144	12 44	55	145	11 49	55	145	10 54	55	145
36	17 42	55	143	16 47	55	144	15 52	55	144	14 57	56	145	14 01	55	145	13 06	56	146	12 11	56	146	11 15	55	146
35	18 05	−56	144	17 09	−55	145	16 14	−55	145	15 19	−56	146	14 23	−55	146	13 28	−56	146	12 32	−55	147	11 37	−56	147
34	18 27	56	145	17 31	55	146	16 36	56	146	15 40	55	147	14 45	56	147	13 49	56	147	12 53	56	148	11 57	56	148
33	18 49	56	146	17 53	56	147	16 57	56	147	16 01	56	147	15 05	56	148	14 09	56	148	13 13	56	149	12 17	56	149
32	19 10	56	147	18 14	56	148	17 18	56	148	16 22	56	148	15 26	56	149	14 30	57	149	13 33	56	149	12 37	56	150
31	19 31	57	148	18 34	56	149	17 38	56	149	16 42	57	149	15 45	56	150	14 49	56	150	13 53	57	150	12 56	56	151
30	19 51	−57	149	18 54	−56	150	17 58	−57	150	17 01	−56	150	16 05	−57	151	15 08	−56	151	14 12	−57	151	13 15	−57	152
29	20 10	56	150	19 14	57	150	18 17	57	151	17 20	57	151	16 23	56	152	15 27	57	152	14 30	57	152	13 33	57	153
28	20 29	57	151	19 32	57	151	18 35	56	152	17 39	57	152	16 42	57	152	15 45	57	153	14 48	57	153	13 51	57	153
27	20 47	57	152	19 50	57	152	18 53	57	153	17 56	57	153	16 59	57	153	16 02	57	154	15 05	57	154	14 08	58	154
26	21 05	57	153	20 08	57	153	19 11	57	154	18 14	58	154	17 16	57	154	16 19	58	155	15 21	57	155	14 24	57	155
25	21 22	−57	154	20 25	−57	154	19 28	−58	155	18 30	−57	155	17 33	−58	155	16 35	−57	156	15 38	−58	156	14 40	−58	156
24	21 39	58	155	20 41	57	155	19 44	58	156	18 46	57	156	17 49	58	156	16 51	58	157	15 53	58	157	14 55	57	157
23	21 55	58	156	20 57	58	156	19 59	57	157	19 02	58	157	18 04	58	157	17 06	58	157	16 08	58	158	15 10	58	158
22	22 10	58	157	21 12	57	157	20 15	58	158	19 17	59	158	18 18	58	158	17 20	58	158	16 22	58	159	15 24	58	159
21	22 25	58	158	21 27	58	158	20 29	58	159	19 31	58	159	18 33	59	159	17 34	58	159	16 36	58	160	15 38	58	160
20	22 39	−58	159	21 41	−58	159	20 43	−59	160	19 44	−58	160	18 46	−58	160	17 48	−59	160	16 49	−58	161	15 51	−59	161
19	22 53	59	160	21 54	58	160	20 56	59	161	19 57	58	161	18 59	59	161	18 00	58	161	17 02	59	162	16 03	58	162
18	23 06	59	161	22 07	59	161	21 08	58	162	20 10	59	162	19 11	59	162	18 12	58	162	17 14	59	162	16 15	59	163
17	23 18	59	162	22 19	59	162	21 20	58	163	20 22	59	163	19 23	59	163	18 24	59	163	17 25	59	163	16 26	59	164
16	23 29	59	163	22 30	58	163	21 32	59	164	20 33	59	164	19 34	59	164	18 35	59	164	17 36	59	164	16 37	59	165
15	23 40	−59	164	22 41	−59	164	21 42	−59	165	20 43	−59	165	19 44	−59	165	18 45	−59	165	17 46	−59	165	16 47	−59	166
14	23 50	59	165	22 51	59	165	21 52	59	166	20 53	59	166	19 54	59	166	18 55	60	166	17 55	59	166	16 56	59	166
13	24 00	59	166	23 01	60	166	22 01	59	167	21 02	59	167	20 03	59	167	19 04	60	167	18 04	59	167	17 05	59	167
12	24 09	60	167	23 09	59	167	22 10	59	168	21 11	60	168	20 11	59	168	19 12	60	168	18 12	59	168	17 13	59	168
11	24 17	60	168	23 17	59	169	22 18	59	169	21 19	60	169	20 19	59	169	19 20	60	169	18 20	59	169	17 21	60	169
10	24 24	−59	169	23 25	−60	170	22 25	−59	170	21 26	−60	170	20 26	−59	170	19 27	−60	170	18 27	−60	170	17 27	−59	170
9	24 31	60	170	23 31	59	171	22 32	60	171	21 32	59	171	20 33	60	171	19 33	60	171	18 33	59	171	17 34	60	171
8	24 37	60	172	23 37	59	172	22 38	60	172	21 38	60	172	20 38	59	172	19 39	60	172	18 39	60	172	17 39	60	172
7	24 43	60	173	23 43	60	173	22 43	60	173	21 43	60	173	20 43	59	173	19 44	60	173	18 44	60	173	17 44	60	173
6	24 47	60	174	23 47	60	174	22 47	59	174	21 48	60	174	20 48	60	174	19 48	60	174	18 48	60	174	17 48	60	174
5	24 51	−60	175	23 51	−60	175	22 51	−60	175	21 51	−59	175	20 52	−60	175	19 52	−60	175	18 52	−60	175	17 52	−60	175
4	24 54	60	176	23 54	60	176	22 54	59	176	21 55	60	176	20 55	60	176	19 55	60	176	18 55	60	176	17 55	60	176
3	24 57	60	177	23 57	60	177	22 57	60	177	21 57	60	177	20 57	60	177	19 57	60	177	18 57	60	177	17 57	60	177
2	24 59	60	178	23 59	60	178	22 59	60	178	21 59	60	178	20 59	60	178	19 59	60	178	18 59	60	178	17 59	60	178
1	25 00	60	179	24 00	60	179	23 00	60	179	22 00	60	179	21 00	60	179	20 00	60	179	19 00	60	179	18 00	60	179
0	25 00	−60	180	24 00	−60	180	23 00	−60	180	22 00	−60	180	21 00	−60	180	20 00	−60	180	19 00	−60	180	18 00	−60	180
	15°			16°			17°			18°			19°			20°			21°			22°		

S. Lat. {LHA greater than 180°....... Zn=180−Z
LHA less than 180°........... Zn=180+Z}

DECLINATION (15°-29°) CONTRARY

23°			24°			25°			26°			27°			28°			29°			
Hc	d	Z	Hc	d	Z	Hc	d	Z	Hc	d	Z	Hc	d	Z	Hc	d	Z	Hc	d	Z	LHA
° ′	′	°	° ′	′	°	° ′	′	°	° ′	′	°	° ′	′	°	° ′	′	°	° ′	′	°	
-5 00	48	120	-5 48	48	121																291
-4 27	48	121	-5 15	48	122	-6 03	48	122													292
-3 54	49	122	-4 43	48	122	-5 31	48	123													293
-3 22	48	123	-4 10	49	123	-4 59	48	124	-5 47	49	124										294
-2 49	-49	123	-3 38	-49	124	-4 27	-49	125	-5 16	-48	125										295
-2 17	49	124	-3 06	49	125	-3 55	49	125	-4 44	49	126	-5 33	49	126							296
-1 46	49	125	-2 35	49	125	-3 24	49	126	-4 13	49	127	-5 02	49	127	-5 51	49	128				297
-1 14	49	126	-2 03	50	126	-2 53	49	127	-3 42	50	127	-4 32	49	128	-5 21	49	128				298
-0 43	49	126	-1 32	50	127	-2 22	50	127	-3 12	49	128	-4 01	50	129	-4 51	49	129	-5 40	50	130	299
-0 12	-50	127	-1 02	-50	128	-1 52	-49	128	-2 41	-50	129	-3 31	-50	129	-4 21	-50	130	-5 11	-50	130	300
00 19	50	128	-0 31	50	128	-1 21	51	129	-2 12	50	130	-3 02	50	130	-3 52	50	131	-4 42	50	131	301
00 49	50	129	-0 01	51	129	-0 52	50	130	-1 42	50	130	-2 32	51	131	-3 23	50	131	-4 13	50	132	302
01 19	51	129	00 28	50	130	-0 22	51	131	-1 13	50	131	-2 03	51	132	-2 54	50	132	-3 44	51	133	303
01 48	50	130	00 58	51	131	00 07	51	131	-0 44	51	132	-1 35	50	132	-2 25	51	133	-3 16	51	133	304
02 18	-51	131	01 27	-51	132	00 36	-51	132	-0 15	-51	133	-1 06	-51	133	-1 57	-51	134	-2 48	-51	134	305
02 47	52	132	01 55	51	132	01 04	51	133	00 13	51	133	-0 38	52	134	-1 30	51	134	-2 21	51	135	306
03 15	51	133	02 24	52	133	01 32	51	134	00 41	52	134	-0 11	52	135	-1 02	52	135	-1 54	51	136	307
03 43	51	133	02 52	52	134	02 00	52	134	01 08	51	135	00 17	52	135	-0 35	52	136	-1 27	52	136	308
04 11	52	134	03 19	52	135	02 27	52	135	01 35	52	136	00 43	51	136	-0 08	52	137	-1 00	53	137	309
04 39	-52	135	03 47	-53	135	02 54	-52	136	02 02	-52	136	01 10	-52	137	00 18	-52	137	-0 34	-53	138	310
05 06	53	136	04 13	52	136	03 21	52	137	02 29	53	137	01 36	52	138	00 44	53	138	-0 09	52	139	311
05 33	53	137	04 40	53	137	03 47	52	138	02 55	53	138	02 02	53	139	01 09	53	139	00 16	52	139	312
05 59	53	137	05 06	53	138	04 13	53	138	03 20	53	139	02 27	53	139	01 34	53	140	00 41	52	140	313
06 25	53	138	05 32	53	139	04 39	54	139	03 45	53	140	02 52	53	140	01 59	53	141	01 06	53	141	314
06 50	-53	139	05 57	-53	140	05 04	-54	140	04 10	-53	140	03 17	-54	141	02 23	-53	141	01 30	-53	142	315
07 15	53	140	06 22	54	140	05 28	53	141	04 35	54	141	03 41	54	142	02 47	53	142	01 54	54	143	316
07 40	54	141	06 46	54	141	05 52	54	142	04 58	53	142	04 05	54	142	03 11	54	143	02 17	54	143	317
08 04	54	142	07 10	54	142	06 16	54	142	05 22	54	143	04 28	54	143	03 34	54	144	02 40	54	144	318
08 28	54	142	07 34	55	143	06 39	54	143	05 45	54	144	04 51	55	144	03 56	54	145	03 02	54	145	319
08 51	-54	143	07 57	-55	144	07 02	-54	144	06 08	-55	145	05 13	-54	145	04 19	-55	145	03 24	-55	146	320
09 14	54	144	08 20	55	145	07 25	55	145	06 30	55	145	05 35	55	146	04 40	55	146	03 45	55	147	321
09 37	55	145	08 42	55	145	07 47	55	146	06 52	55	146	05 57	55	147	05 02	56	147	04 06	55	147	322
09 59	56	146	09 03	55	146	08 08	55	147	07 13	55	147	06 18	56	147	05 22	55	148	04 27	55	148	323
10 20	55	147	09 25	56	147	08 29	55	147	07 34	56	148	06 38	55	148	05 43	56	149	04 47	55	149	324
10 41	-56	148	09 45	-55	148	08 50	-56	148	07 54	-56	149	06 58	-55	149	06 03	-56	149	05 07	-56	150	325
11 01	55	148	10 06	56	149	09 10	56	149	08 14	56	150	07 18	56	150	06 22	56	150	05 26	56	151	326
11 21	56	149	10 25	56	150	09 29	56	150	08 33	56	150	07 37	56	151	06 41	56	151	05 45	56	151	327
11 41	56	150	10 45	57	151	09 48	56	151	08 52	56	151	07 56	57	152	06 59	56	152	06 03	56	152	328
12 00	57	151	11 03	56	151	10 07	57	152	09 10	56	152	08 14	57	152	07 17	56	153	06 21	57	153	329
12 18	-56	152	11 22	-57	152	10 25	-57	153	09 28	-57	153	08 31	-56	153	07 35	-57	154	06 38	-57	154	330
12 36	57	153	11 39	57	153	10 42	56	153	09 46	57	154	08 49	57	154	07 52	57	154	06 55	57	155	331
12 54	57	154	11 57	58	154	10 59	57	154	10 02	57	155	09 05	57	155	08 08	57	155	07 11	57	156	332
13 10	57	155	12 13	57	155	11 16	57	155	10 19	58	156	09 21	57	156	08 24	57	156	07 27	58	156	333
13 27	58	156	12 29	57	156	11 32	58	156	10 34	57	156	09 37	58	157	08 39	57	157	07 42	58	157	334
13 42	-57	156	12 45	-58	157	11 47	-58	157	10 49	-57	157	09 52	-58	158	08 54	-58	158	07 56	-57	158	335
13 58	58	157	13 00	58	158	12 02	58	158	11 04	58	158	10 06	58	158	09 08	57	159	08 11	58	159	336
14 12	58	158	13 14	58	159	12 16	58	159	11 18	58	159	10 20	58	159	09 22	58	160	08 24	58	160	337
14 26	58	159	13 28	58	159	12 30	58	160	11 32	58	160	10 34	59	160	09 35	58	160	08 37	58	161	338
14 40	59	160	13 41	58	160	12 43	58	161	11 45	59	161	10 46	58	161	09 48	58	161	08 50	59	162	339
14 52	-58	161	13 54	-58	161	12 56	-59	162	11 57	-58	162	10 59	-59	162	10 00	-58	162	09 02	-59	162	340
15 05	59	162	14 06	58	162	13 08	59	162	12 09	59	163	11 10	58	163	10 12	59	163	09 13	59	163	341
15 16	58	163	14 18	59	163	13 19	59	163	12 20	59	164	11 21	58	164	10 23	59	164	09 24	59	164	342
15 27	58	164	14 29	59	164	13 30	59	164	12 31	59	164	11 32	59	165	10 33	59	165	09 34	59	165	343
15 38	59	165	14 39	59	165	13 40	59	165	12 41	59	165	11 42	59	166	10 43	59	166	09 44	59	166	344
15 48	-59	166	14 49	-59	166	13 50	-60	166	12 50	-59	166	11 51	-59	166	10 52	-59	167	09 53	-59	167	345
15 57	59	167	14 58	59	167	13 59	60	167	12 59	59	167	12 00	59	167	11 01	59	167	10 02	60	168	346
16 06	60	168	15 06	59	168	14 07	59	168	13 08	60	168	12 08	59	168	11 09	59	168	10 10	60	169	347
16 14	60	169	15 14	59	169	14 15	60	169	13 15	59	169	12 16	59	169	11 17	60	169	10 17	59	169	348
16 21	59	170	15 22	60	170	14 22	60	170	13 22	59	170	12 23	60	170	11 23	59	170	10 24	60	170	349
16 28	-60	170	15 28	-59	171	14 29	-60	171	13 29	-60	171	12 29	-59	171	11 30	-60	171	10 30	-59	171	350
16 34	60	171	15 34	59	172	14 35	60	172	13 35	60	172	12 35	59	172	11 36	60	172	10 36	60	172	351
16 39	59	172	15 40	60	172	14 40	60	173	13 40	60	173	12 40	59	173	11 41	60	173	10 41	60	173	352
16 44	60	173	15 44	59	173	14 45	60	173	13 45	60	174	12 45	60	174	11 45	60	174	10 45	59	174	353
16 48	59	174	15 49	60	174	14 49	60	174	13 49	60	174	12 49	60	175	11 49	60	175	10 49	60	175	354
16 52	-60	175	15 52	-60	175	14 52	-60	175	13 52	-60	175	12 52	-60	175	11 52	-59	176	10 53	-60	176	355
16 55	60	176	15 55	60	176	14 55	60	176	13 55	60	176	12 55	60	176	11 55	60	176	10 55	60	176	356
16 57	60	177	15 57	60	177	14 57	60	177	13 57	60	177	12 57	60	177	11 57	60	177	10 57	60	177	357
16 59	60	178	15 59	60	178	14 59	60	178	13 59	60	178	12 59	60	178	11 59	60	178	10 59	60	178	358
17 00	60	179	16 00	60	179	15 00	60	179	14 00	60	179	13 00	60	179	12 00	60	179	11 00	60	179	359
17 00	-60	180	16 00	-60	180	15 00	-60	180	14 00	-60	180	13 00	-60	180	12 00	-60	180	11 00	-60	180	360
23°			24°			25°			26°			27°			28°			29°			

d / ′	1	2	3	4	5	6	7	8	9	10	11	12	13	14	15	16	17	18	19	20	21	22	23	24	25	26	27	28	29	30
0	0	0	0	0	0	0	0	0	0	0	0	0	0	0	0	0	0	0	0	0	0	0	0	0	0	0	0	0	0	0
1	0	0	0	0	0	0	0	0	0	0	0	0	0	0	0	0	0	0	0	0	0	0	0	0	0	0	0	0	0	0
2	0	0	0	0	0	0	0	0	0	0	0	0	0	0	0	1	1	1	1	1	1	1	1	1	1	1	1	1	1	1
3	0	0	0	0	0	0	0	0	0	0	1	1	1	1	1	1	1	1	1	1	1	1	1	1	1	1	1	1	1	2
4	0	0	0	0	0	0	0	1	1	1	1	1	1	1	1	1	1	1	1	1	1	1	2	2	2	2	2	2	2	2
5	0	0	0	0	0	0	1	1	1	1	1	1	1	1	1	1	1	2	2	2	2	2	2	2	2	2	2	2	2	2
6	0	0	0	0	0	1	1	1	1	1	1	1	1	1	2	2	2	2	2	2	2	2	2	2	2	3	3	3	3	3
7	0	0	0	0	1	1	1	1	1	1	1	1	2	2	2	2	2	2	2	2	2	3	3	3	3	3	3	3	3	4
8	0	0	0	1	1	1	1	1	1	1	1	2	2	2	2	2	2	2	3	3	3	3	3	3	3	3	4	4	4	4
9	0	0	0	1	1	1	1	1	1	2	2	2	2	2	2	2	3	3	3	3	3	3	3	4	4	4	4	4	4	4
10	0	0	0	1	1	1	1	1	2	2	2	2	2	2	2	3	3	3	3	3	4	4	4	4	4	4	4	5	5	5
11	0	0	1	1	1	1	1	1	2	2	2	2	2	3	3	3	3	3	3	4	4	4	4	4	5	5	5	5	5	6
12	0	0	1	1	1	1	1	2	2	2	2	2	3	3	3	3	3	4	4	4	4	4	5	5	5	5	5	6	6	6
13	0	0	1	1	1	1	2	2	2	2	2	3	3	3	3	3	4	4	4	4	5	5	5	5	5	6	6	6	6	6
14	0	0	1	1	1	1	2	2	2	2	3	3	3	3	4	4	4	4	4	5	5	5	5	6	6	6	6	7	7	7
15	0	0	1	1	1	2	2	2	2	2	3	3	3	4	4	4	4	4	5	5	5	6	6	6	6	6	7	7	7	8
16	0	1	1	1	1	2	2	2	2	3	3	3	3	4	4	4	5	5	5	5	6	6	6	6	7	7	7	7	8	8
17	0	1	1	1	1	2	2	2	3	3	3	3	4	4	4	5	5	5	5	6	6	6	7	7	7	7	8	8	8	8
18	0	1	1	1	2	2	2	2	3	3	3	4	4	4	4	5	5	5	6	6	6	7	7	7	8	8	8	8	9	9
19	0	1	1	1	2	2	2	3	3	3	3	4	4	4	5	5	5	6	6	6	7	7	7	8	8	8	9	9	9	10
20	0	1	1	1	2	2	2	3	3	3	4	4	4	5	5	5	6	6	6	7	7	7	8	8	8	9	9	9	10	10
21	0	1	1	1	2	2	2	3	3	4	4	4	5	5	5	6	6	6	7	7	7	8	8	8	9	9	9	10	10	10
22	0	1	1	1	2	2	3	3	3	4	4	4	5	5	6	6	6	7	7	7	8	8	8	9	9	10	10	10	11	11
23	0	1	1	2	2	2	3	3	3	4	4	5	5	5	6	6	7	7	7	8	8	8	9	9	10	10	10	11	11	12
24	0	1	1	2	2	2	3	3	4	4	4	5	5	6	6	6	7	7	8	8	8	9	9	10	10	10	11	11	12	12
25	0	1	1	2	2	2	3	3	4	4	5	5	5	6	6	7	7	8	8	8	9	9	10	10	10	11	11	12	12	12
26	0	1	1	2	2	3	3	3	4	4	5	5	6	6	6	7	7	8	8	9	9	10	10	10	11	11	12	12	13	13
27	0	1	1	2	2	3	3	4	4	4	5	5	6	6	7	7	8	8	9	9	9	10	10	11	11	12	12	13	13	14
28	0	1	1	2	2	3	3	4	4	5	5	6	6	7	7	7	8	8	9	9	10	10	11	11	12	12	13	13	14	14
29	0	1	1	2	2	3	3	4	4	5	5	6	6	7	7	8	8	9	9	10	10	11	11	12	12	13	13	14	14	14
30	0	1	2	2	2	3	4	4	4	5	6	6	6	7	8	8	8	9	10	10	10	11	12	12	12	13	14	14	14	15
31	1	1	2	2	3	3	4	4	5	5	6	6	7	7	8	8	9	9	10	10	11	11	12	12	13	13	14	14	15	16
32	1	1	2	2	3	3	4	4	5	5	6	6	7	7	8	9	9	10	10	11	11	12	12	13	13	14	14	15	15	16
33	1	1	2	2	3	3	4	4	5	6	6	7	7	8	8	9	9	10	10	11	12	12	13	13	14	14	15	15	16	16
34	1	1	2	2	3	3	4	5	5	6	6	7	7	8	8	9	10	10	11	11	12	12	13	14	14	15	15	16	16	17
35	1	1	2	2	3	4	4	5	5	6	6	7	8	8	9	9	10	10	11	12	12	13	13	14	15	15	16	16	17	18
36	1	1	2	2	3	4	4	5	5	6	7	7	8	8	9	10	10	11	11	12	13	13	14	14	15	16	16	17	17	18
37	1	1	2	2	3	4	4	5	6	6	7	7	8	9	9	10	10	11	12	12	13	14	14	15	15	16	17	17	18	18
38	1	1	2	3	3	4	4	5	6	6	7	8	8	9	10	10	11	11	12	13	13	14	15	15	16	16	17	18	18	19
39	1	1	2	3	3	4	5	5	6	6	7	8	8	9	10	10	11	12	12	13	14	14	15	16	16	17	18	18	19	20
40	1	1	2	3	3	4	5	5	6	7	7	8	9	9	10	11	11	12	13	13	14	15	15	16	17	17	18	19	19	20
41	1	1	2	3	3	4	5	5	6	7	8	8	9	10	10	11	12	12	13	14	14	15	16	16	17	18	18	19	20	20
42	1	1	2	3	4	4	5	6	6	7	8	8	9	10	10	11	12	13	13	14	15	15	16	17	18	18	19	20	20	21
43	1	1	2	3	4	4	5	6	6	7	8	9	9	10	11	11	12	13	14	14	15	16	16	17	18	19	19	20	21	22
44	1	1	2	3	4	4	5	6	7	7	8	9	10	10	11	12	12	13	14	15	15	16	17	18	18	19	20	21	21	22
45	1	2	2	3	4	4	5	6	7	8	8	9	10	10	11	12	13	14	14	15	16	16	17	18	19	20	20	21	22	22
46	1	2	2	3	4	5	5	6	7	8	8	9	10	11	12	12	13	14	15	15	16	17	18	18	19	20	21	21	22	23
47	1	2	2	3	4	5	5	6	7	8	9	9	10	11	12	13	13	14	15	16	16	17	18	19	20	20	21	22	23	24
48	1	2	2	3	4	5	6	6	7	8	9	10	10	11	12	13	14	14	15	16	17	18	18	19	20	21	22	22	23	24
49	1	2	2	3	4	5	6	7	7	8	9	10	11	11	12	13	14	15	16	16	17	18	19	20	20	21	22	23	24	24
50	1	2	2	3	4	5	6	7	8	8	9	10	11	12	12	13	14	15	16	17	18	18	19	20	21	22	22	23	24	25
51	1	2	3	3	4	5	6	7	8	8	9	10	11	12	13	14	14	15	16	17	18	19	20	20	21	22	23	24	25	26
52	1	2	3	3	4	5	6	7	8	9	10	10	11	12	13	14	15	16	16	17	18	19	20	21	22	23	23	24	25	26
53	1	2	3	4	4	5	6	7	8	9	10	11	11	12	13	14	15	16	17	18	19	19	20	21	22	23	24	25	26	26
54	1	2	3	4	4	5	6	7	8	9	10	11	12	13	14	14	15	16	17	18	19	20	21	22	22	23	24	25	26	27
55	1	2	3	4	5	6	6	7	8	9	10	11	12	13	14	15	16	16	17	18	19	20	21	22	23	24	25	26	27	28
56	1	2	3	4	5	6	7	7	8	9	10	11	12	13	14	15	16	17	18	19	20	21	21	22	23	24	25	26	27	28
57	1	2	3	4	5	6	7	8	9	10	10	11	12	13	14	15	16	17	18	19	20	21	22	23	24	25	26	27	28	28
58	1	2	3	4	5	6	7	8	9	10	11	12	13	14	14	15	16	17	18	19	20	21	22	23	24	25	26	27	28	29
59	1	2	3	4	5	6	7	8	9	10	11	12	13	14	15	16	17	18	19	20	21	22	23	24	25	26	27	28	29	30

TABLE 5.—Correction to Tabulated Altitude for Minutes of Declination

31	32	33	34	35	36	37	38	39	40	41	42	43	44	45	46	47	48	49	50	51	52	53	54	55	56	57	58	59	60	*d* / ′
0	0	0	0	0	0	0	0	0	0	0	0	0	0	0	0	0	0	0	0	0	0	0	0	0	0	0	0	0	0	0
1	1	1	1	1	1	1	1	1	1	1	1	1	1	1	1	1	1	1	1	1	1	1	1	1	1	1	1	1	1	1
1	1	1	1	1	1	1	1	1	1	1	1	1	1	2	2	2	2	2	2	2	2	2	2	2	2	2	2	2	2	2
2	2	2	2	2	2	2	2	2	2	2	2	2	2	2	2	2	2	2	2	3	3	3	3	3	3	3	3	3	3	3
2	2	2	2	2	2	2	3	3	3	3	3	3	3	3	3	3	3	3	3	3	3	4	4	4	4	4	4	4	4	4
3	3	3	3	3	3	3	3	3	3	3	4	4	4	4	4	4	4	4	4	4	4	4	4	5	5	5	5	5	5	5
3	3	3	3	4	4	4	4	4	4	4	4	4	4	4	5	5	5	5	5	5	5	5	5	6	6	6	6	6	6	6
4	4	4	4	4	4	4	4	5	5	5	5	5	5	5	5	5	6	6	6	6	6	6	6	6	7	7	7	7	7	7
4	4	4	5	5	5	5	5	5	5	5	6	6	6	6	6	6	6	7	7	7	7	7	7	7	7	8	8	8	8	8
5	5	5	5	5	5	6	6	6	6	6	6	6	7	7	7	7	7	7	8	8	8	8	8	8	8	9	9	9	9	9
5	5	6	6	6	6	6	6	6	7	7	7	7	7	8	8	8	8	8	8	8	9	9	9	9	9	10	10	10	10	10
6	6	6	6	6	7	7	7	7	7	8	8	8	8	8	8	9	9	9	9	9	10	10	10	10	10	10	11	11	11	11
6	6	7	7	7	7	7	8	8	8	8	8	9	9	9	9	9	10	10	10	10	10	11	11	11	11	11	12	12	12	12
7	7	7	7	8	8	8	8	8	9	9	9	9	10	10	10	10	10	11	11	11	11	11	12	12	12	12	13	13	13	13
7	7	8	8	8	8	9	9	9	9	10	10	10	10	10	11	11	11	11	12	12	12	12	13	13	13	13	14	14	14	14
8	8	8	8	9	9	9	10	10	10	10	10	11	11	11	12	12	12	12	12	13	13	13	14	14	14	14	14	15	15	15
8	9	9	9	9	10	10	10	10	11	11	11	11	12	12	12	13	13	13	13	14	14	14	14	15	15	15	15	16	16	16
9	9	9	10	10	10	10	11	11	11	12	12	12	12	13	13	13	14	14	14	14	15	15	15	16	16	16	16	17	17	17
9	10	10	10	10	11	11	11	12	12	12	13	13	13	14	14	14	14	15	15	15	16	16	16	16	17	17	17	18	18	18
10	10	10	11	11	11	12	12	12	13	13	13	14	14	14	15	15	15	16	16	16	16	17	17	17	18	18	18	19	19	19
10	11	11	11	12	12	12	13	13	13	14	14	14	15	15	15	16	16	16	17	17	17	18	18	18	19	19	19	20	20	20
11	11	12	12	12	13	13	13	14	14	14	15	15	15	16	16	16	17	17	18	18	18	19	19	19	20	20	20	21	21	21
11	12	12	12	13	13	14	14	14	15	15	15	16	16	16	17	17	18	18	18	19	19	19	20	20	21	21	21	22	22	22
12	12	13	13	13	14	14	15	15	15	16	16	16	17	17	18	18	18	19	19	20	20	20	21	21	21	22	22	23	23	23
12	13	13	14	14	14	15	15	16	16	16	17	17	18	18	18	19	19	20	20	20	21	21	22	22	22	23	23	24	24	24
13	13	14	14	15	15	15	16	16	17	17	18	18	18	19	19	20	20	20	21	21	22	22	22	23	23	24	24	25	25	25
13	14	14	15	15	16	16	16	17	17	18	18	19	19	20	20	20	21	21	22	22	23	23	23	24	24	25	25	26	26	26
14	14	15	15	16	16	17	17	18	18	18	19	19	20	20	21	21	22	22	22	23	23	24	24	25	25	26	26	27	27	27
14	15	15	16	16	17	17	18	18	19	19	20	20	21	21	21	22	22	23	23	24	24	25	25	26	26	27	27	28	28	28
15	15	16	16	17	17	18	18	19	19	20	20	21	21	22	22	23	23	24	24	25	25	26	26	27	27	28	28	29	29	29
16	16	16	17	18	18	18	19	20	20	20	21	22	22	22	23	24	24	24	25	26	26	26	27	28	28	28	29	30	30	30
16	17	17	18	18	19	19	20	20	21	21	22	22	23	23	24	24	25	25	26	26	27	27	28	28	29	29	30	30	31	31
17	17	18	18	19	19	20	20	21	21	22	22	23	23	24	25	25	26	26	27	27	28	28	29	29	30	30	31	31	32	32
17	18	18	19	19	20	20	21	21	22	23	23	24	24	25	25	26	26	27	28	28	29	29	30	30	31	31	32	32	33	33
18	18	19	19	20	20	21	22	22	23	23	24	24	25	26	26	27	27	28	28	29	29	30	31	31	32	32	33	33	34	34
18	19	19	20	20	21	22	22	23	23	24	24	25	26	26	27	27	28	29	29	30	30	31	32	32	33	33	34	34	35	35
19	19	20	20	21	22	22	23	23	24	25	25	26	26	27	28	28	29	29	30	31	31	32	32	33	34	34	35	35	36	36
19	20	20	21	22	22	23	23	24	25	25	26	27	27	28	28	29	30	30	31	31	32	33	33	34	35	35	36	36	37	37
20	20	21	22	22	23	23	24	25	25	26	27	27	28	28	29	30	30	31	32	32	33	34	34	35	35	36	37	37	38	38
20	21	21	22	23	23	24	25	25	26	27	27	28	29	29	30	31	31	32	32	33	34	34	35	36	36	37	38	38	39	39
21	21	22	23	23	24	25	25	26	27	27	28	29	29	30	31	31	32	33	33	34	35	35	36	37	37	38	39	39	40	40
21	22	23	23	24	25	25	26	27	27	28	29	29	30	31	31	32	33	33	34	35	36	36	37	38	38	39	40	40	41	41
22	22	23	24	24	25	26	27	27	28	29	29	30	31	32	32	33	34	34	35	36	36	37	38	38	39	40	41	41	42	42
22	23	24	24	25	26	27	27	28	29	29	30	31	32	32	33	34	34	35	36	37	37	38	39	39	40	41	42	42	43	43
23	23	24	25	26	26	27	28	29	29	30	31	32	32	33	34	34	35	36	37	37	38	39	40	40	41	42	43	43	44	44
23	24	25	26	26	27	28	28	29	30	31	32	32	33	34	34	35	36	37	38	38	39	40	40	41	42	43	44	44	45	45
24	25	25	26	27	28	28	29	30	31	31	32	33	34	34	35	36	37	38	38	39	40	41	41	42	43	44	44	45	46	46
24	25	26	27	27	28	29	30	31	31	32	33	34	34	35	36	37	38	38	39	40	41	42	42	43	44	45	45	46	47	47
25	26	26	27	28	29	30	30	31	32	33	34	34	35	36	37	38	38	39	40	41	42	42	43	44	45	46	46	47	48	48
25	26	27	28	29	29	30	31	32	33	33	34	35	36	37	38	38	39	40	41	42	42	43	44	45	46	47	47	48	49	49
26	27	28	28	29	30	31	32	32	33	34	35	36	37	38	38	39	40	41	42	42	43	44	45	46	47	48	48	49	50	50
26	27	28	29	30	31	31	32	33	34	35	36	37	37	38	39	40	41	42	42	43	44	45	46	47	48	48	49	50	51	51
27	28	29	29	30	31	32	33	34	35	36	36	37	38	39	40	41	42	42	43	44	45	46	47	48	49	49	50	51	52	52
27	28	29	30	31	32	33	34	34	35	36	37	38	39	40	41	42	42	43	44	45	46	47	48	49	49	50	51	52	53	53
28	29	30	31	32	32	33	34	35	36	37	38	39	40	40	41	42	43	44	45	46	47	48	49	50	50	51	52	53	54	54
28	29	30	31	32	33	34	35	36	37	38	38	39	40	41	42	43	44	45	46	47	48	49	50	50	51	52	53	54	55	55
29	30	31	32	33	34	35	35	36	37	38	39	40	41	42	43	44	45	46	47	48	49	49	50	51	52	53	54	55	56	56
29	30	31	32	33	34	35	36	37	38	39	40	41	42	43	44	45	46	47	48	48	49	50	51	52	53	54	55	56	57	57
30	31	32	33	34	35	36	37	38	39	40	41	42	43	44	44	45	46	47	48	49	50	51	52	53	54	55	56	57	58	58
30	31	32	33	34	35	36	37	38	39	40	41	42	43	44	45	46	47	48	49	50	51	52	53	54	55	56	57	58	59	59

Index